MW00633399

gilbert
LAW SUMMARIES

WILLS

Tenth Edition

Stanley M. Johanson
Professor of Law
University of Texas

HARCOURT BRACE LEGAL AND PROFESSIONAL PUBLICATIONS, INC.

EDITORIAL OFFICES: 176 W. Adams, Suite 2100, Chicago, IL 60603

REGIONAL OFFICES: New York, Chicago, Los Angeles, Washington, D.C.

Distributed by: **Harcourt Brace & Company** 6277 Sea Harbor Drive, Orlando, FL 32887 (800)787-8717

PROJECT EDITOR
Elizabeth L. Snyder, B.A., J.D.
Attorney at Law

QUALITY CONTROL EDITOR
Ann R. Kerns, B.S.

SUMMARY OF CONTENTS

gilbert
capsule summary
wills

I. INTESTATE SUCCESSION

A. INTRODUCTION

1. **Intestacy:** Intestacy statutes govern distribution of the property of a person who dies **without a valid will** or whose will does not completely dispose of the estate.   [1]
2. **Common Law:** At common law, there were separate rules for real property and for personal property . . . .   [2]
3. **Modern Law:** Today, intestate distribution is governed by statutes, and in most states, the rules are the same for real and personal property. "Heirs" and "next of kin" are now synonymous and describe persons who take either real or personal property by intestacy . . . .   [3]
4. **What Law Governs:** Generally, the state where the decedent was **domiciled at death** determines the disposition of **personal property**; disposition of **real property** is determined by the law of the **situs** state . . . .   [4]
5. **Property Subject to Administration:** Intestacy statutes (or a will) apply only to a decedent's **probate** (or testamentary) **estate**. This consists of assets that pass by will or inheritance and which are subject to administration by the decedent's personal representative (*e.g.,* cash, real estate, personal effects) . . . . .   [6]
   a. **Nonprobate assets:** Property that passes under a **contract** (*e.g.,* life insurance proceeds), property held with another with the **right of survivorship** (*e.g.,* joint tenancies), **trust assets** where decedent is a trustee or beneficiary, and assets over which decedent holds a **power of appointment** pass outside of probate, and the laws of intestate succession do not apply . .   [7]

B. PATTERNS OF INTESTATE DISTRIBUTIONS

1. **Rules Vary from Jurisdiction to Jurisdiction:** Intestacy laws differ, even among some of the states that have adopted the Uniform Probate Code ("U.P.C."). This summary covers the general patterns of intestate distribution of many states, both common law and community property states. (Separate property in community property states is covered by these general rules; community property is governed by other intestacy statutes) . . . .   [11]
2. **Intestate Share of Surviving Spouse:** If a decedent is survived by a spouse and descendants, the spouse usually takes **one-third or one-half** of the estate. If there are no descendants, the spouse usually inherits the **entire** estate . . .   [14]
3. **Intestate Share of Children and Other Descendants:** The remainder of the estate after the spouse's share (or where there is no surviving spouse) passes to decedent's children and descendants of deceased children. Note that decedent's parents and collateral kin do **not** inherit if decedent is survived by children or their descendants . . . .   [20]
   a. **Grandchildren take by representation:** If there are surviving children, grandchildren take a share only if they are children of a deceased child of the intestate. Such grandchildren take the share that their parent would have taken had he survived (*i.e.,* by representation or "per stirpes") . . . .   [21]
      (1) **Survived by grandchildren only:** Where decedent is survived by grandchildren only (*i.e.,* no surviving children) jurisdictions are split as to whether distribution should be made by representation or per capita (*see infra,* §73) . . . .   [23]
4. **Not Survived by Spouse or Descendants:** Here, decedent's parents inherit the estate (majority rule) . . . .   [24]

II. INHERITANCE RIGHTS AS AFFECTED BY STATUS OF CHILD OR SIBLING

A. ADOPTED CHILDREN

1. **Early Law:** Absent a relevant statute, most courts permitted an adopted child to inherit from the adopting parents (but not from their relatives). Usually, the adopt-

ed child continued to have inheritance rights from and through the natural
parents .... [50]
  2. **Modern Law**
    a. **Adopting parents:** Today, all relevant statutes allow an adopted child to
have the **same inheritance rights** as a natural child .... [52]
    b. **Natural parents—majority rule:** An adopted child (and her issue) have
no inheritance rights from or through the natural parents. An exception is
made when a child is adopted by the spouse of a natural parent; the relationship between that parent and the child is not affected. The Uniform Probate
Code provides that such an adoption has no effect on the relationship between the child and either natural parent .... [54]

B. CHILDREN BORN OUT OF WEDLOCK

At common law, such a child had no inheritance rights from either parent. Today, all
states permit the child to inherit from and through his natural **mother**. Also, the child
can inherit from and through the natural **father** upon certain proof of paternity (*e.g.,*
adjudication or formal acknowledgment) .... [59]

C. POSTHUMOUS CHILDREN

Under both the common law rules and statutory authority, a child born (typically within
280 days) after his father's death is considered the decedent's child for inheritance
purposes .... [65]

D. STEPCHILDREN

In general, a stepchild has **no** inheritance rights from the foster parents. An exception
occurs under the doctrine of adoption by estoppel (*i.e.,* in cases involving an unperformed agreement to adopt) .... [69]

E. DO GRANDCHILDREN TAKE PER STIRPES OR PER CAPITA?

  1. **In General:** Most intestacy statutes provide for distribution to descendants per
stirpes. However, if **only grandchildren** are surviving, distribution may be per
capita or per stirpes .... [73]
  2. **Majority Rule—Per Capita with Representation:** In most states (and under
the U.P.C.), the stirpital shares are determined at the first generational level that
has living takers (*e.g.,* grandchildren). Thus, each grandchild would take one
share, and the descendants of a deceased grandchild would equally divide that
grandchild's share .... [74]
  3. **Minority Rule—Strict Per Stirpes:** In a few states, the stirpital shares are
always determined at the first generational level even though there are no living
takers at that level .... [75]
  4. **Construction Problem Under Wills and Trusts:** The same problem of determining by which manner grandchildren should take can be encountered under
wills and trusts. In such cases, courts look to the intestacy statutes, and in a
majority of cases, a per capita with representation distribution is made .... [76]

F. INHERITANCE BY BROTHERS AND SISTERS OF THE HALF-BLOOD

The English common law rule that wholly excluded half-blood relatives from inheriting
has been statutorily abolished in all American jurisdictions. Today, in most jurisdictions,
no distinction is made between siblings of the half-blood and whole blood, although
some states provide that half-bloods take half as much as whole bloods .... [79]

III. SUCCESSION PROBLEMS COMMON TO INTESTACY AND WILLS

A. SIMULTANEOUS DEATH

  1. **Uniform Simultaneous Death Act:** All jurisdictions (except Ohio and Louisiana) have adopted this act or the equivalent 120-hour survival rule of the U.P.C.

The Act provides that when there is no sufficient evidence that the parties have died otherwise than simultaneously, the property of each person is disposed of as if he had survived . . . . [86]

    a. **Application:** In cases of simultaneous deaths, intestate estates, testamentary assets under a will, and life insurance proceeds pass as though the "owner" survived the "heir" . . . . [88]

    b. **But note:** In cases involving joint tenancies, tenancies by the entireties, or community property, one-half of the property passes as though one party survived and the other half passes as though the other party survived . . [89]

    c. **Evidence of survival:** Remember that if there is sufficient evidence that one party survived the other, even for a brief interval, the Act does **not** apply. Nor does the Act apply where decedent's will (or other instrument) has a contrary survival provision . . . . [91]

  2. **Uniform Probate Code:** The U.P.C. addresses the problem of deaths in quick succession by stating that a person must survive the decedent by **120 hours** in order to take as an heir or will beneficiary. This rule does not apply if it would result in an escheat to the state or to survivorship estates (*i.e.,* joint tenancies, tenancies by the entireties) . . . . [96]

B. ADVANCEMENTS; SATISFACTION OF LEGACIES

  1. **Advancement of Intestate Share**

    a. **Common law:** At common law and in many states today, a lifetime gift to a **child** is **presumed** to be an advance payment of the child's intestate share of the donor's estate . . . . [103]

    b. **Modern law:** Most state statutes permit advancements to be made to **any heir** (*e.g.,* spouse or sister). More importantly, these statutes reverse the common law presumption and provide that a lifetime gift to an heir is **not** an advancement unless so proved. In many states, such proof must be shown by an express declaration or acknowledgment in a writing signed by the donor or the donee . . . . [104]

    c. **Procedure:** Where an advancement is found, the value of the property given to the advancee is added to the estate in determining the intestate shares. This is done only if the advancee elects to share in the intestate distribution. Note that the advancee never has to return the property . . . . [108]

    d. **Partial intestacy:** The advancement doctrine does not apply if decedent left a will that does not make a complete disposition of the estate . . . . . . [111]

    e. **Advancee predeceases intestate:** In such cases, at common law and in most states, the advancement doctrine is applicable to the advancee's heirs. [112]

  2. **Satisfaction of Legacies**

    a. **Majority rule:** At common law and in states without relevant statutes, a gift to a child of the testator is **presumed** to be in partial or total satisfaction of any gifts made to the child in a **previously executed** will. This presumption usually applies also to the child's descendants (*e.g.,* grandchild), but not to other will beneficiaries (*i.e.,* someone other than a child or descendant). [116]

      (1) **General legacy:** The above rule applies to general legacies (*i.e.,* legacies payable out of the general assets of the estate and which do not require delivery of a particular item) . . . . [117]

      (2) **Specific bequest:** Such a bequest can be satisfied only by delivery of a particular item of property described in the will. Whether the doctrine of satisfaction of legacies is applicable depends on the circumstances . [118]

        (a) **Ademption by extinction:** The satisfaction doctrine does **not** apply when the bequeathed item is no longer in a testator's estate at his death (*e.g.,* when the gift was given to the heir before death of testator). Instead, **ademption** applies. . . . . [119]

        (b) **Satisfaction of legacy:** A lifetime gift can be in satisfaction of a bequest if it is shown that this was the testator's intent. This intent

E. **NONRESIDENT ALIENS**
Contrary to common law, most states give aliens an ***unrestricted right*** to inherit or hold title to real or personal property within the state .... [170]

IV. **RESTRICTIONS ON THE POWER OF TESTATION: PROTECTION OF THE FAMILY**

A. **INTRODUCTION**
A testator's generally unrestricted right to dispose of property may be limited by rules designed to prevent disinheritance of the testator's family .... [177]

B. **PROTECTION OF THE SPOUSE—COMMON LAW**
1. **Spouse Was Not an Heir:** A surviving spouse's ***only*** right in a decedent's estate was dower (for a widow) or curtesy (for a widower) .... [178]
2. **Dower:** Upon the husband's death, the widow was entitled to a ***life estate*** in an ***undivided one-third*** in all lands owned by the husband at death and in all lands conveyed during marriage without her joinder .... [179]
3. **Curtesy:** Upon a wife's death, the husband received a ***life estate*** in all of the lands of which the wife was seized during marriage. However, curtesy rights arose ***only if*** issue were born of the marriage .... [185]
4. **As Limitation on Testamentary Power:** Dower and curtesy rights could be asserted regardless of the decedent's will .... [186]
5. **As Limitation on Lifetime Transfers:** Lifetime transfers (*e.g.,* sale to a bona fide purchaser) were ***ineffective*** to limit dower or curtesy rights (unless the spouse had joined in the conveyance). The spouse's interest also superseded claims of decedent's creditors .... [187]
6. **Modern Status:** Although most states have replaced dower and curtesy with statutory rules, these common law estates still exist in a few states .... [188]

C. **PROTECTION OF THE SPOUSE—ELECTIVE SHARE STATUTES**
1. **Protection Against Disinheritance:** Most jurisdictions have enacted statutes that allow the surviving spouse to elect a statutory share of decedent's estate in lieu of taking under the will. In most states, this statutory share may be claimed regardless of the will's provisions .... [189]
    a. **As limitation on lifetime transfers:** Most elective share statutes apply only to property owned by decedent at death; thus, a lifetime transfer ***may*** cut off a surviving spouse's statutory share with respect to that property. (However, some courts have widened the scope of the elective share right to encompass certain lifetime transfers) .... [191]
    b. **Community property states:** Because the community property system has a built-in protection against disinheritance of spouses, none of the community property states has an elective share statute .... [192]
2. **Amount of Elective Share:** In most states, the elective share amount is ***one-third*** of the net estate if decedent was survived by descendants, and ***one-half*** of the net estate if decedent was not survived by descendants .... [194]
3. **Property Subject to Elective Share:** The elective share applies to decedent's ***net estate***, which is the probate estate after payment of administrative expenses and creditor's claims and after the family allowance, homestead right, and any exempt personal property is set aside for the surviving spouse .... [195]
    a. **Situs rule:** The situs rule limits the elective share of real property to that located within the state. The elective share applies to ***all*** of decedent's ***personal property*** wherever located .... [196]
    b. **Settlement agreement with former spouse:** In most states, a former spouse's right to accrued and unpaid alimony payments or a right secured by a property settlement agreement takes precedence over the surviving spouse's elective share .... [198]
    c. **Property subject to contractual will:** Property received by the decedent

b. **Abatement of gifts:** To the extent that assets which, but for the election, would have passed outright to the spouse are insufficient, the elective share is paid pursuant to the abatement rules that apply to creditors' claims. Thus, property passing by partial intestacy is first applied; then the residuary estate; then general legacies; demonstrative legacies; and specific bequests [227]

   (1) **Minority and U.P.C. rule:** The elective share is ratably apportioned among recipients of decedent's estate in proportion to the value of their interests therein, after first applying any property which has passed outright to the surviving spouse .... [228]

D. LIFETIME TRANSFERS TO DEFEAT THE ELECTIVE SHARE

1. **Case Law:** Although most elective share statutes do not apply to property transferred during the decedent's lifetime or to nontestamentary transfers, courts have developed various doctrines under which a surviving spouse may challenge a particular lifetime transfer .... [229]

  a. **Illusory transfer:** If the transferor retained a *significant degree of control* over the property so that the transfer was "illusory," the elective share statute applies .... [230]

   (1) **Special problem—bank account dispositions:** Most courts have held that Totten trust bank accounts and joint bank accounts are *not* illusory and thus not subject to the elective share despite the degree of control and access to the funds retained by the depositor .... [231]

  b. **Motive or intent to defeat share:** Some courts have held that a lifetime transfer is subject to the surviving spouse's elective share *if* the motive or intent of the transfer was to defeat the elective share—especially if the estate has little or no property .... [235]

  c. **Weigh the equities:** Other courts favor a balancing approach, considering: (i) the completeness of the transfer; (ii) the transferor's motive; (iii) whether it was a "brink of death" transfer; (iv) participation of the transferee in the alleged fraud; and (v) the degree to which the surviving spouse is stripped of benefits in the decedent's estate by the transfer .... [236]

  d. **Revocable inter vivos trust:** The courts are divided as to whether property in a revocable trust is subject to the surviving spouse's elective share. [237]

2. **Uniform Probate Code**

  a. **Augmented estate:** Under the U.P.C., the elective share applies to decedent's "augmented estate," which consists of the net probate estate *plus* the value of lifetime transfers to persons other than the decedent's spouse, for less than full consideration, *if* the transfer falls into one of the following categories: (i) retained life estate; (ii) retained control; (iii) transfers within two years of death; or (iv) survivorship estates .... [238]

  b. **Intestacy:** The U.P.C.'s elective share statute applies when a decedent dies intestate as well as when a decedent dies testate .... [239]

  c. **Transfers to spouse:** The augmented estate also includes the value of property given by decedent to the spouse during the marriage. This includes such property owned by the spouse at decedent's death, such property given by the spouse to third parties, a beneficial interest given to the spouse in a trust created by the decedent during lifetime, and property passing to the spouse by decedent's exercise of a power of appointment .... [240]

   (1) **Life insurance proceeds and employee benefits:** The augmented estate includes life insurance proceeds and employee benefits paid to the spouse, to the extent that decedent or decedent's employer paid premiums or made contributions .... [242]

   (2) **Burden of proof:** The surviving spouse has the burden of establishing that property owned by the spouse at decedent's death was derived from a source other than gifts from decedent .... [243]

  d. **Not part of augmented estate:** The augmented estate does not include

considered pretermitted if testator's spouse, who is the parent of the testator's children, is the principal beneficiary under the will .... [296]

3. **Operation of Statute**
   a. **Majority rule:** The pretermitted child takes an *intestate share* of the parent's estate. In most jurisdictions, the child's share comes first out of intestate property (if any), then the residuary estate, etc. In some states, all testamentary gifts abate proportionately .... [298]
   b. **Minority rule:** Several states apply the majority rule if the testator had other children at the time the will was executed. If not, and if no exceptions to the statute apply, the *entire will is void* .... [301]
   c. **New York statute:** Under this statute, the pretermitted child takes the same share of the parent's estate as testator's other children, and the other children's testamentary gifts are reduced ratably .... [302]

G. HOMESTEAD, EXEMPT PERSONAL PROPERTY, FAMILY ALLOWANCE
1. **Homestead:** Homestead laws are designed to protect the family residence or farm from creditors' claims. Representative features of these laws are: ...... [303]
   a. **Protection from creditors' claims:** Except for valid liens on the homestead itself, the property cannot be reached by creditors .... [304]
   b. **Spouse's joinder required:** There is no effective conveyance of any interest in the homestead unless both spouses join .... [305]
   c. **Probate homestead:** In several states, the surviving spouse is entitled to occupy the homestead as a residence for as long as he chooses to occupy it .... [306]
   d. **Restrictions on devise of homestead:** In a few states, the homestead laws operate to restrict the owner's power of testamentary disposition. But these rules have no application if the homestead is held in a tenancy by the entireties. In such a case, title passes to the surviving spouse by right of survivorship .... [307]
   e. **What property qualifies as a homestead:** A homestead is the property acquired for actual or intended use as a *primary residence*. Many jurisdictions have either an acreage or dollar limit on the amount of property that can qualify .... [308]
   f. **Homestead allowance:** Rather than giving the surviving spouse or minor children a right to occupy decedent's property, several jurisdictions provide a *cash award* free of creditors' claims .... [309]
2. **Exempt Personal Property:** Some statutes exempt certain items of tangible personal property from creditors' claims. This exemption typically applies to household furnishings, appliances, personal effects, farm equipment, and in some states, automobiles up to a certain value .... [310]
3. **Family Allowance:** In many states, the surviving spouse or minor children may petition for a family allowance, to provide for their maintenance while decedent's estate is in administration. The family allowance usually takes precedence over all claims except funeral expenses and estate administration expenses, and it is not chargeable against any benefit or share passing to the surviving spouse (or children) by intestate succession, elective share, or the will .... [312]
   a. **Personal right:** The death of the person entitled to the allowance terminates the right to any remaining part of the allowance .... [316]

H. TESTAMENTARY GIFTS TO CHARITY
At early common law, mormain restrictions were placed on the right to make testamentary gifts to the church. Today, most states do not place restrictions on charitable devises and bequests .... [317]

V. FORMAL REQUISITES OF WILLS

A. WHAT CONSTITUTES A WILL

1. **Nature of a Will:** A will is an instrument executed with certain formalities that directs the disposition of testator's property at death, and is effective **only upon the testator's death** . . . . [320]

   a. **Exception:** Generally, a beneficiary has only an **expectancy** unless the testator executed a will pursuant to a contract, in which case, the beneficiary may have a right under **contract law** to enforce the bargained-for testamentary disposition even though the will was amended or revoked . . . . . . [322]

   b. **Codicil:** A codicil is a supplement to a will . . . . [323]

2. **Other Functions of a Will:** A will may be an instrument that does any **one** of the following, regardless of whether it disposes of any property: revokes an earlier will; appoints a personal representative; exercises a power of appointment; or gives directions concerning disposition of the testator's body or part thereof . . [325]

3. **Types of Wills**

   a. **Attested will:** Generally, this is a will signed by the testator and witnessed by two (sometimes three) witnesses pursuant to a formal attestation procedure . . . . [332]

   b. **Holographic will:** Recognized by about half of the states, a holographic will is entirely in the testator's **handwriting**, signed by testator, and is **unattested** (*i.e.,* unwitnessed) . . . . [333]

   c. **Oral wills:** Oral (nuncupative) wills are valid in some states but in very limited circumstances . . . . [334]

4. **Formal Requirements:** The will must have been executed with **testamentary intent;** testator must have had **testamentary capacity;** the will must have been executed **free of fraud, duress, undue influence, or mistake;** and it must have been **duly executed** . . . . [335]

B. GOVERNING LAW

1. **Uniform Probate Code:** A minority of the states have adopted the U.P.C. substantially or in its entirety. A few states have made selective adoptions of some of the U.P.C. provisions while other states have retained their own rules . . . . . [337]

2. **Legislative Control of Right to Make a Will:** Except in Wisconsin, the right to make a will is not a "natural right." Thus, the right to make a will is subject to the legislature's plenary control . . . . [339]

3. **Effect of Change in Law After Execution:** Generally, a will is admitted to probate if it satisfies either the law in effect when the will was executed **or** the law in effect when the testator died . . . . [341]

4. **Conflict of Laws Principles:** Disposition of **real property** is determined by the law of the **situs** of the property; disposition of **personal property** is governed by the law of testator's **domicile** at the time of death . . . . [343]

   a. **Uniform Execution of Foreign Wills Act:** This Act admits a will to probate if the will was executed in accordance with the law of that jurisdiction, the law of the state where it was executed, the law of the testator's domicile at the time of execution, **or** the law of the testator's domicile at death . . . [345]

   b. **Uniform Probate Code:** The Code also allows the testator to select the particular state law unless application of that law contravenes public policy of the testator's state of residence . . . . [346]

C. TESTAMENTARY INTENT

1. **In General:** A testator must have subjectively intended that the particular words in question constitute her will at the time she executed the instrument . . . . [347]

2. **Legal Test:** Testamentary intent exists where the testator intended to **dispose of property,** the disposition was intended to **occur only upon death,** and

      a. **Where signed:** Generally, the testator's signature can appear anywhere on the will. A few states require it at the end of the will .... [400]

      b. **In witnesses' presence:** Many states require the testator to either sign the will or acknowledge her earlier signature in the witnesses' presence. Some states allow the testator to sign the will in one witness's presence and then allow the testator to later acknowledge her signature in the other witness's presence. A few states require the testator to sign in the presence of both witnesses at the same time .... [411]

5. **Publication Requirement:** The *majority* rule requires *no* publication; *i.e.,* the witnesses do not need to know they are attesting to a will. A few states require a testator to declare to the witnesses that they are attesting to a will .... [414]

6. **Order of Signing:** A majority of jurisdictions do not specify the order of signatures as long as the execution ceremony is part of *one contemporaneous transaction.* Others require the testator to sign first .... [417]

7. **When Signing in Someone's "Presence" Is Required:** In many states, each witness must sign in the testator's presence but not necessarily in each other's presence. Other states require the witnesses to sign in the testator's and each other's presence .... [419]

      a. **"Presence" tests:** The majority of states use the *conscious presence* test, wherein a witness has signed in the testator's presence if the testator was conscious of where the witness was and what he was doing, *and* the testator *could have seen* the witness by a slight physical exertion on her part. A few states use the *line of sight test* and require the witness and the will to be within the testator's scope of vision at all times .... [420]

F. WITNESSES

1. **Competency of Witnesses—In General:** Competency of witnesses is determined at the time of the will's execution and generally means that a witness must be mature enough and of sufficient mental capacity to understand the *nature of the act* so that she could testify in court if necessary .... [422]

2. **Interested Witnesses—In General:** At common law, an attesting witness who was also a beneficiary was not a competent witness and the will was invalid. However, generally today, most statutes (called "purging" statutes) consider the witness to be competent and merely *void the gift* to the interested witness. The U.P.C. has abolished the interested witness rule .... [426]

3. **Exceptions to Purging Statutes' Operation:** In some states, if a beneficiary is a "supernumerary" witness (*i.e.,* third witness where only two are required), the bequest is *not* purged if the will can be proved without that witness's testimony. Additionally, if the witness-beneficiary would be an intestate heir if there had been no will, many states allow the witness to take the *lesser* of the intestate share or the bequest amount .... [429]

4. **Purging Statutes—What Constitutes Beneficial Interest:** To have a beneficial interest, a witness must be a *beneficiary* under a will or trust created by a will; *i.e.,* the interest must be a direct, pecuniary one .... [432]

      a. **Indirect interests:** Executors, attorneys, relatives of beneficiary, creditors of beneficiaries, and takers under a lapse statute are indirect beneficiaries, and a purging statute does not apply .... [433]

5. **Subsequent Testamentary Instrument:** A codicil that *reduces* a gift to a witness to the codicil is not affected by a purging statute; similarly, a codicil making a gift to a witness to the will who was not a witness to the codicil is not affected. However, the statute does apply where a codicil increases the attesting witness's gift under the will .... [440]

G. ATTESTATION CLAUSE

1. **Recites Facts of Due Execution:** An attestation clause recites in detail the performance of the statutory requirements for execution of a will and is always

VI. REVOCATION OF WILLS

A. INTRODUCTION

B. REVOCATION BY OPERATION OF LAW

C. REVOCATION BY SUBSEQUENT TESTAMENTARY INSTRUMENT

D. REVOCATION BY PHYSICAL ACT

VIII. CONTRACTS RELATING TO WILLS; JOINT WILLS

takers if there exists a specified degree of relationship between the testator and predeceased beneficiary, ***and*** the beneficiary left descendents surviving the testator .... [660]

    a. **Scope of lapse statutes:** The scope varies greatly from state to state: *e.g.,* limited to testator's descendents, only collateral kin of beneficiary can take a lapsed gift (U.P.C. view), any relative of the testator, etc. However, most states apply a lapse statute only if the predeceasing beneficiary left descendents surviving the testator—*i.e.,* gift by substitution .... [661]

3. **Lapse of Specific Gift or General Legacy:** Absent a contrary will provision, a lapsed specific, demonstrative, or general bequest that is not saved by a lapse statute falls into the residuary estate .... [669]

    a. **Residuary clause:** If there is no residuary clause or if the clause is not stated broadly enough to encompass the gifts, lapsed gifts pass by ***intestate succession*** .... [671]

4. **Lapse of Residuary Gift:** Where one of several residuary beneficiaries predeceases the testator, the majority hold that the lapsed share does ***not*** pass to the surviving residuary beneficiary unless the will so provides; instead it passes by intestacy rules .... [673]

    a. **Minority rule:** A growing minority of states hold that the surviving residuary beneficiary takes the predeceased beneficiary's share .... [675]

    b. **Remember:** The above rules are inapplicable if the language of the will provides for the contingency or if the lapse statute applies .... [676]

5. **Void Gifts:** This is a testamentary gift that was ***never*** valid from the moment of the will's execution because either the beneficiary was dead when the will was executed or the gift violates public policy or a rule of property law .... [677]

    a. **Effect:** Generally, a void gift is treated as though it were a lapsed gift. Whether a lapse statute is applicable depends on the statute's language. [681]

B. CLASS GIFTS

1. **Definitional Problems:** Absent a controlling will provision, the following rules govern what persons are included in class designations .... [685]

    a. **"Children":** This includes descendants in the ***first degree only*** (not grandchildren) and includes children by all marriages of the specified person .... [686]

        (1) **Adopted children:** Most jurisdictions today presume that a gift to someone's children ***includes*** adopted children. A similar rule applies to ***adopted adults*** .... [688]

        (2) **Children born out of wedlock:** The majority rule ***excludes*** such children from the "children" designation unless the will shows an intent to include them. Extrinsic evidence is admissible to show the testator's intention .... [693]

    b. **"Issue"; "descendants":** These terms are generally held to be synonymous and include lineal descendants of any degree. Modern law includes adopted offspring but excludes children born out of wedlock. The living issue take ***per stirpes*** absent a contrary intent .... [697]

    c. **"Heirs":** These include persons who would take the decedent's estate if decedent had died ***intestate*** .... [700]

    d. **Other family terms:** Words such as "relatives," "family," or "kin" are construed to mean "heirs." Brothers and sisters include half-siblings. "Cousins" means first cousins only .... [701]

2. **Constructional Problems:** Sometimes problems arise in determining the takers of a class gift .... [705]

    a. **Death of class member in testator's lifetime:** A testamentary gift to a class of persons, of which one member predeceases the testator, passes to the ***surviving*** class members, absent a contrary will provision (class gift rule) .... [706]

E. STOCK SPLITS AND STOCK DIVIDENDS

F. EXONERATION OF LIENS

X. WILL CONTESTS AND RELATED MATTERS

A. GROUNDS FOR CONTESTING WILL

B. PROCEDURAL ASPECTS

C. TESTAMENTARY CAPACITY

involves coercion while fraud involves deception. Similarly, fraud is distinguishable from duress (*i.e.,* element of threat) .... [824]

2. **Fraud in the Execution:** Situations such as a testator being tricked into signing a writing while not knowing it was a will involve *no testamentary intent* and constitute fraud in the execution .... [827]

3. **Fraud in the Inducement:** This type of fraud occurs where there is testamentary intent, but the testator is fraudulently induced into making a will. The misrepresentation must be the *sole inducement* and there is no fraud if the testator knew the true facts .... [828]

   a. **Note:** The fact that the fraud was perpetrated on the testator by someone other than the beneficiary generally is immaterial. The innocent beneficiary's gift will still be set aside .... [831]

4. **Fraudulent Prevention of Will:** In such cases, there is *no legal remedy,* and the estate passes by intestate succession rules .... [834]

   a. **Other remedies:** Many courts will impose a *constructive trust* for the persons who would have been beneficiaries. Some jurisdictions recognize an action for tort liability for a wrongful interference with an expectancy [835]

5. **Revocation Prevented by Fraud:** Where a testator is tricked into believing her will has been revoked, the will is still *admitted to probate* because there was no valid revocation. However, upon proof of the fraud, a constructive trust would probably be imposed .... [837]

G. MISTAKE

1. **In General:** Parol evidence is usually admissible in cases involving an alleged mistake in a *will's execution* because it relates to testamentary intent. The admissibility of parol evidence is less likely if the alleged mistake relates to the will's *contents* .... [838]

   a. **Compare:** Relief is much more freely given where a mistake as to *revocation* is shown .... [839]

2. **Mistake in Execution of Will**

   a. **Nature of instrument:** Extrinsic evidence is *always* admissible to show that the testator was mistaken as to the nature or effect of the writing he signed. If mistake is proved, probate is denied for lack of testamentary intent .... [840]

   b. **Wrong will signed:** This usually occurs where reciprocal wills are involved. The modern trend is to grant relief since the existence and nature of the mistake is so obvious .... [841]

3. **Mistake in the Inducement:** Absent fraud, *no relief* is granted where the mistake induced the testator to make the will or particular provisions therein. Thus, if testator makes a mistake as to the relationship or status of a beneficiary (T thinks B is his nephew, but B is no relation), the mistake has no effect on the will; it will be given effect as written .... [842]

4. **Mistake as to Contents of Will:** Generally, parol evidence is inadmissible to show that a provision was mistakenly omitted or that a provision in the will was not what testator intended .... [845]

   a. **Mistake as to meaning of terms:** The majority hold that unambiguous terms must be construed according to their *plain meaning* .... [848]

   b. **Mistake in description:** A mistake in describing a beneficiary or item of property has no effect on the will. The gift will be given effect as written. [850]

   c. **Mistake as to legal effect:** It is immaterial that the testator was allegedly mistaken as to the legal effect of the will's language .... [851]

   d. **Liberal (minority) view:** Some courts ignore the plain meaning rule and admit extrinsic evidence to show that the testator meant something other than that indicated by the words' plain meaning .... [852]

   e. **Mistake in recital of facts of execution:** Such mistakes, if of a *minor or purely formal nature,* may be corrected by the courts .... [853]

giving notice to and paying claims of creditors; payment of taxes; and, after paying funeral and administrative expenses, the distribution of the remaining assets.   [888]

3. **Court Supervised vs. Unsupervised Administration:** In most jurisdictions, virtually all steps in probate administration are subject to the court's supervision and control. The personal representative is considered a representative of the court. Several states now permit estate administration without court supervision .   [900]

     a. **Uniform Probate Code:** The U.P.C. provides for two types of administration—unsupervised and supervised. Under a supervised administration, court approval is necessary before an estate can be distributed, but a personal representative may exercise other administrative powers (*e.g.,* pay claims, sell property) ***without*** court approval. Under the U.P.C., all administrations are unsupervised unless a supervised administration is requested by the representative or by any interested party . . . .   [902]

     b. **Informal procedures:** In many jurisdictions, no formal administration or court supervision may be necessary for very modest estates . . . .   [907]

4. **Jurisdiction and Venue:** The primary probate jurisdiction is the state of decedent's ***domicile at the time of his death.*** A probate proceeding is ***in rem***; *i.e.,* it determines who inherits decedent's property, which determination is conclusive as to all other persons . . . .   [908]

     a. **Venue:** Usually, venue lies in the ***county*** of decedent's domicile at the time of death. As to a nonresident, venue is in any county in which the decedent owned property ***or*** where any debtor of the decedent resides . . . .   [910]

     b. **Ancillary administration:** Ancillary probate and administration proceedings in another state are required where a decedent owned property in the other state . . . .   [912]

B. PROOF OF WILLS IN PROBATE

1. **Duty to Produce Will:** A person in possession of a decedent's will must present it to the probate court within a statutorily specified time or face civil, and perhaps criminal, liability . . . .   [914]

2. **Who May Offer Will for Probate:** ***Any*** person ***interested*** in the estate (*e.g.,* beneficiary, creditor, executor) may offer the will for probate . . . .   [915]

3. **Time Within Which Will Must Be Probated:** All states require that a will be offered for probate within a specified time limit. The U.P.C. time limit is three years after decedent's death. If the time limit is not met, the decedent is presumed to have died intestate . . . .   [916]

4. **Informal vs. Formal Probate**

     a. **Uniform Probate Code:** The U.P.C. follows the basic common law forms: An ***informal*** probate proceeding is ex parte with no notice but is held before a registrar rather than a court; and an interested party may bring a ***formal*** testacy proceeding . . . .   [921]

     b. **Majority rule:** In most states, a formal probate proceeding with ***notice*** is always required . . . .   [925]

5. **Burden of Proof:** In the ***offering*** of a will for probate, the will proponents must show due execution. ***After*** the will is admitted to probate, the will contestants carry the burden of proof . . . .   [926]

     a. **Note:** Proof of proper execution ***cannot*** be waived even if all interested parties want the will probated . . . .   [928]

6. **Proof:** Whether a will was validly executed is a question of fact. Usually, both attesting witnesses must testify. If a witness is dead or incompetent, the testimony of the remaining witness is usually sufficient. Depositions may be used as a substitution for a nonresident witness. If no attesting witnesses are available, proof of the testator's and at least one of the witnesses' handwriting is usually required . . . .   [929]

     a. **Attestation clause:** This is ***prima facie evidence*** of the facts recited therein. However, it is not a substitute for the attesting witnesses' testimony.

TEXT CORRELATION CHART

Gilbert Law Summaries Wills	Clark, Lusky, Murphy **Gratuitous Transfers** 1985 (3rd ed.)	Dukeminier, Johanson **Wills, Trusts and Estates** 1984 (3rd ed.)	McGovern **Wills, Trusts and Future Interests** 1983	Ritchie, Alford, Effland **Decedents' Estates and Trusts** 1982 (6th ed.)	Wellman, Waggoner, Browder **Trusts and Succession** 1983 (4th ed.)
I. INTESTATE SUCCESSION					
A. Introduction	59-64	89	40	87	17-20
B. Patterns of Intestate Distributions	64-74	89-101	40-57	88-103, 111-112	20-38
C. Intestate Distributions— Community Property States		90, 416-418	57-68	112-113	
II. INHERITANCE RIGHTS AS AFFECTED BY STATUS OF CHILD OR SIBLING					
A. Adopted Children	88-101	111-113	12-24	104-106	42-43, 52-54
B. Children Born Out of Wedlock	101-116	113-116	3-11	106-108	42-52, 55-60
C. Posthumous Children	117	109-110		108	39
D. Stepchildren	94	92	19-24		41-42
E. Do Grandchildren Take Per Stirpes or Per Capita?	74-82	101-109	48-52	95-103	26-33
F. Inheritance by Brothers and Sisters of the Half-Blood	82-88	98	53	103, 108	41
III. SUCCESSION PROBLEMS COMMON TO INTESTACY AND WILLS					
A. Simultaneous Death	116	356-358, 1027-1028	389-394	988-991	39
B. Advancement, Satisfaction of Legacies	119-120, 358-359	128-129, 381	198-202	116-119	60-63
C. Disclaimer by Heir or Will Beneficiary		132-136, 710-717	204-209	124-130	
D. Killer of the Decedent	7-18, 118-119	120-126	209-213	131-141	63-72
E. Nonresident Aliens		126-128		142-150	41
IV. RESTRICTIONS ON THE POWER OF TESTATION—PROTECTION OF THE FAMILY					
A. Introduction	42-44, 121-124	391-397	69-74	151-153	73-76
B. Protection of the Spouse— Common Law	139-141	397-399	83-85	111-112, 157-159	76-78
C. Protection of the Spouse— Elective Share Statutes	128-132, 142	399-408	85-101	159-168	76-93
D. Lifetime Transfers to Defeat the Elective Share	142-173	408-416		164-168	93-96
E. Protection of Spouse— Community Property States	123, 175-181	416-441	85-104, 183-187	169-170	77-78, 96-102
F. Pretermitted Child Statutes	181-192	441-450	77-80	179-185	121-123
G. Homestead, Exempt Personal Property, Family Allowance	125-128	393-397	74-77	185-187	103-114
H. Testamentary Gifts to Charity	124-125, 192-194	254	80-82	186	123-125
V. FORMAL REQUISITES OF WILLS					
A. What Constitutes a Will					
B. Governing Law	45-49, 582-609	204-205		188-192	127-128
C. Testamentary Intent				370-376	201-212
D. Capacity to Make a Will	202	137-142		356-365	168-178
E. Execution of Attested Wills	265-291	183-198, 204-207	105-106, 111-121	192-209, 220-254	129-157
F. Witnesses	291-298	198-204	116-119	227-232	146-154
G. Attestation Clause	318-319	206-207	116	236	137-138
H. Self-Proving Affidavit	318-319	207-211		249-253	133-134
I. Holographic Wills	299-307	230-240	106-111	254-257	157-167
J. Oral Wills	308-309	186	121	209-211	157-158
K. Conditional Wills		228-230	111		

Gilbert Law Summaries Wills	Clark, Lusky, Murphy **Gratuitous Transfers** 1985 (3rd ed.)	Dukeminier, Johanson **Wills, Trusts and Estates** 1984 (3rd ed.)	McGovern **Wills, Trusts and Future Interests** 1983	Ritchie, Alford, Effland **Decedents' Estates and Trusts** 1982 (6th ed.)	Wellman, Waggoner, Browder **Trusts and Succession** 1983 (4th ed.)
VI. REVOCATION OF WILLS					
A. Introduction		240		258-262	227
B. Revocation by Operation of Law	353-354	260-268	135-137	283-293	257-269
C. Revocation by Subsequent Testamentary Instrument	342-348	240-247	134-135	262-270	227-232
D. Revocation by Physical Act	336-342	240-247	122-132	270-283, 294-304	232-243, 252-256
E. Proof of Lost Wills	342	211-213, 242	126	280-282	243-252
F. Revival of Revoked Wills	342-348	252-253	129-131	304-318	269-276
G. Dependent Relative Revocation	348-352	247-259	132-134	318-325	276-292
VII. COMPONENTS OF A WILL					
A. Integration	321	268-269		213-220	605-606
B. Incorporation by Reference	321-323	270-281	224-228	794-801	599-620
C. Facts of Independent Significance	323	281-283	226-228	801-806	607-611
D. Pour-Over Gift to Inter Vivos Trust	323	516-525	224-228	806-814	612-620
E. Codicil	343-348	269-270		305-309	606-607
VIII. CONTRACTS RELATING TO WILLS; JOINT WILLS					
A. Contract to Make a Gift by Will		291-292	350-351	822-826	308-309
B. Joint Wills	324-330	291-292, 300-306	351-354	829-835	293-308
C. Contract Not to Revoke a Will	324-336	291-306	347-354	827-835	293-308
D. Contract Not to Make a Will		291-292	349-350	822	293
IX. CHANGES IN BENEFICIARIES AND PROPERTY AFTER EXECUTION OF WILL					
A. Lapsed Gifts	360-361	357-364	377-382	935-936, 976-991	310-311, 352-362
B. Class Gifts	802-807	361-367, 738-767	382-399	1003-1027	52-54, 361-366
C. Classification of Testamentary Gifts	359-360	367		937-939	311, 325-326
D. Ademption	354-358	367-374	355-362	939-955	312-325
E. Stock Splits and Stock Dividends		383-389	361-363	960-964	326-328, 332-343
F. Exoneration of Liens		382-383	366-367	955-960	
X. WILL CONTESTS AND RELATED MATTERS					
A. Grounds for Contesting Will		55, 137		356-415	
B. Procedural Aspects		55-62	527-533	327	167-168
C. Testamentary Capacity	202-220	137-150	242-249	357-370	168-178
D. Testamentary Intent				370-376	201-212
E. Undue Influence	220-253	150-168	249-257	376-387	179-194
F. Fraud	258-264	176-183		387-396	194-198
G. Mistake	253-258	213-228	132-134, 244	396-404	367-414
H. Ambiguity	257-258	346-353	215-220	404-415	372-388
I. No-Contest Clause	244-249	170-171	255-256	352-356	
J. Tort Liability for Wrongful Interference With Expected Inheritance		182-183			193-194
XI. PROBATE AND ESTATE ADMINISTRATION					
A. Overview of Estate Administration Process	621-628	33-62, 393-394	535-544	66-86, 1166-1189, 1197-1201	
B. Proof of Wills in Probate	613-621	33-37, 49-54	524-535	66-83, 326-343	6-16, 127-128
C. Appointment and Qualification of Personal Representative	632-644	34	544-554	1202-1218	
D. Duties and Liabilities of Personal Representative	656-690	37-51, 62-70, 869-882, 892-893	554-598	1218-1230, 1261-1339	753-801
E. Creditors' Claims	644-656	38		1300-1314	
F. Abatement	359-360	374-375	363-371	965-976	343-346

Gilbert Law Summaries **Wills**	Clark, Lusky, Murphy **Gratuitous Transfers** 1985 (3rd ed.)	Dukeminier, Johanson **Wills, Trusts and Estates** 1984 (3rd ed.)	McGovern **Wills, Trusts and Future Interests** 1983	Ritchie, Alford, Effland **Decedents' Estates and Trusts** 1982 (6th ed.)	Wellman, Waggoner, Browder **Trusts and Succession** 1983 (4th ed.)
G. Source of Payment of Death Taxes	948-950	962-963, 1058-1060	367-373	975-976	346-347
H. Entitlement to Income During Period of Administration			373-376	1334-1374	
I. Informal Administration Procedures	622-623	42-51	536-538	1175-1181	114-121

Essay questions in a Wills or Decedents' Estates exam usually follow one of two patterns. The first (and most commonly encountered) type of question includes several will clauses making various gifts, and raises separate issues with respect to each gift. Such a question actually consists of several short-answer subquestions because, more often than not, the issues raised by one of the clauses are independent from the issues raised by the other clauses. (*See, e.g.,* Sample Exam Question I.)

If, for example, the will in the question includes this gift, "I devise Blackacre to my brother John," you can be sure that something is going to happen either to Blackacre or to brother John. Read the remaining facts carefully, because you will be expected to discuss and resolve the proper disposition of the gift to John. While it is possible that a few of the will clauses in the question do not raise any issues calling for discussion (*i.e.,* the clause is a "red herring"), this is the exception rather than the rule. Read (and reread) the facts carefully before you decide that no problems are raised with respect to the particular gift.

The second type of question does not contain a number of will gifts, but instead, involves a "rolling fact situation" in which a series of facts or events are presented sequentially. (*See, e.g.,* Sample Exam Question IV.) Each sentence or paragraph presents a new fact or event that will call for discussion in your answer. In such a question, if you have read three or four sentences and no issue comes to mind, go back and reread those sentences, because you may have overlooked something.

Sometimes both of these elements (separate will clauses and a chronological sequence of events) are contained in the same exam question.

Set out below are some important issues that you should be prepared to identify and discuss.

Execution of Wills

1. **Was the Will Validly Executed?** If the question states that "T left a duly executed will," or other such language, or if the question gives no facts concerning the will's execution, there is no need to discuss the requisites for execution of a will. However, questions may raise an issue as to whether the requirements for due execution were satisfied. If so, you probably should discuss the "due execution" issue first because, if the will was not validly executed, **none of its provisions are valid**. But if the issue is a close one, don't put all your eggs in one basket and conclude that since the will was not validly executed, there is no need to discuss the issues raised by the will's terms. Unless the will's execution is clearly invalid, continue your discussion by saying, "If the court were to hold that the will was validly executed, the following issues would be raised. . . ."

   If the facts do raise an issue as to due execution, set out the steps required by the controlling state statute and then discuss whether all these requisites were satisfied. Watch for these issues:

   a. **Did the testator properly sign the will?** The test is: Did testator intend the mark to be his mark? Remember also that the will can be signed by another person at testator's direction and in testator's presence.

b. **Did the testator sign the will "at the end thereof"?** This is an issue to watch for since some states require the signature to be at the end. But if the facts raise this issue, you should discuss the point even if the controlling law does not have a "signature at the end" requirement.

c. **Did the testator acknowledge his earlier signature?** If the testator signed the will at an earlier point in time, in most states it is necessary for the testator to acknowledge his earlier signature to the witnesses.

d. **Did the witnesses know they were witnessing a will?** In several states, the testator must communicate to the witnesses that they are witnessing a will as distinguished from some other legal document. (The U.P.C. and statutes in many states do not have a "publication" requirement.)

e. **Did the witnesses sign in the testator's presence and did testator sign the will (or acknowledge his previous signature) in the witnesses' presence?** Understand the difference between the liberal "conscious presence" test and the "line of sight" test.

f. **Did any of the witnesses sign before the testator signed?** Most courts hold that the exact order of signing is not critical, so long as the execution ceremony is all one contemporaneous transaction.

2. **Were Any of the Attesting Witnesses Also Beneficiaries Under the Will?** If so, remember that the "interested witness" rule *never* results in denial of the will to probate, but the bequest to the witness is usually purged. In states (including U.P.C. states) that have abolished the interested witness rule, you should point out that no problem is raised by the fact that a beneficiary is also an attesting witness.

3. **Is the Will a Conditional Will?** If so, keep in mind that the will does not take effect unless the event occurs, although most courts like to find that the so-called condition was merely the motive that prompted the testator to write a will, meaning that an intestacy is avoided even if the stated event does not occur.

4. **Is a Holographic Instrument Involved?** If the will is handwritten and unattested, consider whether it is valid as a holographic will. In states that recognize holographic wills, remember that the will's material provisions must be in testator's handwriting and the instrument must be signed by the testator. (Remember the signature test above.) Be sure however to look for testamentary intent—*i.e.,* whether the particular writing was itself intended to be a will. Casual statements may be included in a letter with no intent that they were to be considered testamentary in effect.

If your state does not recognize holographic wills, mention that fact in your answer.

Revocation of Wills

1. **Was the Will Revoked by Operation of Law?** Think about this if the testator married or was divorced after the will was executed.

2. **Did the Testator Attempt To Revoke the Will by a Later Instrument?** Remember that the instrument of revocation must be executed with the same formalities as are required for a will, and that a testator must meet the test for testamentary capacity.

3. **Did the Testator Attempt To Revoke the Will by Physical Act?** The physical act must deface or otherwise affect the entire will or at least its material provisions (although striking out the testator's signature is usually held to be a revocation of the entire will) and the intent to revoke must accompany the physical act of destruction. If the will is accidentally destroyed and the testator subsequently decides that he wanted to revoke the will anyhow, there is no effective revocation.

   a. **Was the physical act of destruction made by another person at the testator's direction and in his presence?** If so, it is a valid revocation.

   b. **Do the facts give rise to a presumption of revocation?** For example, if a will was last seen in testator's possession and control but cannot be found after death, there is a presumption that the reason the will can't be found is that the testator destroyed the will with the intent to revoke it. Think about who was in possession of the will to determine whether a presumption arises.

   c. **Was an attempt made to "revive" an earlier will?** Remember that, in most states, revocation of a second will does not, by itself, "revive" an earlier will that was revoked by the second will. (But under the U.P.C. and in several states an intent to revive may be shown.)

   d. **Should the doctrine of dependent relative revocation be applied?** In the "no revival of revoked wills" situation, be ready to discuss DRR. Under this doctrine, a revocation by physical act can be disregarded if it is shown to have been based on a mistake of law as to the validity of another disposition *and* it is shown that testator's intent will more nearly be effectuated if the revocation is disregarded.

4. **Should the "Proof of Lost Wills" Statute Be Applied to Allow Probate of the Will as a Lost Will?** Remember that the "proof of lost wills" rules are very stringent.

5. **Did the Testator Attempt To Partially Revoke the Will by Physical Act?** Changes on the face of a will are a common source of exam issues. In states that do not recognize partial revocations by physical act, the change is disregarded and the will is read as it was originally executed. However, most states do recognize partial revocations by physical act.

   a. **Did testator write in new provisions on the face of the will?** If the will as executed says, "I bequeath $5,000 to Sue," and the testator subsequently strikes the "$5,000" and writes in "$10,000," the attempted increase of the gift is ineffective (unless the will is reexecuted) since it was not part of the duly executed will. Given that the "$5,000" was stricken from the will with an intent to revoke the gift in that amount, these facts would invoke DRR (if the state recognizes partial revocations). But if the testator strikes "Sue" and writes in "Bill," the bequest to Sue is revoked and DRR should *not* be applied, since the intent to revoke the gift to Sue was independent of the intent to make the (ineffective) gift to Bill.

b.   **Were the changes made on a holographic will?** Unlike attested wills, changes made on the face of a holographic will are valid if they are shown to be in the testator's handwriting, because a holographic will does not have to be written at one sitting.

Issues Raised if Testator Was Married

1.   **Did Testator Marry After the Will Was Executed?** If the state has a "pretermitted spouse" statute, and the testator marries after executing a will, the will is revoked so as to give the spouse an intestate share of the decedent's estate. In states without statutes, it is generally provided that marriage following execution of a will has no effect on the will, but the new spouse has rights under the elective share statute (or, in community property states, under the community property system), homestead laws, exempt personal property set-aside, and family allowance.

2.   **Was Testator Divorced After the Will Was Executed?** If so, the divorce revokes all gifts and administrative appointments in favor of the ex-spouse, and the will is read as though the ex-spouse predeceased the testator. But if the parties later reconcile and remarry, the "revocation by divorce" rule does not apply.

3.   **Should the Spouse File for an Elective Share?** In any question involving a husband and wife, determine whether the surviving spouse should file an election to take a statutory share of the decedent's estate. You probably should discuss this issue even if an election is not warranted, showing that you have considered the issue but found that it would not be advantageous for the spouse to so elect.

   a.   **Are any lifetime transfers subject to the elective share?** In determining the amount of the elective share, carefully assess any facts relating to lifetime transfers by the decedent spouse. The U.P.C. and several states apply the elective share to certain lifetime transfers.

4.   **Should the Spouse Assert a Claim to a Homestead, Family Allowance, or Exempt Personal Property Set-Aside?** While the scope of these rights varies markedly from state to state, you should remember that they may afford a means of partially reordering the testator's dispositive plan by shifting more assets to the surviving spouse's "pile." These rights, along with the elective share, are particularly important if the testator attempted to disinherit his spouse. And remember that these rights ordinarily take precedence over creditors' claims, and the benefits accorded are over and above the amounts passing to the spouse under the elective share, by intestate succession, or under the will. In most states, these rights are also available to minor children.

5.   **Community Property Issues:** Keep in mind that, in a community property state, one spouse can fully dispose of all of his *separate* property (unless it was acquired in another state and is subject to a quasi-community property statute), but that he can dispose of only *his one-half* of the couple's community assets. If one spouse purports to dispose of the entire interest in community assets, an "election will" issue is raised. But note that the courts are reluctant to find that the will put the spouse to an election unless the facts clearly call for an election. Also watch for lifetime gifts of community property made by one spouse. These gifts are subject to challenge by the surviving spouse.

6. **Conflict of Laws Issues:** Did the testator and his spouse move *from a common law state to a community property state*? In California and Idaho, any imported assets would be classified as quasi-community property, and special rules apply to their disposition at death. Most of the other community property states have a quasi-community property rule that applies to divisions upon divorce, but *not* to dispositions at death. In these states, the imported assets would be the acquiring spouse's separate property. Or did the testator and his spouse move *from a community property state to a common law jurisdiction*? You should know whether your state has enacted the Uniform Disposition of Community Property Rights at Death Act. If so, the statute recognizes the surviving spouse's ownership rights in any imported community assets. If not, the surviving spouse's rights should be recognized under a resulting or constructive trust theory.

Changes in Beneficiaries After Will's Execution

1. **Was Testator Married or Divorced After the Will's Execution?** If so, this may have an effect on the will. (*See* discussion above.)

2. **Did Testator Have Children After the Will Was Executed?** Under most states' pretermitted child statutes, a child born or adopted after the will's *execution* is entitled to take an intestate share of the decedent's estate unless the will shows an intent not to make provision for such children. (In a few states, the statute applies to children alive at the time the will was executed as well as to afterborns.) But watch for factors that take the pretermitted child statute out of the question:

    a. **Was the child provided for by lifetime settlement?** A lifetime gift, a bank account in the child's favor, and even a life insurance policy naming the child as beneficiary are generally held to be lifetime settlements within the meaning of the statute.

    b. **Was testator's spouse principal beneficiary under the will?** If so, in many states this factor will prevent the operation of the statute—as long as the spouse was parent of all of testator's children.

    c. **Did testator later execute a codicil to her will?** Under the doctrine of "republication by codicil," a will is deemed to have been executed on the date of the last codicil thereto, meaning that the child would no longer be considered an afterborn child.

3. **Did Any Beneficiary Die During Testator's Lifetime?** You can count on the fact that, in some question on the exam, one or more of the named beneficiaries is going to die during the testator's lifetime. Probably no other issue is tested upon with greater frequency than the "lapsed gift" issue. If a beneficiary predeceases the testator, the gift lapses — unless the state's lapse statute applies to the gift.

    a. **Does the state's lapse statute apply?** The most important facts to look for are the beneficiary's relationship to the testator and the scope of your state's lapse statute. Make sure that the predeceased beneficiary was within the required relationship to the testator or the statute won't apply. Also be sure that the predeceased beneficiary left descendants who survived the testator. The lapse statute does *not* save the gift for the beneficiary's estate, but rather, his descendants take by substitution under the lapse statute.

b. **Was the gift contingent on the beneficiary's survival?** If the gift was made to the beneficiary "if she survives me," the lapse statute does not apply. In most states, this is true even though no alternate gift was made in the event of the beneficiary's nonsurvival.

c. **Did the testator and beneficiary die simultaneously, or did the beneficiary die shortly after the testator?** If the Uniform Simultaneous Death Act is applicable, and there is no sufficient evidence that the parties died otherwise than simultaneously, the beneficiary is deemed to have predeceased the testator, invoking the lapsed gift rules. (But watch for evidence of survival, even for a short period of time.) Likewise, if the U.P.C.'s 120-hour rule controls, and if the beneficiary fails to survive the testator by 120 hours, the beneficiary is deemed to have predeceased the testator. But remember that if the gift is conditioned on the beneficiary's surviving the testator, the 120-hour rule does *not* apply, and the beneficiary takes the gift even though she survived the testator by only a few hours or minutes.

d. **Was the beneficiary who predeceased testator a residuary beneficiary?** It is important to know whether your state applies the "no residue of a residue" rule (the lapsed gift "falls out of the will" and passes by intestacy to the testator's heirs) or has a "surviving residuary beneficiaries" rule (the remaining residuary beneficiaries take). But under either rule, the lapse statute applies if the predeceasing residuary beneficiary was within the scope of the statute *and* left descendants who survived the testator.

4. **Was Any Beneficiary Dead at the Time the Will Was Executed?** This is a "void" gift but most states (and the U.P.C.) apply their lapse statutes in this situation.

5. **Does the Will Make a Class Gift?** If the beneficiaries are described as a class (*e.g.,* "Mary Smith's children"), and one of the class members predeceases the testator, under the class gift rule the remaining class members who survive the testator take the gift. *But note:* In most states the lapse statute trumps the class gift rule if the predeceasing class member was within the scope of relationship covered by the statute *and* left descendants who survived the testator.

a. **Was the gift to a "class" or to individuals?** Make sure that the gift really is to a class. The class gift rule ("surviving class members take") does not apply if the beneficiaries are individually named (*e.g.,* "to Ann, Betty, and Carl, the children of Mary Smith"). Here, if one of the named beneficiaries predeceases the testator, the "lapsed gift" rules discussed above apply.

b. **When does the class close?** If the will makes an outright gift to a class of beneficiaries, the class "closes" at testator's death. Only class members alive (or in gestation) at that time share in the gift. Later-born class members are excluded by the "rule of convenience." If the class gift is of a future interest (*e.g.,* "to my husband Hank for life, and on his death to the children of Mary Smith"), the class does not close until the life tenant's death.

Changes in Property After Will's Execution

1. **Does the Doctrine of Ademption Apply to Any Gifts in the Will?** If the will makes a specific bequest of property and the property is not owned by the testator at death (*e.g.,* it was

lost, destroyed, stolen, or sold during testator's lifetime), the gift fails. *But remember:* Ademption applies only to specific devises and bequests. It does not apply to general legacies ("$5,000 to Nellie") or to demonstrative legacies ("$10,000, to be paid from the proceeds of sale of my Acme stock").

    a.   **Is a bequest of securities involved?** The courts apply some unusual rules of construction to bequests of securities. While a gift of "*my* 100 shares of Zircon stock" is a specific bequest, and ademption applies, a gift of "100 shares of Zircon stock" is classified as a general bequest (for purposes of ademption *only*), and ademption does not apply. Also watch for a change in form: If a corporation is acquired by another corporation and testator's shares of stock are replaced by the new company's stock, in most states the specific beneficiary takes the shares of the acquiring corporation.

    b.   **Does any statutory exception apply?** The U.P.C. and other statutes carve out exceptions to the ademption rule. These statutes give the specific beneficiary any casualty insurance proceeds (to the extent the insurance proceeds are paid after testator's death) and give the beneficiary any remaining contract payments if the testator entered into a contract for sale of the property, and the contract was not fully performed at testator's death.

2.   **Are Any Stock Splits or Stock Dividends Involved?** A specific bequest of stock carries with it any new shares produced by a *stock split* after the will was executed, but states are divided on whether the bequest includes any new shares produced by a *stock dividend*. Note that any new shares issued *after testator's death*, whether from a stock split or a stock dividend, belong to the beneficiary, who owns the shares from the moment of testator's death.

3.   **Is Any Specifically Bequeathed Property Subject to a Lien?** If so, many states require the lien to be "exonerated" by payment from the residuary estate. (The U.P.C. and other states give the beneficiary exactly what the testator owned: title subject to a lien.)

Components of a Will

1.   **Do the Facts Raise an "Integration" Issue?** Although the doctrine of "integration" is rarely tested upon, be aware that only the sheets that are shown to have been present at the time the will was executed comprise the decedent's will. Watch for cases in which the staple has been removed and one of the sheets has a different type face than the other sheets.

2.   **Does the Doctrine of Incorporation by Reference Apply?** Don't overlook the possibility of incorporating an extrinsic document, not present at the time the will was executed, into the will. But make sure that all of the required elements for the doctrine's application can be satisfied.

    a.   **Is a list of tangible personal property involved?** The U.P.C. and statutes in several states carve out an exception to the incorporation by reference doctrine for a list that disposes of *tangible personal property* to named beneficiaries. Such a list, signed by the testator, is given effect even if it is written after the will was executed, and even though it is not witnessed. In states without this special rule, such a list can be given effect only if the incorporation by reference doctrine is satisfied.

3.   **Does the Facts of Independent Significance Doctrine Apply?** Keep in mind that the courts will give effect to the bequest of "the automobile that I own at my death," or "the furniture and

furnishings in my living room" even if later unattested acts of the testator (such as trading in her Honda on a Mercedes, or moving a valuable painting into the living room) affect the gift under the will.

Contractual Wills

1. **Did Testator Allegedly Promise To Make a Gift by Her Will?** A promise to make a gift in the future, if not supported by consideration, is unenforceable. But if consideration was given for the promise, the promise may be enforceable under contract law (not wills law).

2. **Did Testator Allegedly Promise Not To Revoke Her Will?** This is something you should consider if a *joint will* (the will of two persons in a single instrument) is involved. Many state statutes require that the existence of such a contract be referred to in the will. Absent such a statute, it is generally held that the mere execution of a joint will (or of mutual wills containing reciprocal provisions), without more, is **not** sufficient to prove that such a contract existed. And don't forget that if a contract not to revoke is established and one party revokes the will and writes a new will, the new will must be admitted to probate even though it was made in breach of the contract. The beneficiaries of the contract must bring an action outside the probate court, seeking the imposition of a constructive trust.

Will Contests

1. **Does Any Party Have Grounds for Contesting the Will?** An occasional question will present facts concerning the testator's mental and physical condition and the conduct of others in connection with the will's execution. The question then asks whether there are grounds for contesting the will. Generally there will be no clear yes-or-no answer. Fact issues, and not the application of legal doctrines, are involved and so you should keep in mind that a jury would have to decide, on the evidence presented, whether the contestants have met their evidentiary burden. In your answer, consider and discuss each of the facts presented in light of the legal tests of testamentary capacity and undue influence.

    a. **Does the party have standing to contest the will?** To have standing, the party must have an economic interest that would be adversely affected if the will is admitted to probate (generally only decedent's heirs or beneficiaries named in an earlier will have standing).

    b. **Was the contest filed within the prescribed period of time?** (Under the U.P.C., the time period is twelve months.)

2. **Did Testator Have Sufficient Capacity To Make a Will?** The contestants must show that the testator lacked the capacity to know and understand: (i) the nature of the act he was doing (*i.e.*, that he was writing a will), (ii) the natural objects of his bounty, (iii) the nature and value of his property, and (iv) the disposition he was making.

3. **Was the Will the Product of an Insane Delusion?** Even though the testator was otherwise sane (and met the test for capacity), the contestants may be able to show that the will (or a gift therein) was the product of a persistent and irrational belief in supposed facts which have no basis except in testator's perverted imagination, and which the testator adheres to against all evidence and reason.

4. **Did Anyone Exert Undue Influence upon the Testator?** The mere opportunity to influence, susceptibility to influence due to age, illness, or physical condition, or the fact that the will makes an unnatural disposition are factors to be considered but no one is sufficient. The contestants have the burden of establishing (i) the existence of the influence, (ii) its effect of overpowering the mind and will of the testator, and (iii) the product of which was a testamentary instrument that expresses the will, not of the testator, but of the one exerting the influence.

   a. **Did the party who procured the will stand in a confidential relationship with the testator?** Watch out especially for gifts made to the attorney who prepared the will. If a party who was active in procuring the will stood in a confidential relationship with the testator, and if there were suspicious circumstances surrounding either the will's execution or its terms, in many states the burden of proof shifts to the will proponent, who must show that undue influence was ***not*** exerted.

5. **Did Anyone Perpetrate a Fraud on the Testator?** To establish fraud, there must have been false statements of material facts, known by the maker to be false and made with the intention of defrauding the testator, who was actually deceived by the false statements. The fraud may consist of signing the wrong instrument (fraud in the execution), or of inducing a testamentary gift (fraud in the inducement).

6. **Does the Will Contain a No-Contest ("In Terrorem") Clause?** Most states enforce such clauses, but a no-contest clause does not result in a forfeiture ***if*** the court finds that the contesting party had probable cause for bringing the contest, even if the contest was unsuccessful. Be sure the action is a "contest"—*e.g.*, a suit to construe the terms of a will is generally held ***not*** to be a "contest" that triggers a no-contest clause since it does not challenge the validity of the will.

Mistake, Ambiguity

1. **Did Testator Make a Mistake in the Execution of the Will?**

   a. **Was testator unaware that the instrument was a will?** If so, the courts will deny probate because the testator lacked the required testamentary intent.

   b. **Did testator sign the wrong will?** If a husband signs the will prepared for his wife, and the wife signs the will prepared for her husband, be prepared to argue both ways. Some courts have denied relief on the ground that testator lacked testamentary intent with respect to the will he signed, but the better result is to grant relief since both the mistake and what the testator actually intended are so clear.

2. **Was a Testamentary Gift Induced by a Mistake?** If the alleged mistake involves the reasons for making (or not making) a gift, and if no fraud was involved, no relief will be granted.

3. **Was Testator Mistaken as to the Contents of the Will?** It does not matter whether the allegation is that a gift was mistakenly omitted (or mistakenly included) in the will, or that the testator was mistaken as to the import of the will's terms; no relief will be granted. Absent fraud, it is conclusively presumed that the testator read the will, and understood and ***intended*** its contents.

4. **Are Any of the Will's Provisions Ambiguous?** When the will's terms, although clear on the face, are susceptible to more than one meaning when applied to the facts, there is *latent ambiguity; e.g.,* the will names a beneficiary, but two persons (or no person) meet the description. Parol evidence is admissible to cure the ambiguity. When the mistake is apparent on the face of the will, *e.g.,* the will refers to a cousin Bill and a cousin Sandy, and then makes a gift "to my cousin," the courts are divided on whether parol evidence is admissible to cure such a *patent ambiguity,* but the better view is that such evidence is admissible.

Intestate Succession

Be thoroughly familiar with the intestate succession rules that your state applies to commonly encountered family situations. An exam question may call for application of the intestacy rules to the estate of a decedent who died without a will, but it is more likely the intestacy rules will be brought into play in a case where the decedent left a will: There may be a partial intestacy because of a lapse in the residuary clause; or the pretermitted spouse or pretermitted child statute may give an intestate share to a new spouse or an afterborn child.

The rules most likely to be tested upon are the shares of a surviving spouse, child, or parent, but prudence dictates that you also be familiar with the distribution that would occur if the decedent was not survived by any close relations.

1. **Do Grandchildren Take Per Stirpes or Per Capita?** When no children survive the decedent, be sure that you know where the "stirpes" are divided: At the child level (even though there are no living children), or at the first generational level at which there are living takers? (Same for the inheritance by nephews and nieces.)

2. **Are There Any Adopted Children?** Such children have full inheritance rights from their adoptive families, but the states are split on whether the adopted child continues to have inheritance rights from natural parents and grandparents.

3. **Were Any Children Born Out of Wedlock?** Such a child has full inheritance rights from and through his natural mother, but the states apply different tests in determining whether the child has inheritance rights from his natural father.

4. **Are Any Stepchildren Involved?** Remember that such children have no inheritance right from their stepparent unless they were adopted, but watch for facts that might invoke the adoption by estoppel doctrine because of an unperformed agreement to adopt.

5. **Does the State Have a "Laughing Heir" Statute?** Statutes in several states do not grant inheritance rights to remote relations (U.P.C. draws the line at grandparents and descendants of grandparents). Instead, the property escheats to the state.

Other concerns regarding intestate succession include application of the Uniform Simultaneous Death Act (or the U.P.C.'s 120-hour rule) if parties die simultaneously or in close proximity to one another. Also, if more than one state is involved, remember that the law of the decedent's domicile governs personal property wherever located, but that devolution of real property is governed by the law of the situs state.

Other Important Issues

1. **Are Any Nonprobate Assets Involved in the Question?** Nonprobate (or nontestamentary) assets are interests that pass at death other than by will or intestacy, and which are not subject to the personal representative's possession for purposes of administering the estate. However, the elective share statutes found in some states do apply to certain nonprobate assets. You should be familiar with the scope of your state's statute with respect to such assets. The nonprobate assets you are most likely to encounter are:

   a. *Life insurance, employee benefits;*

   b. *Survivorship estates* (joint tenancies, tenancies by the entireties, and joint bank accounts with survivorship provisions); and

   c. *Interests in revocable inter vivos trust drafted so as to continue* in operation after testator's death.

2. **Did the Decedent Make a Lifetime Gift to Any Heir or Will Beneficiary?** If so, in many states the gift is presumed to be an advancement (*i.e.*, an advance payment of a portion of the child's share of his parent's estate) and the value of the advanced property is taken into account in making distribution of the intestate shares. If the gift is to a beneficiary named in the will, the gift is presumed to be in partial satisfaction of the legacy. However, many states have reversed these presumptions, and the U.P.C. declares that an advancement or satisfaction of a legacy can be shown only by a writing signed by either the donor or the donee of the lifetime gift.

3. **Has Any Heir or Beneficiary Attempted To Disclaim an Interest in the Decedent's Estate?** To be valid, such a disclaimer must be in writing and (in most states) must be filed within nine months after the decedent's death. Partial disclaimers are also permitted.

4. **Did an Heir or Beneficiary Murder the Decedent?** Generally a party who wrongfully brought about the death of the decedent cannot take under the decedent's will or by intestate succession, and cannot take as beneficiary of insurance policies on the life of the decedent, or he takes the gift but a constructive trust is imposed. Watch out for a case in which the alleged slayer is tried and found not guilty in criminal proceedings. In most states, this does not preclude a finding in civil proceedings (where the evidentiary standard is "preponderance," not "beyond a reasonable doubt") that the party did wrongfully bring about the death of the decedent.

5. **Was the Attorney Guilty of Negligence in Preparing the Will or in Supervising Its Execution?** You should discuss this issue in any case in which the attorney has bungled the job. Most states hold that the attorney owes a duty of due care, not just to the client, but also to the beneficiaries under the will.

Estate Administration

How much you need to know about the rules governing estate administration will depend on the scope of your course. Coverage of this area varies widely. Some professors make only passing references to the probate process, while others go into considerable detail. At the very least, you should be familiar with these issues:

1. **What Proof Is Required to Probate a Will?** Look for a valid self-proving affidavit executed by the testator and the witnesses at (or after) the will execution ceremony, which will allow the will to be admitted to probate on the strength of the affidavit. If the will was not self-proved, be sure you know the test that must be satisfied (usually, proof of signatures) if the attesting witnesses arc dead or cannot be located.

    a. **When must the will be probated?** Most states require that a will must be probated within a specified time after a decedent's death; otherwise, it is conclusively presumed that the decedent died intestate. (Under the U.P.C., the time period is three years.)

2. **Are Any Alternatives to Court-Supervised Administration Available?** If you are in a U.P.C. state, know the differences between an unsupervised and a supervised administration, and when an unsupervised administration is available. In any state, be familiar with the jurisdiction's small estate administration rules, and any other procedures that may be available for small or uncomplicated estates.

3. **What Powers Can a Personal Representative Exercise Without Court Approval?** How much you are expected to know about this issue will turn on the attention given to probate procedures in your course. At the least, though, you should know that unless an unsupervised (or "independent") administration is involved, most states have detailed rules governing a personal representative's power to sell real property. Also, usually a personal representative does not have the power to continue operation of the decedent's business (*e.g.*, a sole proprietorship) without court approval.

4. **When Must Creditors' Claims Be Filed?** Most states have a special statute of limitations (a "nonclaim statute") applicable to creditors' claims against the estate. Such claims must be filed within a specified period of time or the claims are barred. But be careful: Such statutes do not defeat valid security interests held by a creditor, and they do not apply to the extent that the claim (*e.g.*, a tort claim) is covered by liability insurance. *And note:* A few states do not have nonclaim statutes. In these states, failure to file within the time specified in the statute simply means that the creditor will not be paid until after all timely-filed claims are paid.

5. **Is the Estate Partially Insolvent?** "Abatement" rules apply if there are more creditors than can be satisfied out of the residuary estate. In most states, creditors' claims are satisfied out of estate assets in the following order: (i) any property passing by intestacy, (ii) the residuary estate, (iii) general legacies (which abate pro rata), (iv) demonstrative legacies, (v) specific devises and bequests. Know whether (within any of the five categories) personal property must first be sacrificed before any of the estate's real property can be reached.

I. INTESTATE SUCCESSION

___chapter approach___

The typical Wills exam will contain at least one intestate succession question because, unfortunately, a lot of people die without a valid will. Even when the particular question involves a will, intestate succession laws may be involved in distributing the estate. Therefore, for almost every question, you should at least consider whether the laws of intestate succession apply. Ask yourself:

1. **Is there a valid will disposing of all the property?** If the will is valid, then it rules, but if the decedent in the question has left no will, or the will is invalid for some reason (*e.g.*, not witnessed), or the will does not make a complete disposition of the decedent's property, then the intestate succession statute applies.

2. **Which state's intestate succession statute applies?** For personal property, the law of the *decedent's domicile* governs. For real property, the law of the state in which the *property is located* governs.

3. **What property passes by intestate succession?** Only the "probate estate" can pass by intestacy: *i.e.*, cash, real estate, and personal property owned by the decedent at death. Other assets (*e.g.*, life insurance proceeds, property passing by right of survivorship) pass outside of probate.

4. **How should the property be distributed?** Check the appropriate statute of descent and distribution. If your question doesn't give you the statute, follow the general rules:

   a. *Spouse* gets a share, the size of which depends upon whether descendants survive; usually the spouse takes one-half or one-third if there are descendants, all if not.

   b. *Children* take all if there is no surviving spouse, or a smaller share if the spouse survives the decedent.

   c. *Grandchildren and other descendants* take their parent's share if their parent predeceased the decedent.

   d. *Parents* (or the surviving parent) *or the descendants of parents* take if the decedent left no spouse or descendants.

   e. *Other relatives,* or next of kin take before the state.

   f. *If no other takers,* property escheats to the state.

5. **Is the domicile a community property state?** If so, remember that the above rules apply only to separate property. Different rules apply to community property. Keep in mind that the surviving spouse already owns half of all community property.

A. INTRODUCTION

1. **Intestacy:** [§1]   When a person dies without a valid will, or when the will does not make a complete disposition of the estate, distribution of the deceased's property is governed by the intestacy statutes of one or more jurisdictions.

2. **Common Law:** [§2]   At common law, if a decedent left no will, various Canons of Descent governed the descent and distribution of the decedent's property. These Canons provided separate rules for real property and for personal property: Real property **descended** to the decedent's **heirs,** while personal property was **distributed** to the decedent's **next of kin.**

3. **Modern Law:** [§3]   Today, every jurisdiction has supplanted the common law Canons by enacting statutes that regulate the distribution of property by intestate succession. In nearly all states, the rules governing intestate succession are the **same** for real and personal property. However, a few states have separate schemes for the descent of land and the distribution of personal property. [*See e.g.,* Tex. Prob. Code §38(b); Va. Code §§64.1-1, 64.1-11] In modern usage, the terms "heirs" and "next of kin" are synonymous, although "heirs" is the preferred term for describing persons who take either real or personal property by intestacy.

4. **What Law Governs:** [§4]   In general, the law of the state where the decedent was **domiciled at death** governs the disposition of **personal** property, and the law of the **situs** state governs the disposition of **real** property located within that state. (*See* Conflict of Laws Summary.)

    a. **Example:** N, a New York domiciliary, dies intestate. N owned real property and tangible personal property situated in New York. N also owned real property located in North Carolina and had several stock certificates and two items of valuable jewelry in a safe deposit box in a Boston bank. Devolution of the New York land and **all** personal property (including the contents of the safe deposit box) is governed by the New York intestacy statutes. Devolution of the North Carolina land is governed by the North Carolina intestacy statutes.

5. **Property Subject to Administration:** [§5]   The intestacy statutes (or for that matter a will, if the decedent left one) apply only to the decedent's **probate** or **testamentary** estate.

    a. **Probate estate:** [§6]   The probate estate consists of those assets owned at death that pass by will or inheritance and which are subject to administration by the decedent's personal representative (*e.g.,* real estate, cash, stocks and bonds in the decedent's name, etc.).

    b. **Nonprobate assets:** [§7]   Intestate succession rules do not apply to nonprobate assets, and such assets are not subject to administration by the decedent's personal representative. There are four categories of nonprobate assets:

(1) **Contract:** [§8]   Property that passes at death under a contract or agreement is a nonprobate asset. The most commonly encountered example is life insurance proceeds, which are payable to the beneficiary designated by the insured in his contract with the insurance company. A death benefit paid to designated beneficiaries under an employee pension or profit-sharing plan is also a nonprobate asset.

(2) **Right of survivorship:** [§9]   Property held in a valid joint tenancy with the right of survivorship, property owned by spouses as tenants by the entireties, and funds on deposit in a valid survivorship bank account pass by right of survivorship to the surviving party. Such interests do not pass under the decedent's will, are not subject to estate administration, and are not subject to the intestacy laws.

(3) **Trust:** [§10]   Assets owned by the decedent merely as a trustee or trust beneficiary are nonprobate assets.

 (a) **Example:** O settles assets in a revocable or irrevocable inter vivos trust that names X as trustee. Under the terms of the trust, the trustee shall pay the income to O for life, and on O's death shall distribute the trust principal to O's descendants. Legal title to the trust assets is in the trustee; O and her descendants have equitable interests. On O's death, disposition of the trust corpus is governed by the terms of the trust, and not by O's will or under the intestacy statutes. (*See* Trusts Summary.)

(4) **Power of appointment:** [§11]   If the decedent holds a power of appointment over an asset, that asset is not subject to intestacy laws. (*See* Future Interests Summary.)

 (a) **Example:** T's will devises property in trust to pay the income to B for life, and on B's death, to distribute the trust principal to such one or more of B's descendants as B appoints by will. If B does not exercise the power by will, the property is to pass per stirpes to B's descendants.

 1) *If B dies intestate,* the appointive assets pass to the "takers in default of appointment" specified in T's will (B's descendants, per stirpes). The intestacy statutes have no application to the property.

 2) *If B leaves a will that exercises the power* in favor of B's daughter D, by the appointment B is regarded as having "filled in the blanks" in T's will. Although B's will is the instrument by which the taker of the property is identified, the property is deemed to have passed from T to D. The appointive assets are not part of B's probate estate and are not subject to administration by B's personal representative.

B. PATTERNS OF INTESTATE DISTRIBUTIONS

1. **Rules Vary From Jurisdiction to Jurisdiction:** [§12]   Except for states that have enacted the Uniform Probate Code ("U.P.C."), there are no two states whose intestacy

laws are the same in all details. There are even variations in some of the U.P.C. states, as several of those states have not adopted all of the U.P.C. intestate distribution rules.

a. **Community property states:** [§13] Community property states have two sets of intestacy statutes: one governing community property, and the other governing separate property. In general, separate property passes under the inheritance rules described below. The intestate succession rules applicable to community property are discussed *infra*, §§35 *et seq.*

b. **Representative intestacy statutes:** [§14] The following discussion summarizes the general patterns of intestate distribution found in many states. For the rules of descent of a particular state, it is essential that that state's statutes be consulted. The Appendix to this Summary examines representative intestacy statutes of both common law jurisdictions and community property states. For common law jurisdictions, the Uniform Probate Code and the Florida, Illinois, and New York statutes are summarized. For community property states, the California and Texas statutes are outlined.

2. **Intestate Share of Surviving Spouse**

   a. **Spouse takes as heir in all states**

      (1) **Common law:** [§15] At common law, a spouse was not an heir. The decedent's property passed by intestacy to descendants or (if no descendants) to collateral kin. If the decedent left no blood relations, the estate escheated to the Crown. The surviving spouse took only a dower interest (if a widow) or a curtesy estate (if a widower) in the decedent's property. (*See infra*, §§179–185.)

      (2) **Modern law:** [§16] Under modern law, the surviving spouse takes an intestate share of the decedent's estate in **all** jurisdictions.

   b. **Survived by descendants:** [§17] If the intestate is survived by a spouse and by descendants (children, grandchildren, etc.), in most states the spouse takes **one-third or one-half** of the decedent's estate. Some states (and the Uniform Probate Code) give the surviving spouse a stated dollar amount **plus** one-third or one-half of the balance of the estate. The fraction or the dollar amount often varies depending upon the number of decedent's children and their relationship to the surviving spouse.

      (1) **Example:** W dies intestate in a state that has enacted the U.P.C. She is survived by her husband H, and by their children A, B, and C. Under U.P.C. section 2-102, H takes the first $50,000 plus one-half the balance of W's estate. The remaining estate passes to the children (one-sixth each).

(2) **Terminology:** Some intestacy statutes use the term *descendants* when referring to children and more remote offspring, while other statutes refer to *issue.* The terms "descendants" and "issue" are synonymous. This summary uses the term "descendants" in referring to the children and more remote offspring of a person.

c. **Not survived by descendants:** [§18]   If the decedent is survived by a spouse but not by descendants, in many states the spouse inherits the *entire estate.* [*See, e.g.,* Tex. Prob. Code §38]

   (1) **Exception:** [§19]   If the decedent is survived by parents (and, in some states, by descendants of parents), several jurisdictions limit the above rule by giving the spouse only one-half of the estate (or a dollar amount plus one-half). In these states, the spouse inherits the entire estate only if the decedent is not survived by either parent (or, in some states, the descendants of parents). [U.P.C. §2-102; N.Y. Est. Powers & Trusts Law §4-1.1]

      (a) **Example:** H, a resident of a state that has enacted the Uniform Probate Code, dies intestate. He is survived by his wife W and by his parents. W inherits $50,000 plus one-half of the balance of the estate. The remaining estate passes to H's parents (or to his parent if only one survives). If H's parents do not survive him, W inherits the entire estate.

3. **Intestate Share of Children and Other Descendants:** [§20]   The remaining estate that does not pass to the surviving spouse, or all of the estate if the decedent is not survived by a spouse, passes to decedent's children and descendants of deceased children. Parents and collateral kin never inherit if the intestate is survived by children or more remote descendants.

a. **Example:** W, a widow, dies intestate. She is survived by her three children A, B, and C, by her father F, and by her sister S. In all states, W's entire estate passes to her children (one-third each).

b. **Grandchildren take by representation**

   (1) **Survived by both children and grandchildren:** [§21]   If the intestate is survived by children and grandchildren, the grandchildren will take a share of the estate only if they are children of a *deceased* child of the intestate. Grandchildren take *only by representation; i.e.,* grandchildren will take the share that their parent would have taken had he survived. Thus, grandchildren who are descendants of a living child of the intestate do not share in the estate. (This principle also applies to nephews and nieces and other collateral relations whose parents are living so as to take as heirs.)

      (a) **Example:** H, a widower, dies intestate. He is survived by two children (A and B) and by three grandchildren (A's child, A, Jr.; and X and Y, the children of H's deceased child C). The intestate distribution is: one-third to A, one-third to B, and one-sixth each to X and Y. X and Y take by representation; *i.e.*, they take the share their parent C would have taken had C survived. Grandchild A, Jr. takes nothing because his parent A is alive to take a share.

(b) **"Per stirpes":** [§22]   This type of distribution (by representation) is also called a per stirpes distribution. The literal translation of "per stirpes" is "by the roots," meaning one share for each family line.

(2) **Survived by grandchildren only:** [§23]   If the intestate is not survived by any children but is survived by grandchildren, there is a split of authority on how the distribution should be made among the grandchildren—by representation or per capita (*see infra,* §§73 *et seq.*).

4. **Not Survived by Spouse or Descendants**

a. **Majority rule:** [§24]   If the intestate is not survived by a spouse or by descendants, in most jurisdictions the estate is inherited by the decedent's parents (one-half to each) or surviving parent (who takes all). [U.P.C. §2-103]

b. **Minority rule:** [§25]   In a few states, if only one parent survives, that parent takes one-half of the estate, and the other one-half passes to decedent's brothers and sisters (and the descendants of deceased brothers and sisters). [Tex. Prob. Code §38]

5. **Not Survived by Spouse, Descendants, or Parents**

a. **To descendants of parents:** [§26]   In nearly all states, if the intestate is not survived by a spouse, descendants, or parents, the estate passes to the descendants of the intestate's *parents*—*i.e.,* to the decedent's brothers and sisters (and the descendants of deceased brothers and sisters, per stirpes).

b. **To grandparents and descendants of grandparents:** [§27]   In most states, if the decedent left no brothers or sisters (or descendants of deceased brothers and sisters), one-half of the estate passes to *maternal grandparents* (or their descendants), and the other half passes to *paternal grandparents* (or their descendants).

6. **Intestate Distribution Beyond the Grandparent Level:** [§28]   With respect to inheritance beyond grandparents and their descendants, the rules vary from state to state.

a. **Majority rule:** [§29]   If the decedent is not survived by a spouse, grandparents, or descendants of grandparents, in most states the estate is divided into maternal and paternal shares. One-half of the estate goes to the nearest kin on each side of the family, regardless of how remotely they were related to the decedent. [Tex. Prob. Code §38]

b. **"Laughing heir" statutes:** [§30]   Some states cut off inheritance by "laughing heirs," persons so remotely related to the decedent that they suffer no sense of loss, but only gain, at the news of his death. Generally, these statutes prevent inheritance by persons related to the decedent beyond the grandparent or descendant-of-grandparent level. [U.P.C. §2-103; Fla. Prob. Code §732.103] The estate passes instead to the state (*see* below).

7. **Escheat:** [§31]   If the intestate is not survived by any living relations (in states that do not limit the degree of relationship required for inheritance), or is not survived by grandparents or descendants of grandparents (in states that have a "laughing heir" statute), the estate passes (escheats) to the state.

    a. **Exception:** [§32]   In a few states, if the decedent left no living relations to take as heirs, the estate passes to the heirs of the decedent's previously deceased spouse (if any) before it escheats to the state. [Cal. Prob. Code §6402.5(d); Fla. Prob. Code §732.103(5)]

8. **Ancestral Property:** [§33]   A handful of states apply a special rule to property that the decedent received by gift, will, or inheritance *from a parent or grandparent.* If the decedent is not survived by a spouse or descendants, this "ancestral property" reverts back to the parent or grandparent or (if they are deceased) to their heirs. [Cal. Prob. Code §6402.5(c)]

    a. **Rationale:** [§34] This rule is consistent with the parent's or grandparent's probable intent that the property return and be distributed to other children, rather than go to the decedent's collateral heirs. [Estate of Hanson, 179 Cal. App. 2d 32 (1960)]

C. INTESTATE DISTRIBUTIONS—COMMUNITY PROPERTY STATES

1. **Introduction:** [§35]   There are eight community property states: Louisiana, Texas, New Mexico, Arizona, California, Washington, Idaho, and Nevada. Although the community property laws of the eight states vary markedly in detail, there is agreement on certain basic definitions:

    a. **Separate property:** [§36]   Separate property is defined as property owned by a spouse *before marriage,* and property acquired during marriage *by donation* (gift, will, or inheritance). In five of the states (Arizona, California, Nevada, New Mexico, and Washington), the income from separate property is separate property. In Idaho, Louisiana, and Texas, the income from separate property is community property. In all eight states, separate property passes by intestacy in accordance with the rules described above.

    b. **Community property:** [§37]   Community property is negatively defined as *all* property acquired *during marriage* that is *not* separate property. Under the "community presumption," all property on hand on dissolution of the marriage (whether by divorce or death) is presumptively community property. The burden of establishing that a particular asset is separate property (*i.e.*, owned before marriage, acquired during marriage by donation, or purchased with separate funds) is on the party so contending.

2. **Survived by Spouse But Not Descendants:** [§38] In all of the community property states, if the intestate is not survived by descendants, the intestate's one-half share of the community estate passes to the surviving spouse. (The other one-half of the community estate does ***not*** pass to the spouse by inheritance; it already belongs to the surviving spouse.) As a result, the surviving spouse succeeds to the entire community estate.

3. **Survived by Spouse and Descendants:** [§39] There are two basic patterns for distributions of community property if the deceased spouse is survived by descendants.

   a. **All to surviving spouse:** [§40] In several states, the surviving spouse takes the entire community estate even if the decedent was survived by descendants. [*See, e.g.,* U.P.C. §2-102A; Cal. Prob. Code §6401(a)]

   b. **Decedent's one-half community passes to descendants:** [§41] In other states, the decedent's one-half community share is inherited by his descendants; the surviving spouse takes the entire community estate only if the decedent was not survived by descendants. [Tex. Prob. Code §45] In Louisiana, the decedent's one-half community share is inherited by his descendants, subject to the surviving spouse's usufruct for life or until remarriage. [La. Civ. Code §915]

4. **Quasi-Community Property:** [§42] Quasi-community property is property acquired by one spouse while domiciled in another state which would have been classified as community property had it been acquired while domiciled in the community property state. (Real property situated in another state is not quasi-community property.)

   a. **Quasi-community property statutes:** [§43] Two states have quasi-community property statutes that apply to decedents' estates. [Cal. Prob. Code §6401(b); Idaho Code §15-2-201] These statutes are, in effect, elective share statutes (*see infra,* §189) that restrict the "acquiring spouse's" power of disposition over these imported assets. The acquiring spouse may dispose of only his one-half interest in quasi-community property by will; the other one-half passes to the surviving spouse, who cannot be deprived of this amount by will. If the acquiring spouse leaves no will, all of the quasi-community property is inherited by the surviving spouse. (California's quasi-community property statute is discussed *infra,* §44.)

      (1) **Compare:** Several of the other states apply the quasi-community property principle to distributions made upon ***divorce,*** but not to distributions upon the acquiring spouse's death. In these states, quasi-community property is treated the same as "true" community property for purposes of property divisions upon divorce [Tex. Family Code §3.63; Rau v. Rau, 432 P.2d 910 (Ariz. 1967)]; but if the marriage is dissolved by the death of one spouse, these imported assets are considered the ***separate*** property of the acquiring spouse (*see* below).

b. **Conflict of laws separate property:** [§44]   In the states that do not have quasi-community property statutes that apply to distributions at death, there is a source of separate property not covered by the statutory definitions that is the product of conflict of laws principles.

   (1) **Example:** H and W were married in Minnesota in 1975, and lived there until they moved to Texas in 1983. At the time of the move, H owned securities worth $100,000, acquired from his earnings in Minnesota. Two years after the move, H died intestate. Intestate succession of H's estate is governed by Texas law, since H was a domiciliary of Texas at his death. The $100,000 in securities passes by intestacy under the rules applicable to separate property.

   (2) **Rationale:** Although the securities (in the above example) were acquired during marriage, they were acquired while the couple was domiciled in a common law state, where a husband's salary is his property and a wife's salary is her property. The ownership character of an asset is governed by the laws of the marital domicile at the time the asset was acquired; and that ownership is not altered when the couple moves to another state. Stated another way: Under the Constitution, property rights are not lost by moving to another state. (*See* Conflict of Laws Summary.) Since the securities were "H's" property in Minnesota, they were "his separate property" in Texas.

   (3) **Compare:** In California and Idaho, the $100,000 in securities brought from Minnesota would be classified as quasi-community property.

5. **"Former" Community and Separate Property:** [§45]   California applies a special rule to certain assets *if* the decedent dies intestate *not survived by a spouse or descendants.*

   a. **Former community property:** [§46]   One-half of any property that was formerly the community property of the decedent and a previously-deceased spouse goes to the issue of the previously-deceased spouse or (if no issue) to the parents, brothers, and sisters of the previously-deceased spouse. This includes (i) the decedent's one-half interest in the former community property, and (ii) the deceased spouse's one-half share that passed to the decedent by gift, will, inheritance, right of survivorship, or homestead right. [Cal. Prob. Code §6402.5]

   b. **Former separate property:** [§47]   Any property that was formerly the separate property of the previously-deceased spouse and passed from that spouse to the decedent by gift, will, intestate succession, homestead right, or right of survivorship goes to the issue of the previously-deceased spouse or (if no issue) to the parents, brothers and sisters of the previously-deceased spouse. [Cal. Prob. Code §6402.5(b)]

   c. **Application:** [§48]   Because of these special rules, "former" community and separate property passes to the decedent's parents and collateral kin *only* if there are no living issue, parents, or descendants of parents of the previously deceased spouse.

II. INHERITANCE RIGHTS AS AFFECTED BY STATUS OF CHILD OR SIBLING

chapter approach

Inheritance rights may sometimes be affected by the "status" of the heirs (*e.g.*, an adopted child may inherit from the adopted parent but not from the natural parent). Exam questions covering these issues appear quite often as only a portion of a distribution problem. Therefore, keep a watchful eye out for the following:

1. ***Adopted children***—become the children of the adopting parents, and in most cases lose the right to inherit from the natural parent.

2. ***Children born out of wedlock***—inherit from the mother and her kin, but generally need some additional proof (*e.g.*, adjudication or formal acknowledgment of paternity) to inherit from and through the father.

3. ***Posthumous children***—generally may inherit from the decedent.

4. ***Stepchildren***—may ***not*** inherit from stepparent absent certain circumstances presenting "adoption by estoppel."

5. ***Grandchildren***—take by representation (*see supra*, §21), but if only grandchildren are surviving (*i.e.*, none of decedent's children survive), distribution may be either per capita with representation or strict per stirpes.

6. ***Half-bloods***—in most states take the same as whole bloods, but in some states take only half as much as the whole bloods.

A. ADOPTED CHILDREN

1. **Early Law:** [§49] Although the adoptive relationship was recognized early in Roman and Hebrew law, adoption was unknown to the English common law. Beginning with legislation in Massachusetts in 1851, all of the United States now permit adoptions. However, in many states, the statutes governing inheritance by adopted children were not enacted until the 1900's. As a result, early cases had to deal with the inheritance rights of adopted children without the aid of a statute.

    a. **Stranger to the adoption rule:** [§50] Absent a statute, most courts held that an adopted child could inherit from the adopting parents, but not from the adopting parents' kin. The rationale was that an adoption should not be permitted to make an adopted child the heir of a "stranger to the adoption" (*i.e.*, anyone other than the adopting parent). [Welch v. Funchess, 71 So. 2d 783 (Miss. 1954); Hockaday v. Lynn, 98 S.W. 585 (Mo. 1906)]

b. **Natural parents:** [§51]   It was generally held that an adopted child continued to have inheritance rights from and through the child's natural parents, even though now adopted into a new family. [80 A.L.R. 1398]

2. **Modern Law**

a. **Adopting parents:** [§52]   In all states that have enacted statutes governing inheritance rights of adopted children, an adopted child has the *same inheritance rights* as a natural child. The adopted child and her issue can inherit from the adopting parents and from the adopting parents' kin. Also, the adopting parents and their kin can inherit from and through the adopted child. [U.P.C. §2-109]

b. **Natural parents:** [§53]   There are several patterns in the statutes dealing with this problem.

(1) **Majority rule:** [§54]   In many states, the adoption of the child by a new family severs the parent-child relationship between the child and the natural parents. Thus, an adopted child and her issue have *no* inheritance rights from or through the natural parents, and the natural parents and their kin have no inheritance rights from or through the adopted child.

 (a) **Exception—adoption by natural parent's spouse:** [§55]   Under these statutes, an "exception" to the general rule is simply a sensible qualification of the rule: Adoption of a child by the spouse of a natural parent has no effect on the relationship between the child and that natural parent. [*See, e.g.,* N.Y. Dom. Rel. Law §117]

  1) **Example:** W and H have a child C. W divorces H. W marries J, who adopts C. (In most states, this adoption would require the consent of the natural father H, if he is still alive.) C may inherit from or through his natural mother W and his adoptive father J (and they from and through him). But any inheritance rights concerning H have been severed.

(2) **Uniform Probate Code:** [§56]   Under the U.P.C., an adopted child is the child of an adopting parent and not of the natural parents. The adoption severs the parent-child relationship between the child and the natural parents.

 (a) **Exception—adoption by natural parent's spouse:** [§57]   The U.P.C. provides that the "adoption of a child by the spouse of a natural parent has no effect on the relationship between the child and *either* parent." [U.P.C. §2-109] Thus, under the U.P.C., the child can continue to inherit from or through *both* natural parents, and this is true regardless of whether the marriage of the natural parents was ended by divorce or death.

  1) **Application:** The "either" in the statute solves a problem that is raised by the New York-type statute above. Suppose, in the pre-

vious example, W's marriage to H was terminated by H's death rather than by divorce. Then W marries J, and J adopts C. Thereafter, H's mother (C's "grandmother") dies intestate. Under the New York-type statute, C does not inherit from her "grandmother," because the adoption terminated the parent-child relationship between C and her natural father H. [Estate of Garey, 214 Cal. App. 2d 39 (1963)] Under the U.P.C., C would continue to have inheritance rights from and through H, whether the W-H marriage was severed by divorce or by H's death.

(3) **Minority rule:** [§58]   A few states apply a "one-way street" rule. The natural parents of a child who has been adopted have no inheritance rights from or through the child, but the **adopted child** and her issue continue to have inheritance rights from and through the natural parents. [Tex. Prob. Code §40]

B.   CHILDREN BORN OUT OF WEDLOCK

1. **Common Law:** [§59]   At common law, a child born out of wedlock was *filius nullius* (a child of no one) and had no inheritance rights from either his father or his mother. Only the child's spouse and issue could inherit from the child.

2. **Modern Law—Inheritance From Mother:** [§60]   In all states today, a child born out of wedlock inherits from his natural mother and the mother's kin, and they can inherit from and through the child.

3. **Inheritance From Father:** [§61]   Until recently, many statutes provided that a child born out of wedlock had inheritance rights from and through the father (and vice versa) *only* if the child was legitimated by the marriage of the father and mother after the child's birth. [Ill. Prob. Act §12—before amendment in 1975]

   a. **Constitutional problem:** [§62]   The above statute was held unconstitutional on equal protection grounds. The Court held that a statute fixing the inheritance rights of an illegitimate child can exact a higher standard of proof of fatherhood than of motherhood because of the evidentiary problems involved, but a statute that allows for **no** means of proving fatherhood for inheritance purposes denies equal protection. [Trimble v. Gordon, 430 U.S. 762 (1977)]

   b. **Modern law:** [§63]   Most states have amended their statutes to eliminate the constitutional problem. Generally, these statutes provide that the inheritance rights may be established by one of several means, including the father's marriage (or attempted marriage) to the mother, a formal acknowledgement of paternity, or a judgment in a paternity suit. [*See e.g.,* Tex. Prob. Code §42; N.Y. Est. Powers & Trusts Law §4-1.2] Other states look to the existence of a family relationship or the existence of paternal support to establish inheritance rights. [*See* Cal. Civ. Code §7004]

   c. **Uniform Probate Code:** [§64]   The U.P.C. treats the child as heir of the father if: (i) the father and mother "participate" in a void marriage ceremony before or after the child's birth; or (ii) paternity is established by adjudication during the father's lifetime *or* by clear and convincing evidence after the father's death. *But note:* The father and his kin cannot inherit from or through the child unless the father openly treated the child as his own and did not refuse to support the child. [U.P.C. §2-109]

C. POSTHUMOUS CHILDREN

1. **In General:** [§65]   Under common law principles, and by statute in many states, a child conceived during the father's lifetime but born after the father's death is considered the decedent's child for inheritance purposes. [Ill. Prob. Act §2-3]

2. **Presumption:** [§66] The courts have developed a *rebuttable* presumption that the normal period of gestation is ten lunar months (280 days). Thus, a child born more than 280 days after the decedent's death presumptively was sired by someone else. However, the presumption is rebuttable, and whether the child is the decedent's child even though born more than 280 days after the "father's" death is a jury question. [Byerly v. Tolbert, 108 S.E.2d 29 (N.C. 1959)]

3. **Uniform Probate Code:** [§67]   The U.P.C. extends this rule: Any relations (and not just the decedent's child) in gestation at the decedent's death "inherit as if they had been born in the lifetime of the decedent." [U.P.C. §2-108]

D. STEPCHILDREN

1. **General Rule:** [§68]   In general, a stepchild has *no* inheritance rights from the foster parents. If a woman with a child marries, and her husband does not adopt the child, there is no legal relationship between the stepchild and stepfather. There may be a familial relationship (the child may have lived in the man's home and may have called him "daddy"), but inheritance requires a legal relationship. [Bank of Maryville v. Topping, 393 S.W.2d 280 (Tenn. 1965)]

2. **Exception for Adoption by Estoppel:** [§69]   On the right facts, a number of jurisdictions apply the doctrine of adoption by estoppel (sometimes called "equitable adoption") in cases involving an *unperformed agreement to adopt.* This doctrine, based on estoppel principles, allows a stepchild to inherit from the foster parent just as though the child had been adopted.

    a. **Example:** Foster parents obtain custody of a child based on an agreement with the natural parent that they will adopt the child and "give him our name." After obtaining custody, the foster parents do not perform their agreement. One of the foster parents dies intestate. The child may inherit from the decedent. Just as the foster parent would, in equity, be estopped to deny performance of the agreement, so also are the foster parent's natural kin estopped to deny that an adoption took place. [Barlow v. Barlow, 463 P.2d 305 (Colo. 1969)]

    b. **Minority rule:** [§70]   Some jurisdictions do not recognize the adoption by estoppel doctrine, and thus the child has no right to inherit from or through the foster parent. [Bank of Maryville v. Topping, *supra*]

c. **Applies only to estate of foster parent:** [§71] Since the basis of the estoppel is the foster parent's conduct in failing to perform the agreement to adopt, only those claiming through the foster parent are estopped. Thus, if the sister of one of the foster parents dies intestate, the foster parent's stepchild has no interest in his "aunt's" estate. [Shaeffer v. Shaeffer, 292 N.W. 789 (Iowa 1970)]

d. **One-way street:** [§72] The doctrine only works against the foster parent. Suppose there is an unperformed agreement to adopt, but it is the stepchild who dies intestate, single, and wealthy. The foster parents do **not** inherit from the child. Application of the doctrine of adoption by estoppel does not result in the creation of an adoptive parent-adoptive child relationship; rather, it operates to estop the foster parent (and his kin) from denying that an adoption took place. The child would not have done anything to give rise to an estoppel. [Heien v. Crabtree, 369 S.W.2d 28 (Tex. 1963)]

E. DO GRANDCHILDREN TAKE PER STIRPES OR PER CAPITA?

1. **In General:** [§73] Most intestacy statutes provide that when an intestate's estate is inherited by descendents, they take "per stirpes" (*see supra,* §21). When there is at least one taker at the first generational level (*i.e.,* the child level), there is no dispute as to what "per stirpes" means. But what if there are no takers at the child level?

   a. **Example:** W, a widow, dies intestate leaving the following surviving descendants: her son A (and A's child U); grandchildren V and Q (children of her deceased son B); and grandchildren X, Y, and Z (children of her deceased daughter C):

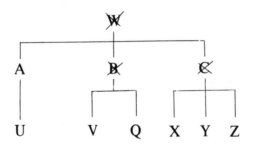

   Since there is one living taker at the child level, the stirpital shares are divided at the child level in all jurisdictions. A takes a one-third share. B's and C's children take the shares their parent would have taken had the parent survived to be an heir. Thus V and Q take one-sixth each, and X, Y, and Z take one-ninth each. (*See supra,* §21.)

   b. **Compare:** Suppose, however, that A also predeceases W, meaning that there are no living takers at the child level. Are the stirpital shares determined at the child level or at the grandchild level?

2. **Majority Rule—Per Capita With Representation:** [§74] In most states, the stirpital shares are determined at the first generational level at which there are living takers. Each

descendant at that generational level takes one share, and the share of each deceased person at the generational level is divided among his descendants by representation. [Restatement of Property §303] This form of distribution, called "per capita with representation," is adopted by the Uniform Probate Code. [U.P.C. §2-106] Thus, in the above example, if all three of W's children predeceased W, the six grandchildren would each take a one-sixth share of W's estate. [*In re* Martin's Estate, 120 A. 863 (Vt. 1923)]

3. **Minority Rule—Strict Per Stirpes:** [§75]   A few states apply a "strict per stirpes" rule. Under this rule, the stirpital shares are *always* determined at the first generational level even though there are no living takers at that level. Applying a strict per stirpes distribution to the above example, if all three of W's children predeceased her, U would take one-third, V and Q would take one-sixth, and X, Y, and Z would take one-ninth of W's estate. [Tex. Prob. Code §45—community property; Maud v. Catherwood, 67 Cal. App. 2d 636 (1945)]

4. **Construction Problem Under Wills and Trusts:** [§76]   The same problem of determining whether grandchildren take under the strict per stirpes rule or per capita with representation can be encountered under wills and trusts, where a gift is made "to my descendants then living, per stirpes," and there are no children alive at the time the distribution is to be made. In fact, the problem is more likely to be encountered under a will or trust than in an intestacy situation. Under intestacy statutes, the heirs are determined at death, and it is relatively rare for a person to outlive all of her children, leaving only grandchildren and more remote descendants as heirs. On the other hand, it is not uncommon for a trust to continue for the lifetime of the settlor's children, with a further provision that "on the death of my last surviving child the trust estate shall be distributed among my descendants then living, per stirpes." Of necessity, under such a provision there will be no children alive when the distribution among descendants is to be made.

    a. **Constructional approach—look to intestacy statutes:** [§77]   In such a case, if the will or trust does not give a clear indication of how the distribution should be made, the courts look to the intestacy statutes of the state to determine what meaning should be given to "per stirpes." In a *majority* of states, a *per capita with representation* distribution is made. [U.P.C. §2-106]

    b. **Drafting suggestion:** [§78] In drafting a will or trust which provides that the remainder shall pass to descendants (or issue), it is not enough to state that the descendants shall take per stirpes. The instrument should provide, in unambiguous language, whether the distribution among descendants is to be on a strict per stirpes basis or on a per capita with representation basis.

F.   INHERITANCE BY BROTHERS AND SISTERS OF THE HALF-BLOOD

1. **In General:** [§79]   A problem is presented when a distribution is to be made among siblings of the half-blood (one common parent) and siblings of the whole blood (two common parents).

a. **Example:** Consider the following family tree:

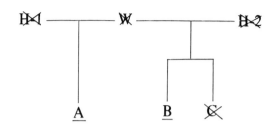

Suppose that C dies intestate, leaving as her nearest relations, her half-brother A and her ''whole'' sister B. What distribution should be made?

2. **Common Law Rule:** [§80]   The English common law rule wholly excluded relatives of the half-blood from inheritance. This rule has been *abolished* by statute in all American jurisdictions.

3. **Majority Rule:** [§81]   Most jurisdictions now ignore the common law and make *no distinctions* between siblings of the whole blood and half-blood. In these states, A and B in the example above would take equal shares of C's estate. [U.P.C. §2-107; Gradwohl v. Campagna, 46 A.2d 850 (Del. 1946)]

a. **Exception for ancestral property:** [§82]   Several jurisdictions that have adopted the majority position abolishing the distinction between half-bloods and whole bloods make an exception for ''ancestral property.'' Kindred of the half-blood inherit equally with those of the whole blood in the same degree, unless the property came to the intestate by devise or gift from one of her ancestors, in which case, all of those who are not of the whole blood of such ancestor are excluded from inheritance in favor of those who are. [Cal. Prob. Code §6406]

4. **Other Solutions**

a. **Half-bloods excluded:** [§83]   In some states, siblings of the same ancestral blood are preferred over siblings of the half-blood. (Thus, in these states, C's entire estate would pass by intestacy to B.) *But note:* Half-bloods are not entirely excluded from inheritance; they take only if the decedent was not survived by siblings of the whole blood (or descendants of such siblings). [Conn. Gen. Stat. Ann. §45-276]

b. **Half-bloods take half as much as whole bloods:** [§84]   In some states, siblings of the half-blood may inherit, but they take only half as much as the siblings of the whole blood (*e.g.*, B would inherit two-thirds of C's estate and A would inherit one-third). [*See, e.g.,* Fla. Prob. Code §732.105; Tex. Prob. Code §41(b); Va. Code §64.1-2]

III. SUCCESSION PROBLEMS COMMON TO INTESTACY AND WILLS

—chapter approach—

This chapter covers certain problems common to intestacy and wills. Some topics are more likely than others to be tested, but all deserve some careful consideration. Consider especially the following:

1. When the **decedent and an heir or will beneficiary die together or in quick succession**, be sure to check whether your question has a statute concerning **simultaneous death** (either the Uniform Simultaneous Death Act or the Uniform Probate Code 120-hour rule), because if there is an applicable statute, it will affect distribution of the estate. Also, look for will provisions requiring survival because these will keep the statute from applying.

2. When your question has the decedent make a **lifetime gift to an heir or will beneficiary**, consider whether the gift might be an **advancement** or **partial satisfaction of a legacy.** If so, it may affect the donee's share of the estate. Remember that the intent of the decedent controls whether the gift is an advancement or in partial satisfaction of a legacy, and that if the gift exceeds the share that the donee would inherit or take under the will, the donee need **not** give back the property.

3. Always remember that an heir or will beneficiary can **disclaim** a share but that the disclaimer must meet the state **and** federal requirements or it may not be (i) valid or (ii) tax-free.

4. Occasionally, a question has an heir or will beneficiary **cause the death of the decedent.** By statute, or under a constructive trust theory, a killer can lose the interest in the estate, but the killing must be intentional and unjustified.

5. This chapter also covers a nonresident alien's right to take property. This right may be limited by statute, but the statute cannot violate United States treaty or constitutional provisions.

A. SIMULTANEOUS DEATH

1. **In General:** [§85]   A person cannot take as an heir or will beneficiary unless he survives the decedent for at least an instant of time. However, it is often difficult to determine whether the person survived the decedent (*e.g.*, when the person and decedent are both fatally injured in an accident). To solve this problem, nearly all states have statutes dealing with simultaneous death or deaths in quick succession.

2. **Uniform Simultaneous Death Act:** [§86]   All jurisdictions except Louisiana and Ohio have enacted the Uniform Simultaneous Death Act (or its Uniform Probate Code equivalent, the 120-hour survival rule). Under the Act, where the title to property or the

devolution thereof depends upon priority of death and there is no sufficient evidence that the parties have died otherwise than simultaneously, the **property of each person shall be disposed of as if he had survived**. [Cal. Prob. Code §220]

a. **Example:** If property owner A and beneficiary B die simultaneously, the Act will cause A's property to pass under A's will or by intestacy to A's kin, rather than through B's estate to B's kin.

b. **Purposes of the Act:** [§87]   The Act is designed to allow property to pass through its owner rather than through an heir or will beneficiary who never lived long enough to enjoy ownership. The Act also tends to avoid administration of the same assets in two estates in quick succession and may avoid double estate and inheritance taxation of the same assets in two estates.

c. **Application**

(1) **Intestate succession, wills, life insurance policies:** [§88]   In the case of simultaneous deaths, an intestate estate is distributed as though the owner survived the heir, testamentary assets are distributed as though the testator survived the will beneficiary, and life insurance proceeds are paid as though the insured survived the beneficiary (absent a contrary provision in the will or insurance policy).

(a) **Example:** A is the insured under a $25,000 life insurance policy that names B as primary beneficiary "if she survives the insured," and C as contingent beneficiary. A's will devises his residuary estate "to B if she survives me; otherwise to D." B has no will. A and B die simultaneously in the crash of a private plane. The life insurance proceeds are payable to C, and A's residuary estate passes to D, since A is deemed to have survived B. For purposes of distributing B's intestate estate, B is deemed to have survived A.

(2) **Joint tenancies, tenancies by the entireties:** [§89]   If joint tenants or tenants by the entireties die simultaneously, **one-half** of the property passes as though one party survived and the other half passes as though the other survived, regardless of which party furnished the consideration for the joint property's acquisition. *Rationale:* There is no evidence of survival to trigger the right of survivorship.

(3) **Community property:** [§90]   If a husband and wife die simultaneously, **one-half** of the community property passes as though the husband survived, and the other half passes as though the wife survived.

d. **Evidence of survival—Act does not apply:** [§91]   Remember that the Act applies only when there is no sufficient evidence that the parties died other than simultaneously. If there is sufficient evidence that one party survived the other, even for a brief period of time, the Simultaneous Death Act does not apply.

(1) **Example:** Mother M and daughter D are fatally injured in an automobile accident. M is pronounced dead at the scene of the accident; D dies at a local hospital seventy-one minutes later. Since there is clear evidence of survival, for purposes of distributing M's estate D is deemed to have survived M. [White v. Taylor, 286 S.W.2d 925 (Tex. 1956)]

(2) **Example:** H and W are killed instantly in the crash of a private plane. An autopsy reveals that H's brain was smashed and there was no carbon monoxide in H's blood stream. W's brain was intact. Carbon monoxide in W's blood stream indicated that she was breathing when fire broke out after the crash. According to one court, this constituted sufficient evidence that W survived H. [Matter of Bucci, 57 Misc. 2d 1001 (1968)]

(3) **Comment:** [§92] Finding sufficient evidence of survival based on an autopsy, as in above example, undercuts the policy of the Simultaneous Death Act. However, the problem does not lie with the courts' accepting such evidence, but with the Act itself. The Act covers only simultaneous deaths and not deaths in quick succession (such as the seventy-one minute example), even though these cases raise the same concerns about double administration and possibly double taxation of the same assets.

e. **Contrary provision—Act does not apply:** [§93] The presumption raised by the Simultaneous Death Act does not apply if the decedent's will or other instrument makes some other provision regarding survival.

(1) **Planning recommendation:** [§94] In drafting wills, it is advisable to make a beneficiary's taking contingent on surviving the testator by a specific period of time (*e.g.*, thirty days). Such a provision would produce a satisfactory result in the seventy-one minute case and the plane crash case described in the above examples.

(2) **Marital deduction:** [§95] In making a federal estate tax marital deduction gift by will, it is advisable to reverse the Simultaneous Death Act presumption to preserve the deduction. Such a *reverse presumption clause* is given effect for federal tax purposes. (*See* Estate & Gift Tax Summary.)

(a) **Example:** W's will makes a marital deduction gift to her husband H "if he survives me." The will further provides: "for purposes of the marital deduction gift, if my husband and I die under such circumstances that there is no sufficient evidence as to which of us survived, my husband shall be considered to have survived me." This clause would secure the marital deduction for W's estate if she and her husband died simultaneously.

3. **Uniform Probate Code:** [§96] The U.P.C. deals with the problem of deaths in quick succession by providing that a person must survive the decedent by *120 hours* in order to

take as heir or will beneficiary (absent a contrary will provision). Several states that have not adopted the U.P.C. have also adopted the 120-hour survival rule. [*See, e.g.,* Tex. Prob. Code §47]

a. **Intestacy—heir must survive by 120 hours:** [§97]   A person who fails to survive the decedent by 120 hours is deemed to have predeceased the decedent for purposes of intestate succession, homestead allowance, and exempt personal property set-aside. [U.P.C. §2-104]

   (1) **Where alternative is escheat—rule does not apply:** [§98]   The 120-hour survival rule does *not* apply if the result of its application would be an escheat to the state. In such a case, even if the person survives the decedent but by less than 120 hours, he takes as heir.

b. **Will beneficiary must survive by 120 hours:** [§99]   A will beneficiary who does not survive the testator by 120 hours is deemed to have predeceased the testator (absent a contrary will provision). [U.P.C. §2-601]

   (1) **Contrary will provision:** [§100]   The 120-hour rule does not apply if the will contains language explicitly dealing with simultaneous deaths or deaths in a common disaster, or requiring that the devisee survive the testator or survive him for a stated period in order to take under the will. [U.P.C. §2-601]

      (a) **Example:** T's will devises Blackacre "to B if she survives me." T dies; B dies 48 hours later. The 120-hour rule does not apply because the will contains a provision dealing with survival. Since B met the condition attached to the testamentary gift (survival of T), Blackacre passes to B (and thence through B's estate to B's successors).

c. **Joint tenancies:** [§101]   The U.P.C.'s 120-hour rule does *not* apply to joint tenancies with right of survivorship or tenancies by the entireties. *But note:* Several states that have adopted the rule have *extended* its application to survivorship estates, and the property passes one-half as though one party had survived and one-half as though the other had survived. [*See, e.g.,* Tex. Prob. Code §47]

   (1) **Example:** A and B own 1,000 shares of Acme Corp. common stock as joint tenants with right of survivorship. A dies; B dies 36 hours later. If the U.P.C. rule applies, title to the Acme stock passes to B by right of survivorship since B survived A. If the Texas 120-hour rule applies, a one-half interest in the stock passes under A's will as though A survived B, and the other one-half interest passes under B's will as though B survived A.

d. **No proof of time of survival:** [§102]   If the time of death of the decedent and the other person cannot be determined, and it cannot be established that the person survived by 120 hours, it is *presumed* that the person *failed to survive* for the required period.

B. ADVANCEMENTS; SATISFACTION OF LEGACIES

1. Advancement of Intestate Share

a. **Common law:** [§103]   At common law and in a number of states today, any lifetime gift to a *child* is *presumed* to be an advancement (*i.e.,* an advance payment) of the child's intestate share, to be taken into account in distributing the intestate's property at death. The burden of establishing that a lifetime gift is *not* an advancement is on the party so contending. In many states, the presumption of advancement also applies to gifts to more remote descendants (*e.g.,* grandchildren). The common law presumption of advancement does not apply to gifts to *collateral* kin (*e.g.,* a sister).

b. **Modern law:** [§104]   Many states have statutes governing advancements. Most statutes provide that an advancement can be made to *any heir* (*e.g.,* a spouse or a sister), and not just to a child or other descendant. However, the most important effect of these statutes is to reverse the common law presumption. The statutes follow several patterns:

(1) **Common law presumption reversed:** [§105]   Some statutes merely provide that a lifetime gift to an heir is not an advancement unless proved to be an advancement. Proof of intent to make an advancement can be based on oral testimony or on written evidence. [Tex. Prob. Code §44]

(2) **Written evidence of advancement:** [§106]   In many states, a lifetime gift to an heir can be treated as an advancement only if (i) expressly declared as such in a writing signed by the donor, *or* (ii) acknowledged as such in a writing signed by the donee. A finding of advancement cannot be based on oral testimony.

(a) **Timing of written evidence:** [§107]   Under statutes requiring written evidence of an advancement, the timing of the writing may be important.

1) In several states and under the U.P.C., a writing signed by the *donor* must be *contemporaneous* with the gift, but a written acknowledgment of the advancement by the *donee* can be made *at any time.* [U.P.C. §2-110; Fla. Prob. Code §733.806]

2) In other states, the writing signed by the donor *or* the acknowledgment signed by the donee must be *contemporaneous* with the gift in order to be admissible as establishing an advancement. [N.Y. Est. Powers & Trusts Law §2-1.5]

3) In yet another group of states, the written evidence of advancement (whether a statement by the donor or an acknowledgment by the donee) can be made *at any time.* [Ill. Prob. Act §2-5]

c. **Procedure if advancement found:** [§108]   If an advancement is established, the advancee must allow the value of the advanced property to be "brought into hotch-pot" in order to share in the intestate estate. ("Hotchpot" is the common law terminology that is still used by many courts to describe the advancement computation.) This does not mean that the advancee must give the property back. It simply means that the value of the property is added to the estate, in an accounting sense only, to determine the intestate shares.

   (1) **Example:** W, a widow, gives land to her son A. Thereafter, W dies intestate survived by three children: A, B, and C. W leaves an estate worth $90,000. The gift to A is determined to be an advancement, and the property's value for advancement purposes is $30,000. This figure is added to W's estate:

   $90,000   W's intestate estate
   +30,000   value of advancement to A
   $120,000

   The total amount ($120,000) is then divided into three shares of $40,000, and A is deemed already to have received $30,000 of his share. Thus W's intestate estate is distributed: $10,000 to A, $40,000 to B, and $40,000 to C.

   (2) **Compare—value of advanced property exceeds intestate share:** [§109] Suppose, in the above example, the value of the property given to A was $60,000 and not $30,000. The value of the advanced property would exceed A's one-third share of the estate as augmented by the advancement (*i.e.*, $90,000 plus $60,000). Would A have to give any portion of the property back? No. A must allow the advanced property to be brought into hotchpot only if he wishes to share in the intestate distribution. Here A would not come into hotchpot. A would keep the land, and B and C would take the intestate estate in equal shares of $45,000 each.

d. **When valuation of advancement is made:** [§110]   The states are divided on whether the advanced property is brought into hotchpot at its date-of-death value [Tex. Prob. Code §44], its estate-tax value [N.Y. Est. Powers & Trusts Law §2-1.5], or its date-of-gift value [D.C. Code Ann. §19-319; Ill. Prob. Act §2.5]. Under U.P.C. section 2-110, the property is valued at the time the heir came into possession of the property or at the decedent's death, whichever first occurs. [Cal. Prob. Code §6409]

e. **Partial intestacy:** [§111]   The advancement doctrine does ***not*** apply if the decedent left a will that does not make a complete disposition of the estate. (This could occur if the will did not contain a residuary clause, or if a gift to a residuary beneficiary lapsed; *see infra*, §§673-676.)

   (1) **Rationale:** It is presumed that the testator had all the lifetime gifts he had made in mind at the time he executed the will. (However, the doctrine of satisfaction of legacies, discussed below, might be applicable to any gifts made after the will's execution.)

f. **Advancee predeceases intestate:** [§112]   A problem arises when the person receiving the advancement predeceases the intestate. For example, suppose that W gives land to her child A, intending the gift as an advancement, and then A dies in W's lifetime. Thereafter, W dies intestate, survived by children B and C and by grandchild A, Jr. Is the lifetime gift to A treated as an advancement against A, Jr.'s intestate share?

  (1) **Majority rule:** [§113]   At common law and in most states, the advancement doctrine applies. Since A, Jr. takes by representation through A, the gift to A *is* taken into account in determining A, Jr.'s intestate share. [Brown v. Taylor, 62 Ind. 295 (1878); Tex. Prob. Code §44]

  (2) **Minority rule:** [§114]   In most states with statutes requiring that evidence of the advancement be in writing, the advanced property is not taken into account in determining the intestate share of the advancee's descendants unless the written declaration or acknowledgment so provides. [U.P.C. §2-110]

2. **Satisfaction of Legacies:** [§115]   Suppose that a person writes a will, and thereafter makes a lifetime gift to one of the beneficiaries named in the will. Is the gift treated as being in partial or total satisfaction of the legacy?

  a. **Majority rule:** [§116]   At common law, and in states that have not enacted statutes dealing with the question, a gift to a child of the testator is *presumptively* in partial or total satisfaction of any gifts made to the child in a previously executed will. [Carmichael v. Lathrop, 66 N.W. 350 (Mich. 1896)] In most of these states, a gift to a more remote descendant (*e.g.*, grandchild) is also presumptively in satisfaction of a legacy to the descendant. But a gift to any other will beneficiary (*i.e.*, someone *other than* a child or descendant) is treated as in satisfaction of the legacy *only* if it is shown to have been intended as such by the testator. [Johnson v. McDowell, 134 N.W. 419 (Iowa 1912)]

    (1) **General legacy:** [§117]   The above rule applies to general legacies (*i.e.*, legacies payable out of the general assets of the estate and which do not require delivery of a particular item of property). [26 A.L.R. 9]

      (a) **Example:** T's will includes legacies of $20,000 to her daughter D and $10,000 to her niece N. Thereafter, T gives her daughter $5,000, and gives her niece $3,000. The gift to the daughter is presumptively in partial satisfaction of the $20,000 legacy. The gift to the niece is treated as being in partial satisfaction of the $10,000 legacy only if it is shown that T intended this result.

    (2) **Specific bequest:** [§118]   A specific bequest is one that can be satisfied only by delivery of a particular item of property described in the gift. Whether the doctrine of satisfaction of legacies applies depends on the circumstances:

      (a) **Ademption by extinction:** [§119]   T's will bequeaths "my gold Rolex watch to my brother Bill." Thereafter, T gives the Rolex watch to Bill.

This case does **not** involve the doctrine of satisfaction of legacies but, rather, results in **ademption by extinction** (*see infra*, §727 *et seq.*) since the watch will not be in T's estate at his death.

(b) **Satisfaction of legacy:** [§120] Suppose the same will provision as above, except that T gives his brother Bill a set of diamond cuff links which are of substantially equal value to the Rolex watch. The gift may be held to be in satisfaction of the bequest of the Rolex watch **if** it is shown that the testator **intended** this result. *And note:* When a specific bequest is involved, the requirement that the gift be shown to have been intended as in satisfaction of the bequest applies to gifts to testator's children as well as to other beneficiaries.

(3) **Residuary bequest:** [§121] A residuary bequest disposes of all property not otherwise disposed of in the will. Early cases held that there could not be satisfaction of a legacy that was indefinite in amount. Therefore, since the amount of the residuary bequest could not be determined until the estate was settled, under this rule, a lifetime gift could **not** be in partial satisfaction of a residuary bequest. *But note:* It is now generally held that a lifetime gift to a residuary legatee **can** be held to be in partial satisfaction of the residuary bequest **if** it is shown to have been so intended. [Carmichael v. Lathrop, *supra*]

b. **Testator's intent controls:** [§122] Under the common law and majority rule, application of the satisfaction doctrine depends on the testator's intention. In ascertaining intent, courts look to statements made in the will itself or to **extrinsic evidence,** particularly to declarations by the testator at or near the time of the gift. Also, the courts have developed certain presumptions.

(1) **Compare—ademption:** By contrast, the doctrine of ademption is generally applied without regard to testator's intent. (*See infra*, §731.)

(2) **Loco parentis presumption:** [§123] If the legatee is a child of the testator or has been so treated by the testator (*e.g.*, a foster child), there is a rebuttable presumption that the gift was intended to work a satisfaction of the legacy. [Wallace v. Dubois, 65 Md. 153 (1886)]

(a) **Limitation:** This presumption was developed to protect against unintentional favoritism of one child over others; therefore, it does **not** apply when there are no other children.

(3) **Specific purpose presumption:** [§124] If a bequest was made for a specific purpose (*e.g.*, "to buy a house for my sister"), and a lifetime gift is made for the same purpose, it is presumed that the gift was in partial or total satisfaction of the bequest. [Austin v. Austin, 22 N.W.2d 560 (Neb. 1946)]

(4) **Ejusdem generis presumption:** [§125]   If the nature of the lifetime gift is basically different from the nature of the testamentary bequest, it is presumed that the gift was *not* intended to be in satisfaction of the bequest. [Vincent v. Vincent, 217 N.W. 65 (Mich. 1928)] However, the presumption can be overcome if it is shown that testator did intend the gift to be in partial or total satisfaction of the legacy.

c.   **Statutory solutions:** [§126]   Most states with statutes governing advancements (*supra,* §§104-107) have another statute that applies the identical rules to satisfaction of legacies. If the state requires that an advancement be proved by a writing signed by the donor or a written acknowledgment by the donee, another statute requires proof of satisfaction of legacies in the same manner.

(1) **Timing of written evidence:** [§127]   As with advancements, some statutes require that the *donor-testator's* statement that the gift is intended as being in satisfaction of the legacy be written *contemporaneously* with the gift, but the *donee's* acknowledgment of the gift as a satisfaction may be written *at any time.* [U.P.C. §2-612; Fla. Prob. Code §732.609]   In other states, *both* the donor's written statement and the donee's acknowledgment must be made *contemporaneously* with the gift. [N.Y. Est. Powers & Trusts Law §2-1.5]   In still other states, the written statement by the testator or acknowledgment by the donee can be made *at any time.*

(2) **Written evidence not required:** [§128]   Some statutes require proof that the gift was intended to be in satisfaction of the legacy, but do not specify what form the proof must take; oral testimony is admissible on the issue of intent. [D.C. Code Ann. §18-307]

d.   **Will beneficiary predeceases testator:** [§129]   Sometimes a named beneficiary under a will predeceases the testator. If the beneficiary had received a lifetime gift from the testator, is that gift treated as a partial satisfaction of the legacy as against the beneficiary's heir? For example, suppose that T's will makes a $25,000 bequest to her son A. Thereafter, T gives A $10,000; then A dies before T, leaving a child G. Since T does not change her will, G takes the bequest to A under the state's lapse statute (*see infra,* §660). If the gift to A was intended as in partial satisfaction of the $25,000 bequest, the gift to G will also be reduced by $10,000.

(1) **Rationale:** Since G takes by representation under the lapse statute, G cannot take any more than A would have taken had A survived the testator. [U.P.C. §2-612, Official Comment]

(2) **Compare:** In the comparable situation involving advancements, under the majority view, the same result would be reached. However, under the Uniform Probate Code, the gift to an heir apparent who predeceases the intestate ordinarily would *not* result in a reduction of the intestate share passing to the intestate's descendants. (*See supra,* §§112-114.)

C. DISCLAIMER BY HEIR OR WILL BENEFICIARY

1. **Introduction:** [§130] No one can be compelled to be a donee of a gift against his will; thus, it has always been held that a will beneficiary can disclaim any testamentary gift. If a beneficiary makes a valid disclaimer, the disclaimed interest passes as though the *disclaimant predeceased the testator.*

   a. **Reason for making disclaimer—tax advantage:** [§131] Although there may be other reasons to disclaim a gift, the vast majority of disclaimers are made for tax purposes.

      (1) **Example:** T dies leaving a will that devises his $250,000 estate to his daughter D if she survives T, otherwise to D's children. D, who is forty years old, already has a substantial estate and enjoys a substantial income. If D accepts the bequest, it will aggravate her own estate tax and estate planning problems and will give her more income to be taxed in the highest tax bracket. D could accept the bequest and then give the property to her children, but this would result in a taxable gift for federal gift tax purposes. Thus, the better solution is for D to disclaim the bequest in whole or in part. The disclaimed interest will pass from *T* to D's children as though D predeceased T. The effect of the disclaimer is to cause the property to pass to the next generation free of any gift tax.

   b. **Statutory requirements for disclaimer**

      (1) **Federal disclaimer statute:** [§132] To be effective for gift tax purposes, a disclaimer must satisfy the federal gift tax statute governing disclaimers. The most important requirements are that the disclaimer must be (i) *in writing,* (ii) *irrevocable,* and (iii) *filed within nine months* after the decedent's death. [Internal Revenue Code ("I.R.C.") §2518; *and see* Estate and Gift Tax Summary]

      (2) **State disclaimer statutes:** [§133] Many states have enacted statutes listing the interests that can be disclaimed and setting forth the procedure that must be followed to make a valid disclaimer. Consequently, to be a valid disclaimer for both local law purposes and tax purposes, the requirements of *both* the state statute and the federal tax statute must be satisfied. Most of the state statutes have been drafted so as to conform to the requirements of Internal Revenue Code section 2518. [U.P.C. §2-801; Cal. Prob. Code §260-295; Tex. Prob. Code §37A]

         (a) **But note:** Some statutes impose additional procedural requirements that are not required under the federal statute—*e.g.,* that the instrument of disclaimer must be acknowledged before a notary public. [Fla. Prob. Code §732.801; N.Y. Est. Powers & Trusts Law §2-1.11]

c. **Terminology:** [§134]   At common law, an inter vivos donee or a testamentary beneficiary *disclaimed* the gift; an heir *renounced* his intestate share. In modern parlance, the terms "disclaimer" and "renunciation" are synonymous and are used interchangeably. The term used by the federal statute and by most state statutes is "disclaimer." This is also a more convenient terminology, as it permits one to refer to the "disclaimant," rather than to a "renunciator."

2. **Interests That May Be Disclaimed**

   a. **Testamentary gifts:** [§135]   Even before statutes were enacted dealing with disclaimers, it was held that a will beneficiary could disclaim a testamentary gift without making a taxable gift. [Brown v. Routzahn, 63 F.2d 914 (6th Cir. 1933)] Now, however, for the disclaimer of a testamentary gift to be valid, it must be in a form that satisfies both the state and the federal statutes.

   b. **Intestate shares**

      (1) **Common law:** [§136]   At common law, an intestate heir could not make a tax-free disclaimer of her intestate share because it was held that title to the intestate's property "is cast upon his heirs by force of law"; *i.e.,* the title to the intestate shares passed to the heirs at the moment of the intestate's death.

         (a) **Example:** H dies intestate, survived by his wife W and by his two children: S and D. W and D, generous as well as rich in their own right, disclaim their intestate shares with the result, under the state's laws, that the entire estate passes to S. Under the principle that title to the intestate's property passes to W and D at the moment of H's death, their subsequent "renunciation" constitutes an assignment of *their* property to S, and thus, each made a taxable gift of their property. [Hardenburgh v. Commissioner, 198 F.2d 68 (8th Cir. 1952)]

      (2) **Modern law:** [§137]   Federal law now recognizes that a disclaimer of an intestate share is valid for federal gift tax purposes (*i.e.,* *no gift tax* will be assessed) *if* the disclaimer is made within nine months after the decedent's death. [I.R.C. §2518] All states with disclaimer statutes expressly authorize disclaimer of an intestate share.

   c. **Life insurance and employee benefit proceeds:** [§138]   Most state statutes permit a beneficiary to disclaim the proceeds of a life insurance policy or an employee death benefit plan if the disclaimer is made within nine months after the decedent's death. The disclaimer of such an interest is valid for federal gift tax purposes. [I.R.C. §2518]

   d. **Joint tenancies:** [§139]   Statutes in a number of states permit the surviving joint tenant (or surviving tenant by the entireties) to disclaim within nine months after the first tenant's death. However, the Internal Revenue Service takes the position that such a disclaimer is *not* valid for gift tax purposes unless made within nine months *after the interest is created* (*i.e.,* when the joint tenancy property is acquired).

e. **Life estates:** [§140]   If a life tenant disclaims the life estate, the future interests following the life estate are accelerated (*i.e.*, they vest in possession) unless the testator has made other provision for what is to happen if the life tenant disclaims. [N.Y. Est. Powers & Trusts Law §2-1.11(d)]

f. **Future interests:** [§141]   Disclaimer statutes in many states permit the holder of a future interest to disclaim that interest within nine months after the future interest ***vests in possession.*** *But note:* Under current federal gift tax law such a disclaimer would have ***gift tax consequences*** (*see* below).

   (1) **Former law—*Keinath* case:** [§142]   T died in 1944, leaving a will that devised property in trust: income to wife W for life, and on W's death, per stirpes to W's descendants then living. On T's death in 1944, his son S (then in his 20's) gave no thought to disclaiming his share of the remainder interest. W died in 1963; S (who had become wealthy in the meantime) disclaimed his share of the remainder, which passed to S's children as a result of the disclaimer. The disclaimer was held valid for gift tax purposes since the disclaimer was made within a reasonable time after the future interest vested in possession. [Keinath v. Commissioner, 480 F.2d 57 (8th Cir. 1973)]

   (2) **Current law:** [§143]   The result in the *Keinath* case was legislatively overturned when section 2518 of the Internal Revenue Code was enacted in 1976, and was judicially overturned by the United States Supreme Court in *Jewett v. Commissioner*, 455 U.S. 305 (1982). To be tax-free for gift tax purposes, a future interest must be disclaimed within nine months ***after the interest is created*** (on the *Keinath* facts, when T died in 1944), even though the interest is a contingent remainder.

g. **Partial disclaimers:** [§144]   Under most disclaimer statutes, an heir or beneficiary can make a partial as well as a total disclaimer (*e.g.*, by disclaiming one-half or two-thirds of the interest that otherwise would pass to her). Partial disclaimers are recognized as valid for federal gift tax purposes.

3. **Disclaimer by Personal Representative or Guardian**

a. **Common law:** [§145]   In the handful of cases that have considered the question without the aid of a statute, it is generally held that a decedent's personal representative or an incompetent person's guardian can, **with court approval,** make a disclaimer on behalf of the decedent or incompetent beneficiary. [Estate of Hoenig v. Commissioner, 66 T.C. 471 (1976)]

b. **Statutes:** [§146]   Nearly all state disclaimer statutes now permit a personal representative or guardian to disclaim upon a court finding that it is in the interest of the decedent's estate or the ward to do so. [U.P.C. §2-801; N.Y. Est. Powers & Trusts Law §2-1.11; Tex. Prob. Code §37A]

c. **Application:** [§147]   H dies leaving a $750,000 estate and a will that devises "all my property to my wife W if she survives me; otherwise to my children." W survives H, but by only three months. Because of the unlimited federal estate tax marital deduction, there is no estate tax on H's estate. But W is left with an estate greater than $750,000 and no marital deduction available to reduce the federal estate tax. W's executor could disclaim one-half of the gift from H's will; the disclaimed one-half would bypass W and go directly to the children. H and W each would have a taxable estate of $375,000. Because of the federal estate tax unified credit, no estate tax would be due from either estate. (*See* Estate and Gift Tax Summary.)

4. **Estoppel:** [§148] A beneficiary or heir cannot disclaim an interest after having *"accepted"* the property or any of its benefits. Thus, a person will be estopped from disclaiming if he has received a partial distribution of the property, he transfers or encumbers the property, or he enters into a contract for the property's sale, because in these situations, he has "accepted" the property.

5. **Creditors' Claims**

   a. **Majority rule:** [§149] In most states, a disclaimer *can* be used to defeat creditors' claims. If an heir or beneficiary disclaims an interest in the decedent's estate, the property passes as though the heir or beneficiary predeceased the decedent, and thus the heir or beneficiary has no interest that can be reached by creditors. [Estate of Oot, 95 Misc. 2d 72 (1978)]

   b. **Minority rule:** [§150] In a minority of jurisdictions, a disclaimer is *not* effective as against the creditors of the disclaimant. The creditors can reach the property as though the disclaimer had not been made. [Fla. Prob. Code §732.801]

D. KILLER OF THE DECEDENT

1. **Common Law:** [§151] Suppose that an heir (or will beneficiary) murders the decedent. Should that person be entitled to inherit from the estate? Working without the aid of statutes, the courts have developed various solutions to this problem.

   a. **Minority rule:** [§152] Some courts have held that the legal title passes to the slayer and can be retained by him in spite of the crime. [Bird v. Plunkett, 95 A.2d 71 (Conn. 1953)]

      (1) **Rationale:** Devolution of a decedent's property is controlled entirely by the statutes of descent and distribution. Furthermore, denial of inheritance rights because of the crime would be imposing additional punishment not provided for by the criminal statute and would violate constitutional provisions against corruption of blood (*see infra,* §§168-169). [Wall v. Pfanschmidt, 106 N.E. 785 (Ill. 1914)]

      (2) **Critique:** This position is generally discredited, and most jurisdictions now *bar* a killer from succeeding to his victim's property. [McGovern, *Homicide and Succession to Property,* 68 Mich. L. Rev. 65 (1969)] In several cases in which the killer was allowed to inherit, legislation was immediately enacted to

address the problem. [*In re* Duncan's Estate, 246 P.2d 445 (Wash. 1952); Wash. Laws ch. 141, §613]

b. **Majority rule:** [§153]   Under the equitable principle that a person should not be allowed to profit from his wrongful conduct, most courts hold that one who wrong-fully brings about the death of a decedent **forfeits** any interest in the decedent's estate. The property passes as though the killer predeceased the victim. There are two lines of decision that have reached this result:

(1) **Title does not pass to killer:** [§154]   Some courts have held that legal title does not pass to the killer because of the equitable principle that no one should profit from his wrong or crime. Rather, legal title passes to the persons who would take if the killer had predeceased the victim. [Riggs v. Palmer, 115 N.Y. 506 (1889); Price v. Hitaffer, 165 A. 470 (Md. 1933)]

(a) **Critique:** This approach has been criticized as judicially engrafting an exception on the statutes that control the devolution of title. [Wall v. Pfanschmidt, *supra;* Estate of Mahoney, 220 A.2d 475 (Vt. 1966)] Modernly, most courts that bar the killer do so under constructive trust reasoning (below).

(2) **Constructive trust imposed:** [§155]   Using a constructive trust theory, le-gal title "passes" to the killer pursuant to the legal rules, but to disgorge unjust enrichment, equity holds him to be a constructive trustee of the property. [Kelley v. State, 196 A.2d 68 (N.H. 1963); Dutill v. Dana, 113 A.2d 499 (Me. 1952)] This approach does not disturb the statutory laws of descent and distribution, because title does pass to the killer. But because of the unconscio-nable mode by which he acquired title, equity treats the killer as a constructive trustee, and he does not enjoy the benefits of the property. [39 A.L.R.2d 477]

(a) **Note:** A constructive trust does not give rise to a true trust relationship under which the trustee holds legal title for the benefit of others. "Con-structive trust" is, instead, the name given to a flexible equitable remedy designed to disgorge unjust enrichment. In the same decree that imposes a constructive trust, the court compels a conveyance to the persons who would have taken had the killer predeceased the victim.

c. **Nature of homicide:** [§156]   For the killer to lose his interest in the estate, he must have wrongfully brought about the victim's death. Thus, murder would cer-tainly trigger a constructive trust. If the slayer is found guilty of manslaughter and not murder, some courts have held that a constructive trust should not be imposed. [Restatement of Restitution §187, comment (e); Estate of Kirby, 162 Cal. 91 (1912)] However, most courts draw a distinction between **voluntary** and **involun-tary** manslaughter, and refuse to impose a constructive trust only in the latter situation. [Estate of Mahoney, *supra*] A slayer who is found not guilty by reason of insanity does **not** forfeit his rights. [Blair v. Travelers Insurance Co., 174 N.E.2d 209 (Ill. 1961)]

UNIVERSITY CO-OP
EAST

JOHAN/WILLS GILB 0159000408n   19.95

Subtotal   19.95
Sales Tax   1.65

TOTAL   21.60
CHECK   21.60
     Acct: 12551385

YOUR RECEIPT
THANK YOU!
01/29/96 14:18 0001-0008 8404   #4110
****

UNIVERSITY CO-OP
EAST
UNIVERSITY AIR DISPOSADODA   19.95

Subtotal   19.95
Sales Tax   1.65

TOTAL   21.60

CHECK   21.60

ACCT   4155135X

** SAVE THIS RECEIPT FOR YOUR REBATE **
MUST BE TURNED IN BEFORE JUNE 30, 1995.
ONLY UT/AUSTIN STUDENTS, FACULTY & STAFF
ARE ELIGIBLE FOR THIS REBATE.
YOUR RECEIPT
THANK YOU!
0127048 1618 0001-0008 8404   #440

2. **Statutory Solutions:** [§157]   Many states now have statutes that govern the right of a killer to receive property from the victim's estate. [41 Ohio St. L.J. 907 (1980)] The statutes vary in their scope.

    a. **Conviction required:** [§158]   In some states, the statute applies only if the heir or will beneficiary is *convicted* of intentionally and unlawfully killing the decedent. [Vt. Stat. Ann. tit. 14, §551(6)]

    b. **Conviction not required:** [§159]   In other states, a final judgment of conviction of murder is conclusive, but even in the absence of conviction, the court may determine by a *preponderance* of the evidence that the killing was unlawful and intentional. [Fla. Prob. Code §732.802]

    c. **Effect of statute:** [§160]   Where a statute governs the effect of slaying the decedent, there is no occasion for applying the two-step reasoning involved in the imposition of a constructive trust (*i.e.,* that title passes to the killer, who holds as constructive trustee). Rather, *title* to the decedent's property *passes directly* to the persons who would take if the killer predeceased the victim.

3. **Forms of Disposition Affected:** [§161]   Case decisions and statutes dealing with this problem do not limit application of the rule to cases involving an intestate distribution.

    a. **Wills and life insurance policies:** [§162]   Forfeiture is applied where the killer is a legatee under the decedent's will [36 A.L.R.2d 960], or a beneficiary under an insurance policy on the life of the victim [Swavely v. Prudential Insurance Co., 157 A. 394 (N.J. 1931); Beck v. West Coast Life Insurance Co., 38 Cal. 2d 643 (1952); 26 A.L.R.2d 979 (1952)].

    b   **Joint tenancy or tenancy by the entireties:** [§163]   Where the killer and the victim owned property as joint tenants or as tenants by the entireties, in most states the tenancy is *severed.* The killer takes one-half of the property, and the other one-half passes as though the killer predeceased the victim. [Bradley v. Fox, 129 N.E.2d 699 (Ill. 1955); 32 A.L.R.2d 1099]

        (1) **Rationale:** While the killer should not profit from his wrongful conduct, neither should he forfeit his one-half interest in the property based on speculation as to who might have survived. [Estate of Matye, 645 P.2d 955 (Mont. 1982)]

        (2) **Note—other solutions:** [§164]   Some courts award everything but the actuarial value of the killer's life income interest in one-half of the property to the victim's estate on the ground that the killer deprived the victim of the chance to be the surviving tenant. [Neiman v. Hurff, 93 A.2d 345 (N.J. 1952); Hargrove v. Taylor, 389 P.2d 36 (Or. 1964)]

4. **Uniform Probate Code:** [§165]   U.P.C. Section 2-803 applies where the killer *feloniously and intentionally* kills the decedent and provides that the property passes as though the killer predeceased the victim. The statute applies to cases of intestacy, wills,

life insurance policies, or any other acquisition of property by reason of the decedent's death.

    a. **Joint tenancies or tenancies by the entireties:** [§166] With respect to joint tenants, tenants by the entireties, survivorship bank accounts, and similar arrangements, the slaying effects a *severance* so that the killer takes one-half of the property and the other half passes as though the killer predeceased the victim.

    b. **Conviction not required:** [§167] Conviction of a felonious and intentional killing is conclusive, but in the absence of a conviction the court may determine by a *preponderance* of the evidence whether the killing was felonious and intentional.

5. **Corruption of Blood**

    a. **Common law:** [§168] At common law, a felon forfeited his real and personal property, which passed by *escheat* and not to his heirs or distributees.

    b. **Modern law:** [§169] Nearly all states have eliminated the common law rule by constitutional or statutory provision. Except where the felony involves killing the person whose property is being distributed (in which case the above rules would apply), conviction of a felony does not result in corruption of the blood, forfeiture, or escheat. [*See, e.g.,* Tex. Prob. Code §41(1d)]

E. NONRESIDENT ALIENS

1. **Common Law:** [§170] At common law, aliens were **denied** the right to inherit **real property** either by will or intestate succession.

2. **Modern Law:** [§171] In most states, there are **no restrictions** on the right of an alien to inherit or hold title to real or personal property within the state. [*See, e.g.,* Fla. Prob. Code §732.1101]

    a. **Minority view:** [§172] Several states have statutes that prohibit nonresident aliens from inheriting land. [Neb. Rev. Stat. §76-402—rural lands only; N.H. Rev. Stat. §477.20] In other states, aliens can inherit land but must sell it within a specified time. [Ill. Ann. Stat. ch. 6, §2; Okla. Stat. Ann. tit. 60, §123] *But note:* If the United States government has extended inheritance rights to nonresident aliens by treaty, the **treaty prevails** over any statute to the contrary. [De Tenorio v. McGowan, 364 F. Supp. 1051 (S.D. Miss. 1973)]

    b. **Iron curtain statutes:** [§173] Some states have enacted **reciprocity statutes** that bar inheritance by a nonresident alien unless the alien's country grants reciprocal rights to American citizens. [N.C. Gen. Stat. §64-3; Iowa Code §567.8] Other states have enacted **impounding statutes** under which the inheritance will be impounded if the court determines that the alien would not get the benefit of use and enjoyment of the property. [N.Y. Surr. Ct. Proc. Act §2218; Mich. Stat. Ann. §27.3178 (30)(a)]

(1) **Constitutional problem:** [§174]   Some of these statutes have met with constitutional objections. For example, an Oregon reciprocity statute was held unconstitutional on the facts presented, on the ground that a state court's inquiry into whether a foreign government is communist or nondemocratic constitutes an invasion into the field of foreign affairs reserved exclusively to the federal government. [Zschernig v. Miller, 389 U.S. 429 (1968)]

(2) **Testamentary gifts:** [§175]   A gift in a will conditioned on an alien's being able to freely and fully enjoy the benefits of the property in his homeland is valid and requires a court determination that the condition has been met and a distribution can safely be made. [Estate of Kosek, 31 N.Y.2d 475 (1973)]

c. **Uniform Probate Code:** [§176]   Under the U.P.C., *no person is disqualified* to take as an heir because he or a person through whom he claims is or has been an alien. [U.P.C. §2-112]

IV. RESTRICTIONS ON THE POWER OF TESTATION—PROTECTION OF THE FAMILY

chapter approach

Whenever you encounter an exam question in which a testator is survived by a spouse or children, you must consider whether any of the limitations on testation designed to protect the family apply:

1. **Protection of Spouse**

    a. **Common law states:** Although dower and curtesy are usually not exam topics (because these common law rights have been abolished in most states), the **elective share statute** is a likely source of exam questions. You should always keep the statute in the back of your mind, to draw out as a viable alternative to a small (or nonexistent) gift under the will. Remember that the amount of the share and the procedure to be followed are set by statute, and thus statutory terms must be followed. Remember too that generally only the spouse can make the election, and that **lifetime transfers** may be challenged as illusory, voidable under the "motive" or "equities" tests, or included in the estate by statute.

    b. **Community property states:** Similar to the elective share is the **election will** in community property states. The election may be forced or voluntary, and even accidental. In any case, note that if the spouse elects against the will, he loses all gifts under the will.

2. **Protection of Children:** Pretermitted child questions frequently turn up on Wills exams. Follow the statute carefully, as most apply only to children born or adopted **after** execution of the will, but some apply to previously existing children. Don't forget that the statute does **not** apply if: the child was intentionally omitted, the child was provided for by a lifetime settlement, or the spouse (parent of the child) is the principal beneficiary.

3. **Protection of Spouse and Children:** Statutes in many states provide for **homestead** rights, **exempt personal property,** and **family allowance** to protect the family. These rights are in addition to the spouse's elective share and gifts under the will, and they are generally safe from creditors.

A. INTRODUCTION [§177]

A testator's right to dispose of property as the testator chooses is subject to few substantive restrictions. Although a testator must comply procedurally with the formalities required for will execution in order to make an effective disposition, the law imposes few limitations on how, or to whom, a testator may bequeath the estate. This chapter outlines those restrictions on the power of disposition which are designed to protect the testator's family against disinheritance.

B. PROTECTION OF THE SPOUSE — COMMON LAW

1. **Spouse Was Not an Heir:** [§178]   At common law, a surviving spouse never took as an heir. A decedent's estate passed by intestacy to his descendants, or if not survived by

descendants, to his parents or collateral kin. If a decedent was survived by his spouse but no kindred, his estate escheated to the Crown. A surviving spouse's only rights in a decedent's estate were dower (if a widow) or curtesy (if a widower).

2. **Dower:** [§179]   Dower was the provision the law made for a widow out of the husband's property. Unlike a husband's curtesy estate (*see infra,* §185), dower did ***not*** depend upon issue being born to the marriage.

   a. **One-third life estate:** [§180]   Upon the husband's death, the widow was entitled to a life estate in an ***undivided one-third*** of the husband's lands.

   b. **Property subject to dower:** [§181]   A wife had dower in all lands of which her husband was ***seised*** of an ***estate of inheritance*** during marriage. Thus, dower applied to lands owned by the husband at the time of the marriage as well as to land acquired during the marriage. In effect, dower applied to ***all lands owned by the husband at death*** and also to lands ***conveyed during the marriage*** without his wife's joinder.

      (1) **Joint tenancy:** [§182]   Dower did ***not*** apply to land held in joint tenancy with the right of survivorship, because this was not an inheritable estate. [Jezo v. Jezo, 129 N.W.2d 195 (Wis. 1964)]

      (2) **"Undivided" interest:** [§183]   Although dower gave the widow an undivided one-third interest in each separate tract of land, when it was feasible to do so, the widow was assigned dower in metes and bounds so as to give her a "whole" life estate in one-third of each tract (rather than an undivided one-third life estate in the entirety of each tract). If such a division was impractical, or several tracts of land were involved, some courts assigned to the widow a life estate in the whole of some of the tracts, so as to give her a "whole" life estate in one-third of all lands in terms of acreage and value. [Byars v. Mixon, 299 So. 2d 262 (Ala. 1964)]

         (a) **Example:** H owns two tracts of land at his death: one of 1,000 acres and one of 500 acres. A court would likely assign W a life estate in the 500-acre tract, rather than a one-third life estate in ***both*** tracts. Alternatively, if H owns one 1,500-acre tract, some courts prefer to assign dower as a life estate in 500 acres of the tract, rather than a one-third life estate in the entire 1,500 acres.

   c. **Inchoate dower:** [§184]   The wife's dower interest was "inchoate" until her husband died, which means that she had no right of possession or other right as long as her husband was alive. If the wife predeceased her husband, her inchoate dower was extinguished.

3. **Curtesy:** [§185]   A husband had a comparable interest in his wife's lands. Upon a wife's death, her husband's curtesy right gave him a ***life estate*** in ***all*** (and not just an undivided one-third) of the lands of which the wife was seised during marriage. However, a husband's curtesy estate arose ***only if issue were born*** to the marriage.

4. **As Limitation on Testamentary Power:** [§186]   Dower and curtesy rights could be asserted regardless of the decedent's will. Thus, a wife's dower interest in her husband's land was not affected by the fact that the husband had devised the land to another. To this extent, then, each spouse's power of testamentary disposition over property was limited by the other's dower or curtesy right.

5. **As Limitation on Lifetime Transfers:** [§187]   Nor could the rights of the surviving spouse be defeated by lifetime conveyance. Even a sale to a bona fide purchaser was ineffective to cut off the spouse's dower or curtesy right (unless the spouse had joined in the conveyance). Similarly, a spouse's dower or curtesy interest was superior to the claims of the deceased spouse's creditors.

6. **Modern Status:** [§188]   The common law dower and curtesy estates still exist in several states. In some of these jurisdictions the rules governing dower and curtesy have been assimilated. The estate is called "dower" or "statutory dower," and the surviving spouse (whether wife or husband) takes a one-third life estate in all of the decedent's lands. [*See, e.g.,* D.C. Code Ann. §19-102] However, most states have **abolished** dower and curtesy in favor of the statutory substitutes discussed below. Note that dower and curtesy never were a part of the law in the eight community property states (*supra,* §35).

C.   PROTECTION OF THE SPOUSE — ELECTIVE SHARE STATUTES

1. **In General:** [§189]   Nearly all of the common law jurisdictions have enacted elective share statutes designed to give the surviving spouse some protection against disinheritance. These statutes give the spouse an election to take a statutory share (usually one-third or one-half) of the decedent's estate **in lieu of** taking under the decedent's will.

   a. **As limitation on testamentary power:** [§190]   As with dower or curtesy, elective share statutes operate as a restriction on the decedent's power of testation. The surviving spouse has a right to claim a designated share of the decedent's net estate regardless of the will.

      (1) **Comment:** Cases in which the surviving spouse actually elects to take a statutory share are relatively infrequent. In large part, this is because most spouses leave the bulk of their estates to the surviving spouse. And where a testator is inclined to disinherit the other spouse, the existence of the elective share statute has the salutary effect of inducing the testator to bequeath at least the elective share amount to the surviving spouse.

   b. **As limitation on lifetime transfers:** [§191]   Under most statutes, the elective share applies only to property owned by the decedent **at death,** meaning that a lifetime transfer of property is ordinarily effective to cut off the surviving spouse's statutory share with respect to that property. However, courts in several states have extended the scope of the elective share right to encompass certain lifetime transfers (*see infra,* §§229-237), and some statutes define the estate subject to the elective share to include certain lifetime transfers (*see infra,* §§238-256).

c. **Community property states:** [§192]   None of the community property states has an elective share statute because of the built-in protection against disinheritance given to spouses by the community property system (*supra*, §§38 *et seq.*).

(1) **Exception:** [§193]   The quasi-community property statutes found in California and Idaho are a form of the elective share statute that applies to certain imported assets. (*See supra*, §43.)

2. **Amount of Elective Share:** [§194]   The elective share amount varies from state to state. In most states, the amount is **one-third** of the decedent's net estate if the decedent was survived by descendants, and **one-half** if the decedent was not survived by descendants. [D.C. Code Ann. §19-113; Ill. Prob. Act §2-8; N.Y. Est. Powers & Trusts Law §5-1.1] In some states, the amount is one-third of the estate regardless of whether the decedent was survived by descendants [U.P.C. §2-201], and in Florida, the statutory share is always thirty percent of the net estate [Fla. Prob. Code §732.201].

3. **Property Subject to Elective Share:** [§195]   In most states, the elective share applies to the decedent's net estate: the **probate** estate (*supra*, §6) after payment of expenses of administration and creditors' claims. However, in some states, the elective share fraction is applied to the decedent's "augmented estate," a concept that is designed to include certain lifetime transfers (*see infra*, §238).

a. **Situs rule:** [§196]   The elective share applies to all of the decedent's **personal** property wherever located. However, because of the "situs rule," the elective share applies only to real property located within the state. [Fla. Prob. Code §732.206; N.Y. Est. Powers & Trusts Law §5-1.1(d)(8)]

b. **Family allowance and exempt property set-aside:** [§197]   The elective share statute applies to the decedent's net estate **after** the family allowance, homestead right, and any exempt personal property (*see infra*, §§303-316) are set aside for the surviving spouse. [U.P.C. §2-202; Fla. Prob. Code §732.208] Thus, the spouse who elects to take against the will is entitled to a family allowance, etc., **and** the statutory share.

c. **Settlement agreement with former spouse**

(1) **Arrearages:** [§198]   Most courts hold that a former spouse's right to accrued and unpaid alimony payments **takes precedence** over the surviving spouse's elective share. Moreover, if the property settlement agreement binds the decedent's estate to continue to make payments to the former spouse during her lifetime, such claim is superior to the surviving spouse's elective share right. The rationale is that with regard to such payments, agreed to pursuant to a contract, the former spouse is a creditor of the decedent's estate, and creditors' claims are deducted before determining the net estate subject to the elective share. [*In re* Lewis' Will, 4 Misc. 2d 937 (1953)]

(a) **Minority view:** [§199] In a minority of jurisdictions, the elective share takes precedence over the former spouse's claim on the ground that the elective share right, granted by the legislature, cannot be contracted away in a property settlement agreement with a former spouse. [Estate of Donner, 364 So. 2d 742 (Fla. 1978)]

(2) **Compare—promise to make testamentary gift:** [§200] Even the majority jurisdictions hold that the elective share takes precedence over the decedent's promise (contained in a property settlement agreement) to make a bequest to the former spouse. Here the former spouse is regarded as a legatee, not a creditor, and thus her rights are subordinate to the surviving spouse's right of election. [*In re* Lewis' Will, *supra*]

d. **Property subject to contractual will:** [§201] Property received by the decedent from a former spouse under a contractual will, giving the decedent the full use of the property for life with the remainder on his death to pass to others, is **not** subject to the surviving spouse's elective share. Because of the terms of the contractual will, the decedent had no property interest at death to which the elective share could attach. [Rubenstein v. Mueller, 19 N.Y.2d 228 (1967)]

4. Who May Elect

a. **Decedent's domicile:** [§202] A particular state's elective share statute is available to the surviving spouse only if the decedent was a domiciliary of that state at the time of death. [Fla. Prob. Code §732.205] The surviving spouse has a right of election even if she is **not** a domiciliary of that state; it is the decedent's domicile that controls.

b. **Surviving spouse:** [§203] In nearly all states, the right of election is given to both husbands and wives; that is, to widowers as well as to widows.

(1) **Divorce decree not final:** [§204] To be entitled to elect, the surviving party must be a surviving *spouse.* If the marriage was terminated before death by a **final** decree of divorce or annulment, there is no right of election. However, if an interlocutory decree of divorce had been entered, but was not final on the decedent's death, or if a decree of divorce had been entered but the decree was not final because the time for appeal had not expired, the surviving spouse has a right of election. [Estate of Lueke, 78 Misc. 2d 904 (1974)]

(2) **Death before election made:** [§205] In general, the right of election can be exercised only by the surviving spouse. Thus, if the spouse dies before the election is made, there is no right of election. The spouse's personal representative **cannot** make an election on behalf of the spouse's estate. [U.P.C. §2-203; 83 A.L.R.2d 1077]

c. **Incompetent or minor spouse:** [§206] It is generally provided that the guardian of an incompetent or minor spouse may make an election on behalf of the spouse, but only upon a finding by the court that the election is in the spouse's best interest.

[3 A.L.R.3d 6] Under the Uniform Probate Code, the right of election on behalf of a protected person may be exercised only by order of the court in which protective proceedings are pending, after a finding that exercise is necessary to provide adequate support for the spouse during his or her probable life expectancy. [U.P.C. §2-203]

5. When Right of Election Not Available

a. **In general:** [§207]   In most jurisdictions, a surviving spouse can make an election even if the effect is to give the spouse *less* property than is bequeathed to her by the decedent's will. In some cases, this may be advantageous for the surviving spouse.

   (1) **Example:** H dies leaving a one million dollar estate and a will that bequeaths all his property to his wife W if she survives him, otherwise to the couple's children. Under this will, H's estate will qualify for an unlimited marital deduction under the federal estate tax, and there will be no estate tax on his estate. However, the million dollars received from H's estate, together with W's own estate, will lead to substantial estate taxes on her death. Thus, W could make an election, the effect of which (under the particular state's laws) would be to give her only one-half of H's estate, or $500,000. As a result of W's election, H's estate would qualify for only a $500,000 marital deduction, but there would be no estate taxes on H's death because of the unified estate tax credit available to H's estate. (*See* Estate & Gift Taxation Outline.) W's election would reduce the projected taxes on her estate upon her subsequent death.

   (2) **Comment:** In the above example, W could also reduce the projected taxes on her estate by making a partial disclaimer (*see supra*, §§130-131) rather than by electing to take her statutory share.

b. **New York statute:** [§208]   The New York statute is fundamentally different from the elective share statutes found in other states. Under the New York elective share statute, the surviving spouse has **no right of election** if he is left an amount of **qualifying dispositions** equal to or exceeding the elective share (one-third if decedent was survived by issue, one-half if no surviving issue). Also, dispositions that give the spouse only a life estate can be used to satisfy the elective share and thus eliminate the right of election. [N.Y. Est. Powers & Trusts Law §5-1.1]

   (1) **Rationale:** The basic purpose of the New York statute is to avoid disruption of the decedent's testamentary plan, while assuring that the surviving spouse receives the income from at least one-third or one-half of the decedent's estate. If the spouse is left this amount in a qualifying way, the surviving spouse has no right of election.

   (2) **Limited right of election:** [§209]   If the decedent left some assets to the spouse, but the value of those assets is less than the elective share amount, the surviving spouse has a limited right of election: He must accept the dispositions that have been made by the decedent, and then by electing take the

difference between the elective share amount and the value of the qualifying dispositions.

(3) **Qualifying dispositions:** [§210]   In general, two forms of disposition qualify as being in satisfaction of the elective share in New York: (i) absolute dispositions that pass into the spouse's **outright ownership** —these include testamentary gifts, intestate shares, and "testamentary substitutes" (*see infra*, §§248-251) such as the decedent's share of property passing to the spouse by right of survivorship or by Totten trust; and (ii) dispositions that give the spouse an **indefeasible income interest for life.** The indefeasible income interest can be in trust, or it can be a legal life estate. If the sum of (i) absolute dispositions plus (ii) the corpus of a trust (or the property subject to the life estate) in which the spouse is given an indefeasible income interest **equals or exceeds** the elective share amount, the spouse has **no right of election.** If the aggregate of (i) and (ii) is **less** than the elective share amount, the surviving spouse has a **limited right of election** to take the difference between such aggregate and the amount of the elective share. [N.Y. Est. Powers & Trusts Law §5-1.1(c)]

(4) **Limited right of withdrawal:** [§211]   Under the New York statute, if the decedent (i) made no absolute dispositions to the surviving spouse, or if the total of such dispositions is less than $10,000; and (ii) created an indefeasible income trust for her spouse, the corpus of which, when added to the absolute dispositions, equals or exceeds the one-third or one-half elective share amount (meaning the spouse has no right of election), the surviving spouse has a limited right of withdrawal. He can elect to take, outright, the difference between $10,000 and the absolute dispositions made to him. Such amount "shall be deducted from the principal of the trust [for the spouse] and the terms of the instrument making the testamentary provision shall remain otherwise effective." [N.Y. Est. Powers & Trusts Law §5-1.1(c)]

   (a) **Rationale:** The limited right of withdrawal insures that the surviving spouse has access to at least some cash or liquid assets. Otherwise, the decedent could satisfy the elective share statute by completely "trusteeing" the surviving spouse, making the spouse totally dependent upon the trust income interest for all his cash needs.

   (b) **Example:** W dies leaving a net estate of $300,000. Her will bequeaths $4,000 cash to her husband H, and $100,000 to the trustee of a trust to pay income to H for life, on his death to distribute the principal to W's daughter C. W's will gives her residuary estate to her sister S. Since W is survived by issue, the elective share amount is one-third of $300,000 or $100,000. Although the sum of (i) $4,000 outright disposition and (ii) $100,000 corpus of trust giving H an indefeasible life estate exceeds the elective share amount, H can file a notice of election to withdraw $6,000 from the corpus of the trust. If H does so, he will end up with $10,000 cash, and the corpus of the trust giving him an indefeasible life estate will be reduced to $94,000.

c. **Waiver of right of election:** [§212]   By statute in most states and by case law in other states, a spouse may waive the right of election (and also the right to an intestate share, a homestead allowance, exempt personal property set-aside, and family allowance) either before or during the marriage. [U.P.C. §2-204; Kan. Stat. Ann. §59-602]

    (1) **Writing required:** [§213]   To be valid, a waiver must be in writing and *signed* by the spouse. In some states, the waiver also must be acknowledged before a notary public. [N.Y. Est. Powers & Trusts Law §5-1.1(f)]

    (2) **No consideration but fair disclosure required:** [§214]   Under most states' laws, a waiver is valid even though there is no consideration for the waiver, but there must be fair disclosure as to the effect of the waiver. That is, the spouse must be apprised generally of the consequences of the waiver: the size and value of the other spouse's estate, etc. In a few states, fair disclosure is required for waivers made during the marriage, but not for waivers that are a part of an antenuptial agreement. [Fla. Prob. Code §732.702]

d. **Surviving spouse disqualified**

    (1) **Majority rule:** [§215]   In most states, the surviving spouse is entitled to an elective share even though he abandoned his spouse, refused to support her, has committed adultery, or is guilty of some other misconduct. [13 A.L.R.3d 446, 485]

        (a) **Rationale:** The right of election is granted by statute. If the legislature has not conditioned the surviving spouse's taking upon his good conduct, the courts should not read such a condition into the statute. [Fogo v. Griffin, 551 S.W.2d 677 (Tenn. 1977)]

    (2) **Minority rule:** [§216]   In a few states, the surviving spouse has no right of election (or right to take an intestate share, family allowance, or exempt personal property set-aside) if: (i) the surviving spouse abandoned the deceased spouse; (ii) the surviving spouse failed or refused to support the deceased spouse; (iii) the surviving spouse procured a divorce or annulment in another jurisdiction that is not recognized as valid in the domiciliary state; or (iv) a final decree of separation was rendered against the surviving spouse. [N.Y. Est. Powers & Trusts Law §5-1.2] In these states, neither cruelty nor adultery, by itself, bars the right of election. However, open and notorious cohabitation with another woman constitutes abandonment. [Estate of Loeb, 77 Misc. 2d 814 (1974)]

6. **Procedure Governing Election:** [§217]   To take a statutory share, the surviving spouse must file a *notice of election* (and under many statutes must deliver a copy of the notice to the decedent's personal representative) within the time period fixed by statute.

a. **Exception to notice requirement:** [§218]   In a few jurisdictions, the surviving spouse does not have to file a notice of election if the decedent did not make any gifts to the spouse in his will. The right to an elective share is automatic. [D.C. Code Ann. §19-113]

b. **Time period for filing notice of election:** [§219]   The time periods for making the election range from four months [Fla. Prob. Code §732.212] to six months [N.Y. Est. Powers & Trusts Law §5-1.1] to one year [3 A.L.R.3d 6].

    (1) **When time period commences to run:** [§220]   Under most statutes, the time period commences to run from the date the administration is opened by the granting of letters of administration to the personal representative. In some states, the time period begins to run on the date of the first publication of notice of administration.

    (2) **Uniform Probate Code:** [§221]   Under the U.P.C., the election must be made within nine months after the decedent's death or within six months after probate of the decedent's will, whichever is later. [U.P.C. §2-205(a)]

    (3) **Extension of time period:** [§222]   A few statutes expressly provide that the probate court can extend the time period for electing, upon a showing of good cause for the extension. [N.Y. Est. Powers & Trusts Law §5-1.1] In several states, the time period is automatically extended if the probate proceedings are contested (*e.g.*, a will contest) or if a will construction suit is filed. [Fla. Prob. Code §732.212]

c. **Three-way election:** [§223]   In the handful of jurisdictions that have an elective share statute **and** common law dower or its equivalent, the surviving spouse has a three-way election: He can take (i) under the will, (ii) an elective share, or (iii) dower. [D.C. Code Ann. §19-113]

    (1) **Comment:** Ordinarily, dower would be the least attractive option since it gives the surviving spouse only a one-third life estate in the decedent's lands. However, the dower right might be of greater value to the spouse (i) if the decedent's estate is insolvent—only dower takes precedence over creditors' claims, or (ii) if the decedent had made lifetime transfers of valuable lands without the spouse's joinder.

7. **Effect of Election**

a. **Testamentary gifts to the spouse**

    (1) **General rule:** [§224]   In most states, the elective share is first paid in cash or in kind from assets passing under decedent's will which **would have passed** outright to the surviving spouse but for the election. [Fla. Prob. Code §733.209] The purpose of this rule is to prevent disruption of the decedent's testamentary plan insofar as is possible.

(2) **Life estate**

    (a) **Majority rule:** [§225]   If the decedent's will gave the surviving spouse a life estate (*e.g.*, a trust income interest), in most states the life estate is not counted as being in partial satisfaction of the statutory share because the elective share entitles the spouse to outright ownership of assets. Instead, the spouse who elects to take a statutory share is deemed to have renounced the life estate, and the remainder interest following the life estate is accelerated.

    (b) **Minority rule:** [§226]   Under the Uniform Probate Code, a life estate is counted as being in partial satisfaction of the elective share. The value of the life estate is computed as if it is worth one-half of the total value of the property subject to the life estate, unless a higher or lower value is established by proof. [U.P.C. §2-207(a)] In New York, an indefeasible life estate given to the surviving spouse can be used to satisfy the elective share. (*See supra*, §208.)

b. **Abatement of gifts**

    (1) **Majority rule:** [§227]   As noted above, the elective share is first paid in cash or in kind from assets passing under the will which, but for the election, would have passed outright to the surviving spouse. To the extent that such assets are insufficient, the elective share is paid pursuant to the abatement rules that apply to creditors' claims (*see infra*, §998 *et seq.*): That is, property passing by partial intestacy is first applied; then the residuary estate; then general legacies, demonstrative legacies, and specific bequests are abated (in that order). [Fla. Prob. Code §733.209] Thus, in the ordinary case, the burden of the elective share falls entirely on the decedent's residuary estate.

    (2) **Minority rule:** [§228]   Under the Uniform Probate Code and in several non-U.P.C. states, the elective share is ratably apportioned among recipients of the decedent's estate in proportion to the value of their interests therein, after first applying any property which has passed outright to the surviving spouse. [U.P.C. §2-207; N.Y. Est. Powers & Trusts Law §5-1.1]

D. LIFETIME TRANSFERS TO DEFEAT THE ELECTIVE SHARE

1. **Case Law:** [§229]   Most elective share statutes apply to the decedent's **net estate**, which is construed to mean the testamentary or probate estate. Thus, most statutes do not apply to property transferred during the decedent's lifetime or to nontestamentary transfers. As a consequence, absent judicial intervention, a husband or wife might make substantial lifetime transfers, perhaps even a transfer with a retained life estate or other retained economic benefits, then die leaving a modest probate estate, and thereby defeat the surviving spouse's elective share right. In response, the courts have developed various doctrines under which the surviving spouse may be able to challenge a particular lifetime transfer.

a. **Illusory transfer:** [§230] A substantial number of courts apply the "illusory transfer" doctrine, under which the transferred property is subject to the elective share statute *if* the transferor retained so many controls over the property that the transfer was "illusory." This test does not depend on the motive that may have prompted the transfer, but rather looks to the *degree of control* retained by the transferor. [Newman v. Dore, 275 N.Y. 371 (1937)]

(1) **Example:** H executes a will that devises one-third of his estate (the elective share amount) to his wife W. However, shortly before his death, H transfers the bulk of his estate to the trustee of a revocable trust, retaining trust income for life, the power to revoke or amend the trust, and the power to control the trustee in its administration of the trust. As to the latter, the trustee cannot take any significant actions in administering the trust without H's prior approval. The trust is to terminate on H's death, and the trust principal is to be distributed to H's sister. Because nearly all of H's estate is settled in the trust (and not in the probate estate), on H's death, W is entitled to one-third of zero. On these and similar facts, and particularly because of the controls over the trustee, some courts have held that such a transfer is illusory; *i.e.,* the transfer is colorable and not real. Thus, the trust assets are subject to the surviving spouse's elective share. [Newman v. Dore, *supra*]

(2) **Criticism:** The illusory transfer doctrine has been criticized because of its vagueness and imprecision. Concepts such as "illusory" and "colorable" have no inherent meaning and do not provide a basis for analysis or predicting the outcome of decisions. In states that have adopted the illusory transfer doctrine, there has been considerable litigation over whether particular forms of transfer are or are not illusory.

(3) **Special problem—bank account dispositions**

(a) **Majority rule:** [§231] Despite the degree of control and access to the funds retained by the depositor, most courts have held that Totten trust bank accounts [*In re* Halpern's Estate, 303 N.Y. 33 (1951)] and joint bank accounts [Inda v. Inda, 288 N.Y. 315 (1942)] are not illusory and thus are *not subject to the elective share.* The rationale is that these are valid forms of transfer that are given recognized legal effect.

(b) **Minority rule:** [§232] The problem with the majority rationale is that it begs the question. The surviving spouse is not challenging the validity of the bank account as such. Rather, she is asserting that the bank account disposition, while generally valid, should not be allowed to defeat the purpose of the elective share because of the depositor's retained controls. For this reason, a substantial minority of courts have held that such bank account arrangements *are* subject to the surviving spouse's elective share. [Montgomery v. Michaels, 301 N.E.2d 465 (Ill. 1973)]

(c) **Restatement of Trusts:** [§233] Some courts have adopted the position of the Restatement (Second) of Trusts section 58: Amounts deposited under Totten trust bank accounts are counted for purposes of determining the "estate" against which the elective share fraction applies. However, the Totten trust beneficiaries receive the funds on deposit unless the general assets in the decedent's estate are insufficient to satisfy the elective share. [Jeruzal v. Jeruzal, 130 N.W.2d 473 (Minn. 1964)]

(d) **Example of three views:** [§234]   W dies leaving a will that leaves nothing to her husband H but, instead, bequeaths her $50,000 estate to her sister S. In addition, at W's death, $10,000 was on deposit in several Totten trust bank accounts W had created; the accounts name W's brother B as beneficiary. H files for his elective share, which is one-third of W's estate. Under the majority rule, the Totten trust accounts are not subject to the elective share statute; H takes one-third of the $50,000 estate. Under the minority rule, H takes one-third of the $50,000 estate, and also one-third of $10,000 Totten trust deposits. Under the Restatement rule, H takes one-third of ($50,000 + $10,000 =) $60,000, but the $20,000 comes out of the probate estate; brother B takes the $10,000 Totten trust accounts.

b. **Motive or intent to defeat share:** [§235]   Instead of using the "illusory transfer" doctrine, a number of courts have held that a lifetime transfer is subject to the surviving spouse's elective share *if* the motive or intent of the transfer was to defeat the elective share right. [Wansrath v. Kappel, 201 S.W.2d 327 (Mo. 1947); Patch v. Squires, 165 A. 919 (Vt. 1933)] In other states, the intent to deprive a surviving spouse of the elective share is deemed material only when the estate contains little or no other property to which the election might attach. [Conner v. Nationwide Maintenance Corp., 44 So. 2d 684 (Fla. 1950)]

c. **Weigh the equities:** [§236]   Still other courts have eschewed the "illusory transfer" and "motive" tests in favor of a "balancing" approach that considers the equities on a case-by-case basis. Under this approach, in deciding whether a particular transfer is subject to the elective share, the court considers:

   (i)   The *completeness of the transfer* (revocable or irrevocable; who was trustee);

   (ii)   The transferor's *motive;*

   (iii)   Whether it was a *"brink of death" transfer;*

   (iv)   *Participation of the transferee* in the alleged fraud; and

   (v)   The *degree* to which the surviving spouse is *deprived of benefits* in the decedent's estate by the transfer.

[Whittington v. Whittington, 106 A.2d 72 (Md. 1954); Windsor v. Leonard, 475 F.2d 932 (D.C. Cir. 1973)]

d. **Revocable inter vivos trusts:** [§237]   Absent a statute on the question, the courts are divided as to whether property in a revocable trust, in which the settlor has retained the income for life and the right to revoke or amend the trust, is subject to the surviving spouse's elective share right. A number of courts have subjected such assets to the right of election, on the ground that the powers and benefits retained by the settlor are tantamount to ownership. [39 A.L.R.3d 14] Other courts have ruled that since revocable trusts constitute valid transfers under state law, they are not subject to the elective share statute. [Johnson v. LaGrange State Bank, 383 N.E.2d 185 (Ill. 1978)]

2. **Uniform Probate Code**

a. **Augmented estate:** [§238]   Under the U.P.C., the elective share statute applies to the decedent's "augmented estate." The augmented estate consists of the net probate estate *plus* the value of property transferred *to persons other than the decedent's spouse* during lifetime for less than adequate and full consideration, if the transfer falls into one of the following categories:

   (i) *Retained life estate*—transfers in which the decedent retained the right to possession or enjoyment of, or the income from, property;

   (ii) *Retained controls*—transfers in which the decedent retained the right to revoke, or to invade, consume, or dispose of the principal for his own benefit;

   (iii) *Transfers within two years of death*—gifts made within two years of death, to the extent that such gifts to any one donee in any year exceeded $3,000; or

   (iv) *Survivorship estates*—transfers whereby property is held at the time of decedent's death by decedent and another with right of survivorship.

   [U.P.C. §2-202]

b. **Intestacy:** [§239]   The U.P.C.'s elective share statute applies when the decedent died intestate as well as when the decedent left a will. The purpose of this provision is to prevent avoidance of the augmented estate rules. Otherwise, a spouse could make massive gifts shortly before death, or gifts with the retained power to revoke, etc., and then die intestate, leaving the surviving spouse with a right of election in an estate of zero.

c. **Transfers to spouse:** [§240]   The augmented estate also includes the value of property given by the decedent to the spouse during the marriage (but not the income from such property).

   (1) **Rationale:** If the decedent provided for the spouse by gifts during the marriage, such gifts should be taken into account in determining the amount to which the spouse is entitled at death. Including such gifts in the augmented estate reduces the amount passing to the spouse under the elective share. While the inclusion has the effect of increasing the amount against which the one-third elective share fraction applies, such gifts count dollar for dollar as in partial satisfaction of the elective share amount.

   (2) **Transfers included:** [§241]   Under this rule, the augmented estate includes such property owned by the spouse at the decedent's death and also such property *given by the spouse to third parties.* The augmented estate also

includes a beneficial interest given to the spouse in a trust created by the decedent during lifetime, and property passing to the spouse by the decedent's exercise of a power of appointment.

(3) **Life insurance proceeds and employee benefits:** [§242] The augmented estate includes life insurance proceeds and employee benefits (other than Social Security benefits) paid to the spouse, *to the extent that the decedent or decedent's employer paid premiums* or made contributions.

(4) **Burden of proof:** [§243] The surviving spouse has the burden of establishing that property owned by the spouse at decedent's death (and property given by the spouse to others during decedent's lifetime) was derived from a source *other than* gifts from the decedent.

d. **Not part of augmented estate:** [§244] The augmented estate does not include any life insurance, joint annuity, or pension benefit payable to a person *other than* the surviving spouse.

e. **Waiver by spouse:** [§245] A transfer to a person other than the spouse is excluded from the augmented estate if made with the spouse's *written* consent or joinder.

f. **When valued:** [§246] Property included in the augmented estate is valued as of the decedent's death, except that property given irrevocably to a donee during lifetime is valued as of the date the donee came into possession and enjoyment, if that occurred before the decedent's death.

3. **Other Statutory Solutions**

a. **New York statute:** [§247] The New York elective share statute takes an approach similar to the U.P.C. by applying the elective share statute to the decedent's net probate estate *plus testamentary substitutes.* [N.Y. Est. Powers & Trusts Law §5-1.1]

(1) **Testamentary substitutes:** [§248] The following dispositions are defined as testamentary substitutes:

(a) **Gifts causa mortis:** [§249] These are gifts made in fear of impending death that are automatically revoked if the donor survives the apprehended peril.

(b) **Survivorship estates:** [§250] Survivorship estates include Totten trust bank accounts, joint bank accounts with survivorship provisions, joint tenancies with right of survivorship, and tenancies by the entireties.

(c) **Transfers with retained controls:** [§251] Testamentary substitutes also include inter vivos transfers in which the deceased spouse retained the power to revoke or the power to consume, invade, or dispose of principal.

(2) **Burden of proof:** [§252]   If the joint bank account, joint tenancy, etc., was between the decedent and the surviving spouse, the spouse has the burden of showing the amount of consideration she furnished for the property's acquisition (*e.g.*, the amount in the bank account attributable to her deposits). If the testamentary substitute was between the decedent and a third party, the surviving spouse has the burden of showing the amount of consideration the decedent furnished for the property's acquisition.

(3) **Intestacy:** [§253]   As with the Uniform Probate Code's elective share statute, the New York statute applies when the decedent died intestate as well as when decedent left a will (*see supra*, §239).

(4) **Dispositions that are not testamentary substitutes:** [§254]   By statute, the following dispositions are expressly declared ***not*** to be testamentary substitutes, and thus are not subject to the New York elective share statute: life insurance proceeds; pension plan benefits; U.S. government bonds; and irrevocable lifetime transfers with ***no*** retained power to revoke, or to invade, consume, or dispose of principal.

(5) **Effective date:** [§255]   The New York testamentary substitute rules apply ***only if*** (i) the decedent's will (if she left one) was executed on or after September 1, 1966; (ii) the testamentary substitute was created after September 1, 1966; and (iii) the testamentary substitute was created after the marriage.

b. **Other states' statutes:** [§256]   Several states have statutes that are less comprehensive (and considerably less complicated) than the U.P.C. and New York models. These statutes reach lifetime transfers in which the decedent retained a testamentary power of appointment, a power to revoke, or a power to consume the property. [*See* Minn. Stat. Ann. §525.213; Pa. Stat. Ann. tit. 20, §301.11] One major consequence of such statutes is to prevent the use of revocable trusts to defeat the surviving spouse's right of election.

E. PROTECTION OF SPOUSE—COMMUNITY PROPERTY STATES

1. **No Elective Share Statutes:** [§257]   In general, none of the eight community property states has an elective share statute. Each spouse has the power of testamentary disposition over only his or her one-half community interest. The surviving spouse automatically owns one-half of the community estate on the first spouse's death, and there is no perceived need for a statutory scheme to protect against disinheritance.

a. **Exception:** [§258]   California and Idaho have enacted "quasi-community property" statutes, a form of elective share statute that applies to certain assets acquired by the couple before they moved to California or Idaho. (*See supra*, §43.)

b. **Separate property:** [§259] Each spouse has the **unrestricted power** of testamentary disposition over his or her separate property.

2. **Election Wills:** [§260] In a community property state, the surviving spouse is put to an election if the deceased spouse leaves a will that purports to dispose of the **entire interest** in community property, and not just the one-half community interest over which he or she has the power of testamentary disposition. These are often referred to as "widow's election wills," because (i) husbands tend to write such wills more often than wives, and (ii) in any event, wives tend to outlive their husbands.

   a. **Example:** Language that puts the surviving spouse to an election might read as follows: "It is my intention by this will to dispose of the entire interest in the community property of my wife and myself, and not just the one-half share over which I have the power of disposition. . . ." A typical dispositive plan under such a will is to devise the family residence and tangible personal property outright to the spouse (free of any election), and then leave the remaining community estate in trust: income to the surviving spouse for life, remainder to descendants.

   b. **Forced election will:** [§261] Under a forced election will, the trust created by the will is to be **irrevocable** as to both the decedent's and the surviving spouse's one-half community interests. Such a will puts the surviving spouse to an election.

      (1) **Election against the will:** [§262] Since the decedent does not have testamentary power over the survivor's one-half community interest, the surviving spouse does not have to go along with the arrangement. She can elect to take the one-half community to which she is entitled by law, rejecting the will's terms. If she does so, however, she **relinquishes all testamentary gifts** in her favor made in the will. [Estate of Murphy, 15 Cal. 3d 907 (1976)]

         (a) **Analysis:** In effect, the decedent through his will is saying, "I will give you a life income interest in my one-half of our community property **if** you will allow my will to govern the disposition of **your** one-half of our community estate." If the survivor elects against the will, she takes her one-half community as in the ordinary case; **but** she gives up the life income interest in the decedent's one-half community.

      (2) **Election to take under the will:** [§263] If the surviving spouse elects to take under the will, the decedent's will operates to transfer the surviving spouse's one-half community interest, as well as his own.

      (3) **Tax consequences:** [§264] If the survivor elects to take under the will, she is treated as having **transferred** her one-half community share **in exchange for** receiving an interest in her husband's one-half community share. Although the decedent's will contains the terms of the transfer, as to her one-half community interest, the surviving spouse is treated as a transferor for federal gift tax and estate tax purposes. (In the disposition given in the example above (§260), she will have made a transfer with a retained life estate.) [Commissioner v. Chase Manhattan Bank, 259 F.2d 231 (5th Cir. 1958)] *But note:* The

surviving spouse made the transfer *for consideration,* and so may be entitled to a "consideration offset" for federal tax purposes. [Commissioner v. Siegel, 250 F.2d 339 (9th Cir. 1957)] (*See* Estate & Gift Tax outline.)

c. **Voluntary election will:** [§265]   Under a voluntary election will, the trust funded with the surviving spouse's one-half community property is *revocable by her* at any time. She also receives the interests in the decedent's property passing under the will whether she leaves her one-half community in the trust or withdraws it by exercising the revocation power. Unlike the forced election will, which puts the survivor to a hard choice, a voluntary election will is merely an invitation to the spouse to have her one-half community share settled in the trust created by the decedent's will, with no penalty if the surviving spouse chooses not to do so.

d. **Elective share statutes compared:** [§266]   Under the elective share statutes found in many common law jurisdictions (*see supra,* §§189 *et seq.*), the surviving spouse who exercises the right of election takes a statutory share of *the decedent's* property. Under a community property widow's election will, the spouse who elects to take "against" the will takes *her* share of property that she owns under the community property system.

e. **When election will is used**

(1) **Trust settlement desired:** [§267]   The couple may have decided that, because of age or infirmity, or because of one spouse's inexperience in managing and investing property, a trust settlement of the entire community estate is preferred to leaving the spouse with outright ownership of her one-half community interest.

(2) **Unified management:** [§268]   The couple may own, as community property, assets (*e.g.,* a business interest) for which it is desired to have unified management of the property.

(a) **Example:** H and W own, as community property, all 100 shares of stock in a closely held corporation. H wants a trust settlement of the interest. If H leaves a will that devises "all my property" to a bank as trustee of a testamentary trust, his will would operate on only his one-half community interest, or fifty shares. The bank as trustee would own fifty shares of the stock, and the surviving spouse would own the other fifty shares. This could lead to awkwardness in management of the business through voting the stock. An election will could be used to transfer all 100 shares to the bank as trustee.

(3) **Compare—revocable trust:** [§269]   Another means of making a trust settlement and unified disposition of both halves of the community estate (without using an election will) is a revocable trust that is funded with community property during the spouses' lifetimes. (*See* Trusts outline.)

f. **Accidental election wills:** [§270]   The example in §260, *supra*, involved a deliberate attempt to dispose of the surviving spouse's one-half community interest. However, the election situation may arise unintentionally.

   (1) **Example:** H's will includes this provision: "I own Blackacre, my farm in Hunt County, as my separate property. I devise the fee simple title thereto to my brother Bill." However, Blackacre is actually the community property of H and his wife W. Since the will purports to dispose of the entire fee simple title in Blackacre, W is put to an election. If W elects against the will, she takes her one-half interest in Blackacre (and will be a tenant in common with Bill); **but** she must give up all gifts made to her by H's will. If W wants to take the interests given to her by the will, she must allow the will to operate to transfer her one-half interest in Blackacre to Bill. [*In re* Johnson's Estate, 178 Cal. App. 2d 826 (1960)]

   (2) **Compare:** However, a gift of "all of my property, of all kinds and wherever located, in which I have an interest at the time of my death," does **not** put the surviving spouse to an election. Such a will disposes of only the interests over which the decedent had the power of disposition; *i.e.*, his separate property and his one- half community interest. There is a presumption that the decedent by his will did not intend to dispose of property that he did not own (*i.e.*, his spouse's one-half community interest). [Estate of Wolfe, 48 Cal. 2d 570 (1957); 60 A.L.R.2d 736]

   (3) **Life insurance proceeds:** [§271]   An unintentional election may occur by the naming of a life insurance beneficiary.

      (a) **Example:** H is the insured under a $100,000 life insurance policy that is owned by the community because it was taken out after marriage and paid for out of H's salary. H names, as primary beneficiary of the policy proceeds, "the trustee named in my will," a valid beneficiary designation under state law. (*See* Trusts outline.) This beneficiary designation makes H's will a widow's election will since H by his will is purporting to transfer W's one-half community interest in the policy proceeds. [Martin v. Moran, 32 S.W. 904 (Tex. 1895)]

   (4) **Joint tenancy property:** [§272]   An election may be required where testator's will purports to dispose of property which he held in joint tenancy with the surviving spouse or with another party.

      (a) **Example:** T's will purports to devise the entire interest in property which he holds in joint tenancy with W, "one-half to my daughter D, and the other half to W," and bequeaths his residuary estate to W. W is put to an election to assert her right to the whole of the joint tenancy property (*i.e.*, by right of survivorship), or to accept the gifts provided in the will (half of the joint tenancy property plus the residue). [Waters v. Jennings, 24 Cal. App. 3d 81 (1972)]

(b) **Note:** Such an election involving a joint tenancy property or a tenancy by the entireties property can also arise in a common law state. [60 A.L.R.2d 736]

g. **Common law election will:** [§273] An election will situation can also arise in a common law state.

(1) **Example:** T leaves a will that states, "I devise Blackacre to A, and I devise Whiteacre to B." T owns Blackacre, but A owns Whiteacre, which T has purported to devise to B. A can assert his ownership right to Whiteacre—but if he does so, he must relinquish the devise of Blackacre to him. If A wants to take Blackacre under T's will, he must allow the will to operate to transfer Whiteacre to B. In effect, A would make a gift to B in exchange for receiving the gift under T's will. [60 A.L.R.2d 736]

3. **Lifetime Gifts of Community Property:** [§274]   Suppose that one spouse gives community property to a third party without the other spouse's joinder or consent. Can the other spouse set aside the transfer?

a. **Majority rule:** [§275]   Most of the community property states take the position that one spouse can make "reasonable" gifts of community property, so long as such gifts are not "in fraud of the other spouse's community rights." [Gristy v. Hudgens, 203 P. 569 (Ariz. 1922); Howard v. Howard, 96 So. 2d 345 (La. 1957)] This is often referred to by courts as the "fraud on the wife" doctrine since the husband was until recently the sole "manager" of the community estate, and most of the litigated cases involved gifts by the husband. However, a lifetime gift of community property by a wife may be found to be in fraud of the husband's community rights. [Cockerham v. Cockerham, 527 S.W.2d 162 (Tex. 1975)]

(1) **Criticism:** The "fraud on the spouse" test has the advantage of flexibility, but the concomitant disadvantage of not providing clear guidelines for predicting the outcome of cases. Also, while the rule has a historical basis (*i.e.*, it is applied under the Spanish and French community property systems), it is difficult to justify a *gift* of community property as being within the power to *manage* such assets.

(2) **"Fraudulent" transfer:** [§276]   An actual intent to defraud need not be proved; a particular transfer may be "constructively" fraudulent. [Davis v. Prudential Insurance Co., 331 F.2d 346 (5th Cir. 1964)] The following factors are considered by the courts in determining whether a particular transfer should be held to be in fraud of the other spouse's community rights.

(a) **Amount of gift:** [§277]   One factor is the amount of the gift in relation to the size of the community estate. Thus a husband's gift of $30,000 to his children by a former marriage might seem excessive when considered by itself, but in the context of a $250,000 community estate, it may be considered reasonable. [Brown v. Brown, 282 S.W.2d 90 (Tex. 1955)]

(b) **Relationship of donee:** [§278]   That the donee is a close relation to the donor (*e.g.*, child, parent, sibling) is a factor that tends to support upholding the gift. [Kemp v. Metropolitan Life Insurance Co., 220 F.2d 952 (5th Cir. 1955)] On the other hand, if the donee is not related to the donor, there is a strong *presumption* that the gift is constructively fraudulent. [Givens v. Girard Life Insurance Co., 480 S.W.2d 412 (Tex. 1972)]

(c) **Amount of remaining community estate:** [§279]   If the remaining community estate is sufficient to make ample provision for the surviving spouse, this factor tends to support the gift. [Krueger v. Williams, 359 S.W.2d 48 (Tex. 1962)]

(3) **Nontestamentary transfers:** [§280]   In the majority rule states, life insurance dispositions and interests passing by right of survivorship are considered lifetime transfers for purposes of these rules; *i.e.*, they are subject to the "fraud on the spouse" test, and not the surviving spouse's right of election. Thus, if they are not "reasonable" gifts of community property, they may be set aside.

(a) **Example:** H is the insured under a $100,000 life insurance policy that names his mother M as the primary beneficiary. On H's death, W cannot set the beneficiary designation aside as to her one-half community interest in the policy proceeds unless she establishes that naming M beneficiary was in fraud of her community rights.

b. **Minority rule:** [§281]   In several states, lifetime transfers of community property are treated the same way as testamentary transfers under an election will: Except for *de minimis* gifts, the spouse who does not join in or consent to such a transfer can *elect* to set the transfer aside (or receive reimbursement from other community assets) as to her one-half community share. [Cal. Civ. Code §172; Marston v. Rue, 159 P. 111 (Wash. 1916)]

4. **Community Property Brought to Common Law State:** [§282]   Suppose that a husband and wife live in a community property jurisdiction for a number of years and then move to a common law state, bringing community property assets with them. Suppose further that the community funds are invested in new assets, title to which is taken in the husband's name. What is the ownership status of such assets acquired with "imported community property"? It should be clear that since the wife owned an undivided one-half interest in the community property before the move, those property rights should not be lost even though title is taken in the husband's name. Under established conflict of laws principles, the ownership of marital assets is determined under the laws of the marital domicile *at the time the assets are acquired.* Such ownership interests, once acquired, are not lost upon a move to another jurisdiction.

a. **Case decisions:** [§283]   Surprisingly, there are relatively few case decisions dealing with imported community property. This may be because the possible significance of the community history of such assets has been overlooked, since the general rule in common law jurisdictions is that ownership is determined by the manner in which title is held or registered. In the handful of reported cases in which the wife has asserted an ownership interest, she has been successful under either a constructive trust theory [Edwards v. Edwards, 233 P. 477 (Okla. 1925)] or a resulting trust theory [Quintana v. Ordono, 195 So. 2d 577 (Fla. 1967)]. Where, however, the issue has been state inheritance taxation of the husband's interest at death, the courts in the new state have tended not to recognize the wife's one-half ownership interest. [*In re* Kessler's Estate, 203 N.E.2d 221 (Ohio 1964); *but see* People v. Bejarano, 358 P.2d 866 (Colo. 1961)]

b. **Uniform Disposition of Community Property Rights at Death Act:** [§284]   Several jurisdictions have enacted a uniform act that recognizes both spouses' interests in such imported community property, regardless of how title is taken in the new state. [*See, e.g.,* Ky. Rev. Stat. §391.210; N.Y. Est. Powers & Trusts Law §6-6.1; Or. Rev. Stat. §112.705] The Act applies to all property which was acquired as community property under the laws of another jurisdiction or was acquired with the income from or the proceeds of sale of such community property. Under the Act, upon the death of one spouse, only one-half of such property is subject to testamentary disposition or intestate distribution. The remaining one-half of the property belongs to the surviving spouse and does not pass through the decedent's estate.

F.   PRETERMITTED CHILD STATUTES

1. **In General:** [§285]   Except for Louisiana with its forced heirship rules [La. Civ. Code art. 1493], it is possible for a testator to **disinherit** her children. A parent need not bequeath anything to the children—not even the proverbial one dollar. However, many states have statutes, called "pretermitted child" statutes, designed to protect children who may have been **accidentally** omitted from the will.

   a. **Majority rule:** [§286]   In most states, the statute operates only in favor of children born or adopted **after the will's execution.** [U.P.C. §2-302(a); Tex. Prob. Code §67; Va. Code §64.1-70]

      (1) **Example:** T has a child C at the time she executes a will that bequeaths her estate one-third to her husband H and two-thirds to her sister S. The will makes no mention of C or of any future children that T might have. There is nothing to indicate that C's omission was intentional. Thereafter, T and her husband have another child D. T then dies without having revoked or modified her will. D takes an intestate share of T's estate as a pretermitted child, but C takes nothing since he was alive at the time the will was executed.

   b. **Minority rule:** [§287]   In several states, the pretermitted child statute applies to children alive when the will was executed, as well as to afterborn and after-adopted children. [84 Okla. Stat. §132] This is a very different type of statute, as it requires a testator to name or at least refer to her children in order to prevent the statute's operation.

      (1) **Example:** In these states, C **and** D in the above example would each take an intestate share of T's estate.

c. **Grandchildren:** [§288]   In most states, the pretermitted child statute operates only in favor of children, and not grandchildren, of the testator. [U.P.C. §2-302(a)] However, in a substantial minority of states, the statute also applies to the descendants of a **deceased** child of the testator. [84 Okla. Stat. §132]

2. **When Statute Does Not Apply:** [§289]   Under the typical pretermitted child statute, the child takes an intestate share of the decedent's estate **unless** one of the exceptions written into the statute is applicable.

   a. **Intentional omission:** [§290]   A number of statutes provide that the child is not protected if it appears that the omission was intentional.

      (1) **Majority rule:** [§291]   A majority of such states require that the decedent's intention to omit the child must appear **on the face of the will.** If the will does not speak to the situation, extrinsic evidence is **not** admissible to show that the omission was intentional. [Estate of Glomset, 547 P.2d 951 (Okla. 1976)] Such statutes raise the issue of what language is required in the will to evidence such intent.

         (a) **Specific disinheritance clause:** [§292]   In such states, where the will specifically disinherits "my son B," this is a sufficient mention to establish that the failure to provide for B was intentional, and hence B is not pretermitted. (But if B were already dead at the time the will was executed, or later predeceased the testator, an express disinheritance of "my son B" would **not** be a sufficient mention of B's descendants; and in states whose statutes apply to grandchildren, B's grandchildren may be pretermitted (*supra,* §288).

         (b) **General disinheritance and incontestability clauses:** [§293]   The trend of authority is to uphold even rather sparse provisions as being a sufficient "mention" of the testator's children to prevent pretermission. [152 A.L.R. 723] In minority rule states, in which the statute applies to children alive when the will was executed, the testator's children need not be individually named. Thus, "I leave the sum of $1.00 to any of my children who contest this will," or "I disinherit all of my children," would be sufficient mention so that no child is a pretermitted heir. [Estate of Fanning, 8 Cal. 2d 229 (1937)]

            1) **Example:** Many cases hold that a disinheritance clause applicable to "all my relatives" or even "all my heirs" is a sufficient mention to prevent operation of the pretermitted child statute. [152 A.L.R. 723]

            2) **Compare:** A provision disinheriting "any other person or persons," or "anyone who may contest this will," is frequently held **not** a sufficient mention to show that testator had her children in mind. [Estate of Gardner, 21 Cal. 3d 620 (1978)] On the other hand, a disinheritance clause applicable "to any person who, if I died intes-

tate, would be entitled to share in my estate" has been held equivalent to "heirs"; and hence sufficient mention to prevent pretermission of a child. [Van Strien v. Jones, 46 Cal. 2d 705 (1956)]

(2) **Minority rule:** [§294]   Some courts admit *extrinsic evidence* on the issue of whether the testator intended to disinherit her children. [88 A.L.R.2d 616]

b. **Child provided for by settlement:** [§295]   Under a number of statutes, the child who otherwise would be protected by the statute is not pretermitted if provided for by a lifetime settlement.

(1) **Example:** T executes a will that bequeaths his estate one-third to his wife W and two-thirds to his son S. Thereafter, T and W have another child: D. Two years after D's birth, T creates a trust for D's benefit; then T dies survived by W, S, and D. D is not a pretermitted child within the meaning of the statute because she was provided for by a lifetime settlement.

(2) **Comment:** It is the *existence* of the settlement, not its amount, that controls. If, in the above example, the trust was funded with assets worth $10,000 and T left a $3 million estate, D would take considerably less than her sibling S (who would take $2 million under the will). The purpose of the pretermitted child statutes is to cover *accidental omission* of a child who is not provided for by settlement, *not* to provide equality of treatment among siblings.

c. **Spouse is principal beneficiary:** [§296]   Under several statutes, even if a child was born after the will was executed and was not provided for by settlement, the pretermission statute does not apply if the testator's spouse, who was the parent of testator's children, was the principal beneficiary under the will. [Tex. Prob. Code §67]

(1) **Example:** T's will devises his entire estate "to my wife if she survives me; otherwise to my daughter D." Thereafter, T and W adopt a child S; then T dies, and his will is admitted to probate. Even though S was adopted after the will's execution and was not provided for by lifetime settlement, S does not take as a pretermitted child since T's entire estate passed to his surviving spouse.

(2) **Compare:** But if W predeceased T, meaning that D would be the sole beneficiary under the will, the pretermitted child statute would operate in S's favor.

d. **Uniform Probate Code:** [§297]   Under U.P.C. section 2-302(a), there is *no* pretermission of an afterborn or after-adopted child if:

(i) It appears from the will that the omission was *intentional;*

(ii) The testator had one or more children when the will was executed and devised substantially all of his estate to the other *parent* of the omitted child; or

(iii) The testator provided for the omitted child by *transfer outside the will* and the *intent* that the transfer be in lieu of a testamentary bequest is shown by T's statements, the amount of the transfer, or other evidence.

3. Operation of Statute

a. **Majority rule:** [§298]   Under most statutes, the pretermitted child takes an ***intestate share*** of the deceased parent's estate—*i.e.,* the share the child would have taken if the parent had died intestate. The child takes an intestate share, and the will operates on the remaining assets.

   (1) **Abatement:** [§299]   In most jurisdictions, in making up the pretermitted child's share, the ordinary rules of abatement apply (*see infra,* §998 *et seq.*): The child's share comes first out of intestate property (if any), then the residuary estate, etc. [U.P.C. §§2-302(c), 3-902]

   (2) **Pro rata abatement:** [§300]   In some states, the residuary estate is not burdened with the entire cost of the pretermitted child's share. All testamentary gifts abate proportionately unless this would defeat the testator's obvious intent with respect to some specific gift.

b. **Minority rule:** [§301]   Several states apply the majority rule ***if*** the testator had other children at the time the will was executed. If, however, the testator had ***no other children*** at the time the will was executed and then has or adopts a child, and if none of the exceptions to the statute's operation applies (*see supra,* §§290-296), ***the entire will is void.*** That is, the will is revoked by operation of law. [Tex. Prob. Code §67; Va. Code §64.1-71]

c. **New York statute:** [§302]   Under the New York statute, the pretermitted child who is not provided for by lifetime settlement does not take an intestate share; neither is the will void. Instead, to the extent feasible, the pretermitted child takes the same share of the parent's estate as testator's other children, and the other childrens' testamentary gifts are ***reduced ratably*** in making up the pretermitted child's share. [N.Y. Est. Powers & Trusts Law §5-3.2]

   (1) **Comment:** Unlike most statutes, the New York scheme ***does*** attempt to provide equality of treatment of all of testator's children–those given gifts in the will and those born or adopted thereafter. Only the gifts to testator's other children are reduced; no other beneficiary is affected by the pretermission.

   (2) **Example:** T, a resident of New York, bequeaths $60,000 to each of his children A and B, and devises his residuary estate to his sister S. Thereafter, T adopts a child C, who is not provided for by lifetime settlement. The gifts to A and B are reduced in C's favor; each takes $40,000. Sister S takes the residuary estate.

G. HOMESTEAD, EXEMPT PERSONAL PROPERTY, FAMILY ALLOWANCE

1. **Homestead:** [§303]   Many states have homestead laws designed to protect the family residence or farm from creditors' claims. In a number of these jurisdictions, the homestead laws also give some form of protection to the surviving spouse or minor children of a deceased homestead owner. Homestead laws differ so markedly from jurisdiction to

jurisdiction that easy generalizations are not possible. Representative features of several states' homestead laws are summarized below.

a. **Protection from creditors' claims:** [§304]   The most common feature of the various states' homestead laws is that property that qualifies as a homestead cannot be reached to satisfy creditors' claims *except for valid liens on the homestead* itself (*e.g.*, purchase money or other mortgage lien, real property ad valorem taxes, and merchants' or materialmens' liens). In most jurisdictions, this homestead protection applies to claims asserted by creditors of the decedent's estate if the decedent was survived by a spouse or minor children.

b. **Spouse's joinder required:** [§305]   In many jurisdictions, conveyance of any interest in the homestead is not effective unless the conveyance is signed by the other spouse.

c. **Probate homestead:** [§306]   In several states, the surviving spouse (or, if there is no surviving spouse, the decedent's minor or dependent children) is entitled to *occupy the homestead* as a residence for as long as he or she chooses to occupy it. [Tex. Const. art. 16, §52] This right of occupancy is personal to the spouse (or children) and cannot be assigned. If the spouse or children cease to occupy the homestead as a residence, the so-called probate homestead is said to be "abandoned," and the property is free of any homestead occupancy claim. The homestead right in favor of minor children terminates when the children reach legal age.

    (1) **Example:** H owns the family residence, which qualifies as a homestead, in fee simple. H dies leaving a will that devises "all my property," including his interest in the residence, to his sister S. Legal title to the residence passes to S. However, under the state's probate homestead laws, W has the exclusive right to occupy the residence as a homestead for as long as she chooses to do so.

d. **Restrictions on devise of homestead:** [§307]   In a few states, the homestead laws do not merely give the surviving family members a right of occupancy but, instead, operate to *restrict the owner's power* of testamentary disposition. For example, in Florida, the homestead cannot be devised if the decedent is survived by a spouse or by minor children:

    (i) If the decedent is survived by his *spouse and a minor child,* the spouse takes a life estate with a vested remainder in the decedent's *lineal descendants* (not just minor children).

    (ii) If the decedent is survived by his *spouse and by adult children* (but no minor children), the homestead can be devised to the spouse only. If the homestead is devised to anyone else, the devise is ineffective; the spouse takes a life estate, with a vested remainder in lineal descendants.

    (iii) If the decedent is survived by his *spouse but not by lineal descendants,* the homestead cannot be devised. Instead it passes to the spouse in fee simple.

(iv) If the decedent is *not survived by his spouse* but is survived by *minor* children, the homestead cannot be devised; it passes to the lineal descendants (and not just the minor children).

(v) If the decedent is *not survived by a spouse or by minor children,* then and only then does he have the power of testation.

[Fla. Const. art. 10, §4(c)]

(1) **But note:** These rules restricting the power of disposition have no application if the homestead is held in a *tenancy by the entireties* between the spouses. In such a case, title passes to the surviving spouse by right of survivorship.

e. **What property qualifies as a homestead:** [§308]   In general, to qualify as a homestead the property must have been acquired for *actual or intended use as a primary residence.* In many jurisdictions, there is either an acreage limit or a dollar limit on the amount of property that can qualify for homestead protection. For example, in Texas, the homestead qualification is limited to one acre of land if an "urban" homestead is involved; or 200 acres of land (without regard to the value of improvements) if a "rural" homestead is involved. [Tex. Const. art. 16, §51] In Florida, the homestead exemption is limited to one acre for land located within a city or town, and 160 acres for rural lands. [Fla. Const. art. 10, §4(c)]

f. **Homestead allowance:** [§309]   Several jurisdictions do not give the surviving spouse or minor children any right to occupy the decedent's real property, but instead provide a "homestead allowance," *i.e.,* a *cash award* that is free of creditors' claims. [Utah Code §75-2-401—$10,000]

(1) **Compare:** Some of the states that give the spouse and minor children a "probate homestead" right of occupancy also provide for a homestead allowance. But, in these states, the homestead allowance serves a very different function. It is an allowance *in lieu of* homestead, and is available only if the decedent did not own a homestead (*e.g.,* was an apartment dweller). [Tex. Prob. Code §273—$10,000 allowance in lieu of homestead]

2. **Exempt Personal Property:** [§310]   Related to the homestead laws are statutes that exempt certain items of *tangible* personal property from execution or levy in satisfaction of creditors' claims. Typically, the exemption applies to household furnishings, furniture, appliances, personal effects, farm equipment, and, in a number of states, automobiles up to a stated value. [Cal. Civ. Proc. Code §690]

a. **Personal property set-aside:** [§311]   As with the homestead laws, in many states the exempt personal property statutes give added protection to the surviving spouse and minor children of a deceased owner: Items that are exempt from creditors' claims during the owner's lifetime are "set aside" for the spouse or children. Typically, the statute lists the types or categories of items that are eligible for the set-aside [Cal. Prob. Code §§6500, 6510, 6520; Fla. Prob. Code §732.402], and there may be a dollar limit on the items within each category that are eligible for a set-aside. [N.Y. Est. Powers & Trusts Law §5-3.1]

b. **Set-aside not automatic:** [§312]   The specified items of personal property are awarded to the spouse (or, if there is no spouse, to the minor children) only if petition is made for a set-aside. In most estates, the right to a personal property set-aside is not asserted.

(1) **Example:** W dies leaving a will that bequeaths "all of my real and personal property" to her husband H, who survives her. Since all of W's personal property passes to H under the will, H has no reason to petition for a set-aside—unless W's estate is insolvent; in that case, the set-aside will secure protection of the assets from creditors' claims.

(2) **Example:** H's will bequeaths five dollars to W, his wife of twenty years, and bequeaths the rest of his estate "to my secretary and dear, dear friend, M." In addition to her right to take an elective share of H's estate, W can increase the amount of H's property passing to her by petitioning for a personal property set-aside and a family allowance, both of which are over and above the amount left to W by the will or the amount of W's elective share. (*See supra,* §197.)

3. **Family Allowance:** [§313]   In many states, the surviving spouse or minor children are entitled to petition for a family allowance, to provide for their maintenance during the period in which the decedent's estate is in administration. After notice and hearing, the court may order the allowance to be paid as a lump sum or in periodic installments. [U.P.C. §2-403] In some states, the allowance is limited to a stated dollar amount. [Fla. Prob. Code §733.707—$6,000; D.C. Prob. Act §20-906—$10,000] In other states, the allowance is the amount needed to maintain the spouse or children for a year [Tex. Prob. Code §287], or is specified as a "reasonable" amount to be fixed by the court [Cal. Prob. Code §§680-682].

a. **Allowance takes precedence over other claims:** [§314]   Typically, the allowance takes precedence over all claims except funeral expenses (up to a stated dollar amount) and expenses of estate administration.

b. **Allowance in addition to other benefit or share:** [§315]   The family allowance is not chargeable against any benefit or share passing to the surviving spouse (or children) by intestate succession, elective share, or the will of the decedent.

c. **Personal right:** [§316]   Typically, the death of the person entitled to the allowance terminates the right to any remaining part of the allowance not already paid. [Fla. Prob. Code §732.403]

H. TESTAMENTARY GIFTS TO CHARITY

1. **Common Law:** [§317]   At early common law, *"mortmain"* restrictions were placed on the right to make testamentary gifts to a *church.* The reasons were twofold: (i) testators otherwise might be inclined to favor the church over their heirs, in wills made shortly before death, out of a concern for increasing their chances in the hereafter; and (ii) the sovereign was concerned about great accumulations of wealth by the church.

2. **Present Law:** [§318]   Most states place no restriction on charitable devises and bequests. However, a handful of states still have statutes restricting testamentary gifts to **charity** (not just churches). [6 A.L.R.4th 603] The restrictions take the form of either **voiding** all charitable bequests in wills executed within a short time before death [Fla. Prob. Code §732.803—six months], or **limiting** testamentary gifts made within the specified period to a fixed percentage of the estate [Page's Ohio Rev. Code Ann. §2107.06—six months, one-fourth of estate].

3. **Constitutionality:** [§319]   Two such statutes, voiding gifts in wills made within thirty days of death, were recently held to violate the Equal Protection Clause. The courts reasoned that a statute voiding gifts in a will made twenty-nine days before death but upholding such gifts in a will made thirty-one days before death was arbitrary, and was not fairly or substantially related to the legislative purpose of protecting testator's family members from excessive charitable gifts. [*In re* Estate of Cavill, 329 A.2d 503 (Pa. 1974)] One of the statutes, which applied only to religious gifts, was held unconstitutional on the further ground that there was no rational basis for voiding religious gifts but not gifts to other charities. [Key v. Doyle, 365 A.2d 621 (D.C. 1976)]

V. FORMAL REQUISITES OF WILLS

chapter approach

In all likelihood, you will see some of the topics covered in this chapter on your exam because the formal requirements of a will are a rich source of exam questions. In particular, watch for the following issues:

1. **Is the writing a will?** Although some states allow oral wills in limited circumstances, the typical situation involves a writing. But is the writing a will? Other writings (*e.g.,* a list of property to be distributed, a letter expressing a desire to give the property to someone, a deed, etc.) purport to be wills but are not written with testamentary intent. Remember that a will must take effect only on the death of the testator, and it may, but **need not,** dispose of the testator's property. (If the writing has certain other functions—*e.g.,* revokes an earlier will—it is a will regardless of whether it disposes of property.)

2. **Did the testator intend the writing as a will?** If not, it is not a will. Look for an intent (i) to dispose of property; (ii) that the disposition take place only at death, and (iii) that this writing accomplish the disposition of property. If a document is ambiguous, extrinsic evidence may be used to show testamentary intent.

3. **Did the testator have capacity to make a will?** The key time for judging capacity is **at the time testator executed the will.** Don't be fooled by questions where testator is incompetent before execution or becomes so afterwards; if testator has capacity at the time of execution, the will is valid. Also keep in mind that the test for capacity is an **easy one.** Testator can be mentally retarded, suffering from the afflictions of extreme old age, even intoxicated; but if testator (i) knows he is making a will; (ii) knows the relationship between himself and the "natural objects of his bounty" (*e.g.,* family, friends); (iii) knows the nature of and extent of his property; and (iv) understands the disposition he is making, the will is valid.

4. **Were the statutory requirements of a will met?** For example, was the will signed by testator in the presence of the required number of witnesses? These requirements vary from state to state so be sure to read your question carefully to determine what the particular state requires, then follow those requirements. If the requirements are not met, the will cannot be admitted to probate.

5. **If the statute requires that the will be attested to by witnesses, were those witnesses "competent"?** Besides the general competency requirements (maturity, mental capacity, etc.), watch out for the "interested witness"—a witness who is also a beneficiary under the will. If the witness is "interested," she may **lose her gift** under the will (due to a purging statute), but the **will itself is still valid.** Be aware too that some statutes **allow** the interested witness to take in certain circumstances (*e.g.,* if the beneficiary would take as an heir if there were no will).

6. **If there are no attesting witnesses, can the will be valid as a holographic will** (one entirely in the testator's handwriting)? Be sure the will meets the state's specific requirements for holographs. If the state does not recognize holographic wills, be sure to mention that a handwritten, signed "will" is not valid unless it is properly witnessed.

Finally note that the issues above should be considered for a **codicil** as well as a will.

A. WHAT CONSTITUTES A WILL

1. **Nature of a Will:** [§320]   A will (other than an oral will, *infra*, §§471 *et seq.*) is an instrument executed in accordance with certain formalities that directs the disposition of a person's (the "testator's") property at his death. A will, therefore, is an instrument that operates to transfer title to real or personal property at the testator's death.

    a. **Effective only on death:** [§321]   The principal distinction between a will and any other type of conveyance is that a will takes effect only upon the death of the maker. A will is sometimes referred to as an "ambulatory" document. This means that a will has ***no operative effect*** during the testator's lifetime; it is fully revocable or amendable at any time and does not establish any property rights until the testator's death. The beneficiaries named in a living person's will have no rights or benefits thereunder until the testator dies; until that time, they have nothing but an ***expectancy***.

        (1) **Exception for contractual wills:** [§322]   A beneficiary may have greater rights where the testator has executed his will pursuant to a contract with the beneficiary or some other person. In such a case, the beneficiary may have rights and remedies—but ***under contract law, not wills law***—to compel the bargained-for testamentary disposition even though the testator subsequently amends or revokes his will. (*See infra*, §§613 *et seq.*)

    b. **Codicil:** [§323]   A codicil is a supplement to a will. It may add to, take from, or alter the will's provisions, or it may confirm the will in whole or in part. [N.Y. Est. Powers & Trusts Law §1-2.1] In states that have a statutory definition of a will, it is generally provided that the term "will" includes codicil unless a particular statute provides otherwise. [Tex. Prob. Code §3ff; N.Y. Est. Powers & Trusts Law §1-2.18]

    c. **Terminology—testator or testatrix:** [§324]   At common law, a male will-maker was referred to as a "testator," while a female will-maker was called a "testatrix." Although many lawyers and courts continue to follow this practice, using gender-based terminology to refer to persons who make wills is as inappropriate as referring to a female doctor as "doctress." Following the modern and better practice, this Summary uses the term "testator" when referring to either a male or a female will-maker.

2. **Other Functions of a Will:** [§325]   Generally, a will disposes of a person's property at death, but an instrument that does ***not*** dispose of property may still be a will. By majority rule, and by statute in many states, a will is defined as an instrument that does any ***one*** of the following things—regardless of whether it disposes of property.

    a. **Revokes an earlier will:** [§326]   Assuming that the instrument meets the formal requisites for making a will, it is admissible to probate as a will even though it does nothing more than revoke an earlier will. [Tex. Prob. Code §3ff]

    b. **Appoints a personal representative:** [§327]   A testamentary instrument will be given effect even if it does nothing more than name an executor or make some other provision for administration of the decedent's estate. In this situation, the will is admitted to probate, the designated person is appointed as personal representative, and the decedent's estate passes by **intestate succession** to the heirs. [Conoway v. Fulmer, 54 So. 624 (Ala. 1911); *In re* Hickman's Estate, 101 Cal. 609 (1894)]

c. **Exercises a power of appointment:** [§328]   An instrument that merely exercises a power of appointment can be a will. [N.Y. Est. Powers & Trusts Law §1-2.18]

d. **Directions regarding testator's body or part thereof:** [§329]   In some states, an instrument can be probated if it does nothing more than dispose of the testator's body or a part thereof (*e.g.*, a kidney). (In some states, oral declarations concerning the disposition of organs are also valid if the requirements of an oral will are met. [N.Y. Est. Powers & Trusts Law §1-2.18])

e. **New York's "negative bequest" rule:** [§330]   By statute in New York, a will (or a provision in a will) is valid if it does nothing more than direct how property shall **not** be disposed of. This is called the "negative bequest" statute. [N.Y. Est. Powers & Trusts Law §1-2.18]

   (1) **Example:** T, a New York resident, dies leaving a will that devises all his real property to B and further provides: "I hereby direct that my son John shall not take any part of my estate." The will contains no residuary clause, meaning that there is a partial intestacy as to T's personal property. The "negative bequest" to John is given effect. T's personal property passes to T's heirs as though son John predeceased T.

   (2) **Note:** This is decidedly a **minority** position. At common law and in nearly all states, on the above facts, son John would take an intestate share of the personal property; the words of disinheritance would not be given effect. The theory is that when a person dies partially intestate, the affected property passes "by force of law" under the intestacy statutes, and the will has no operative effect on property passing by intestacy. [Kimley v. Whittaker, 306 A.2d 443 (N.J. 1973)]

3. **Types of Wills:** [§331]   A valid will may take one of three forms.

   a. **Attested will:** [§332]   The standard form of will is one that is signed by the testator and witnessed by two (and in some states three) witnesses pursuant to a formal attestation procedure. (*See infra,* §§384 *et seq.*)

   b. **Holographic will:** [§333]   About half the states recognize holographic wills. A holographic will is an **unattested** (*i.e.*, unwitnessed) will that is entirely in the testator's **handwriting** and signed by the testator. (*See infra,* §§455 *et seq.*)

      (1) **Compare:** An attested will may be handwritten. There is no requirement that an attested will be typed, as long as it is signed by the testator and attesting witnesses pursuant to the prescribed formalities. "Holograph," however, is a term of art that refers to handwritten, **unattested** wills that are recognized as valid in some, but not all, states.

c. **Oral wills:** [§334]   A number of states give effect to oral ("nuncupative") wills but only in very limited circumstances. (*See infra*, §471.)

4. **Formal Requirements:** [§335]   There are four main requirements to the formation of a valid will:

   (i)   The will must have been executed with *testamentary intent*;

   (ii)   The testator must have had *testamentary capacity*;

   (iii)   The will must have been executed *free of fraud, duress, undue influence, or mistake*; and

   (iv)   The will must have been *duly executed*.

   These requirements are discussed in detail below.

B. GOVERNING LAW

1. **Uniform Probate Code:** [§336]   In 1969, a Uniform Probate Code ("U.P.C.") was approved by the National Commissioners on Uniform State Laws. The basic thrust of the U.P.C. is to simplify the requirements and procedures relating to the formation of wills and administration of estates.

   a. **U.P.C. states:** [§337]   Unlike many other uniform acts (*e.g.*, the Uniform Commercial Code), the Uniform Probate Code has been adopted by only a minority of jurisdictions. It has been adopted, in whole or in substantial part, in Alaska, Arizona, Colorado, Idaho, Maine, Michigan, Minnesota, Montana, Nebraska, New Jersey, New Mexico, North Dakota, Pennsylvania, and Utah.

   b. **Other states:** [§338]   The Uniform Probate Code has been used as a model for statutory reform in other states that did not adopt the U.P.C. Thus, the probate codes of a few states (*e.g.*, Florida, Texas) have made selective adoptions of some of the U.P.C.'s substantive law provisions. Other states (*e.g.*, California, Illinois, New York) have chosen not to adopt the Uniform Code but have retained their existing rules, modifying them where necessary.

2. **Legislative Control of Right to Make a Will:** [§339]   The right to make testamentary disposition of one's property has never been regarded as a "natural right." A will must meet the statutory requirements. Hence, a property owner's right to dispose of property by will is subject to the legislature's plenary control; the legislature can withhold or condition the right as it chooses. [Irving Trust Co. v. Day, 314 U.S. 556 (1942); Estate of Emerson, 183 N.W. 327 (Iowa 1921)]

   a. **Minority view:** [§340]   The courts of Wisconsin have taken the position that the right to dispose of property by will is a natural right which cannot be taken away or substantially impaired by legislative action. [Nunnemacher v. State, 108 N.W. 627 (Wis. 1906)]

3. Effect of Change in Law After Execution

a. **Common law:** [§341]   While some cases declare that the validity of a will's execution is determined under the law in effect when the will was executed, and others apply the law in effect at testator's death, the decisions are in fact harmonious. If the requirements of due execution were *increased* by the later statute, the courts apply the statute in existence when the will was executed. If the requirements were *liberalized* by the later statute, the courts apply the law in effect at testator's death. The effect is to admit the will to probate if it satisfies either the law in effect when the will was executed or the law in effect when the testator died. [111 A.L.R. 910]

b. **Statutory solutions:** [§342]   Statutes in several states expressly provide that a will is valid if it satisfies the law in effect at the time of death *or* at the time of execution. [U.P.C. §2-506; Cal. Prob. Code §6113]

4. Conflict of Laws Principles

a. **Real property:** [§343]   The validity and effect of a will, insofar as it disposes of real property, are determined by reference to the law of the *situs* of the real property. [Restatement (Second) of Conflicts §240]

b. **Personal property:** [§344]   With respect to dispositions of personal property, the law of the testator's *domicile* at the time of her death generally governs the validity and effect of the will. [Restatement (Second) of Conflicts §263]

c. **Uniform Execution of Foreign Wills Act:** [§345]   Many states have enacted the Uniform Execution of Foreign Wills Act or its equivalent. Under the Act, a will is admissible to probate in the jurisdiction if it has been executed in accordance with:

(i)   The law of that jurisdiction;

(ii)   The law of the state in which the will was executed;

(iii)   The law of the testator's domicile at the time the will was executed; *or*

(iv)   The law of the testator's domicile at death.

[U.P.C. §2-506]

d. **Uniform Probate Code:** [§346]   The Uniform Probate Code also allows the testator to select the particular state law to be applied to dispositions under the will, unless application of that law would be contrary to the public policy of testator's state of residence. [U.P.C. §2-602]

C. TESTAMENTARY INTENT

1. **In General:** [§347]   A will must be executed with testamentary intent. The testator must have subjectively intended that the particular words in question constitute her will at the time she executed the instrument. In the ordinary case, testamentary intent is established on the face of the will (*e.g.*, "I, Martha Green, do hereby declare this instrument to be my Last Will and Testament . . ."). Most of the cases dealing with the issue of testamentary intent have involved instruments that contain no such recital but, instead, are ambiguous as to whether they were intended to be testamentary or nontestamentary. However, testamentary intent may be put in issue even if the instrument contains a recital to the effect that "this is my will." [21 A.L.R. 2d 319]

2. **Legal Test:** [§348]   A person is held to have testamentary intent only if she in fact intended the words executed to operate as her will. Such intent thus consists of three elements:

   (i)   The testator must have intended to **dispose of property**;

   (ii) The testator must have intended the disposition to **occur only upon death**; and

   (iii) The testator must have intended the **instrument in question to accomplish the disposition**.

3. **Document Testamentary on Its Face**

   a. **Older view—conclusive presumption:** [§349]   In a number of cases, the courts have stated that a document containing a recital that it is intended to be testamentary (*e.g.*, "this is my last will and testament") raises a conclusive presumption of testamentary intent, and that extrinsic evidence is inadmissible to show that the document was not testamentary. [*In re* Kennedy's Will, 124 N.W. 516 (Mich. 1910); Estate of Smith, 31 Cal. 2d 563 (1948)]

   b. **Modern (majority) view—rebuttable presumption:** [§350]   Later cases from these same jurisdictions support the overwhelming majority view that such evidence *is* admissible notwithstanding the will's recitals. [*In re* Cosgrove's Estate, 287 N.W. 456 (Mich. 1939); Estate of Sargavak, 35 Cal. 2d 93 (1950)] Thus, the prevailing view is that such a recital raises a presumption of testamentary intent, but the presumption can be **overcome** by extrinsic evidence, provided the evidence is clear, convincing, and cogent. [Madden v. Madden, 118 S.E.2d 443 (S.C. 1961)]

      (1) **Rationale:** "If the fact is plainly and conclusively made out, that the paper which appears to be the record of a testamentary act, was in reality the offspring of a jest, or the result of a contrivance to effect some collateral object, and never seriously intended as a disposition of property, it is not reasonable that the court should turn it into an effective instrument." [Lister v. Smith, 164 Eng. Rep. 1282 (1863)]

(2) **Sham wills—examples:** [§351] Thus, extrinsic evidence has been admitted to show that a person made out a will naming his girlfriend as beneficiary to induce her to sleep with him [Fleming v. Morrison, 72 N.E. 499 (Mass. 1904)], that the maker intended the instrument as a deed [Belgarde v. Carter, 146 S.W. 964 (Tex. 1912)], that the instrument was executed as part of a ceremonial initiation into a secret order [Shiels v. Shiels, 109 S.W.2d 1112 (Tex. 1937)], and that the maker was merely showing how brief a will could be [Nichols v. Nichols, 161 Eng. Rep. 1113 (1814)].

4. **Ambiguous Document:** [§352] Where a document might reasonably be construed as either a will or some other type of instrument, it is universally held that extrinsic evidence is admissible on the issue of whether the document was written with testamentary intent. [21 A.L.R.2d 319] The many cases on this issue have involved letters containing testamentary noises [*In re* Briggs' Estate, 134 S.E.2d 737 (W. Va. 1964)]; informal memoranda containing the names of persons and lists of property, but nothing else [Hopson v. Ewing, 353 S.W.2d 203 (Ky. 1961)]; documents that appear to be partial drafts of a will [Estate of Stickney, 101 Cal. App. 2d 361 (1951)]; instruments having characteristics both of wills and of deeds of gift [Estate of Estes, 27 So. 2d 854 (Miss. 1946)]; and powers of attorney [Stewart v. Stewart, 59 N.E. 116 (Mass. 1901)].

5. **Character of Evidence**

    a. **Testator's own statements:** [§353] Most courts admit statements made by the testator before or after execution of the instrument, on the issue of whether she regarded it as her will. [Estate of Sargavak, *supra*, §350] The parol evidence may be used to disprove or contradict statements of intent made in the will itself. Thus, even though the will recites, "this is my last will and testament," parol evidence is admissible to show that the maker in fact did ***not*** intend the instrument as her will. [Fleming v. Morrison, *supra*]

    b. **Drafter's testimony:** [§354] The testimony of the drafter of the document is admissible to show the testator's intent. [*In re* Kemp's Will, 186 A. 890 (Del. 1936)]

    c. **Surrounding circumstances:** [§355] Evidence may be admitted to show the circumstances attendant to the document's execution [*In re* Sharp's Estate, 183 So. 470 (Fla. 1938)—lodge initiation] and the maker's attitudes and family relationships at the time [*In re* Kauffman's Estate, 76 A.2d 414 (Pa. 1950)].

    d. **Imminence of death:** [§356] The fact that the maker was near death, or was about to undergo a serious operation, is admissible as a relevant circumstance bearing on testamentary intent. [Chambers v. Younes, 399 S.W.2d 655 (Ark. 1966)]

6. **Intent to Make Future Will:** [§357] Where the instrument indicates that the maker did not intend these particular words to be her will, but rather that her will would be executed in the future, there is no testamentary intent.

    a. **Example:** In a jurisdiction that recognizes holographic wills, T writes and signs a handwritten letter to her attorney: "Dear Mr. Smith: Please prepare a will for me. I want all of my property to go to my husband, John, if he survives me; otherwise to my daughter Agnes. I also want my husband John to be my executor, to serve without bond. After you prepare the will, I will come into town to sign it. /s/ T." Although the letter sets forth a complete dispositive plan and meets all of the formal requirements of a holographic will, it is not admissible to probate. It is clear from the letter that T did not intend **this instrument** to be her will, but instead looked to the preparation of another document that was to be executed by her with testamentary intent. [Price v. Huntsman, 430 S.W.2d 831 (Tex. 1968)]

b.   **Compare:** If it is shown that the person **intended** her instructions to be given effect as her will until a more formal document embodying those instructions could be prepared, the document will be given effect as a will (assuming the document otherwise satisfies the formalities of the Statute of Wills). [Nelson v. Nelson, 30 S.W.2d 893 (Ky. 1930)]

7.   **Conditional Will:** [§358]   A will may be expressly made contingent upon the happening of a specified event. If the specified event does not occur, the will is denied probate. If, however, the court interprets the conditional language as merely expressing the testator's **motive** for executing the will, probate will be granted. (*See infra*, §§478 *et seq.*)

8.   **Ineffective Deeds as Wills:** [§359]   If a deed is validly executed but fails as an inter vivos conveyance because it is not delivered, it cannot be admitted to probate as a will because it was not executed with testamentary intent. To be effective as a will, the testator must have intended the instrument to be effective at her death, not during her lifetime.

D.   CAPACITY TO MAKE A WILL

1.   **Requirement:** [§360]   In addition to testamentary intent, the testator must have had testamentary capacity, as defined in the rules set out below, **at the time he executed the will.** Similarly, the testator must have testamentary capacity at the time he executes a **codicil** to the will or attempts to revoke a will. The testator's capacity before or after execution is not controlling. [*In re* Reardon's Will, 36 Misc. 2d 307 (1962)]

2.   **Mental Capacity:** [§361]   Mental capacity for testamentary purposes is a completely different concept from mental capacity for other purposes (*e.g.*, criminal capacity, ability to contract, etc.). In general, it takes **less capacity** to make a will than to do any other legal act. Perfect sanity is not required. Even an **adjudication of incompetency** does not conclusively show that a person lacks mental capacity for testamentary purposes, although such an adjudication is evidence (and in many states raises a presumption) of lack of testamentary capacity.

a.   **Example:** An adult testator who is mentally retarded, has the mental capacity of a ten-year-old child, and has been adjudicated an incompetent, nonetheless has sufficient capacity to make a will if the jury finds that the four-point test below is met. [Estate of Teel, 483 P.2d 603 (Ariz. 1971)]

b. **Four-point test:** [§362] In order to establish that the testator had the requisite capacity to make a will, it must be shown that the testator:

(1) **Knew the nature of the act he was doing:** [§363] The testator must have the ability to understand that he is executing a will, and not some other legal document.

(2) **Knew the natural objects of his bounty:** [§364] The testator must have the capacity to understand the relationship between himself and those persons he ought to have in mind at the time of making his will.

(3) **Knew the nature and extent of his property:** [§365] The testator must have the ability to understand the nature and approximate value of the estate that will be affected by the will.

(4) **Understood the disposition he was making:** [§366] The testator must have had the capacity to relate the previous factors and formulate an orderly scheme of disposition. [Gilmer v. Brown, 44 S.E.2d 16 (Va. 1947); Estate of Bullock, 140 Cal. App. 2d 944 (1956)]

c. **Statutory modifications:** [§367] A few jurisdictions have modified the above test for testamentary capacity. In some states, the testator must be "of sound and disposing mind and capable of executing a valid deed or contract." [D.C. Code Ann. §17-102]

d. **Relation to will contests:** [§368] The issue of testamentary capacity is invariably raised in the context of a will contest. Therefore, more extended discussion of this topic is given *infra*, §§780-795.

3. **Testator's Status as Affecting Capacity:** [§369] At common law, a testator's status sometimes affected his capacity to distribute property by will.

a. **Minority**

(1) **Common law:** [§370] At common law, any male over age fourteen and any female over age twelve could write a will.

(2) **Modern law:** [§371] In all states today, the age at which a person can write a valid will is fixed by statute. In almost all states, a person must be at least age eighteen to make a will. [*See, e.g.,* Cal. Prob. Code §6100; Fla. Prob. Code §732.501; N.Y. Est. Powers & Trusts Law §3-1.1] Some states set a different minimum age for devises of land than for bequests of personal property, and several states impose no age requirement for married persons and persons serving in the armed forces. [Tex. Prob. Code §59]

b. **Marriage:** [§372] At early common law, a married woman did not have the capacity to dispose of real property by will, although she did have capacity to dispose of personal property as long as her husband made no objection. This distinction has been abolished in every American jurisdiction. [9 A.L.R.2d 505]

c. **Aliens:** [§373]   At common law, an alien could devise real or personal property, but the sovereign was given powers of confiscation within a year and a day. This restriction has been eliminated under all modern statutes.

d. **Felons:** [§374]   At common law, a person convicted of a serious crime was deprived of testamentary capacity. Again, this is no longer true in most states.

e. **Drunkenness, eccentricity, physical infirmity:** [§375]   These elements do not, by themselves, constitute incapacity. There must be something further to establish a lack of testamentary capacity.

   (1) **Drunkenness:** [§376]   Even habitual and extreme intoxication does not automatically constitute testamentary incapacity. There must be additional proof that at the time of the will's execution the "natural intelligence, memory, and judgment were paralyzed or perverted or the power of volition inactive because of the intoxication." [*In re* Heaton's Will, 224 N.Y. 22 (1918)]

   (2) **Eccentricities:** [§377]   Even though a person is eccentric and arbitrary, if he is also capable of managing his affairs, he has testamentary capacity regardless of how different he may be from others. [Dobie v. Armstrong, 160 N.Y. 584 (1899)]

   (3) **Physical infirmities:** [§378]   As long as the requirements for testamentary capacity are met, characteristics of old age such as physical infirmity, lack of memory, or even childishness are not significant. [*In re* Clearwater's Will, 2 N.Y.S. 99 (1888)]

   (4) **Mental illness:** [§379]   A court will not infer a lack of capacity from psychiatric treatment or an attempted suicide. [Estate of Hatzistefanou, 77 Misc. 2d 594 (1974)]

E. EXECUTION OF ATTESTED WILLS

1. **Statutory Requirements Must Be Met:** [§380]   For a will to be valid and admissible to probate, the testator must meet the formal requirements of due execution imposed by the statutes of the appropriate state. These statutes are sometimes referred to as the Statute(s) of Wills. Failure to satisfy the requirements of due execution makes the will **void**—not merely voidable. Thus, if the will is signed by the testator but witnessed by less than the required number of witnesses, the will is not admissible to probate even though all of the beneficiaries thereunder and all of testator's heirs join in the petition for probate and fervently desire to have the instrument probated. *Rationale:* Since the prescribed formalities have not been satisfied, the instrument **is not a will**.

2. **Functions of Required Formalities**

   a. **Ritual:** [§381]   One function of the formalities is to impress upon the testator the significance of the act; *i.e.,* that she is performing a legally binding act, the effect of which will be to dispose of all of her property at death. If the required formalities are met, the courts will conclude that the decedent deliberately intended the result.

b. **Evidentiary:** [§382]   By meeting the requirements of the Statute of Wills, the testator provides the proof that the instrument expresses her intent. A written instrument signed by the testator in front of attesting witnesses avoids the problems inherent in oral evidence and tends to reduce the chances of mistake and perjury.

c. **Protective:** [§383]   The formalities tend to protect the testator against undue influence and other forms of imposition by requiring competent, disinterested witnesses.

3. **Requirements—In General:** [§384]   The formal requirements for execution of a will vary from state to state. The variations are largely due to the fact that England had two statutes governing the execution of wills, each with different requirements: the Statute of Frauds (1677) and the Wills Act (1837). American jurisdictions tended to borrow from one or the other of the English statutes, and sometimes borrowed a little from each statute or added a new wrinkle of their own.

a. **Formalities that may be required:** [§385]   The following is a list of the formalities that may be required in a particular state.

(1) **Signed by testator:** [§386]   The will must be signed by the testator (or signed for the testator by another person at the testator's direction and in her presence).

(2) **Signature at the end:** [§387]   Several states have adopted the requirement of the English Wills Act that testator's signature be "at the foot or end" of the will.

(3) **Testator signs in the presence of attesting witnesses:** [§388]   The testator may be required to sign the will (or acknowledge her earlier signature) in the presence of all attesting witnesses (the witnesses must all be present at the same time).

(4) **Testator "publishes" will:** [§389]   In several states, the testator must declare to the witnesses that the instrument is her will or must otherwise communicate this to the witnesses so that they know that they are witnessing a will as distinguished from some other legal document.

(5) **Number of attesting witnesses:** [§390]   Most states require only *two* attesting witnesses. However, three witnesses are required in Maine, New Hampshire, South Carolina, and Vermont.

(6) **Signature of witnesses:** [§391]   Usually, witnesses must sign in the testator's presence and sometimes must sign in each other's presence.

(7) **Execution ceremony must be completed within thirty days:** [§392]   Only New York requires that the two attesting witnesses each must sign within thirty days of each other. [N.Y. Est. Powers & Trusts Law §3-2.1(a)(4)]

b. **Variations from state to state:** [§393]   No jurisdiction requires all of the above formalities. Thus, it is necessary to consult the statutes of a particular state to determine what particular formalities are required. Some jurisidictions have much more liberal will execution statutes than others.

    (1) **Example—strict statutes:** [§394]   The Florida statute is fairly strict. The testator must sign the will (or have it signed for her by another person at testator's direction and in her presence) *at the end* of the will (or must acknowledge her previous signature) *in the presence* of two attesting witnesses, both present *at the same time.* The two attesting witnesses must sign the will in testator's presence *and* in the presence of each other. [Fla. Prob. Code §732.502] Thus, the only requirements found in some states but not required in Florida are that the testator publish the will and that there be three attesting witnesses.

    (2) **Example—liberal statutes:** [§395]   Under the Uniform Probate Code, all that is required for due execution of an attested will is that the testator sign the will (or have it signed for her by another person at testator's direction and in her presence), that there be two attesting witnesses, and that the witnesses witness *either* testator's signing *or* testator's acknowledgment of her previous signature of the will. [U.P.C. §2-502] Note that the U.P.C. does *not* require: the testator to sign (or acknowledge her previous signature) in the presence of both attesting witnesses at the same time, the testator's signature to be at the end of the will, the testator to publish the will, the witnesses to sign in the testator's presence, the witnesses to sign in each other's presence, or the execution ceremony to be completed by any particular time.

c. **Planning tip:** [§396]   Even though a will is executed in a state that has a liberal will execution statute, the better practice is to have the will executed in a manner that satisfies the seven-point maximum formalities listed above. The testator may move and then die in a state with a more stringent will execution statute. Or the testator may own real property in another state, meaning that ancillary probate may be required (*see infra,* §912). Although many states have enacted the Uniform Execution of Foreign Wills Act or its equivalent (*see supra,* §345), not all states have done so.

    (1) **Exception:** Unless the will is *executed* in one of the four states requiring three witnesses (Maine, New Hampshire, South Carolina, or Vermont), it is *not* necessary to have three attesting witnesses. All of these states have enacted the Uniform Execution of Foreign Wills Act or its equivalent (*see supra,* §345).

4. **Signature Requirement**

a. **What constitutes signature:** [§397]   Most courts take a liberal position on what constitutes the testator's signature. The signature requirement is satisfied by testator's signing her first name or nickname, her initials, "Mom," or by the X of an illiterate person—provided that the mark was intended to be testator's signature or mark and it was made by testator's volitional act. [98 A.L.R.2d 841] Testator's fingerprints constitute a valid signature. [28 A.L.R.2d 1157] A few courts have even held that the signature requirement is satisfied by a rubber-stamped or type-written name, but this is decidedly the minority position. [98 A.L.R.2d 893]

b.   **Assistance in signing:** [§398]   The signature requirement is satisfied even though testator's hand was guided or steadied by another because the testator was blind, illiterate, or palsied—as long as the testator desired and intended to sign the instrument. [98 A.L.R.2d 824]

c.   **Signature by another person:** [§399]   Consistent with the Wills Act of 1837, most statutes expressly provide that the testator's signature may be made by another person at testator's direction and in testator's presence. A few statutes require that, where this procedure is followed, the person signing testator's name (i) must also sign his or her own name, and (ii) cannot serve as one of the required attesting witnesses. [N.Y. Est. Powers & Trusts Law §3-2.1(a)(1)(C)]

d.   **Where signed**

(1)   **Majority rule:** [§400]   In most states, there is no requirement that the testator *subscribe* his signature (*i.e.,* sign at the foot or end of the will). The signature can appear anywhere on the will, provided it was intended by the testator to be her signature. [Potter v. Richardson, 230 S.W.2d 672 (Mo. 1950)]

(2)   **Minority rule:** [§401]   A substantial minority of states have retained the Wills Act requirement of a "subscription" for formal wills, *i.e.,* a signing at the end of the will. [N.Y. Est. Powers & Trusts Law §3-2.1(a)(1)] In such jurisdictions, two main questions arise: (i) where is "the end" of the will; and (ii) what is the effect of provisions appearing after the testator's signature?

(a)   **What constitutes "end" of will:** [§402]   In states that require the testator to sign at the end of the will, two tests have been applied to locate "the end":

1)   **Physical end:** [§403]   A few courts apply a purely *objective test* and require the testator's signature to be on the last line of the document in a physical sense (except for the attestation clause and signatures of the attesting witnesses).

2)   **Logical or literary end:** [§404]   However, most courts apply a *subjective test* and hold that even if a portion of the will (other than the attestation clause) follows the testator's signature, it will not invalidate the will as long as that portion can be read as a logical or literary part of the will itself. Under this test, the question is whether the testator subjectively thought that she was signing at the end of the will.

a) **Example—"folded sheet" case:** Under the "logical or literary end" test, a will is deemed to be subscribed at "the end" thereof where testator began the will on the first page of a folded sheet, continued the will on what ordinarily would be paginated as the third page, and then completed the will and signed it on the second page. [*In re* Stinson's Estate, 77 A. 807 (Pa. 1910)]

b) **Compare:** In states that apply the objective test, probate would be denied in the "folded sheet" case described above. [*In re* Andrews' Will, 162 N.Y. 1 (1900)]

(b) **Effect of provisions appearing after testator's signature:** [§405] In states that require the testator's signature to be at the end of the will, what is the result of provisions following testator's signature?

1) **Majority view:** [§406] Subject to the "surplusage" rule (below), if anything appears after the testator's signature (other than the attestation clause), the **entire will is void.** [Estate of Seaman, 146 Cal. 455 (1905)]

2) **Minority view:** [§407] Everything appearing **before** the signature is given effect; only the provisions that follow the signature are void.

a) **Exception:** [§408] If the matter following the signature is so material that deletion of it, and giving effect only to the matter preceding the signature, would subvert the general testamentary plan, the **entire will** is void. [N.Y. Est. Powers & Trusts Law §3-2.1(a)(1)(A)]

3) **Surplusage:** [§409] In applying the "signature at the end" rule, many courts hold that items of a purely informal or nondispositive nature following the testator's signature can be disregarded as surplusage (*e.g.,* provisions regarding burial or compensation of the executor). [*In re* McConihe's Estate, 123 Misc. 318 (1924)] However, a provision following testator's signature that **names** an executor is **not** surplusage; thus, the will was not signed at the end. [*In re* Winter's Will, 302 N.Y. 666 (1951)]

4) **Compare—provisions added after execution:** [§410] The previous discussion assumes that the provisions in question were part of the will at the time testator signed it. Provisions added **after** the will is executed are **disregarded** in all states (unless they can be given effect as a codicil), since they were not part of the duly executed will. In such a case, the will itself is valid since it has been signed at "the end."

a) **Note:** Some courts adopt a rebuttable presumption that any provisions appearing below the testator's signature were added after the will was executed. [*In re* Taylor's Estate, 79 A. 632 (Pa. 1911)]

e. **Signature (or acknowledgment of earlier signature) in witnesses' presence:** [§411]   Many states require that the testator either sign the will or acknowledge her earlier signature in the witnesses' presence. In some states, this requirement is met by the testator signing in one witness's presence and then later acknowledging that signature in the presence of the other witness. A few states require that the signature (or acknowledgment of the earlier signature) be in the presence of witnesses **present at the same time.**

(1) **Acknowledgment of earlier signature:** [§412] It is generally held that a profferring of the will with testator's signature clearly visible constitutes a sufficient acknowledgment of the signature; testator does not have to make verbal reference to her signature. [*In re* Levine's Will, 2 N.Y.2d 757 (1956)] If, however, testator proffers the will folded over so that the fold-over covers her signature and only the witnesses' signature lines are visible, there has been no acknowledgment of the signature, and the will has not been validly executed. [*In re* Weinstock's Will, 78 Misc. 2d 182 (1974)]

(2) **Uniform Probate Code—acknowledgment of will:** [§413]   The U.P.C. requires only that each witness must witness either testator's signing, testator's acknowledgment of her earlier signature, **or** testator's acknowledgment **of the will.** [U.P.C. §2-502] Thus, in a U.P.C. state, the will would be validly executed even in the "fold-over situation" (*i.e.*, where the witness could not see testator's signature) if the testator acknowledged the instrument as her will.

(a) **Problem:** In this latter situation, how can a court be sure that testator's signature was actually on the will when the witnesses signed? *Answer:* There is a **rebuttable presumption** that testator's signature was affixed prior to the attestation; the burden of persuasion is on the contestants to prove otherwise. [Bullock v. Morchouse, 57 App. D.C. 231 (1927)]

5. **Publication Requirement**

a. **Majority rule:** [§414]   In most states, there is **no** "publicaton" requirement; *i.e.*, there is no requirement that the witnesses know they are attesting witnesses to a **will**. All that is required is that the witnesses sign and satisfy the other requirements imposed by the particular state. [Estate of Beakes, 306 So. 2d 99 (Fla. 1974); Estate of Brantlinger, 210 A.2d 246 (Pa. 1965); 71 A.L.R.3d 877] Publication is not required by the Uniform Probate Code.

b. **Minority rule:** [§415]   Publication of a will is required by statute in several states. [Cal. Prob. Code §6110; N.Y. Est. Powers & Trusts Law §3-2.1(a)(3)] Where required, the testator must publish (*i.e.*, declare) to the attesting witnesses that the instrument which they are requested to attest is a will, so that they know that they are serving as witnesses to a **will** rather than some other legal document. [60 A.L.R.2d 165]

(1) **Example:** T asks two bank safe deposit vault guards to "witness my signature. I am going away on a trip. I have some instructions here that I want carried out if anything happens. With all the accidents you have nowadays, you never know what may happen." The guards saw T sign the document; then they added their signatures. However, the instrument contained no attestation clause, and the witnesses testified they did not know whether they were signing a will, a power of attorney, or some other document. Thus, the will was not validly executed. [*In re* Pulvermacher's Will, 305 N.Y. 378 (1953)]

(2) **Note:** The attesting witnesses need not know the contents of the will; all that is required is that they know they are serving as witnesses to a will.

(3) **Publication on behalf of testator:** [§416] Publication may be made by someone on the testator's behalf. For example, suppose testator is in the hospital, in bad shape. In the presence of the testator and the witnesses, a nurse says, "This is **her** last will and testament, and she wants you to witness her signature." This would constitute a valid publication since the nurse's statement was made in the testator's presence and with her acquiescence.

6. Order of Signing

a. **Majority rule:** [§417] Most courts have held that it makes no difference whether the testator or an attesting witness signs first, as long as the execution ceremony is part of **one contemporaneous transaction.** Nor is it material that the signatures of the attesting witnesses are positioned in the will ahead of the testator's signature. [Gordon v. Parker, 104 So. 77 (Miss. 1925); Clark v. Turner, 183 F.2d 141 (D.C. Cir. 1950)] And this is true even in states that require the testator to sign "at the end" of the will (*supra,* §401). The requirement to sign at the end usually refers to the dispositive provisions of the will, and hence it is immaterial that the witnesses' signatures appear ahead of the testator's.

b. **Minority rule:** [§418] A few states follow the English rule, which requires the testator to sign first even though the signings occur in a single transaction. [Marshall v. Mason, 57 N.E. 340 (Mass. 1900)] *Rationale:* The witnesses cannot attest to the testator's signature unless the testator signs first.

7. **When Signing in Someone's "Presence" Is Required:** [§419] A signing in someone's "presence" is a requirement under many statutes, although the requirement takes various forms. In many states, each witness must sign in the testator's presence (but not necessarily in each other's presence). In other states, the attesting witnesses must sign in the testator's presence **and** in the presence of each other. [Fla. Prob. Code §732.502(1)] In still other states, the witnesses do not have to sign in the testator's presence, but the testator must sign the will or acknowledge her previous signature in the presence of each witness. [N.Y. Est. Powers & Trusts Law §3-2(1)(a)] Under such statutes, there may be a question as to what is meant by "presence."

a. **Minority rule—line of sight test:** [§420]   Some courts have held that a witness has not signed in the testator's presence if the testator could not see the witness at the time the witness signed. Thus, when the witness signs the will, it must appear that he and the will were within the testator's scope of vision **at all times.** [Green v. Davis, 153 So. 240 (Ala. 1934)] Fortunately, the courts that take this approach carve out an exception for blind testators. [*In re* Allred's Will, 86 S.E. 1047 (N.C. 1915)]

b. **Majority rule—conscious presence test:** [§421]   A number of states adopt a more liberal test. A witness has signed in the "presence" of testator (or vice versa) if the testator was **conscious** of where the witness was and what he was doing, **and** the testator **could have seen** the witness by a slight physical exertion on her part. [Cunningham v. Cunningham, 83 N.W.2d 58 (Minn. 1900); Demaris' Estate, 110 P.2d 571 (Or. 1941)]

(1) **Example:** Testator signs her will while lying in a hospital bed. A screen separates the testator from the doorway where the witnesses are standing, which is twelve feet away. A nurse takes the will around the screen to the witnesses, where they sign. Since the testator was conscious of where the witnesses were and of what they were doing, the witnesses signed in the testator's presence. [Nichols v. Rowan, 422 S.W.2d 21 (Tex. 1967)]

F.   WITNESSES

1. **Competency of Witnesses—In General:** [§422]   Witnesses must possess certain minimal qualifications or their attestation may be legally insufficient, and the will may fail for lack of due execution.

a. **Competency:** [§423]   All jurisdictions require that a witness be competent. [U.P.C. §2-505] This generally means that at the time the will is executed the witness must be mature enough and of sufficient mental capacity to understand and appreciate the **nature of the act** she is witnessing and her attestation, so that, if need be, she could testify in court on these matters. [Wallace v. Harrison, 65 So. 2d 456 (Miss. 1953)]

b. **When determined:** [§424]   As in the case of the testator, competency of an attesting witness is determined at the **time the will is executed.** The fact that a competent witness subsequently becomes incompetent does not render her attestation invalid. [Bruce v. Shuler, 62 S.E. 973 (Va. 1908)] Conversely, if the witness was incompetent at the time the will was executed, the attestation is invalid regardless of subsequent events by which competency is restored. [Vrooman v. Powers, 24 N.E. 267 (Ohio 1890)]

c. **Age:** [§425]   In several states, statutes provide that a person must be a certain minimum age in order to serve as an attesting witness. [*See, e.g,* Tex. Prob. Code §59—age 14] However, most states do not impose a minimum age requirement.

2. **Interested Witnesses—In General**

a. **Common law:** [§426]   At common law, if an attesting witness was also a beneficiary under the will, the witness-beneficiary was **not a competent** witness. Thus, if the beneficiary was one of the two necessary attesting witnesses, the will was **denied probate** because it was not signed by two competent witnesses.

b. **Majority rule today:** [§427]   The harsh common law rule has been abolished in all but a handful of states. Most jurisdictions have "interested witness" statutes, which provide that if an attesting witness is also a will beneficiary, the **gift to the witness is void** (with certain exceptions, discussed below), but she is a competent witness and the will may be probated. [Cal. Prob. Code §6112; D.C. Code §18-104] These laws are called **"purging" statutes** because they eliminate the problem of interest by purging the bequest to the witness. Under these statutes, the will is never denied probate because of the interest of the witness; the only result is that the witness-beneficiary may lose the bequest.

c. **Uniform Probate Code:** [§428]   The Uniform Probate Code **abolishes** the interested witness rule: Neither the will nor any of its provisions is affected by the fact that an attesting witness is also a beneficiary under the will. [U.P.C. §2-505] Several non-U.P.C. states have enacted similar statutes. [Fla. Prob. Code §732.504]

   (1) **Rationale:**   A person who uses improper means to get himself a gift in the will probably is shrewd enough to have disinterested persons serve as witnesses to the will. Thus, purging statutes do not reach cases of improper overreaching; instead, they tend to void gifts to family members, innocently made, in wills whose execution is not supervised by an attorney.

3. **Exceptions to Purging Statutes' Operation:** [§429]   The purging statutes enacted in many states do not in all cases purge legacies to attesting witnesses. Several exceptions to the purging rule have been written into the statutes [*see, e.g., Iowa Code Ann §633.281*] or have been recognized by case decision.

   a. **Supernumerary exception:** [§430]   If (in a state that requires two attesting witnesses to a will) a beneficiary is one of three attesting witnesses, **and if** the will can be proved without the witness-beneficiary's testimony, the bequest is not purged. The beneficiary is a "supernumerary" witness; she was not needed to have a validly executed will.

   b. **Beneficiary would be heir—"whichever is least" exception:** [§431]   If the witness-beneficiary would be an heir if there were no will, to the extent of his intestate share he has no interest in having the will admitted to probate. Thus, a number of statutes expressly provide that, in this situation, the witness-beneficiary takes the **lesser** of (i) his intestate share of the estate if there were no will or (ii) the amount of the bequest. [Cal. Prob. Code §6112(c); Tex. Prob. Code §61]

      (1) **Example:** T, who is single, dies leaving a typewritten will that devises $10,000 to his sister Sue and his residuary estate to his mother. T leaves an estate worth $40,000. Sister Sue is one of the two attesting witnesses to the will. Under the state's intestacy statutes, if T had died intestate, his estate would have passed one-half to his mother and one-half to his sister. Since Sue would take more by intestacy than under the will, the interested witness statute does not apply, and Sue may take the $10,000 legacy.

(2) **Compare:** If, however, T's will gave a legacy of $10,000 to mother and the residuary estate to sister Sue, and Sue was one of the two attesting witnesses, Sue's intestate share would be less than the amount of her bequest. Under the "whichever is least" rule, Sue would take $20,000. T's mother would also take $20,000: $10,000 under the will, and $10,000 (the amount of the purged legacy) by inheritance.

(3) **And note:** In states whose statutes do not contain this exception, the above result has been reached by court decision.

4. **Purging Statutes—What Constitutes Beneficial Interest:** [§432] Under the purging statutes, it is generally held that, for a person to be "beneficially interested" in the will, the interest must be a direct, pecuniary one. That is, the witness must be a *beneficiary* under the will or under a trust created by the will.

   a. **Executor, trustee, attorney:** [§433] A person designated as executor, testamentary trustee, or attorney for the estate is *not* a beneficiary (unless he is also given a bequest in the will). While executors, trustees and attorneys receive money from the estate, this is compensation for services rendered, not a gift. [74 A.L.R.2d 297]

   b. **Family member of beneficiary:** [§434] If a spouse, parent, or other relative of a will beneficiary is an attesting witness, the purging statute does not apply, and the beneficiary is entitled to the gift. [Speer v. Johnson, 113 N.E. 622 (Ill. 1916)] *Rationale:* The interests of family members are only *indirect*—as prospective heirs or donees of the one who is the named beneficiary.

   c. **Creditors:** [§435] A will beneficiary does not lose his gift merely because one of his creditors is an attesting witness. [D.C. Code §18-106] Similarly, creditors of the *testator* are deemed competent witnesses; even though they may be paid from the testator's estate, they do not take under the will and hence have no "beneficial interest" in it.

   d. **Taker of other indirect benefits:** [§436] By majority rule, a witness is not disqualified by indirect benefits he may receive as an officer or member of a church, fraternal society, or other charitable corporation named as a beneficiary in the will. [Estate of Tkachuk, 73 Cal. App. 3d 14 (1977); Estate of Jordan, 519 S.W.2d 902 (Tex. 1975)]

   e. **Taker under lapse statute:** [§437] If a witness takes under the will only because of a lapse statute, the purging statute does not apply. For example, suppose a will makes a bequest to testator's daughter B, and B's son S is one of the two attesting witnesses. B dies in the testator's lifetime; on testator's death, S takes the bequest to B under the state's lapse statute (*see infra*, §§660-668). The purging statute does not apply because S is not a *beneficiary* under the will. Thus, S may take the bequest. [*In re* Ackerina's Estate, 195 Misc. 383 (1949)]

5. **Subsequent Testamentary Instrument:** [§438] The operation of a purging statute may be affected by a later will or codicil. This is illustrated by the following examples.

a. **Codicil that reduces gift:** [§439]   If the codicil reduces the attesting witness' gift under the will, the statute does not apply.

   (1) **Example:** W's will devises real property outright to H; the will is witnessed by two neighbors. Thereafter, W executes a codicil devising the same real property to H for life, with the remainder on H's death to pass to C. H is one of the two attesting witnesses to the codicil. The purging statute does not apply to the codicil because H did not receive a beneficial devise under the codicil since the codicil *reduced* the gift to H made by the will. [*In re* Moore's Will, 32 Misc. 2d 429 (1961)]

b. **Codicil that does not make gift to witness:** [§440]   If the codicil makes a gift to a witness who attested to the *will* (but not the codicil), the statute does not apply because the codicil making the gift is attested to by two disinterested witnesses.

   (1) **Example:** T executes a will that makes various gifts (but none to B); B is one of two attesting witnesses. Thereafter, T executes a codicil that gives $5,000 to B. B is not a witness to the codicil. The purging statute does not apply. B may take the $5,000 because she was not an attesting witness to the codicil that made the beneficial disposition.

c. **Compare—codicil that increases gift:** [§441]   If the codicil increases the attesting witness' gift under the will, the purging statute does apply.

   (1) **Example:** T executes a will that makes a legacy to Jones and bequeaths the residue of the estate to D. Later, T executes a codicil that *revokes* the legacy to Jones, with D acting as one of the two attesting witnesses to the codicil. D cannot take the accretion to T's residuary estate caused by the revocation of the gift to Jones because the purging statute applies: By revoking the gift to Jones, in effect the codicil made a new gift to D. [*In re* Hunt's Estate, 122 N.Y.S.2d 765 (1953)]

d. **Effect of republication by codicil:** [§442]   A disqualified witness may still receive the gift if a later testamentary document *republishes the will* in which the gift is provided.

   (1) **Example:** T's will leaves his entire estate to B, who is one of the two attesting witnesses. At this point, the gift to B would be void. However, T later duly executes a codicil that is witnessed by two disinterested persons; the codicil makes a minor change in the will (*e.g.,* names a new executor). Execution of the codicil has the effect of republishing the earlier will under the doctrine of "republication by codicil" (*see infra,* §§607-610), thus validating the otherwise void gift to B.

G.   ATTESTATION CLAUSE

1. **Recites Facts of Due Execution:** [§443]   An attestation clause is a provision that appears immediately below the testator's signature line and immediately above the

signature lines for the attesting witnesses, and recites in detail the performance of the statutory requisites for execution of a will (*e.g.*, testator's subscription or acknowledgment, publication, presence of witnesses, etc.). Although an attestation clause is not legally required, it is always included in a well-drafted will.

a. **Example:** An attestation clause might read as follows: "On the above date, _____, the testator, declared to us, the undersigned, that this instrument was his last will, and he asked us to sign as attesting witnesses to it. He then signed the will in our presence, we being present at the same time. Each of us then signed the will in the testator's presence and in the presence of each other."

2. **Prima Facie Evidence:** [§444]   An attestation clause is prima facie evidence of the facts recited therein [Gaff v. Knight, 206 P.2d 992 (Okla. 1948)], thus placing the burden of proving the lack of any required formality on those contesting the will. Such clauses are particularly useful in two situations:

a. **Witness with bad memory:** [§445]   Suppose that both attesting witnesses testify that they recognize their signatures, but that they have no recollection of signing and that they do not believe that they ever met the testator. If the will contains an attestation clause, the will can be admitted to probate on the strength of its recitals. Probate of a will does not depend on the memory of the attesting witnesses. [Jones v. Whiteley, 533 S.W.2d 881 (Tex. 1976)]

b. **Hostile witness:** [§446]   The probate court may admit a will to probate even though one attesting witness testifies that (i) she had not signed in the testator's presence, and (ii) the signature on the will was not the testator's signature, if the court finds that the evidence given by the attestation clause, and not the witness's testimony, is to be believed. [Estate of Koss, 228 N.E.2d 510 (Ill. 1967)]

3. **Compare—In Some States Signatures Alone Raise Presumption of Due Execution:** [§447]   Many states recognize a *rebuttable presumption* of due execution simply upon proof of the genuineness of the signatures of the attesting witnesses. [40 A.L.R.2d 1223; Estate of Pitcairn, 6 Cal. 2d 730 (1936)] In such states, it is not necessary to rely on an attestation clause for the presumption of due execution. Still, the inclusion of such a clause is good practice. Its presence lends added weight to the presumption of due execution, and it may serve to impeach a witness attempting to give testimony contrary to the facts recited in the clause.

H.   SELF-PROVING AFFIDAVIT

1. **In General:** [§448]   In recent years, a number of states have enacted self-proving affidavit statutes. Under such a statute, the testator and the witnesses sign the will in the usual manner, and then the testator and the witnesses sign a *sworn affidavit* (usually on a separate piece of paper) before a notary public. The sworn affidavit recites all the elements of due execution and serves as a *substitute for the live testimony* of the attesting witnesses in open court. The will is admitted to probate on the strength of the recitals in the affidavit. [Tex. Prob. Code §59]

a. **Uniform Probate Code:** [§449]   As noted above, in most states the testator and the witnesses sign the will (which contains an attestation clause), **and then** they sign the self-proving affidavit, which is notarized. The Uniform Probate Code recognizes this two-step procedure (which would be used, in a U.P.C. state, if the will is not self-proved at the time of its execution). However, the U.P.C. also permits the attestation clause itself to be in affidavit form. Under this procedure, the testator and the witnesses sign only once. Testator signs the will; then the attesting witnesses sign beneath the attestation clause, which is in affidavit form; then the notary public signs and affixes the notarial seal. [Fla. Prob. Code §732.503; U.P.C. §2-504]

2. **Purpose of Self-Proving Affidavit:** [§450]   Where a will is not self-proved, practical difficulties and minor irritants are often encountered in proving up a will—even though, in most cases, no one challenges the will's due execution. The attesting witnesses must be located and made to appear in probate court, where they sit around waiting for the docket call. If a witness resides outside the county or state, her testimony must be obtained by deposition or interrogatory. The self-proving affidavit procedure recognizes that most probates are harmonious, nonlitigious proceedings in which no one is questioning whether the will was duly executed. Even when wills are contested on grounds of lack of capacity or undue influence, valid execution of the will is seldom challenged. Thus, use of the affidavit as evidence of due execution eliminates the need to locate the witnesses and secure their testimony.

a. **Challenges to affidavit:** [§451]   Of course, it would be possible for a will opponent to establish that "the affidavit lies"—that the witnesses did not sign in the testator's presence, etc. [Estate of Mackaben, 617 P.2d 765 (Ariz. 1980)] However, the burden of proof is on the opponent to overcome the evidence provided by the affidavit.

3. **Improper Execution:** [§452]   Suppose, in a non-U.P.C. state, that the testator signs the will, but the witnesses do not; the signature lines below the attestation clause are left blank. However, the self-proving affidavit, on a separate piece of paper, is duly signed by the testator and the witnesses and is acknowledged by a notary public. Can the will be admitted to probate?

a. **Majority rule:** [§453]   When presented with the above facts, most courts have admitted the will to probate by counting the witnesses' signatures on the affidavit as the signatures needed for a duly executed will, since the affidavit recites that the execution formalities were complied with. [Estate of Charry, 359 So. 2d 544 (Fla. 1978)]

b. **Minority rule:** [§454]   A few courts have denied probate on the ground that the self-proving provisions attached to the will are not a part of the will but concern the matter of its proof only; *i.e.,* that the affidavit is not part of the instrument that must be executed with testamentary intent. "A testamentary document, to be self-proved, must first be a will." [Boren v. Boren, 402 S.W.2d 728 (Tex. 1966)]

I. HOLOGRAPHIC WILLS

1. **In General:** [§455]   About half the states recognize holographic wills, *i.e.,* wills entirely in the ***testator's handwriting*** and which have ***no attesting witnesses.*** [Tex. Prob. Code; U.P.C. §2-503] (North Carolina imposes the additional requirement that the holographic will be found among the testator's valuable papers. [N.C. Gen. Stat. §31-3.4(3)]) Where holographic wills are recognized, they may generally be made by any testator who has capacity, although a few states limit the making of holographic wills to soldiers, sailors, and mariners at sea. [N.Y. Est. Powers & Trusts Law §3-2.2]

2. **Testator's Handwriting:** [§456]   To be a valid holographic will, the instrument must be written entirely in the testator's handwriting (or block printing). To be admissible to probate, witnesses who know the testator's writing must testify in probate court (or by deposition) that the instrument was written by the testator's hand. [Tex. Prob. Code §84] Additionally, one state requires that the holographic will must have been found among the testator's valuable papers or effects. [*In re* Gilkey's Will, 124 S.E.2d 155 (N.C. 1962)]

    a. **Material provisions typed:** [§457]   The general rule is that the will must be ***entirely*** in the testator's handwriting. But suppose that a testator begins to type his will, then, for some reason, he takes the sheet out of the typewriter and completes the will in his handwriting. The instrument is signed by the testator but it is not witnessed. This instrument is generally ***not*** admissible to probate because it is not entirely in the testator's handwriting. [Hinson v. Hinson, 280 S.W.2d 731 (Tex. 1955)]

    b. **Surplusage rule:** [§458]   However, in the case above, if the typewritten or mechanically reproduced words are not necessary to complete the meaning of the will—*i.e.,* if the handwritten provisions make sense and form a complete will without them—the typewritten or printed words will be disregarded as "surplusage" and the instrument may be admitted. [Will of Parsons, 178 S.E. 78 (N.C. 1935)]

        (1) **Example:** A "will" handwritten on a partially preprinted stationer's will form is valid as a holographic will even though the testator filled in blanks in the form's exordium, executor, and testimonium clauses, since none of the printed matter was material to the substance of the will or essential to its validity. [Estate of Black, 30 Cal. 3d 880 (1982); Fairweather v. Nord, 388 S.W.2d 122 (Ky. 1965)]

    c. **Uniform Probate Code:** [§459]   Under the U.P.C., a holographic will is valid if its ***material provisions*** are in the testator's handwriting. [U.P.C. §2-503]

3. **Testator's Signature:** [§460]   All states require that a holographic will be signed by the testator.

    a. **What constitutes signature:** [§461]   As with attested wills, the courts take a liberal position on what constitutes a valid signature (*see supra,* §397). A testator's initials, first name, and nickname have been held to be a valid signature. However, an engraved monogram is not sufficient, since it is not in the testator's handwriting. [Pounds v. Litaker, 71 S.E.2d 39 (N.C. 1952)]

b. **Where signed:** [§462]   By majority rule, there is no requirement that a holographic will be signed at the end of the will. Testator's signature may appear **anywhere**: in the margin or in the opening caption ("I, Joan Smith, do hereby declare . . ."). [Lawson v. Dawson's Estate, 53 S.W. 64 (Tex. 1899)] If, however, the signature does not appear at the end of the holographic will, the court must be satisfied that the testator intended the signature as his signature, and that the instrument was the **complete** will intended by the testator.

4. **Date of Execution**

a. **Majority rule:** [§463]   In all but a handful of states, there is no requirement that a holographic will be dated in order to be valid. [U.P.C. §2-503]

b. **Minority rule:** [§464]   In a few states, a holographic will must be dated in the testator's handwriting in order to be valid. [La. Civ. Code art. 1588; 84 Okla. Stat. Ann. §54] In these states, to be a valid dating, the day, month, and year must be shown. [Succession of Sarrazin, 65 So. 2d 602 (La. 1953)] *And note:* The date does not have to be correct as long as it is complete! [*In re* Moody's Estate, 118 Cal. App. 2d 300 (1953)] If testator has dated the will 2/8/72 (which could refer either to February 8 or 2 August), the courts have held that this is a valid dating if extrinsic evidence establishes which date was intended. [Succession of Boyd, 306 So. 2d 687 (La. 1975)]

5. **Testamentary Intent:** [§465]   A frequent problem with alleged holographic wills is whether the particular document was written with testamentary intent, *i.e.,* whether the maker intended the writing to be a will. This issue is often raised when a letter or an informal memorandum, entirely handwritten and signed, is offered for probate. Perhaps the writer was only making statements about a will or gifts that she intended to make in the future. Suppose, for example, that the testator writes a three-page letter to B in which she says, among many other things, "After my death, Blackacre will be yours." Is this a valid holograph?

a. **Test:** [§466]   The crux of the problem is whether the testator intended the writing to serve **in and of itself** as her will. If it appears that some future writing was contemplated, then the letter clearly will not suffice. (*See supra,* §357.) Vagueness, an informal or abbreviated signature, discussion of other matters, etc., may all support the conclusion that testamentary intent was lacking, although no one of these factors is conclusive.

(1) **Example:** A memorandum, entirely in J. B. Curtis' handwriting, is found among papers on Curtis' desk after his death. The memo reads:

> Jewel and mother get 1/2 of stock sales.
> Jewel and mother get Greenville property.
> Little brick house.
> 1/2 of oil property.
> 1/2 of bank account.
> /s/ J. B. Curtis

This instrument might have been intended by Curtis to be his will. However, "it is more reasonable to conclude that it was intended as a memorandum from which a will might later be drawn; or of the manner in which he planned to dispose of his property during his lifetime." [Curtis v. Curtis, 373 S.W.2d 367 (Tex. 1963)] Thus, the instrument does not show on its face that it was written with testatmentary intent.

b. **Extrinsic evidence:** [§467]   Extrinsic evidence is admissible to establish that an otherwise ambivalent document was written with testamentary intent.

(1) **Example:** A handwritten note, written while William Kuhlmann was in the hospital, was handed to a nurse with this declaration, "Take care of this; it's my will." The note read:

Dec. 17, To Mrs. Eugenia Poss auto and $5,000 dollars.

/s/ Wm. Kuhlmann

The circumstances of the note's writing, plus the statement to a witness, show it was intended that this brief note was intended to serve as a will. [Poss v. Kuhlmann, 222 S.W. 638 (Tex. 1920)] Thus, in the *Curtis* case, *supra*, if there was any evidence, even parol evidence, that J. B. Curtis intended the memo to be his will, such evidence would be admissible and would support a finding of testamentary intent.

6. **Interlineations:** [§468]   Suppose that a testator writes and signs a valid holographic will that leaves Blackacre to B and the residue of her estate to C. Later, the testator scratches out C's name and writes in the name of another person. What is the effect of the interlineation?

a. **Majority rule:** [§469]   Nearly all states that recognize holographic wills give effect to such interlineations, as long as the evidentiary test for probating holographic wills is met: *i.e.*, the will, including the interlineations, is entirely in the testator's handwriting. Put another way, a testator can write a holographic will in spurts.

b. **Compare:** [§470]   Contrast this with interlineations on a typewritten and witnessed will, which are generally *not* given effect.

J. ORAL WILLS

1. **In General—Limited Use:** [§471]   Borrowing from the Statute of Frauds (1677) and the English Wills Act of 1837, statutes in many jurisdictions permit oral ("nuncupative") wills in very limited circumstances. The statutes vary greatly in detail as to the circumstances under which an oral will is permitted, and also as to the formalities required. In some states, persons who can make oral wills are limited to *soldiers, sailors, and mariners at sea*; with the further limitation, in some states, that the will must be made during a time of declared or undeclared war or other armed conflict. [N.Y. Est. Powers & Trusts Law §3-2.2] In other states, oral wills can be made by any person, but only during

the person's **last sickness** or in **contemplation of immediate death**. [Tex. Prob. Code §65; Ga. Code §§113-501 *et seq.*] In yet another group of jurisdictions, oral wills can be made by soldiers and sailors, but **only** during their last illness. [D.C. Code §18-107]

2. **Uniform Probate Code:** [§472]   The Uniform Probate Code makes **no provision** for oral wills.

3. **Personal Property Only:** [§473]   In nearly all states that allow oral wills, oral wills can dispose of personal property only. However, the Georgia statute allows real (as well as personal) property to pass by oral will [Ga. Code Ann. §113-504], and in a few states the statute does not limit oral wills to personal property dispositions [N.Y. Est. Powers & Trusts Law §3-2.2].

4. **Dollar Limit:** [§474]   In most states that allow oral wills, there is no limit on the amount of personal property that can pass under an oral will. However, a few states impose a dollar limit (*e.g.,* $1,000), and in other states additional formalities must be satisfied if the value of the property passing thereunder exceeds a specified amount [Tex. Prob. Code §65—three witnesses required if amount exceeds $30].

5. **Formalities Required:** [§475]   It is usually provided that there must be *two* (and in some states three) *witnesses* to the uttering of the oral will, although some states require only one witness for a soldier's will. [Gould v. Stafford, 39 Vt. 498 (1866)] Some states impose additional requirements, *e.g.,* that the oral will be reduced to writing by the witnesses within a specified period [D.C. Code §18-107—ten days], and that it be offered for probate within a specified time.

6. **Automatic Revocation:** [§476]   Under some statutes, an oral will automatically expires after a stipulated time. Under one statute, for example, a mariner's will becomes invalid three years after its making, and a soldier's or sailor's will expires one year after discharge from military service. [N.Y. Est. Powers & Trusts Law §3-2.2]

7. **Oral Codicil:** [§477]   Judicial hostility toward oral wills is reflected in cases holding that an oral will cannot be made by a testator who has previously enacted a written, attested will. [*In re* Carlton's Estate, 221 So. 2d 184 (Fla. 1969)] *Rationale:* To give the oral will effect would result in a partial revocation of the attested will, and oral revocations are invalid. [*In re* Grattan's Estate, 138 P.2d 497 (Kan. 1943)] *But note:* A number of states permit oral wills (in effect, oral codicils) even though the effect is to alter the dispositions made by an earlier attested will. [Connor v. Purcell, 360 S.W.2d 438 (Tex. 1962)]

K. CONDITIONAL WILLS

1. **In General:** [§478]   A conditional will is one which expressly provides that it shall be operative only if some condition stated in the will is satisfied (*e.g.,* "This will shall be effective only in the event my wife survives me"). In such a case, testamentary intent exists only if the condition occurs, and if it does not (*e.g.,* if the wife predeceases the testator), the will **fails** for lack of testamentary intent. [Cal. Prob. Code §328.7]

2. **Condition Must Appear on Face of Will:** [§479]   A will that is absolute on its face cannot be shown to have been executed conditionally. Parol evidence is **not admissible** to prove a condition that does not appear on the face of the will. [*In re* Webb's Will, 122 Misc. 129 (1923)]

    a. **Criticism:** This rule is logically inconsistent with the majority view allowing parol evidence to rebut the presumption of testamentary intent arising from proof that a will was duly executed (*see supra,* §350). If a will is executed upon a parol condition and the condition does not occur, then the testator had no testamentary intent—just as in the sham will cases. The rule governing admissibility of parol evidence should be (but is not) the same.

    b. **Response:** The basis for this seeming inconsistency is the reluctance of courts to allow oral proof, the effect of which is to overturn a written, attested will that is unconditional on its face.

3. **Condition vs. Motive:** [§480]   The most commonly litigated question concerning conditional wills is whether the language in the will imposed a condition or, instead, merely expressed the *motive* or inducement for making the will. The litigation occurs when the testator dies some years later, having survived the apprehended peril referred to in the will.

    a. **Example:** The will provides: "I am going on a journey, and I may not ever return. And if I do not, here is how I want my property disposed of. . . ." On these and similar facts, many courts have held that testator's language merely expressed what was on her mind as the occasion and inducement for making a will. "She was thinking of the possibility of death or she would not have made a will. But the possibility at that moment took the specific shape of not returning from her journey, and so she wrote 'if I do not return' before giving her last commands." Thus the will is admissible to probate even though the testator died some years after returning from the journey. [Eaton v. Brown, 193 U.S. 411 (1904); *In re* Taylor's Estate, 119 Cal. App. 2d 574 (1953)]

    b. **Compare:** However, on very similar facts, a number of courts have found the will to be conditional, and have denied probate if the condition did not occur. [*In re* Pascal's Estate, 2 Misc. 2d 337 (1956)]

    c. **Factors supporting finding of absolute will:** [§481]   The tendency of the more recent decisions is to find that the will was not intended to be conditional unless a contrary intent clearly appears. [1 A.L.R.3d 1048] Various factors have been cited in support of a finding that the will was intended to be absolute and not conditional.

        (1) **Intestacy avoided:** [§482]   The fact that a will was executed by the testator is an indication that she did not intend to die intestate (which would be the result if the will were found to be conditional). [Ferguson v. Ferguson, 45 S.W.2d 1096 (Tex. 1931)]

        (2) **Preservation of will:** [§483]   The fact that the testator preserved the document after returning from the journey or surviving the operation is an indica-

tion that the will's operation was not intended to be limited. [Estate of Desmond, 223 Cal. App. 2d 211 (1963)]

d. **Extrinsic evidence:** [§484]   By majority rule, extrinsic evidence is admissible to show whether the testator intended by conditional language to make an absolute or conditional will. [*In re* Taylor's Estate, *supra*; Barber v. Barber, 13 N.E.2d 257 (Ill. 1938)]

4. **Conditional Codicils:** [§485]   A codicil also may be executed subject to a condition. If the condition does not occur, the codicil is not given effect.

a. **As republication of will:** [§486]   However, even where the condition has failed, a conditional codicil may be admissible to probate for the sole purpose of ***republishing*** the will. (On republication by codicil, *see infra,* §§608-610.)

(1) **Example:** T executes a will that leaves all his property to B, but unbeknownst to anyone, the will is invalid because not properly executed. Later, T duly executes a codicil providing that in the event C returns home from China before T's death, B and C are to share the estate equally. C does not return home from China. The terms of the codicil are not effective (because C never returned home), but the codicil is admissible to probate for the purpose of republishing and thus validating the earlier will.

VI. REVOCATION OF WILLS

chapter approach

The issue of whether a will has been partially or totally revoked comes up frequently on Wills exams. You need to keep in mind two important principles:

1. A testator may **always revoke** his will. Even when he has signed a contract not to revoke, the testator is free to do so, although his estate may face a breach of contract action by the beneficiaries of the contract.

2. A will may be revoked by one of **three methods**:

    (i)   **By operation of law**—if the testator gets married or divorced after executing a will, consider whether the change in his status affects the will. Such changes may revoke **all or part** of the will, or may have no effect whatsoever, depending on the particular state's law.

    (ii) **By a later will or codicil**—first of all, be sure that the later instrument is a valid will or codicil (*i.e.,* has met the specific statutory requirements of the state, *see* chapter V). Then look for language that **expressly revokes** the will (in whole or part) or for inconsistent provisions, which **impliedly revoke**.

    (iii) **By a physical act of destruction**—generally burning, tearing, or obliterating a material part of the will or cancelling by writing across the face of the will. Questions about this method of revocation can be tricky. Requirements for the proper act are set by statute. Follow the law of the particular state to the letter, because what may be a valid revocation in one state may not suffice in another. Recall too that another person can do the burning, tearing, etc. for testator, if in the testator's presence and at his direction.

    Note: For all of these methods, the testator must **intend to revoke** the will; however, for the first method (**by operation of law**), the court will **presume** testator's intent to revoke.

This chapter also covers **lost wills, revival of revoked wills,** and the **doctrine of dependent relative revocation** ("DRR"). While proof of lost wills is probably more important for the practicing attorney than the student exam-taker, you should be aware that under certain circumstances, a lost will may be probated by witnesses' testimony and/or a copy of the lost will.

More likely exam question topics are revival or DRR. For revival, remember that, in most states, merely revoking a later will does **not** automatically revive an earlier will; there must be reexecution of the will or republication by codicil, both requiring **full testamentary formalities** (signature, witnesses, etc., *see* chapter V). Think of DRR when you see a situation where testator has revoked a will based on a **mistake of law** that another will is valid; if the requirements for DRR are met, the court will **ignore the revocation** and enforce the will as if it had not been revoked.

Watch for questions in which the testator makes changes on the will after it has been executed. Remember that unless the will is a holograph, such interlineations are **ineffective.** If the testator crossed out an existing gift in making the changes, the strikeout may or may not be an effective partial revocation, depending on the state's laws. If the state recognizes partial revocations, think about whether the revocation can be disregarded under DRR.

A. INTRODUCTION

1. **All Wills Are Revocable by Testator:** [§487]   A testator always has the power to revoke his or her will at any time. Even a testator who has validly contracted **not** to revoke the will may do so, although such action may give rise to a constructive trust or some other remedy in favor of the beneficiaries of the contract. (*See infra* §624.)

2. **Methods of Revocation:** [§488]   Revocation of a will may occur in one of three ways.

    a. **By operation of law:** [§489]   Revocation of a will (or a portion thereof) may occur as the result of a change in the family circumstances of the testator: marriage, birth of issue, or divorce. (*See* below.)

    b. **By subsequent testamentary instrument:** [§490]   A later will or codicil may expressly or impliedly revoke an earlier will (*see infra*, §§516 *et seq.*).

    c. **By physical act:** [§491]   A will may be entirely revoked by an act of destruction performed on the will by the testator (or by another person acting at the testator's direction and in the testator's presence) (*see infra*, §§527 *et seq.*). In a number of jurisdictions, a will may be partially revoked by physical act (*see infra*, §§535-537).

B. REVOCATION BY OPERATION OF LAW [§492]

Changes in the testator's family circumstances since the making of the will may operate to revoke the will, or particular gifts in the will, by operation of law. Despite the testator's lack of affirmative action, the law **presumes an intent to revoke** in certain situations.

1. **Marriage**

    a. **Common law:** [§493]   At common law, marriage following the execution of a man's will had no effect on the will, but **marriage followed by birth of issue** was held to revoke the will. A woman's will was immediately and completely revoked upon her marriage, irrespective of birth of issue. However, the Wills Act of 1837 established a uniform rule: Marriage revoked the prior will of a man or a woman (with certain narrow exceptions).

    b. **Modern law:** [§494]   Most states no longer follow the above common law rules. The states are divided on the effect of marriage on a previously executed will. [97 A.L.R.2d 1026]

        (1) **States without statutes—marriage has no effect on will:** [§495]   About half of the states have no statute dealing with the effect of marriage on a previously executed will. In these states marriage, by itself, does not affect the will. *Rationale:* The new spouse is given adequate protection by dower or an

elective share statute (or, in a community property state, by the community property system).

    (a) **Minority view—marriage followed by birth of issue revokes will:** [§496]   In several states that do not have statutes dealing with the effect of marriage on a will, the courts apply the common law rule: While *marriage alone has no effect* on the will, marriage followed by birth of issue revokes a will executed before the marriage. [Pascucci v. Alsop, 147 F.2d 880 (D.C. Cir. 1945)] In most states, however, this fact setting is covered by the jurisdiction's pretermitted child statute. (*See supra,* §§285-302.)

  (2) **Statutory solutions:** [§497]   About half the states have statutes under which the testator's subsequent marriage has an effect on the will.

    (a) **Majority rule:** [§498]   In most of the states having statutes dealing with marriage's effect on a will, the will is only *partially revoked.* The marriage revokes the will only to the extent of providing the new spouse with an intestate share. After distribution of the spouse's intestate share, the will operates to distribute the remaining assets. [U.P.C. §2-301(a); Cal. Prob. Code §6560] These are sometimes referred to as "pretermitted spouse" statutes. [Fla. Stat. Ann. §732.507(1)]

    (b) **Minority rule:** [§499]   In several states, marriage after the execution of a will revokes the will *in its entirety.* [Conn. Gen. Stat. §45-162; Ga. Code Ann. §113-408; Or. Rev. Stat. §112.305]

    (c) **Exception:** [§500]   Note that the above statutes often provide that the will is *not* partially or totally revoked if: (i) the will makes provision for the new spouse; (ii) the will provides that the spouse's omission was intentional; *or* (iii) it appears that the will was made in contemplation of marriage. [U.P.C. §2-301(a); Mass. Laws Ann. ch. 191, §9]

c. **Attorney liability for negligence:** [§501]   An attorney who fails to take into account a statute dealing with subsequent marriage may be held liable for negligent will drafting. If the attorney knows of the impending marriage at the time the will is executed but fails to provide that the new spouse is to take nothing, the attorney may be held liable to the intended will beneficiaries for the amount passing to the spouse under the statute. [Heyer v. Flaig, 70 Cal. 2d 223 (1969); McAbee v. Edwards, 340 So. 2d 1167 (Fla. 1977)]

2. **Divorce**

a. **Common law:** [§502]   Early common law had no rule dealing with the effect of divorce on a previously executed will. This is not surprising since divorces rarely occurred in that era.

b. **Modern law—states without statutes**

  (1) **Majority rule:** [§503]   In view of the increased frequency of divorce, several courts have adopted a rule that divorce accompanied by a property settle-

ment revokes all dispositive provisions and fiduciary appointments in favor of the ex-spouse. [71 A.L.R.3d 1297] The will may be revived if the couple remarries. [*In re* Estate of Blanchard, 218 N.W.2d 37 (Mich. 1974)]

(a) **Rationale:** Common knowledge and experience indicate that it would be rare for a testator to want his or her former spouse to be benefitted under the will. Hence, the law requires a testator desiring such a result to formally republish the will or execute a new will. [Casewell v. Kent, 186 A.2d 581 (Me. 1962)]

(b) **Note—must be property settlement:** [§504]   If the divorce is not accompanied by a property settlement, the provisions in favor of the former spouse are not revoked. [Luff v. Luff, 359 F.2d 235 (D.C. Cir. 1966)]

(c) **Presumption of revocation is conclusive:** [§505]   In most of these states, the presumption of revocation is conclusive and cannot be overcome by evidence of a contrary intent. [Luff v. Luff, *supra*] However, a few states admit evidence tending to rebut the presumption of revocation. [Estate of Mercure, 216 N.W.2d 914 (Mich. 1974)]

(d) **Effect—property passes as though ex-spouse predeceased:** [§506] In states applying this rule, the will is read as though the former spouse predeceased the testator. [74 A.L.R.3d 1108]

　1) **Example:** W executes a will leaving her estate "to my husband H if he survives me; if H does not survive me, to my brother B." Subsequently, W and H are divorced; the divorce is accompanied by a property settlement. The will is read as though H predeceased W; thus, brother B takes the entire estate.

　2) **Rationale:** Even though the literal condition to B's taking ("if H does not survive me") was not satisfied, the testator would probably want B to take if the gift to H was invalid for any reason. [Jones v. Brown, 248 S.E.2d 812 (Va. 1978)]

(2) **Minority rule:** [§507]   A minority of jurisdictions have held that, absent a statute on the question, divorce has *no effect* on the will [Estate of Patterson, 224 P. 374 (Cal. 1923)], or at least that a divorce does not per se operate to revoke the gift to the former spouse [McKnight v. McKnight, 267 So. 2d 315 (Miss. 1972); 71 A.L.R.3d 1297].

(a) **Rationale:** In view of the ease with which a testator may revoke or alter a will, "it would be a serious matter to invalidate a will because of a supposed change in intention on the part of the testator not given formal expression by him." [Hertrais v. Moore, 88 N.E.2d 909 (Mass. 1949)]

(b) **Gift valid despite beneficiary's designation as spouse:** [§508]   In minority rule states, a gift "to my wife Martha" is effective even though, because of divorce, Martha is no longer the testator's wife. The gift is to Martha; "my wife" is merely descriptive. [18 A.L.R.2d 697]

c. **Modern law—states with statutes:** [§509] There has been a pronounced trend toward statutory recognition of divorce as partially revoking a will. In 1940, only three states had such statutes. Today, a majority of states have enacted such statutes.

(1) **Provisions in former spouse's favor are revoked:** [§510] Under these statutes, a divorce automatically revokes provisions of a will in favor of the former spouse (including dispositions of property, powers of appointment, and appointments as a fiduciary). The will is read as though the former spouse predeceased the testator. [U.P.C. §2-508; Fla. Prob. Code §732.507(2); Ill. Prob. Act §4-7(b)]

(2) **Remarriage:** [§511] Several of the statutes expressly provide that if the couple remarries the revoked provisions are revived. [Tex. Prob. Code §69]

(3) **No effect on life insurance:** [§512] These statutes apply only to wills, not to life insurance policies. If a policy names the insured's spouse as beneficiary and this beneficiary designation is not changed after the divorce, on the insured's death the proceeds are payable to the ex-spouse pursuant to the terms of the contract between the insured and the insurance carrier.

3. **Other Changed Circumstances Have No Effect:** [§513] No change in the testator's circumstances besides marriage, birth of issue, or divorce operates to revoke a will or any portion thereof. [U.P.C. §2-508]

a. **Insanity:** [§514] The testator's *subsequent* insanity does not revoke a will. [World's Gospel Union v. Barnes' Estate, 127 N.W. 37 (Mich. 1910)]

b. **Marked change in testator's circumstances:** [§515] A testamentary gift is not revoked by proof of the testator's changed feelings toward the beneficiary; nor by a huge and unexpected increase in the value of property devised to a beneficiary. [Ater v. McClure, 161 N.E. 129 (Ill. 1923)]

C. REVOCATION BY SUBSEQUENT TESTAMENTARY INSTRUMENT [§516]

All American jurisdictions have statutes providing that a will may be revoked in whole or in part by a later will or codicil. Such revocation may be express or implied. In either case, however, the later instrument must be testamentary; *i.e.,* it must be executed with the necessary formalities by a testator having testamentary capacity. [Maddox v. Mock, 220 N.E.2d 773 (Ind. 1966)]

1. **Express Revocation:** [§517] A later testamentary instrument may explicitly state that it revokes an earlier will in whole or in part.

a. **Need not be dispositive:** [§518] The revoking instrument does *not* have to contain dispositive provisions. Most jurisdictions recognize a duly executed testamentary instrument that does nothing more than revoke an earlier will. [Grotts v. Casburn, 129 N.E. 137 (Ill. 1920); 22 A.L.R.3d 1346]

b. **Revoking language must be explicit:** [§519]   The words used by the testator must indicate an **_intent_** to revoke the earlier will. An express revocation clause ("I hereby revoke all prior wills made by me") is clearly sufficient. However, a later instrument that merely states that "this is my last will" does not revoke an earlier will in its entirety, but only to the extent of **_inconsistent provisions._** [59 A.L.R.2d 11, 70]

c. **Present intent to revoke:** [§520]   Testator's words must show a present intent to revoke. An instruction to another ("Please destroy my will") is insufficient, even if executed with testamentary formalities. The words in the testamentary instrument must themselves accomplish the revocation. [*In re* McGill, 229 N.Y. 405 (1920)]

d. **Holographic instrument:** [§521]   In states that recognize holographic wills, a valid holographic will may revoke a typewritten, attested will. (*See supra,* §455.)

e. **Oral will:** [§522]   Jurisdictions that recognize nuncupative (oral) wills are divided on whether such a will may alter an earlier written will. Some courts give effect to such an oral "codicil" [Connor v. Purcell, 360 S.W.2d 438 (Tex. 1962)]; other courts refuse to do so, on the ground that to hold otherwise would be to permit a partial revocation by oral statement rather than by a writing executed with due formalities [*In re* Carlton's Estate, *supra*, §477].

2. **Implied Revocation by Inconsistency:** [§523]   If a later testamentary instrument does not expressly revoke an earlier will, to the extent possible the second instrument is treated as a codicil. The second instrument revokes the first will **only to the extent** that its provisions are inconsistent with the first will. [Cal. Prob. Code §6120; *In re* Wolfe's Will, 117 S.E. 804 (N.C. 1923)]

a. **Partial inconsistency:** [§524]   A residuary devise in the first will is not revoked by specific devises in a later will, although the specific devises, being a later and partially inconsistent expression of the testator's intent, are given effect. Likewise, a residuary devise in the second will does not revoke specific devises in an earlier will.

(1) **Example:** T's first will leaves all her property to Ron. T's second will makes no mention of the first will; it leaves T's house to Harry and T's car to Carol. When T dies, both wills are read together; that is, the second will is treated as a codicil to the first will. The specific devises are given effect, and Harry takes the house and Carol takes the car, but Ron takes the residuary estate.

(2) **Example:** T's first will leaves her house to Harry and the remainder of her estate to Ron. T's second will does not expressly revoke the first, but it leaves T's antique desk to Pat and the remainder of T's estate to Fred. The change in the residuary devise does not revoke Harry's gift. Harry takes the house, but also, Pat takes the desk, and **Fred** takes the remainder of T's estate. Absent

evidence of contrary intent, the residuary clause in the second will is not deemed inconsistent with the first will's specific devise to Harry, but it does operate to revoke the residuary gift to Ron.

b. **Second instrument totally inconsistent:** [§525] If the later testamentary instrument is entirely inconsistent with the earlier will, the first will is revoked in its entirety. To be entirely inconsistent, none of the dispositive provisions may be the same, and the provisions of the second will must purport to make a complete disposition of the testator's estate. [Gould v. Chamberlain, 68 N.E. 39 (Mass. 1903); 59 A.L.R.2d 11, 21]

c. **Neither will dated:** [§526] If the testator leaves two wills containing inconsistent provisions, each of which declares that it is "my last will and testament," and it cannot be determined when the wills were executed, both instruments are denied probate. [*In re* Westfeldt's Will, 125 S.E. 531 (N.C. 1925)]

D. REVOCATION BY PHYSICAL ACT [§527]

Nearly all statutes provide that a will may be revoked by some physical act, either by the testator or by some third person acting at the testator's direction and in his presence. The physical act must be accompanied by a ***present intent to revoke.*** [Cal. Prob. Code §6120; 24 A.L.R.2d 514]

1. **Requirements**

a. **Physical act:** [§528] The will must be physically acted upon. The statutes prescribe the acts sufficient to revoke a will. [U.P.C. §2-507—"burned, torn, cancelled, obliterated, or destroyed"] However, the act must be shown to have had an ***actual effect*** on the will or its language.

(1) **Burning:** [§529] If a ***material portion*** of the will's language is burned by the testator, the will is revoked. However, merely burning the will's outside cover or singeing its corners is insufficient. [White v. Casten, 46 N.C. 197 (1853)]

(2) **Tearing:** [§530] A tearing or cutting of the will is generally sufficient to revoke it ***if a material part*** (*e.g.*, a dispositive provision or testator's signature) is torn. [Crampton v. Osburn, 201 S.W. 336 (Mo. 1947)]

(3) **Obliteration:** [§531] A revocation by obliteration, as by inking out or erasing, generally requires damage to a ***material part*** of the will. [Cook v. Jeffett, 272 S.W. 873 (Ark. 1925)]

(4) **Cancellation:** [§532] Lining out or writing "void" across the face of the will operates to revoke it ***if*** the line-out at least ***touches the words*** of the will.

(a) **Compare:** T has words of cancellation inscribed on the ***back*** of the will by her attorney. This is not an effective revocation by cancellation since the attorney's writing, although done in T's presence and at her direction, did not cancel or deface the will. [Thompson v. Royall, 175 S.E. 748 (Va. 1934)]

(b) **Example:** T writes in the margin of the will, "I hereby revoke this will." This is not an effective revocation by cancellation because it does not touch the words of the will. [*In re* Berman's Will, 185 Misc. 1037 (1945)] (Note that if signed by the testator, in states that recognize holographic wills, the writing might constitute a holographic will which would expressly revoke the first will.)

b. **Intent:** [§533]   The act must be accompanied by a ***present intent*** to revoke the instrument. If a will is accidentally destroyed, a subsequent expression that testator intended to revoke the will anyhow is ineffective. [Estate of Olmstead, 122 Cal. 244 (1898)]

2. **Physical Act of Another:** [§534]   Many statutes permit revocation of a will by a physical act performed by a third person ***in the testator's presence and at the testator's direction.*** [U.P.C. §2-507] Some states additionally require that the third person's act be ***witnessed*** by two persons besides the testator. [Cal. Prob. Code §6120(b); N.Y. Est. Powers & Trusts Law §3-4.1(a)(2)]

a. **Example:** T's husband accidentally tears T's will while pulling out a desk drawer. When T is later told of the accident, she says it is unimportant because she was planning to revoke the will anyway. There has been no revocation because the physical act was not done in T's presence nor at her direction.

b. **Example:** John writes a letter to his friend Sam, who has possession of John's will, directing Sam to destroy the will. If Sam destroys the will, there is no effective revocation because the physical act was not done in the testator's presence. Moreover, the letter, although entirely in John's handwriting, was not written with a present intent to revoke and hence is not a holographic express revocation by subsequent instrument. [*In re* McGill, *supra,* §520]

c. **Compare:** Even in the handful of states requiring that there be witnesses to a revocation by physical act of a third person, there is no such witness requirement when the act is performed by the testator herself.

3. **Partial Revocation**

a. **Majority rule:** [§535]   Most statutes authorize partial as well as total revocation of a will by physical act. [U.P.C. §2-507; Bigelow v. Gillott, 123 Mass. 102 (1877)]

(1) **Intent:** [§536]   However, with partial revocation, determining testator's intent may be a problem. Did the testator intend only a partial revocation, or did he intend to revoke the entire will, but happened to touch only the part destroyed? Extrinsic evidence is generally admissible to show what testator intended.

(2) **Limitation:** [§537]   Even where partial revocation by physical act is permitted, courts are reluctant to give effect to nontestamentary actions that operate to *increase* the size of a gift to the beneficiary of a *general or specific bequest*.

   (a) **Example:** T's will provides: "I devise Blackacre to Mary for life, remainder to Marsha." If T subsequently strikes the words "for life, remainder to Marsha," the action will be given no effect. *Rationale:* Giving effect to such an act operates to make a new gift of property, by increasing the gift to Mary from a life estate to a fee simple, without complying with testamentary formalities. [Nelen v. Nelen, 161 A. 121 (R.I. 1932)]

   (b) **Compare:**   The testator can always increase the *residuary* gift by cancelling or destroying some general or specific bequest. [Barfield v. Carr, 86 S.E. 498 (N.C. 1915)] Thus in the example above, if T struck the entire devise of Blackacre (*i.e.*, neither Mary nor Marsha takes the property), the residuary gift would increase since Blackacre would become part of the residue. This increase would be enforced.

b. **Minority rule:** [§538]   In the absence of a statute expressly allowing partial revocation, several states refuse to recognize partial revocation by physical act. In these jurisdictions, where the testator attempts to revoke a portion of the will, the act is given *no effect*. Thus in these states, if T crosses out a bequest to John, John takes the bequest despite the attempted cancellation. [N.Y. Est. Powers & Trusts Law §3-4.1; Leatherwood v. Stephens, 24 S.W.2d 819 (Tex. 1930); 34 A.L.R.2d 619] If the destroyed portion cannot be recreated by extrinsic evidence, only the destroyed portion fails; the remainder of the will is given effect. [*In re* Lyons' Will; 75 N.Y.S.2d 237 (1947)]

4. **Effect on Another Testamentary Instrument**

a. **Destruction of codicil:** [§539]   A physical act destroying a codicil is generally held to *revoke only the codicil* and not the prior will. The will is read as though the codicil had never been executed. [Osburn v. Rochester Trust & Safe Deposit Co., 209 N.Y. 54 (1913)]

b. **Destruction of will:** [§540]   A physical act of destruction performed on a will is generally held to *revoke all codicils* to the will if the testator so intended. It is presumed that the will and codicils were interdependent, and that the testator would want the codicils to be revoked along with the will. [Estate of Cuneo, 60 Cal. 2d 196 (1963)]

c. **Destruction of duplicate will:** [§541]   If two copies of a will are *executed* (*i.e.*, signed by the testator and witnessed), destruction by the testator of one executed duplicate will in the testator's possession and control revokes the will, including the untouched duplicate. For this purpose, it is the copy of the executed will in testator's possession and control that counts. [Roberts v. Fisher, 105 N.E.2d 595 (Ind. 1952)] However, destruction of an *unexecuted* copy of the will does not have the effect of revoking the executed will. [*In re* Wehr's Estate, 18 N.W.2d 709 (Wis. 1945)]

5. **Burden of Proof—Presumptions:** [§542]   A testator can destroy a will and thereby revoke it without any witnesses to the act. On the other hand, an accidentally destroyed will is not revoked because there was no intent to revoke. When the will cannot be found after testator's death, or if it is found but it has been torn or mutilated, problems of proof arise as to the testator's actions or intentions. As an aid in solving these problems, the courts have developed various presumptions.

   a. **Presumption of continuity:** [§543]   In many jurisdictions, the proponents of a will have the burden of establishing that the will was not revoked. However, where the will is found after the testator's death and there is nothing to indicate that it might have been revoked (*i.e.*, it is not cancelled or mutilated), the will is presumed to have had a **continuous legal existence** from the time of its execution. This is sometimes called the presumption of continuity.

   b. **Will not found or found in mutilated condition:** [§544]   When the will cannot be found at the testator's death, the courts have developed another presumption.

      (1) **Presumption of revocation:** [§545]   If the will was last seen in testator's possession or under his control, and is found after testator's death in a mutilated condition, the presumption is that the testator was the one who mutilated or destroyed it, and that he did so with the intent to revoke the will. [*In re* Will of Bonner, 17 N.Y.2d 9 (1966)] Similarly, if the will was last known to be in the testator's possession or control and is **not** found after his death, the presumption is that the testator destroyed the will with the intent to revoke it. [*In re* Donigian's Will, 60 N.W.2d 732 (Wis. 1953); 24 A.L.R.2d 514, 522]

      (2) **Evidence to overcome presumption:** [§546]   Where a presumption of revocation arises from the will's nonproduction, extrinsic evidence is admissible to show the testator's intention. Most jurisdictions admit declarations by the testator as to his intent; thus, testator's references to the will and its provisions shortly before his death tend to support a finding that the will was not revoked. [Mimms v. Hunt, 458 S.W.2d 759 (Ky. 1970); 28 A.L.R.3d 994] However, some courts limit testator's declarations concerning the will to statements that are part of the res gestae; *i.e.*, to statements made at the time the physical act is made on the will. [Will of Bonner, *supra*]

      (3) **No presumption of revocation:** [§547]   If the will was last known to be in the possession of a **third person** (*e.g.*, testator's attorney), or if one who would be adversely affected by the will had access to it, the will's loss or damage does **not** give rise to a presumption of revocation. [165 A.L.R. 1188, 1211]

E. PROOF OF LOST WILLS [§548]

To avoid frustration of a testator's intentions when the will has been **inadvertently** lost or destroyed, most states have enacted statutes authorizing probate of a lost will. In states without "lost will" statutes, essentially these same rules are applied by the courts. Generally, probate of a lost will requires the establishment of three elements: (i) valid execution; (ii) the cause of nonproduction; and (iii) the contents of the will.

1. **Due Execution:** [§549]   The will proponents must prove that the will was validly executed. The means of proof are the same as in any other case involving probate of a will (*see infra* §§914-936). The rationale for this requirement is that, otherwise, it would be easier to probate a lost will than an existing one. The case would "derive its strength from its intrinsic weakness." [Tynan v. Paschal, 27 Tex. 286 (1863)] Note that such proof may be impossible if, given that the will is lost, the attesting witnesses cannot be identified.

2. **Cause of Nonproduction:** [§550]   The will proponents must establish that revocation of the will is not the reason for its nonproduction. In this, the proponents may be aided by the presumptions discussed in §§544-547, above.

    a. **Presumption:** [§551]   The fact that the will was last known to be in the possession of someone adversely affected by its contents may create a presumption of nonrevocation.

    b. **Fraudulent destruction:** [§552]   A few statutes require proof that the will was in existence at the time of the testator's death, or was fraudulently destroyed during her lifetime. Generally, such statutes are liberally construed to allow proof of no revocation, thus avoiding intestacy. Some courts have held that the word "existence" in the statute means "legal existence," and that a will not lawfully revoked continues in legal existence until the testator's death. Other courts have ruled that a will destroyed without testator's consent was "fraudulently destroyed," even though no actual fraud was involved. [Estate of Wheaton, 579 P.2d 930 (Utah 1978)]

3. **Contents of Will:** [§553]   All statutes require proof of the contents of the lost will.

    a. **Standard of proof:** [§554]   The standard of proof is generally quite high and is described by words requiring contents to be "substantially proved" [Fla. Prob. Code §733.207], or that ***all*** the will's provisions be "clearly and distinctly proved" [N.Y. Surr. Ct. Proc. Act §1407].

    b. **Means of proof:** [§555]   Most statutes require proof by testimony of persons who had knowledge of the contents of the will, as by having read the will or having heard it read. [Tex. Prob. Code §85] Generally, since these witnesses are proving content and not execution, they are ***not*** disqualified by beneficial interest. (*See supra,* §§426 *et seq.*) [Estate of Reynolds, 94 Cal. App. 2d 851 (1949); *and see* Fla. Prob. Code §733.207] Typically, the statutes require proof by two witnesses, but often allow a true copy of the will to substitute for the testimony of one witness.

4. **Proof to Show Revocation of Prior Will:** [§556]   Even though a lost will is not admissible to probate (*e.g.,* because all of its contents cannot be substantially proved), evidence of the will's due execution plus evidence that it contained language of revocation is admissible to show that an ***earlier*** will, now being offered for probate, was revoked. Proof of execution of such will is ***not*** an offering of the second (now lost) will for probate, but simply to show that the earlier will was revoked. [May v. Brown, 190 S.W.2d 715 (Tex. 1945)]

F. REVIVAL OF REVOKED WILLS [§557]

The issue of revival of revoked wills typically involves the following situation: Testator executes Will #2 which expressly revokes her earlier will (Will #1). However, testator does not destroy the earlier will. Later, unhappy with her second will, testator revokes Will #2. Testator's intention with respect to Will #1 may or may not be known. She may have forgotten entirely about her first will and intended to die intestate. She may, however, have intended that by revoking Will #2, Will #1 would again become effective. What should the court do?

1. **Common Law:** [§558]   The early common law rule, still adhered to in several states, is that no part of a will is effective until the death of the testator. Therefore, if the revoking instrument (Will #2) is itself revoked before the testator's death, Will #1 alone remains in effect and is operative upon the death of the testator. Destruction of Will #2 operates to "revive" Will #1. [Timberlake v. State-Planters Bank, 115 S.E.2d 39 (Va. 1960); 59 A.L.R.2d 11, 53]

2. **Modern Law**

   a. **Majority rule:** [§559]   In most jurisdictions, a will, once revoked, is **not** revived unless republished by (i) **reexecution** or (ii) **a later codicil** under the doctrine of republication by codicil (*see infra,* §§607-610). Hence, revocation of a later will that contained language revoking an earlier will does not, by itself, revive the earlier will or any of its provisions. [N.Y. Est. Powers & Trusts Law §3-4.6]

      (1) **Rationale:** The theory behind the "no revival of revoked wills" rule is that Will #2 operated **immediately** to revoke Will #1, despite the fact that its dispositive provisions would not take effect until the testator's death. Will #1, once revoked, had no further legal existence and could not be resurrected by the revocation of Will #2.

      (2) **Revival by testamentary act:** [§560]   If the testator wishes to reestablish Will #1 as her will, she may do so by one of two means:

         (a) **Reexecution:** [§561]   The will may be reexecuted with full testamentary formalities or reacknowledged before the same attesting witnesses.

         (b) **Republication by codicil:** [§562]   The first will may be revived by the valid execution of a codicil which expressly refers to Will #1. If, however, the first will has been **physically destroyed,** such a reference cannot be effective to revive the will. [Farmers' Bank & Trust Co. v. Harding, 272 S.W. 3 (Ky. 1925)]

   b. **Minority rule:** [§563]   Under the Uniform Probate Code and in a substantial minority of states, destruction of Will #2 and its language of revocation **may** operate to revive Will #1, depending upon the testator's intent. Such intent is established by testator's statements and by reference to all of the circumstances of the case. [U.P.C. §2-509]

G. DEPENDENT RELATIVE REVOCATION [§564]

Dependent relative revocation ("DRR") is an equity-type doctrine under which a court may disregard a revocation if it determines that the act of revocation was premised on a **mistake of law or fact**, and would not have occurred but for the testator's mistaken belief that another disposition of his property was valid. Thus, if the other disposition is for some reason ineffective, the revocation accompanying the attempted disposition also fails and the original will remains in force. [Onions v. Tyrer, 2 Vern. 742 (Ch. 1716)]

1. **Examples**

   a. **Attempted revival of revoked will:** [§565]   T executes Will #1, which gives the residue of his estate to his nephew Andy. T later executes Will #2 which expressly revokes Will #1 and gives the residue of his estate in trust: income to Andy for life with the remainder to Andy's children. However, T does not destroy Will #1. Some time later, T again changes his mind and destroys Will #2 with the intent to revoke it, and with the further intent to revive Will #1. Will #1 cannot be probated because it was revoked by Will #2 and was not revived (*see supra*, §§557-563). Will #2 can be probated under DRR *if* the court finds that its revocation was conditioned and dependent upon the mistaken belief that Will #1 would be revived, and further finds that probating Will #2 more closely effectuates the testator's intent than would an intestate distribution. [Estate of Alburn, 118 N.W.2d 919 (Wis. 1963)]

   b. **Partial revocation:** [§566]   In a jurisdiction that recognizes partial revocations by physical act, T executes Will #1 which makes a bequest to Barbara of $10,000. Later, T strikes through the bequest and writes in the margin, "see codicil." At T's death, Will #1 and the codicil are found. The typewritten "codicil" leaves Barbara $15,000 and is signed by the testator, but it is not witnessed. The codicil cannot be given effect because it was not validly executed. Barbara should take the bequest of $10,000 under DRR. The partial revocation by physical act was premised on the mistaken belief that the codicil was validly executed. Giving effect to the original bequest more closely accomplishes the testator's intent than does eliminating the bequest.

      (1) **Compare:** Suppose, in the example immediately above, the attempted codicil purported to give Barbara $2,000. Here, DRR should *not* be applied because to do so would defeat the testator's intent to substantially reduce Barbara's bequest. [Ruel v. Hardy, 6 A.2d 753 (N.H. 1939)]

2. **Requirements:** [§567]   Before the doctrine of DRR will be applied, four elements must be established.

   a. **Ineffective new disposition:** [§568]   DRR applies only where it is shown that the testator, at the time of revocation, intended to make a new testamentary disposition which for some reason was ineffective. The doctrine will *not* apply if the new disposition is valid, or if no such disposition accompanies the revocation. [Estate of Olmstead, *supra*, §533]

b. **Act of revocation:** [§569]   Before DRR can be applied, there must have been a valid revocation on which the doctrine may act.

    (1) **Physical act:** [§570]   The doctrine may apply where the testator destroyed an earlier will and the destruction was accompanied by an attempt to make a new disposition, or where the testator simply attempted to change some *portion* of her will (*e.g.*, by lining out a bequest and writing in a new amount). [24 A.L.R.2d 514, 554]

    (2) **Later testamentary instrument**

        (a) **Majority view:** [§571]   Most jurisdictions apply the doctrine where the earlier will was expressly or impliedly revoked in some later will or codicil which proves ineffective. [Carter v. First United Methodist Church, 271 S.E.2d 493 (Ga. 1980)]

        (b) **Minority view:** [§572]   Some jurisdictions are reluctant to apply the doctrine where the revocation is by instrument and not by physical act. The rationale for this view is that revocation by physical act is inherently ambiguous. Extrinsic evidence must be used to show the testator's intent; proof that such intent was conditional is, in that case, proper. No such ambiguity exists when the revocation is by later testamentary instrument. [Crosby v. Alton Ochsner Medical Foundation, 276 So. 2d 661 (Miss. 1973)]

        (c) **Mistake must appear on face of will:** [§573]   In any event, courts applying DRR in cases involving revocation by later testamentary instrument require that the mistake appear on the face of the later instrument or at least be inferable from it. If, for example, testator makes a will revoking an earlier bequest to John and the later will leaves the property to Marsha "because John is dead," when John is in fact alive, the doctrine of DRR may operate to nullify the revocation.

c. **Mistake of law:** [§574] The testator's intent to revoke must have been premised or conditioned on a mistaken belief as to the validity of another disposition. Hence, DRR has been applied where a testator mistakenly believes a new will to have been validly executed, or mistakenly believes that the revocation of a later will revived an earlier one. [24 A.L.R.2d 514, 554]

d. **Probable intent of testator:** [§575]   The last and most important element in the application of DRR is that the invalidation of the revocation must be consistent with the testator's probable intent. The doctrine should be applied only when the court concludes that the testator would have preferred a distribution under the "revoked" will over an intestate distribution.

    (1) **Example:** Suppose, in the example *supra* (in §565), nephew Andy would not be an heir, or would be one of several heirs, if T were held to have died intestate. DRR should apply and the revocation of Will #2 should be disre-

garded. Since T tried (but failed) to give his estate outright to Andy, he would prefer a gift in trust for Andy over an intestate distribution among the heirs.

(2) **Compare:** In a jurisdiction that recognizes partial revocation by physical act, T's typewritten will includes a gift of "$10,000 to my brother Bill." Thereafter, T strikes "brother Bill" and writes "niece Nellie" over the strikeout, thereby attempting to make the $10,000 gift to Nellie. The interlineation cannot be given effect because it was not part of T's duly executed will. However, T's revocation of the gift to brother Bill should *not* be disregarded under DRR. T's intent to revoke the gift to Bill was *independent* of his attempt to make a new gift to Nellie. To disregard the partial revocation would be contrary to T's intent.

VII. COMPONENTS OF A WILL

chapter approach

In most cases, a will is a complete, formally executed document that needs no other document or fact to administer the decedent's estate. However, sometimes you will see a will that needs something more—a reference to another document or fact. Whether the court will recognize the other document or fact usually depends on whether it falls within one of the following categories:

1. **Integration:**   Integration problems arise only rarely on Wills exams, but you may see one where heirs are contesting the will or where there are suspicious circumstances (_e.g._, pages that do not seem to fit). The important thing to remember is that all the pages must have been **present** when the testator signed the will and that testator must have **intended** them to be part of the will.

2. **Incorporation by Reference:**   If you cannot "integrate" the particular paper into the will but you believe that testator intended it to be given effect at his death, try applying incorporation by reference. Be sure that the paper was **in existence at the time the will was executed**; that the will **identifies** and refers to the paper **in the present tense**; and that testator's **intent** was to incorporate this paper.

3. **Facts of Independent Significance:**   Sometimes a testator's will requires the court to look outside the document to determine what a gift shall be or who shall receive it (_e.g._, "I give to all full-time employees of my company at the date of my death an equal share of twenty percent of the company's net profits for that year"). The critical issue is whether the fact or event has independent significance, or put another way, is based on a **nontestamentary act**. For instance, the determination of the company's profits serves some valid function **other than** affecting the will.

4. **Pour-Over to Inter Vivos Trust:**   If you see a gift in a will to a **revocable** trust set up during the testator's life, be sure that the trust was in existence **before** or executed **concurrently** with the will's **execution** and that the trust is sufficiently described in the will.

5. **Codicil:**   Some wills questions involve one or more codicils. Besides altering, modifying, or expanding the will, the other important functions of a codicil must be remembered:

    (i)   **Republishing a prior will,** _i.e._, redating and reexecuting it so that the execution date of the prior will is moved up to the date of the codicil (this may be important for interpreting the will or for pretermitted heir statutes);

    (ii) **Validating a prior will that was invalid** (_e.g._, because it was not properly executed); and

    (iii) **Reviving a will** that has been revoked but **not** physically destroyed.

    Remember too that a codicil must be executed with all the formalities of a will or it will be invalid.

A. INTEGRATION

1. **Introduction:** [§576] Integration of a will is the process of embodying several sheets of paper or documents into a *single, entire will,* validated by a *single action of execution.* [Appeal of Sleeper, 151 A. 150 (Me. 1930)] The doctrine of "integration of wills" concerns this question: What sheets were present at the will's execution so as to constitute the decedent's last will that should be admitted to probate?

   a. **Comment:** This doctrine is rarely the subject of litigation, because in the ordinary case, the will is physically connected by a staple and there is an internal integration as well: consecutively numbered clauses on consecutively numbered pages.

   b. **Application:** Problems arise when, for example, the will being executed is casually spread in loose sheets on a coffee table at a cocktail party [Estate of Beale, 113 N.W.2d 380 (Wis. 1962)]; or where pages 1 to 3 and 5 to 6 are typed in an elite typeface and page 4 is in pica, and there is a clear indication that the original staple was removed and the pages were restapled. In these fact settings, the question arises: Were *all* of those pages present when the will was signed by the testator and witnessed by the attesting witnesses?

2. **Requirements for Integration:** [§577] To show that the will being offered for probate was integrated, all the various pages involved must have been *actually present* at the time of execution, and the testator must have *intended* the several pages to constitute his will. [Estate of Beale, *supra*]

3. **Proving Integration:** [§578] The issue of whether the will being offered for probate is an integrated document does not arise unless there are suspicious circumstances or the issue is pleaded by the contestants.

   a. **Presumption of integration:** [§579] There is a strong presumption of integration where the attestation clause recites the total number of pages of the will and where the testator has initialled each page. [30 A.L.R. 427] A presumption of integration also arises if the pages are found *physically connected* to each other by staple or paper clip; if there is a sequence in numbering of consecutive pages [Appeal of Sleeper, *supra*]; or if there is *logical continuity* in thought of the provisions running from one page to another [38 A.L.R.2d 477].

   b. **Extrinsic evidence:** [§580] Even in the absence of any presumption, integration can be proved by the testimony of witnesses or by reference to surrounding circumstances.

B. INCORPORATION BY REFERENCE

1. **Introduction:** [§581] Papers that cannot be "integrated" because they were not present at the will's execution nevertheless may be given effect under the doctrine of incorporation by reference. [U.P.C. §2-510] Basically, this doctrine recognizes that a duly executed will may, by appropriate reference, incorporate into itself any extrinsic document or writing, even though the other document was not properly executed and is not otherwise

of testamentary character. [173 A.L.R. 568] Some jurisdictions do not recognize the doctrine of incorporation by reference [Hatheway v. Smith, 65 A. 1058 (Conn. 1907)], but they represent the minority view.

2. **Requirements for Incorporation by Reference:** [§582]   The doctrine of incorporation by reference enables the court to admit into probate nontestamentary writings that were not part of the duly executed will and that were not executed with statutory formalities. Accordingly, to limit the danger of fraud or substitution, the following conditions must be met:

   a. **Document must be in existence:** [§583]   The document to be incorporated must have been in existence *at the time the will was executed*. [Lawless v. Lawless, 47 S.E.2d 431 (Va. 1948)] As will be seen below, however, where the testator later executes a codicil to the will, it may be sufficient for the document to be in existence at the time the codicil was executed. (*See infra,* §609.)

   b. **Document must be referred to as being in existence:** [§584]   By majority rule, the will also must *expressly refer* to the document in the *present tense* (*i.e.,* as an existing document). Thus, a reference to "a sealed letter which *will be found* with this will," or to "an inventory *to be prepared by me* and deposited herewith" is *insufficient*—even though the document was in existence when the will was executed. [Kellom v. Beverstock, 126 A.2d 127 (N.H. 1956); 152 A.L.R. 1238] Some courts do not insist upon this, as long as the document is proved to have been in actual existence at the time the will was executed.

   c. **Will must identify and describe document:** [§585]   The will must identify and describe the document to be incorporated so clearly that there can be no mistake as to the identity of the document referred to. [*In re* Young's Estate, 123 Cal. 337 (1899)] A mere reference to "the attached document" is *not* a sufficient identification, even if a document is found stapled to the will, since the reference does not unequivocally refer to one and only one document. [Taylor v. Republic National Bank, 452 S.W.2d 560 (Tex. 1970)]

   d. **Will must show intent to incorporate:** [§586]   The testator must have intended to incorporate the extrinsic document as part of the *overall testamentary plan*. [Estate of Hopper, 194 N.W. 237 (Neb. 1912)]

3. **Validation of Invalid Prior Will:** [§587]   The doctrine of incorporation by reference can be used to give effect to an earlier instrument that otherwise would be ineffective because not validly executed. Thus, it has been held that a valid "codicil" which makes appropriate reference to a prior "will" may give effect to that document even though the earlier "will" was not properly witnessed. [21 A.L.R.2d 821] This fact setting does *not* involve the doctrine of "republication by codicil" (*see infra,* §§607-608) because republication applies only to earlier valid wills.

4. **Ineffective Deed as Will:** [§588]   Occasionally, courts are confronted with the situation where a decedent executed a deed purporting to convey property inter vivos but the conveyance failed for some reason (*e.g.,* lack of delivery). The deed is then offered as the decedent's will (*i.e.,* a testamentary disposition) as to such property.

a. **Majority rule:** [§589]   Most courts **deny probate** to such an instrument, on the ground that it was not executed with testamentary intent. That is, since the instrument was intended to be effective during the grantor's lifetime, the grantor did not intend the instrument to operate at his death as a will.

b. **Exception:** [§590]   If the decedent left a valid will that refers to the inter vivos deed (*e.g.,* "I make no provision for my brother Lenny, since I have already deeded my farm to him"), the will may be held to have **incorporated the ineffective deed by reference**. Thus, even though the deed was otherwise invalid, and even though the testator thought the property was no longer in his estate, the reference to the deed in the will is enough to carry out the transfer. [Estate of Dimmitt, 3 N.W.2d 752 (Neb. 1942)]

5. **Uniform Probate Code Exception for List of Tangible Personal Property:** [§591]   The Uniform Probate Code carves out an exception to the requirements for incorporation by reference where a list of tangible personal property is involved. A will may refer to a written statement or list to dispose of items of tangible personal property—other than money, intangibles such as shares of stock, and property used in trade or business—not otherwise specifically disposed of by the will. It is not necessary that the writing have any significance apart from its effect upon the dispositions made in the will. The writing must be **signed** by the testator and must **describe** the items and the devisees with reasonable certainty. It may be referred to as one in existence at the time of the testator's death. The writing may be prepared before **or after** the execution of the will, and it **may be altered** by the testator after its initial preparation. [U.P.C. §2-513] Several non-U.P.C. states have enacted a similar statute. [*See, e.g.,* Fla. Prob. Code §732.515]

6. **Oral Statements Not Incorporated by Reference:** [§592]   Oral instructions (*e.g.,* "I devise Blackacre to B for the purposes I have already communicated to him") **cannot** be incorporated into a will by reference, and in such cases extrinsic evidence is **not** admissible to show the testator's intent. In the absence of fraud, the person designated to take under the will is entitled to the property absolutely and is not bound by the restrictions contained in the testator's instructions.

a. **Compare:** If the testator makes such a provision only after the designated beneficiary has assured testator that he will dispose of the property as the testator has instructed, parol evidence is admissible to show fraud, and a constructive trust may be impressed in favor of the intended beneficiaries. (*See* Trusts Summary.)

C. FACTS OF INDEPENDENT SIGNIFICANCE

1. **Nontestamentary Acts:** [§593]   A testator may refer in the will to extrinsic acts or events that have some **independent legal significance** (*i.e.,* that ordinarily are not testamentary in nature), for the purpose of either designating the beneficiaries (*e.g.,* "I bequeath $1,000 to each of my servants in my employ on the date of my death," or designating the property that is the subject of the gift (*e.g.,* "I bequeath to X an amount equal to the net profit of my business in the year of my death"). Under the "facts of independent significance" doctrine (sometimes called the doctrine of "nontestamentary acts"), these gifts are given effect even though the identity of the beneficiaries or the

property will be determined by resort to unattested acts. [U.P.C. §2-512] The doctrine allows the testator some latitude in describing the intended beneficiaries or the gifts they are to receive.

    a.   **Acts of testator:** [§594]   The acts referred to may be those of the testator: "I bequeath the contents of my hope chest to my sister Sue." [Succession of Maginnis, 104 So. 726 (La. 1925)]

    b.   **Acts of another person:** [§595]   The acts referred to may be the acts of some third person: "I devise Blackacre to the persons named as beneficiaries in my brother's will." [Matter of Fowles, 222 N.Y. 222 (1918)]

2.   **Test:** [§596]   The critical issue in any question involving the facts of independent significance doctrine is whether the extrinsic fact or event in question has a legal significance apart from and independent of its impact on the will. The act or event must be one which ordinarily has some ***nontestamentary utility*** or function.

    a.   **Example:** A bequest of "$1,000 to each person employed in my business at the time of my death" is a valid designation. [Metcalf v. Sweeney, 21 A. 364 (R.I. 1891)] The act of hiring or firing employees is normally done to enhance the business of the testator, not to designate the beneficiaries in a will. The event of employment, therefore, has an "independent significance"—something apart from its effect on the testamentary disposition.

    b.   **Example:** T's will devises "the automobile that I own at my death" to her nephew N. At the time the will was executed, T owned a ten-year-old Volkswagen. Shortly before her death, T traded the Volkswagen in on a new Cadillac, with the result that T died owning a $20,000 car instead of a $2,000 car. The disposition is valid. While T's purchase of the Cadillac had the practical effect of greatly increasing the value of the gift to N, it is unlikely that this motivated her purchase. More probably, she bought the new car because she wanted to own and drive a Cadillac—a lifetime motive for a lifetime act that also had an effect on her will.

    c.   **Compare:** A bequest of "$1,000 to the person bearing a letter from me identifying him or her as my beneficiary" is clearly invalid, since the giving of such a letter has ***no significance*** apart from its effect on the will. Allowing such a gift would enable the testator to change her will up to the moment of death by an unattested act.

D. POUR-OVER GIFT TO INTER VIVOS TRUST

1.   **Introduction:** [§597]   A "pour-over" gift is a testamentary gift to a trust created during the decedent's lifetime, with the testamentary assets to be administered and distributed as part of that trust. For example, T creates a revocable inter vivos trust, and later executes a will devising her residuary estate "to the First National Bank, trustee of the trust which I executed on January 11, 1980." The objective of a pour-over gift is to provide a ***single, integrated trust management and disposition*** of (i) assets transferred to the trust during lifetime, and (ii) assets owned by the settlor at death. (*See* Trusts Summary.)

2. **Validity of Pour-Over Gift—Case Law:** [§598]   In several jurisdictions, early cases invalidated such gifts to a revocable, amendable trust inter vivos on the ground that the settlor could amend the trust after the will's execution, and thus could indirectly change the testamentary gift without complying with testamentary formalities. Other jurisdictions upheld the gift under the theory that the inter vivos trust was incorporated by reference into the will. [21 A.L.R.2d 220] This had the result of giving effect to the testamentary gift to the trust as it existed when the will was executed, without regard to subsequent amendments of the trust. Still other courts upheld the testamentary gift and construed it as a gift to the trust, *including subsequent amendments*, under the facts of independent significance doctrine, at least if the trust had been funded with substantial assets during the testator's lifetime. [Second Bank-State Street Trust Co. v. Pinion, 170 N.E.2d 350 (Mass. 1960)]

3. **Uniform Testamentary Additions to Trust Act:** [§599]   The validity and effect of a pour-over gift to a revocable inter vivos trust is no longer in doubt in most states. Nearly all jurisdictions have enacted the Uniform Testamentary Additions to Trusts Act or its equivalent. [U.P.C. §2-511; *and see* Cal. Prob. Code §6300] The Act validates a testamentary gift to an inter vivos trust created by the testator or by another person, even though the trust is revocable or amendable, and even though the trust is *amended after the will's execution*. The testamentary assets are added to the assets placed in the trust during the testator's lifetime, and the combined assets are administered as one trust under the trust terms as they exist at the testator's death, including any amendments made after the will's execution.

   a. **Trust in existence or executed concurrently with will:** [§600]   Under the Act, the only substantive requirements for a valid pour-over gift are that (i) the trust must be *sufficiently described* in the testator's will, and (ii) the trust must be *in existence before* or *executed concurrently* with the will.

      (1) **Exception:** [§601]   The Act also validates testamentary gifts to a trust *not* in existence when the testator executed the will, *if* the trust was created by the will of another person who predeceased the testator.

         (a) **Example:** T devises her estate "on the terms and conditions of the trust contained in the will of my brother, Bob." If Bob had no will when T executed the foregoing, but he predeceased T and left a valid will with trust terms, T's gift to the trust is valid.

   b. **Added requirements in some states:** [§602]   In some jurisdictions, a revocable, amendable trust must be executed and *acknowledged* before a notary public in order to receive valid testamentary pour-over gifts. [N.Y. Est. Powers & Trusts Law §3-3.7]

   c. **Pour-over to unfunded trust:** [§603]   The size and character of the trust corpus during the testator's lifetime is immaterial. This means that a testator can, during lifetime, create a trust funded with only five dollars, and by subsequent amendments of this token trust control the disposition of assets that will pass under the will. The fact that the amendments are made without testamentary formalities is irrelevant.

The Act specifically validates gifts to funded or unfunded life insurance trusts, even though the testator has reserved all ownership rights in the insurance contracts.

E. CODICIL

1. **Definition:** [§604]   A codicil is a testamentary instrument, executed **subsequent** to the execution of a will, that **alters, modifies, or expands** the provisions of the will in some manner.

2. **Formalities:** [§605]   A codicil must be executed with the same formalities required for execution of a will. However, the codicil does not have to be in the same form as the will it amends. In states that recognize holographic instruments (*see supra*, §§455 *et seq.*), it is possible to have a **holographic codicil** to a typewritten, witnessed will, and vice versa. [40 A.L.R.2d 698]

3. **Separate Document Not Required:** [§606]   The codicil may appear as a separate document, or it may appear on the same piece of paper as the will it amends. For this reason, in jurisdictions that recognize holographic wills, always consider whether an interlineation on the will can be upheld as a valid codicil.

   a. **Example:** The third paragraph of T's typewritten, witnessed will makes a $2,000 bequest to T's niece Nell. Some time later, T writes at the bottom of the page: "I have changed my mind about the gift in paragraph 3. I want Nell to have $5,000 rather than $2,000." T signs and dates this addition. In jurisdictions that recognize holographic testamentary instruments, this is a valid holographic codicil to T's will. (In jurisdictions that do not recognize holographs, T's attempted change of the will would not be effective because it was not witnessed.)

   b. **Compare:** Consider the same will except that, instead of writing a new provision at the bottom of the page, T strikes the "$2,000" and writes in above it "$5,000." T initials and dates the margin alongside this change. The interlineation is not given effect because "$5,000" has no meaning without its context, and the context consists of the typewritten provisions making the gift to Nell. Thus as to the interlineation the requirements of a valid holographic instrument are not satisfied. (*See supra*, §§468-469.)

4. **Effect of Codicil:** [§607]   In addition to whatever modification, alteration, or expansion of the prior will was intended by the testator, a codicil may have one of the following legal effects: (i) it may **republish** a prior valid will; (ii) it may **incorporate by reference** and thus validate a prior invalid will (*see supra*, §587); or (iii) it may **revive** a previously revoked will that is still in existence.

   a. **Republication by codicil:** [§608]   The doctrine of "republication by codicil" concerns the question of when does a will "speak"; *i.e.,* when is a will deemed to have been executed? Under this doctrine, the execution of a codicil has the effect of "republishing" the will itself, so that the will is deemed to have been **redated and reexecuted as of the date of the codicil.** The republication doctrine applies not only to the will, but to all intervening codicils made prior to the codicil now being executed. [87 A.L.R. 839]

(1) **Significance:** [§609]   Although a will is deemed to be effective only upon the death of the testator as to property then included in her estate, the general rule is that a will is to be interpreted in the light of circumstances existing at the time of its execution. Republication, therefore, causes the will to be interpreted as of the ***date of the codicil,*** rather than as of the date the will was originally executed. [Matter of Champion, (1893) L.R. 1 Ch. 101]

   (a) **Example under interested witness statute:** If the original will contains a gift to one of the attesting witnesses, as a general rule that gift will be held invalid (*see supra*, §427). A subsequent codicil, however, republishes the prior will and (assuming there are different attesting witnesses) operates to validate the gift to the beneficially-interested witness under the original will. The earlier attestation is disregarded.

   (b) **Example under incorporation by reference doctrine:** T's will dated March 25, 1970, devises her estate "to the persons named in a letter I have written to Jane Jones, my executor." The next day, T writes a letter to Jane Jones, telling her that this is the letter referred to in T's will and naming those to whom she wants her estate distributed. On January 15, 1971, T executes a codicil to her will. Ordinarily, T's letter to her executor would not be given effect under the theory of incorporation by reference, since it was not in existence when T's will was executed (*see supra*, §583). However, T's codicil of January 15, 1971, republished the will as of that date, and since the letter was in existence ***then***, it is incorporated by reference. [Simon v. Grayson, 15 Cal. 2d 531 (1940)]

   (c) **Example under pretermitted child statute:** In 1965, T executes a will that devises one-half of his estate to his wife W and the remaining one-half to his daughter D. In 1968, a son S is born to T. In 1970, T executes a codicil that changes the alternate executor. The will is deemed to have been executed in 1970; therefore, S is not entitled to any protection under the state's pretermitted child statute, which only protects children born ***after*** the will's execution (*see supra*, §286).

(2) **Limitation:** [§610]   The republication doctrine is not applied mechanically or if the result would be patently inconsistent with the testator's apparent intention. The purpose of the doctrine is to effectuate, not frustrate, the testator's plan. [Tanton v. Keller, 47 N.E. 376 (Ill. 1897)]

   (a) **Example:** Ordinarily a will speaks as of the date of execution for purposes of identifying beneficiaries. Thus, a bequest "to my doctor" would generally be interpreted as meaning the physician attending T at the time the will was executed. If T subsequently executes a codicil, the gift to "my doctor" could be interpreted as meaning T's doctor at the later date. However, this is not very likely where the codicil had nothing to do with the gift in question (*e.g.*, where the codicil merely names a new executor).

b. **Validation of prior invalid will:** [§611]   The doctrine of republication by codicil technically applies only to valid testamentary documents. Thus, wills or intervening codicils that were never valid to begin with (*e.g.,* because not validly executed) cannot be "republished" by a later codicil. However, many courts are willing to construe a codicil as impliedly *incorporating* the prior defective will by reference, thereby validating the otherwise invalid prior testamentary instrument.

(1) **Example:** T signs a will on January 15, 1971, but it is not properly attested. Later, T executes an instrument with proper testamentary formalities which provides simply: "This is a codicil to my will dated January 15, 1971. I hereby nominate my wife to serve as my executor." T then dies. The later instrument is not, in fact, a "codicil" because there is no preexisting valid will. Rather, the later instrument (being properly executed) *is* T's will; and it incorporates by reference the dispositive provisions in the earlier, defective instrument.

c. **Revival of revoked will:** [§612]   Execution of a codicil to a will that previously had been revoked but was not physically destroyed is generally held to "revive" the prior will. [Kimbark v. Satas, 231 N.E.2d 699 (Ill. 1967)] (On revival of revoked wills, *see supra,* §§557-563.)

VIII.   CONTRACTS RELATING TO WILLS; JOINT WILLS

chapter approach

Although the topics in this chapter relate to wills, they actually involve contracts. Specifically:

(i)   A *contract to make a gift* by will;

(ii)   *Joint wills* that may or may not be contractual (if they are, they are subject to a contract not to revoke, *see* below);

(iii)   A *contract not to revoke* a will or a provision in a will; and

(iv)   A *contract not to make a will* at all.

For questions about these topics, keep in mind that *contract law* rather than wills law governs. The will itself is valid and may be probated even though its execution was in breach of contract. But if the contract is valid, contract remedies are available, the most common being *constructive trust* for the benefit of the promisee (this remedy is also called "quasi-specific performance").

A.   CONTRACT TO MAKE A GIFT BY WILL

1.   **Contract Law, Not Wills Law, Controls:** [§613]   A promise or contract to make a will, even if in writing and witnessed, is *never* admissible to probate *as a will*, because there is no expression of *present* testamentary intent (*see supra,* §357) but merely a promise to make the will in the future. In any case involving an alleged promise to make a testamentary gift, contract law rather than the law of wills controls. Thus, there must be an offer, acceptance, and consideration, and the parties must have the capacity to contract. Whatever rights the promisee acquires are contract rights and are enforceable only as such.

    a.   **Example:** T promises to make a will that devises Blackacre to his niece B if B will move in with and take care of him. B performs her part of the bargain, but T dies without having made such a will. To what relief, if any, is B entitled? This commonly litigated fact situation [69 A.L.R. 14] is a contracts problem controlled by contract law, rather than by the law of wills. B cannot simply claim the land in probate court but may sue the estate for breach of contract.

2.   **Consideration:** [§614]   As a general proposition, the promisee has no enforceable contract rights unless she gave sufficient consideration for the testator's promise to name her as a will beneficiary. Without such consideration, the testator's promise is simply a promise to make a gift in the future, and therefore is unenforceable.

3. **Formalities**

   a. **Common law:** [§615]   At common law and in states without statutes dealing with the question, a contract to make a will or to make a gift by will need *not* be in writing unless real property is involved. (If land is involved, the Statute of Frauds applies since the promise is treated as a contract for the sale of land. [Rape v. Lyerly, 215 S.E.2d 737 (N.C. 1975)]) However, the Dead Man's Statute may be applicable to prohibit testimony offered to establish the alleged contract. (*See* Evidence Summary.)

   b. **Statutory solutions:** [§616]   Concerns about spurious claims and the inability of the alleged promisor to refute the promisee's testimony have prompted many states to enact statutes requiring that a contract to make a gift by will (or a contract not to revoke a will) must be in *writing*. In general, the statutes take one of three forms.

      (1) **Promise in writing and signed:** [§617]   In several states, the statutes require that an agreement to make a testamentary provision of any kind or an agreement not to revoke a will must be in writing and signed by the promisor. [N.Y. Est. Powers & Trusts Law §13-2.1] Additionally, some states require that the writing be signed by *two witnesses*. [*See* Fla. Prob. Code §732.701]

      (2) **Reference to contract in will:** [§618]   Some statutes go considerably further and provide that a contract relating to a will can be established *only* by provisions of a will stating that a contract does exist *and* stating the material provisions of the contract. [Tex. Prob. Code §59A]

      (3) **Uniform Probate Code:** [§619]   The U.P.C. requires that a contract to make a will or devise (or not to revoke a will or devise) can be established only by (i) provisions in a will stating the *material provisions* of the contract; (ii) an *express reference* in a will to the contract and extrinsic evidence proving the terms of the contract; *or* (iii) a *writing signed by the decedent* evidencing the contract. [U.P.C. §2-701]

4. **Remedies**

   a. **During testator's lifetime:** [§620]   A contract to make a testamentary gift ordinarily is *not* enforceable during the testator's lifetime, because there is no way of telling whether the testator will perform the contract until after his death. [Warden v. Hinds, 163 F. 201 (4th Cir. 1908)]

      (1) **Anticipatory breach:** [§621]   However, if the promisor repudiates the promise *after substantial performance* by the promisee, this may be construed as an anticipatory breach of contract, entitling the promisee to maintain an immediate action against the promisor. [Smith v. Long, 83 P.2d 167 (Okla. 1983); 7 A.L.R.2d 1166]

      (2) **Equitable relief:** [§622]   Where an anticipatory breach is established, the courts are divided on whether specific performance should be granted. [7

A.L.R.2d 1171] Some courts have granted equitable relief, requiring the promisor (or any non-bona fide purchaser to whom he has deeded the property) to hold the property for the promisor's benefit during his lifetime and convey the property to the promisee upon the promisor's death. [Matheson v. Gullickson, 24 N.W.2d 704 (Minn. 1946)]

(3) **Remedies at law:** [§623]   If the promisor repudiates the contract, the promisee is entitled to *damages* for breach of contract [Spinks v. Jenkins, 43 S.E.2d 586 (Ga. 1947)], or to a *quantum meruit* recovery for the value of the consideration paid or services rendered [Cramer v. McKinney, 49 A.2d 374 (Pa. 1946)].

b.   **After testator's death**

(1) **Remedies:** [§624]   If the promisor fails to make the promised testamentary gift, the promisee has a cause of action against the promisor's estate for *damages* for breach of contract. [*In re* Soles' Will, 253 N.W. 801 (Wis. 1934)] The measure of damages is the *value of the property* promised to be devised or bequeathed. [65 A.L.R.3d 632] However, if the case involves a promise to make a devise or bequest of *specific* property, the usual remedy is to grant a *constructive trust* for the promisee's benefit. [106 A.L.R. 742] Since the effect of this remedy is to give the promisee the very property contracted for, it is sometimes referred to as "quasi-specific performance." [60 A.L.R. 14] (On the constructive trust remedy, *see* Trusts Summary.)

(2) **Early death of promisor:** [§625]   The fact that the promisor dies shortly after the agreement is made, meaning that the promisee was not called upon to furnish much in the way of care and support, does *not* affect enforceability of the contract. There is necessarily an element of uncertainty in such an agreement from both parties' standpoint, and adequacy of consideration and fairness must be viewed in light of the circumstances at the time the contract was made. [Dingler v. Ritzius, 247 P. 10 (Idaho 1926); 49 A.L.R. 601]

(3) **Statute of limitations:** [§626]   The courts are divided as to what statute of limitations applies to a suit seeking to enforce the contract. Some cases hold that the claim must be presented within the "nonclaim" period required for filing creditors' claims; others that the applicable period is the time within which a will contest must be filed; others that the statutes governing actions for the recovery of land are applicable; and still others that the statute of limitations applicable to equitable claims is controlling. [94 A.L.R.2d 810]

c.   **Enforcement by party other than original promisee:** [§627]   In certain cases, someone other than the original promisee may enforce the contract. For example, suppose that T promises to devise real property to his daughter if she will move in with and take care of him. The daughter and her family move in with T, and the daughter cares for T for several years. The daughter dies, but her husband and children continue to live with and care for T. T dies several years later; his will makes no devise to the daughter or her family. The contract is enforceable by the daughter's husband and children. While T could have rescinded the agreement on the ground that it was a personal service contract, his failure to do so and his continued acceptance of benefits from the daughter's successors bound him to perform as promised. [Rape v. Lyerly, *supra*, §615; 84 A.L.R.3d 908]

B. JOINT WILLS

1. **Introduction:** [§628]   The most frequently litigated question concerning joint wills is whether the particular joint will was executed pursuant to a contract—namely, that the surviving party to the joint will agreed not to revoke the will or alter its dispositive provisions. However, other issues concerning joint wills, discussed below, can arise even if it is determined that the particular joint will was not contractual.

2. **Terminology**

   a. **Joint will:** [§629]   A "joint will" is the will of two or more persons executed as a *single* testamentary instrument.

      (1) **Admissibility to probate:** [§630]   A joint will is admissible to probate on the death of *each* of the testators, just as if it had been written on separate pieces of paper. The fact that the document is the will of more than one testator does not affect its admission to probate in each testator's estate.

      (2) **Revocation by one testator:** [§631]   If one of the joint testators has revoked the will, it is no longer admissible to probate as *his* will, but the document still would be admissible to probate as the will of the other.

   b. **Reciprocal wills:** [§632]   In contrast to joint wills, "reciprocal" wills, sometimes called "mirror" wills, are *separate* wills of two or more persons which contain reciprocal provisions.

   c. **Mutual wills:** [§633]   The courts are not uniform in their use of the word "mutual" in connection with joint wills and reciprocal wills. Some courts use the term "mutual" as synonymous with *"contractual."* Under this usage, a "joint and mutual will" is a single instrument executed jointly by two or more testators, the provisions of which are contractual. However, many courts use the term "mutual" as a synonym for *"reciprocal."* Under this parlance, "mutual wills" are separate wills containing reciprocal provisions; and a "joint and mutual will" is a joint will containing reciprocal provisions which *may or may not* be contractual. In reading cases involving joint wills or reciprocal wills, care must be exercised in determining which meaning is intended when the court refers to mutual wills.

3. **Survivor's Rights:** [§634]   What are the surviving party's rights in the property subject to a joint will? This issue can arise even if the joint will is held *not* to be contractual, in which case the issue concerns only the decedent's property that passes under the will to the survivor. The issue also can arise if the will *is* held to be contractual, in which case the question of the survivor's rights concerns not only the decedent's property but *also* the survivor's property that is subject to the contractual obligation. In either case, the issue is

this: Does the surviving party have only a life estate, a life estate with powers of invasion, or a fee simple subject to defeasance on her death? Where the will is found to be subject to a contract not to revoke, there is a greater tendency to find that the surviving party's rights do ***not*** include the power to make lifetime gifts, since the effect of such gifts would be to defeat the rights of the beneficiaries of the contract. [85 A.L.R.3d 8]

a. **Life estate with invasion powers:** [§635]   A life estate with invasion powers may give the survivor a right to invade the principal.

    (1) **Example:** "We and each of us give all of our property, real and personal, to the survivor of us, to be used, possessed, and enjoyed by the survivor during his or her lifetime, and on the death of the survivor all of the property shall pass as follows. . . ."

    (2) **Effect:** A joint will drafted along the above lines gives the survivor a ***life estate*** ("during his or her lifetime"). However, the survivor may not be limited to the income from or the right to possess the property. The life tenant's right of use will depend upon the language employed, and infinite variations in the words used by different testators make generalization difficult. However, the very broad language frequently employed in such wills (*e.g.,* "to be used, possessed, and enjoyed") is often found to give the survivor a right to ***consume the principal*** for her own support and benefit, but does ***not*** permit lifetime gifts with the purpose or effect of defeating the remainder interests. [Thomas v. Thomas, 446 S.W.2d 590 (Tex. 1969)]

b. **Defeasible fee simple:** [§636]   A grant of a defeasible fee may allow the survivor to defeat the rights of the beneficiaries under the contract.

    (1) **Example:** "We give and bequeath to the survivor of us, absolutely, all our property, real, personal, and mixed, to use as he or she may see fit. After the death of both of us, the remainder of our property, of which the survivor shall die seised and possessed, shall go to. . . ." [Harrell v. Hickman, 215 S.W.2d 876 (Tex. 1948)]

    (2) **Effect:** Under a joint will drafted along the above lines ("to the survivor of us, ***absolutely***"), it is generally held that the survivor has all the powers of a fee simple owner during his or her lifetime. This includes the power to make inter vivos gifts, even though such gifts have the intent and effect of defeating the interest of the takers at death. The beneficiaries take only what remains on the survivor's death. [Brack v. Brodbeck, 466 S.W.2d 600 (Tex. 1971)]

C. CONTRACT NOT TO REVOKE A WILL

1. **Introduction:** [§637]   A frequently litigated situation involves an alleged promise that the testator would not revoke the will. Most of the cases involve a joint will or reciprocal wills executed by a husband and wife, but the issue also can arise with respect to wills executed by siblings or by unrelated parties. Of course, the parties could expressly provide that the joint will or mutual wills were not to be revoked by either party.

However, this is decidedly the exception; and proof of the contract usually is based upon the language of the joint will (or reciprocal wills) and upon extrinsic evidence.

a. **Example:** H and W are married, and each has a child by a former marriage. On the same day, H and W execute identical wills. H's will leaves his entire estate to W if she survives him, otherwise one-half to H's son S and one-half to W's daughter D. W's will contains reciprocal terms: to H if he survives W, otherwise one-half to S and one-half to D. H dies, and his entire estate passes to W. Thereafter, W writes a new will that revokes her earlier will, makes a bequest of five dollars to H's son S, and devises "all the remainder of *my* property to my beloved daughter, D." S now contends that H and W executed their wills pursuant to an agreement under which the survivor would not revoke his or her will.

b. **Comment:** [§638]   The case is a difficult and troublesome one. Given the similarity of the wills, it is very likely that H and W discussed the wills before they were prepared and executed; and it may be shown that, after such discussion, they orally "agreed" to write reciprocal wills under which their estates ultimately would pass to their respective children. But should this discussion and "agreement" to write similar wills lead to a finding that H and W entered into an irrevocable commitment and enforceable obligation, the effect of which would be to prevent the survivor from ever changing her will regardless of changed circumstances? If that was their intent, it certainly would have been more appropriate to put their agreement in writing, or to utilize some formal arrangement (such as a trust) whereby their estates would be divided between the two children on the survivor's death.

2. **Formalities:** [§639]   As noted earlier, a number of states have recently enacted statutes requiring that any agreement relating to a will, including a contract not to revoke a will, be in a writing executed with certain formalities (*see supra*, §616). In these states, the statutes have accomplished their avowed objective of eliminating litigation over claims, based on oral testimony or other extrinsic evidence, that a will was executed pursuant to a contract. Still, such cases continue to arise in states that do not have such a statute.

3. **Presumptions:** [§640]   In jurisdictions that do not have statutes requiring that contracts relating to wills be in writing, the courts have developed various presumptions as to whether such a contract exists.

a. **Joint will:** [§641]   It is invariably *stated* (as distinguished from *held*) by the courts that the mere execution of a joint will containing reciprocal provisions, without more, is **insufficient** to support a finding that the joint will was contractual.

(1) **Rationale:** Many husbands and wives execute such wills without intending to irrevocably bind the survivor. "Contracts of this nature are viewed by the courts with caution; they can be established only by full and satisfactory proof; and no presumptions or inferences will be indulged in favor of them." [Magids v. American Title Insurance Co., 473 S.W.2d 460 (Tex. 1971)]

(2) **Comment:** However, more than a few cases, after solemnly stating the above rule, nonetheless uphold findings that a joint will with reciprocal provisions,

coupled with evidence that the parties "agreed" to execute the joint will, **does** establish the existence of a contract, especially when the testators use plural possessive pronouns to make a joint disposition of all of their collective properties. "A will like that could not have been made without agreement between the testators that it should be so made. Its very terms are evidence that an agreement was made." [Nye v. Bradford, 193 S.W.2d 165 (Tex. 1946)] However, the cases, even from the same jurisdiction, are not at all predictable. [169 A.L.R. 9; 17 A.L.R.4th 167]

b. **Reciprocal wills:** [§642]   By the overwhelming weight of authority, the mere execution of reciprocal wills containing identical provisions, drafted by the same attorney and executed on the same day, does **not** constitute evidence that the wills were contractual. [Plemmons v. Pemberton, 139 S.W.2d 910 (Mo. 1940)]

   (1) **Example:** H has two children by his first marriage and two children by his marriage to W. H and W execute reciprocal wills: H's will provides that his estate is to go to W if she survives him; otherwise to the four children. W's will provides that her estate is to go to H if he survives her; otherwise to the four children. H dies; some years later W executes a new will that revokes her earlier will and leaves her entire estate (including the property received from H) to her two children and omits H's other two children. On these and similar facts, it is usually held that the reciprocal wills, by themselves, do not support a finding that the wills were contractual. "The power to dispose of one's property by will is not lightly to be denied. . . . No express promise or representation was proved in writing or orally to have been made by [W] that she would not change her testamentary intent as expressed in the will which she executed contemporaneously with the will of her husband. . . . The law requires clear evidence of the existence of a promise of this nature." [Oursler v. Armstrong, 10 N.Y.2d 374 (1961)]

   (2) **Comment:** Nonetheless, an occasional court has found reciprocal wills to be contractual based on evidence that the parties "agreed" to write such wills. Here, too, the cases are not altogether predictable. [17 A.L.R.4th 224]

4. **Effect of Contract**

   a. **During both parties' lifetimes:** [§643]   It is generally held that either party may revoke a contractual will **provided** she gives notice to the other party to the contract. [Ankeny v. Lieuallen, 113 P.2d 1113 (Or. 1942); 169 A.L.R. 50] Moreover, if one party secretly revokes a contractual will but predeceases the other party, the survivor has no remedy because he has not suffered any loss in reliance on the contract. [Canada v. Ihmsen, 240 P. 927 (Wyo. 1925)] "The only object of notice is to enable the other party to the bargain to alter his or her will also, but the survivor in the present case is not in any way prejudiced. He has notice as from the death." [Stone v. Hoskins, (1905) L.R. Prob. 194]

   b. **Revocation of will by survivor:** [§644]   By the overwhelming weight of authority, if the surviving party to the contract revokes her will and executes a new one, the ***new will is admissible to probate*** notwithstanding the breach of contract. Moreover, the contractual will cannot be probated because it was revoked. This does not mean that the beneficiaries of the contract are without a remedy; it simply means that ***wills law***, and not contract law, determines which will should be probated. The issue of whether a will is contractual cannot be determined in a probate proceeding, as that proceeding concerns only whether the proffered will is the duly executed last will of the decedent. The contractual issue and any resulting remedy must be pursued in a subsequent proceeding. [Estate of Marcucci, 296 N.E.2d 849 (Ill. 1973); 17 A.L.R.4th 180]

c. **Remedies:** [§645]   Since revocation of the contractual will and execution of a new will constitute a breach of contract, the contract beneficiaries have a remedy for the breach. The proper remedy is not damages but a suit to impress a ***constructive trust*** [169 A.L.R. 9], although the remedy is described by some courts as "in the nature of specific performance" or "quasi-specific performance." [O'Connor v. Immele, 43 N.W.2d 649 (N.D. 1950)] The beneficiaries under the new will, which was executed in breach of contract, hold on a constructive trust for the benefit of the contract beneficiaries.

5. Property Subject to the Contract

a. **In general:** [§646]   Since the purpose of a contractual will is to make a unified disposition of both parties' estates regardless of which party dies first, the contract applies to the survivor's ***own property*** as well as to the property that passed to her from the decedent.

b. **After-acquired property:** [§647]   Does the contract not to revoke apply only to property on hand when the first party died, or does it also apply to property ***subsequently acquired*** by the survivor?

(1) **General rule:** [§648]   The contract presumptively applies only to property owned by the two parties ***at the time of death*** of the first decedent. Thus, property thereafter acquired by the survivor could be devised by a later will. If, for example, the will contained language to the effect that "upon the death of the survivor of us, all of our said property" shall be distributed in a particular way, this would lead to a finding that "our ***said*** property" referred only to property on hand at the death of the first party. A will should not be construed to apply to after-acquired property "unless the intention to do so is set forth in the will by very plain, specific, and unambiguous language." [Murphy v. Slaton, 273 S.W.2d 588 (Tex. 1953)]

(2) **Exception:** [§649]   However, the particular language used may lead to a finding that the contract also applies to property acquired by the survivor after the first party's death. Thus, if the contractual will provides that "upon the death of the survivor, ***all of our property*** shall be distributed. . . ," this has been held to connote an intent that the contract was to apply to after-acquired property. [Weidner v. Crowther, 301 S.W.2d 621 (Tex. 1957)]

6. **Effect on Elective Share Right:** [§650]   A joint will that is contractual limits a spouse's elective share right to only that property **not subject** to the contractual will, if any. (*See supra*, §201 for discussion of elective share.)

    a.   **Example:** H and W execute a joint will that is held to be contractual. W dies; thereafter, H remarries. On H's subsequent death, his second wife files an election to take a statutory share of H's estate. H's "estate" against which the elective share applies does **not** include property subject to a contractual will. Under such a will, the survivor "really took but an interest during his life with a power to use or otherwise dispose of principal, and the named beneficiaries [of the contract] took the interest which remained [on his death]. Under such circumstances, he had no property interest in these assets against which the widow's right of election could operate." [Rubenstein v. Mueller, *supra*, §201]

D. CONTRACT NOT TO MAKE A WILL

1. **Introduction:** [§651]   Less frequently litigated are cases involving an alleged promise to die intestate (*i.e.*, to not make a will). Such agreements are **not** against public policy, and they are enforceable if supported by **consideration**. [32 A.L.R.2d 370]

2. **Statute of Frauds:** [§652]   If the property affected by a promise not to make a will includes real property, the courts are divided on whether the agreement must be evidenced by a memorandum that satisfies the Statute of Frauds.

    a.   **Majority rule:** [§653]   Most courts hold that the Statute of Frauds applies, since the agreement constitutes a contract for the sale of land. [Griffin v. Driver, 42 S.E.2d 368 (Ga. 1947); *In re* Heyer's Estate, 12 N.W.2d 520 (Iowa 1944)] Moreover, if the contract is invalid as to real property because of the Statute of Frauds, it is **also invalid** as to **personal** property in the estate; the contract is indivisible. [Wolf v. Rich, 121 P.2d 270 (Kan. 1942)]

    b.   **Minority rule:** [§654]   Several courts have held that the Statute of Frauds does not apply to such a contract, since the agreement has no necessary connection to any specific real property owned by the promisor. [Stahl v. Stevenson, 171 P.1164 (Kan. 1918)]

3. **Remedies:** [§655]   As with cases involving a promise to make a will or not to revoke a will, the remedy most commonly granted for breach of a contract not to make a will is in the nature of quasi-specific performance, under which a constructive trust is impressed against the decedent's personal representative or the beneficiaries under the will. [Asbaugh v. Davis, 227 P.2d 954 (Idaho 1951)]

IX. CHANGES IN BENEFICIARIES AND PROPERTY AFTER EXECUTION OF WILL

chapter approach

From the time a will is executed until the testator's death, a number of things can happen that may have an effect on the will's terms. A well-drafted will should cover all reasonably foreseeable contingencies that could affect the will's terms and should specify what is to happen if the indicated events occur. However, since well-drafted wills are no challenge to students, you will seldom see one on your exam. Rather, the will you are likely to encounter may require you to consider the rules and statutes in this chapter to handle the following contingencies:

1. **Lapsed Gifts:** One or more beneficiaries may predecease the testator, and you will need to determine what happens to their gifts. Watch for a lapse statute, which for certain beneficiaries will save the gift for the beneficiary's descendants. (If the lapse statute does not apply, the gift will usually pass to the residuary beneficiaries.)

2. **Class Gifts:** If the will leaves property to a class (_e.g._, someone's "children"), keep in mind that additional class members may be born or existing members may die. Your task is to identify who is part of the class and when class members are determined. (Here, the rule of convenience may apply, closing the class when any one member is entitled to take a share.)

3. **Ademption:** The will may make a **specific** bequest of property, but by the time the testator dies, the property is gone—either by testator's voluntary act (_e.g._, sale or gift) or through events beyond the testator's control (_e.g._, destruction). The general rule is that if property mentioned in a specific bequest is not in the estate at testator's death, the beneficiary is out of luck. But be sure to discuss the ways that courts sometimes try to avoid application of ademption (as by construing the gift as a general legacy) and the statutes that modify the common law rule.

4. **Stock Splits and Dividends:** The testator's ownership of specifically bequeathed corporate securities may be affected by the corporation's declaration of a stock split or stock dividend. Although the common law gives the beneficiary the additional shares due to a split, the beneficiary does **not** get the dividends. (The U.P.C. and other statutes give the beneficiary the additional stock in both cases.)

5. **Exoneration of Liens:** Testator may leave to a beneficiary a particular piece of property that has a mortgage still owing at testator's death. You need to determine who pays off the mortgage, the beneficiary or the estate (majority rule says the estate).

Remember that all of the above rules apply **only if the will doesn't make provisions** for these contingencies. If the will in your question states the testator's intent in such cases, be sure to follow the will.

A. LAPSED GIFTS

1. **Definition:** [§656]   A lapsed gift is one that was valid when the will was executed, but which fails due to the **subsequent** death, unwillingness, or other incapacity of the beneficiary to take the gift. The most commonly encountered reason for a gift to lapse is the death of a beneficiary during the testator's lifetime. However, a testamentary gift may lapse for some other reason; *e.g.*, the beneficiary may disclaim the gift. (*See supra*, §130.)

    a. **Death of beneficiary in testator's lifetime:** [§657]   If a will beneficiary dies during the testator's lifetime, the gift lapses because onc cannot make a gift to a dead person. A beneficiary must survive the testator to take under the will.

    b. **Uniform Simultaneous Death Act:** [§658]   As for whether a beneficiary has survived the testator, many jurisdictions have enacted the Uniform Simultaneous Death Act (discussed more fully *supra*, §§86-95). Under the Act, if two persons die under such circumstances that there is no sufficient evidence as to which of them survived, the property of each is distributed as though he survived. Thus if a testator and a will beneficiary die simultaneously, the testator's estate is distributed as though the beneficiary failed to survive the testator.

    c. **Uniform Probate Code 120-hour survival rule:** [§659]   Under the Uniform Probate Code and also in several non-U.P.C. states, a will beneficiary who does not survive the testator by 120 hours is deemed to have predeceased the testator (absent a contrary will provision). [U.P.C. §2-601; Tex. Prob. Code §47; *see supra*, §§96-102]

2. **Lapse Statutes:** [§660]   Nearly all jurisdictions have lapse statutes, which provide **substitute takers** if: (i) the predeceasing beneficiary was within a specified degree of relationship to the testator, **and** (ii) the beneficiary left descendants surviving the testator. Such descendants take the gift by substitution. These statutes are sometimes called "anti-lapse" statutes, which is actually a more descriptive title since the purpose of the statutes is to **prevent** gifts from lapsing. In a jurisdiction that has enacted the U.P.C.'s 120-hour survival rule, the lapse statute applies where a beneficiary is deemed to have predeceased the testator by failing to survive the testator by 120 hours.

    a. **Scope of lapse statutes:** [§661]   Not all cases in which a beneficiary predeceases the testator are covered by the lapse statute. The states' statutes vary widely as to their scope.

       (1) **Narrow statutes—descendants of testator:** [§662]   In many states, the lapse statute applies only if the predeceasing beneficiary was a child or other **descendant** of the testator. [Ill. Prob. Act §4-11; Tex. Prob. Code §68]

       (2) **Intermediate statutes—collateral kin:** [§663]   Under the Uniform Probate Code and in several non-U.P.C. states, the statute applies if the predeceasing beneficiary was a **grandparent** or a **lineal descendant of a grandparent** of the testator. [U.P.C. §2-605; Fla. Prob. Code §732-603] It should be noted

that the scope of the U.P.C. lapse statute coincides with the degree of relationship required for inheritance under the Uniform Probate Code. (*See supra,* §§15 *et seq.*) The New York statute, which also applies to certain collateral kindred, is much narrower in scope. It applies if the predeceasing beneficiary was an issue, brother, or sister of the testator. [N.Y. Est. Powers & Trusts Law §3-3.3]

(3) **Broad statutes:** [§664] In several states, the lapse statute applies if the predeceasing beneficiary was a child *or other relation* of the testator. [Mass. Ann. Laws ch. 194, §22; Wis. Stat. Ann. §238.13] Under such a broad statute, the only situation not covered by the lapse statute is one in which the predeceasing beneficiary was not related to the testator. *But note:* The testator's spouse is *not* considered a "relation" within the meaning of the statute. [Estate of Dodge, 84 N.W.2d 66 (Wis. 1957)]

  (a) **Compare:** Some statutes apply when *any beneficiary* (whether related or unrelated to the testator) dies before the testator. [Iowa Code Ann. §633.273; Va. Code Ann. §64.1-64] Thus, for example, if testator's will made a gift to a stepchild whom the testator did not adopt, and the stepchild predeceased the testator leaving descendants, the Massachusetts-type lapse statute would not apply [Estate of Sowash, 62 Cal. App. 512 (1923)], but the Iowa or Virginia statute would apply.

(4) **Example:** T's will devises Blackacre "to my nephew Norman." Norman is a child of T's sister. Norman predeceases T, leaving a child (Nancy) who survives T. If Illinois or Texas law applies (narrow statutes), the lapse statute does not operate because Norman was not a descendant of the testator. Under the Uniform Probate Code and in Florida (intermediate statutes), the statute applies, and Nancy, a descendant of T's grandparent, takes Blackacre by substitution under the lapse statute, but if New York law applies, the statute does not operate since Norman was a nephew (not a brother or sister) of the testator. If Massachusetts, Iowa, or Virginia law (broad statutes) applies, Nancy takes by substitution under the lapse statute.

b. **Substitute takers:** [§665] In nearly all states, the lapse statute operates only if the predeceasing beneficiary left descendants who survived the testator. Such descendants take the gift by substitution.

(1) **Example:** Tom's will bequeaths 1,000 shares of Acme stock "to my daughter Mary." Mary dies in Tom's lifetime, leaving a will that devises "all my property, including all of my interest in my father Tom's estate, to my husband Jack." Mary is survived by Jack and by her son Sam, both of whom also survive Tom. Sam takes the bequest of the Acme stock under the lapse statute. Mary's will cannot bequeath any interest in her father's estate to Jack because Mary had only an expectancy. The lapse statute does not save the gift for the deceased beneficiary's estate but rather designates the beneficiary's descendants as substitute takers.

(2) **Compare:** Consider the same facts as above, except that Sam also predeceases Tom. Thus, none of Mary's descendants survived the testator. The bequest of 1,000 shares of Acme stock lapses. The Acme stock falls into Tom's residuary estate as undisposed-of property.

(3) **Minority view:** [§666] In a few states, the predeceasing beneficiary's "heirs" take the devised property [Iowa Code Ann. §633.273], and in other states the property passes "to those persons who would have taken if the legatec had died, *testate or intestate,* owning the property" [Md. Est. & Trusts Code §4.403].

c. **Contrary will provision:** [§667] The lapse statute does not apply if the gift is contingent on the beneficiary's surviving the testator. For example, if the will makes a gift "to such of my children as are living at my death," this is a clear indication that only those children are to take; thus, the lapse statute does not operate in favor of the descendants of a child who predeceases the testator. [Estate of Leuer, 84 Misc. 2d 1087 (1976)]

(1) **Example:** T's will devises Blackacre "to my son John if he survives me." John predeceases T, leaving two children who survive T. The lapse statute does not operate in the children's favor. The gift to John was conditioned upon his surviving T. Since this condition was not satisfied, the gift fails according to its terms. [Rossi v. Rossi, 448 S.W.2d 162 (Tex. 1970); 63 A.L.R.2d 1172]

(2) **Minority view:** [§668] A handful of states would apply the above rule only if the will makes an alternate gift (*e.g.*, "to my son John if he survives me; but if he does not survive me, to my sister Sue"). If (as in the example immediately above) no alternate gift is made in the event of the beneficiary's nonsurvival, the beneficiary's descendants take under the lapse statute. The theory underlying this minority view is that lapse statutes are remedial and should receive a liberal construction in favor of the deceased beneficiary's descendants unless the testator has directed a different disposition. [Detzel v. Nieberding, 219 N.E.2d 327 (Ohio 1966)]

3. **Lapse of Specific Gift or General Legacy:** [§669] Absent a contrary will provision, a specific, demonstrative, or general bequest that lapses (and is *not* saved by the jurisdiction's lapse statute) falls into the residuary estate. [U.P.C. §2-606(a)]

a. **Residuary beneficiaries take:** [§670] If the will contains a residuary clause, the lapsed gifts pass to the residuary beneficiaries as undisposed-of property.

b. **Exception if narrow residuary clause:** [§671] Lapsed gifts pass under the residuary clause *only if* the clause is broad enough to encompass them. If, for example, the residuary clause makes a gift of "all of my remaining property, *other than the property I have referred to above,*" lapsed gifts in the preceding will provisions would not be caught by the residuary clause.

c. **No residuary clause:** [§672] If the will does not contain a residuary clause, or if gifts fall outside the clause (as above), lapsed gifts pass by *intestate succession*.

4. **Lapse of Residuary Gift:** [§673]   Suppose that testator's residuary estate is devised to two or more beneficiaries, one of the residuary beneficiaries predeceases the testator, and neither the will nor the state's lapse statute covers the situation. Does the share of the deceased beneficiary go to the remaining residuary beneficiaries, or does it pass by intestate succession?

   a. **Majority rule—no residue of a residue:** [§674]   At common law and in a majority of states today, the share of the deceased residuary beneficiary does **not** pass to the remaining residuary beneficiary unless the will so provides. Instead, that share "falls out of will" and passes by **intestacy** to the testator's heirs. [36 A.L.R.2d 1117] This is commonly referred to as the "no residue of a residue" rule, the theory being that the residuary clause cannot "catch" property that is itself a part of the residuary estate. The rule is also said to rest on the testator's intent that the residuary beneficiaries were to receive the indicated shares and no more.

   b. **Minority rule—surviving residuary beneficiaries take:** [§675]   The "no residue of a residue" rule has been criticized as being merely a play on words, and as inconsistent with the testator's general intent in most cases. The very fact that the testator has written a will is an indication that she probably would want her estate to go to the designated testamentary beneficiaries who survive her rather than to her heirs. Thus, the "no residue of a residue" rule has been rejected by a handful of courts [*see, e.g., In re* Frolich Estate, 295 A.2d 448 (N.H. 1972)], and an increasing number of states have enacted statutes providing that if the residue is devised to two or more persons and the share of one of the residuary devisees fails for any reason, his share passes to the other residuary devisees in proportion to their interests in the residue [U.P.C. §2-606(b); N.Y. Est. Powers & Trusts Law §3-3.4].

   c. **Caveat:** [§676]   It should be remembered that neither of the foregoing rules applies if the will contains *language covering the contingency* or if the *lapse statute* applies.

   (1) **Examples:** T's will devises her residuary estate "in equal shares to my daughter Ann, my brother Bill, and my cousin Charlie." Ann predeceases T, leaving a child (Arnie) who survives T. Bill also predeceases T, leaving no descendants. T dies; she is survived by Arnie and by Charlie.

      (a) *In a jurisdiction applying the "no residue for a residue" rule*, Charlie takes one-third of the residuary estate under the will, Arnie takes one-third under the lapse statute, and the one-third share devised to Bill passes by intestacy. (If T was a widow and Arnie was her only surviving descendant, Arnie would take another one-third share by intestate succession.)

      (b) *In a state applying the "surviving residuary beneficiaries" rule*, Arnie (substituted for Ann under the lapse statute) would take one-half of the residuary estate and Charlie would take the remaining one half.

      (c) *But the best solution* would have been careful drafting of T's will, providing for the above contingencies.

5. **Void Gifts:** [§677]   A void testamentary gift is one that was **never** valid, such that the gift could not be given effect even if the testator had died the moment after the will was executed.

    a. **When gift is void:** [§678]   A gift may be void for either of two reasons:

        (1) **Beneficiary dead when will executed:** [§679]   A testamentary gift is void if the beneficiary was dead or legally incapable of taking the gift at the time the will was executed. [3 A.L.R. 1673]

        (2) **Gift violates policy rule:** [§680]   A gift is void if it violates public policy or some rule of property law (*e.g.,* Rule Against Perpetuities) or violates some statutory rule (*e.g.,* statute restricting testamentary gifts to charities, *see supra,* §318).

    b. **Effect:** [§681]   In general, a void gift is treated the same as a lapsed gift. In the absence of statute or a controlling will provision, void specific gifts and general legacies fall into the residuary estate, while void residuary gifts either pass to the other residuary legatees or pass by intestate succession (*see above*).

    c. **Application of lapse statute:** [§682]   Whether a lapse statute applies to a void gift depends upon the language of the particular statute. For example, suppose that T executes a will that devises Blackacre "to my daughter Mary." Unbeknownst to T, Mary is dead at the time the will is executed. Thus, the gift is void. T dies some time later; he is survived by Mary's two children. Do the children take Blackacre by substitution under the state's lapse statute? The answer will turn on the wording of the statute. If the lapse statute applies "if a beneficiary dies **after the will is executed** but during the testator's lifetime," by its terms the statute does not cover the case of a void gift. On the other hand, if the statute covers "a beneficiary who predeceases the testator," it is at least possible to construe the statute as applying to void gifts.

        (1) **Majority rule:** [§683]   In a majority of states, the lapse statute applies to void gifts if the other requisites to the statute's operation are met. In several states, the statute expressly applies to cases in which the named beneficiary was dead when the will was executed. [U.P.C. §2-605; N.Y. Est. Powers & Trusts Law §3-3.3] (The rule may be different, however, if a class gift, rather than a gift to an individually-named beneficiary, is involved; *see below*.) In states in which the lapse statute does not explicitly cover void gifts, courts point to the remedial nature of the statute and conclude that the testator probably would want the property to pass to the designated beneficiary's descendant under the statute.

        (2) **Minority rule:** [§684]   In a minority of states, the lapse statute has been held **not** to apply to void gifts. As noted above, in some states the literal wording of the statute precludes its application to a situation where the beneficiary was dead when the will was executed. In cases in which the statute is unclear, some courts have held that a void gift cannot lapse because, being void, it was never a gift.

B. CLASS GIFTS

1. **Definitional Problems:** [§685] When a gift is made to a class of persons, such as the "children," "brothers and sisters," "descendants," or "heirs" of a named beneficiary, questions sometimes arise as to what persons were intended to be included within the class designation. This section outlines the rules applied by the courts *in the absence of a controlling will provision.*

    a. **Children**

        (1) **Grandchildren not included:** [§686] A gift to someone's "children" includes descendants *in the first degree only.* Such a gift does not include grandchildren unless the will as a whole shows an "unmistakable intent" that the term "children" has been used in other than its dictionary meaning, *i.e.,* that it has been used synonymously with "issue" or "descendants." [Villalonga's Will, 6 N.Y.2d 477 (1959); Barnum's Will, 29 App. Div. 2d 945 (1968)]

        (2) **Children by all marriages included:** [§687] In the absence of a contrary indication, a gift to A's "children" includes children of all of A's marriages, and not just the children of A's present marriage.

        (3) **Adopted children**

            (a) **Former law—"stranger to the adoption" rule:** [§688] Adoption, which derives from Roman law, was unknown to the common law. The first American jurisdiction to recognize adoptive status was Massachusetts (by statute in 1851). Even after the adoptive relationship came to be widely recognized, for a long time judicial decisions favored relations by blood over relations by adoption. Thus, until the 1960's, in most states a gift to someone's "children," "descendants," "issue," etc., presumptively included adopted children *only* if the will, deed, or trust being construed was that of the *adopting parent*—the idea being that the adopting parent would intend to include his adopted children along with natural children. But if the will, etc., being construed was that of a "stranger to the adoption" (*i.e.,* anyone other than the adopting parent), a gift to someone's children, etc., presumptively did *not* include adopted offspring. [86 A.L.R.2d 12]

            (b) **Majority rule today:** [§689] In most states today, either by statute or case law, a gift to someone's "children," "issue," "descendants," etc., presumptively *includes* adopted children. [U.P.C. §2-611; N.Y. Est. Powers & Trusts Law §2-1.3(a); Estate of Coe, 201 A.2d 571 (N.J. 1964); Vaughn v. Gunter, 461 S.W.2d 599 (Tex. 1970)]

                1) **But note:** Where a will creates various gifts for A's existing children and provides for additional trusts for children "*born to* my son after my death," the reference "born to" has been held to *preclude*

adopted children from sharing in the trusts. [Vaughn v. Vaughn, 337 S.W.2d 793 (Tex. 1960)]

(c) **Adoption of adult:** [§690]   What if a person adopts an adult for the purpose of allowing him to inherit? For example, suppose that a will creates a trust: "Income to my son John for life, and on John's death, principal to his children" (or "issue"). After the testator's death, John, who is childless, adopts his adult nephew for the purpose of making the nephew a remainderman. Should the adopted person be allowed to take the remainder interest?

1) **Majority rule:** [§691]   Most courts have allowed the adopted adult to take, as long as the controlling law does not preclude the adoption of adults. [Estate of Stanford, 49 Cal. 2d 120 (1957); Estate of Fortney, 611 P.2d 599 (Kan. 1980)]

2) **Minority rule:** [§692]   Other courts have ruled otherwise, reasoning that the adoption of an adult for the sole purpose of enabling the person to take under the will was not within the testator's intent or contemplation. [Estate of Tafel, 296 A.2d 797 (Pa. 1972)—rule codified in Penn. Stat. Ann. §2514(7)] In some states, an adopted adult is included within a class gift only if raised as a member of the adopting parent's household from the age of fifteen or before. [Wis. Stat. Ann. §851.51(3)]

(4) **Children born out of wedlock**

(a) **Majority rule:** [§693]   At common law and by majority rule today, a gift to someone's "children," "issue," and the like does *not* include children born out of wedlock unless the will shows an intent that they were to be included. [34 A.L.R.2d 4]

1) **Extrinsic evidence admissible:** [§694]   Testator's intention to include children born out of wedlock can be shown by express statements or by necessary implication from words in the will. Such an intent also can be shown by surrounding facts and circumstances. For example, if the child was raised as a member of a person's family, a gift to the person's "children" may be construed as including the illegitimate child. [*In re* Trust of Parsons, 203 N.W.2d 40 (Wis. 1957)]

2) **Only illegitimate children at execution:** [§695]   If the named person had only illegitimate children when the will was executed, some cases have taken the position that a gift to "children" includes children born out of wedlock, the theory being that these must have been the children that the testator had in mind.

(b) **Minority rule:** [§696]   The Uniform Probate Code adopts a rule of construction that a gift to "children" presumptively *includes* children born out of wedlock to the **mother**, but a child born out of wedlock is **not** treated as the child of the father unless openly and notoriously so treated by the father. [U.P.C. §2-611] Some courts have cited "changing societal attitudes" toward illegitimate children in ruling that a gift to somcone's children presumptively includes children born out of wedlock. [Will of Hoffman, 53 App. Div. 2d 55 (1976)]

b. **"Issue"; "descendants":** [§697]   A gift to someone's "issue" presumptively includes lineal descendants of any degree (children, grandchildren, etc.). The terms "issue" and "descendants" are generally held to be synonymous.

   (1) **Limited to legitimate or adopted issue:** [§698]   Under the traditional view, "issue" and "descendants" were interpreted as meaning natural, legitimate issue only, thereby excluding adopted or illegitimate offspring. [86 A.L.R.2d 12] But as indicated above (§689), by majority rule today a gift to "issue" or "descendants" presumptively **includes adopted offspring** [U.P.C. §2-611; N.Y. Est. Powers & Trusts Law 1-2.10(a)]; however, illegitimate children are **not** included.

   (2) **Per stirpes distribution:** [§699]   Whenever a gift is made to the "issue" or "descendants" of someone, absent a contrary expression of intent, the issue or descendants who are alive when the distribution is to be made (testator's death, if an outright gift by will; death of life tenant, if a remainder interest) take per stirpes; *i.e.,* by representation. [Clark v. Clark, 159 A.2d 362 (Md. 1960); Wilkes v. Wilkes, 488 S.W.2d 398 (Tex. 1972)]

c. **"Heirs":** [§700]   A gift to someonc's "hcirs" is interpreted as meaning those persons who would take the person's estate if she had died **intestate**. As a general rule the courts refer to the laws of intestate succession in effect at the time of the testator's death. [65 A.L.R.2d 1408]

d. **Other family terms:** [§701]   Other terms such as "relatives," "family," or "kin" are generally interpreted as being synonymous with "heirs"—those who would take the named person's estate according to the laws of descent and distribution—unless, of course, there is a showing of contrary intent by the testator. [N.Y. Est. Powers & Trusts Law §2-1.1]

   (1) **Compare—"friends":** [§702]   Terms such as "relatives" and the like represent the outer limit on how far a court will go in giving meaning to "class gift" terms used by a testator in a will. A gift to a person's *"friends"* is beyond the pale. It is **void** for vagueness, and the gift fails for want of clearly identified beneficiaries. Extrinsic evidence is **not** admissible to show whom the testator intended to include within the term "friends."

e. **Brothers and sisters:** [§703]   By majority rule, a gift to someone's "brothers and sisters" is construed to include half-brothers and half-sisters as well as siblings of the whole blood, in the absence of a contrary expression of intent.

f. **"Cousins"; "nieces and nephews":** [§704]   A gift to someone's "cousins" includes *first cousins only* (*i.e.,* children of aunts and uncles), absent a contrary expression of intent. The words "nieces and nephews" presumptively refer to the children of brothers and sisters.

2. **Constructional Problems:** [§705]   Besides deciding what is meant by the terms "issue," "children," etc., the courts sometimes face problems in determining who is to be included in the class. For example, suppose T executes a will that devises Blackacre "to the children of my brother John." At the time the will is executed in 1975, John has two children, A and B. Between 1975 and T's death in 1986, A dies, and John has another child C. Two years after T's death, John has another child D. Who takes Blackacre? If the will had made a disposition "to the children of my brother John *who are living at my death*," there would be no problem in identifying the takers of the gift: B and C would take. But all too often, the will does not specify the time to determine which persons qualify as takers of the class gift (the "members" of the class). This section outlines the rules of construction applied by the courts in determining the takers under a gift to a class.

a. **Death of class member in testator's lifetime—class gift rule:** [§706]   If a testamentary gift is made to a class of persons and some class member predeceases the testator, and if the will does *not* cover the contingency, the class members who *survive the testator* take the gift. This is called the "class gift rule." The gift is interpreted as applying to the members of the class alive at the testator's death. [33 A.L.R.2d 242]

(1) **Rationale:** The best way to understand the rationale of the class gift rule is to contrast it with the treatment of a gift to named individuals. Suppose that in the example above T's will devises Blackacre "to my brother John's children, A, B, and C in equal shares," and devises T's residuary estate to the American Cancer Society. A predeceases T, and assume that the case is not covered by the state's lapse statute. The gift of A's one-third share lapses and falls into the residuary estate (*see supra,* §669). The Cancer Society becomes a tenant in common with B and C. The rationale of the class gift rule is that where the testator did not name the beneficiaries individually, but instead designated a "class" of persons as beneficiaries, she would not want that result to occur. Thus, in this example, where John's child A died in T's lifetime, T probably would not want A's share of the gift to lapse and fall into the residuary estate, for that would mean that a "stranger to the class" would own a share of Blackacre. Instead, T probably wanted the children of John, as a class constituted at her death, *and only that group*, to share in the ownership of Blackacre.

(2) **Lapse statute:** [§707]   If the class member who predeceases the testator is within the degree of relationship covered by the state's lapse statute, and if he left descendants who survived the testator, do the descendants take by substitution under the lapse statute?

(a) **Majority rule:** [§708]   Many lapse statutes expressly apply to class gifts, as long as the other elements of the statute are met. [U.P.C. §2-605;

Cal. Prob. Code §6147(b); Fla. Prob. Code §732.602; Va. Code Ann. §64.1-64] In the majority of states in which the lapse statute does not expressly refer to class gifts, cases have held that the statute does apply to such gifts. In these states, the class gift rule ("surviving class members take") gives way to the lapse statute if the predeceasing class member is within the degree of relationship covered by the statute. [56 A.L.R.2d 948]

1) **Example:** T's will devises Blackacre "to the children of my daughter Mary." At the time the will is executed, Mary has three children, Ann, Bill, and Carl. Carl predeceases T, leaving two children, Celia and Cedric. On T's death, Celia and Cedric take one-sixth shares under the lapse statute and are tenants in common with Ann and Bill (who take one-third each).

    a) **Note:** If Carl did not leave any descendants who survived T, the lapse statute would not apply. Ann and Bill would take Blackacre under the class gift rule since they are the class members alive at T's death.

(b) **Minority rule:** [§709]   A minority of courts hold that the lapse statute does not apply to class gifts. Since under the "class gift" rule the surviving class members take the bequest, there is no lapse on which the statute can operate.

b. **Death of class member before will's execution:** [§710]   A problem arises as to whether the lapse statute should apply to a case where the class member dies before the will is executed. For instance, suppose that T executes a will that bequeaths property "to my brothers and sisters." T has two living brothers and two sisters at the time the will is executed, but another brother had died leaving two children. If "brothers and sisters" are within the scope of the jurisdiction's lapse statute (*see supra*, §§661-664), does the lapse statute operate in favor of the predeceased brother's two children?

(1) **Majority rule:** [§711]   In most states, the lapse statute does ***not*** apply in this situation. [N.Y. Est. Powers & Trusts Law §3-3.3] The reason is that it is more logical to assume that the testator intended to benefit only her living brothers and sisters, and did not intend to confer a benefit on a deceased brother (or the brother's descendants). [Drafts v. Drafts, 114 So. 2d 473 (Fla. 1959)]

(2) **Uniform Probate Code:** [§712]   The U.P.C.'s lapse statute applies to a class member (who was the testator's grandparent or descendant of a grandparent) "whether his death occurred before or after the execution of the will." [U.P.C. §2-605] "It still seems likely that the testator would want the issue of a person included in a class term but dead when the will is made to be treated like the issue of another member who was alive at the time the will was executed but who died before the testator." [U.P.C. §2-605, Comment]

c. **Closing the class—the rule of convenience:** [§713]   In determining the "member-ship" of the class (*i.e.,* the maximum number of takers to share in the class gift), the common law courts worked out the "rule of convenience." This is a rule of construction that applies in the absence of a contrary expression of intent. Under the rule, a class closes, which simply means that later-born class members are excluded from sharing the gift, when *some member* of the class is *entitled to a distribution* of his share of the class gift. [6 A.L.R.2d 1342] The class closes at that time so that the minimum size of each class member's share can be determined, permitting a distribution that will not be subject to recall or rebate later on.

(1) **Outright gift by will:** [§714]   If a will makes an outright gift to a class, *the class closes on the testator's death* if any members of the class are alive at that time. Thus, in the example of a gift "to the children of my brother John" in §705, *supra,* the class closes at T's death, and D is excluded from sharing in the gift. D loses out because he was born after the time for distribution of the gift had arrived.

(a) **Rationale:** The above result is based on the presumed intent of the ordinary testator. Since this was a gift to a class and not to named individuals, the testator probably intended to include all members who fit the description, whenever born, *as long as this would not cause any undue inconvenience.* The rule of convenience closes the class at testator's death because the testator would probably want as early a distribution as possible, so that the beneficiaries can begin enjoying the property. Any alternative solutions (making partial distributions but withholding some property to provide for John's future children; making a full distribution but requiring the distributees to return a portion if John has any more children) are inconvenient and disruptive to property ownership and enjoyment. Unless the class is closed at testator's death, final determination of ownership will be delayed—possibly for a very long time.

1) **Example:** In the example giving Blackacre to the children of T's brother John, an additional class member, C, was born prior to T's death. C is included in the class because she fits the description ("the children of my brother John") and because no inconvenience results from including her. But D, born two years after T's death, loses out. The class closes at T's death so that B and C can begin enjoying the property. It would be inconvenient to hold the class open (or make a partial distribution, etc.) to include other children born to John. In fact, John could live a long time and have many more children. To avoid this problem of waiting to distribute the property until John's death (the only time one can be sure that John will have no more children), courts use the rule of convenience.

(b) **Child in gestation:** [§715]   Under the gestation principle, children in gestation at the time for closing the class, if later born alive, are treated as being alive at the time the class closed. Thus, if D had been born within 280 days after testator's death, he presumptively would have been included in the class.

(c) **No class members:** [§716] If there are no class members in existence when the will is executed or on the testator's death, all class members, ***whenever born***, are included in the class. The theory here is that the testator knew that there was the possibility that no class members would be alive at her death, and that distribution and enjoyment might be postponed beyond her death.

(2) **Postponed gifts:** [§717] The rule of convenience applies to postponed gifts—*i.e.*, gifts that take effect some time after testator's death. The class closes at the time some member is entitled to a distribution.

  (a) **Example:** T's will creates a trust, to pay the income to her husband H for life, and on H's death to distribute the corpus "to the children of my sister Sue." At the time T executes her will, Sue has two children (A and B). After T's death, but during the lifetime of her husband H, Sue has another child, C. Then H dies; two years later Sue has another child, D. Under the rule of convenience, the class closes and its maximum membership is determined when H dies and his life estate comes to an end. A, B, and C each take a one-third share.

  (b) **Note:** In this case, there is no need to close the class at the testator's death, because the class gift is not to be distributed at that time. There was no inconvenience in leaving the class open until the life tenant's death, for the time has not yet come for distribution of the corpus. But when H dies, it is time to make a distribution, and the class closes. D is excluded by the rule of convenience (unless he was in gestation at the time of W's death) because he was born after the time set for distribution. (*See* Future Interests Summary.)

(3) **Per capita gifts:** [§718] The rule of convenience may apply to per capita gifts. For instance, suppose T's will makes legacies of $10,000 "to each of my brother John's children." This is ***not*** a class gift, because the size of each beneficiary's gift will not fluctuate and is not determined by the number of children that John has. However, the identity of the beneficiaries is determined by reference to a class. The problem thus is a different one: How many gifts of $10,000 are to be made? The size of the residuary estate cannot be determined, and the residuary gift cannot be distributed, until the number of legacies is known. If the class were to remain open after the testator's death, distribution of the entire estate would be postponed until John died, for John could have or adopt children until his death. Hence, courts prefer a rule of construction that immediately determines the number of class members.

  (a) **Living children:** [§719] If there are children living at the ***testator's death***, the class closes at that time. Those children (including children in gestation) take legacies. Later-born children are excluded.

  (b) **No children:** [§720] If there are no children of John living at testator's death, the ***gift fails.*** This is again based on the supposed inconvenience of postponing determination of the class membership. The principle of prompt distribution controls, and the per capita gift to John's children fails, in order to facilitate the administration and distribution of the testator's estate. [Rogers v. Mutch, 10 Ch. Div. 25 (1878)]

(c) **Compare—contrary intent in will:** [§721]   If the testator in her will indicates that all children of John, whether born before **or after** her death, shall have $10,000 legacies, then the executor must set aside enough money to meet such legacies; the gift does not fail. All of these "rules of convenience" are rules of construction based on presumed intent, not rules of law. The constructional rules apply in the absence of a clear expression of intent.

C.   CLASSIFICATION OF TESTAMENTARY GIFTS

1. **Importance of Classification:** [§722]   There are four classes of testamentary gifts: specific, demonstrative, general, and residuary. Classification of testamentary gifts may be important for one of the following reasons: Classification establishes the **order of distribution and abatement** if the estate's assets, after the payment of creditors' claims, are insufficient to satisfy all of the gifts made by the will. (*See infra*, §§998 *et seq.*) The doctrine of ademption by extinction is applicable only to specific devises and bequests. Also, the doctrine of satisfaction of legacies (*supra*, §§115 *et seq.*) is generally applicable only to certain classes of testamentary gifts.

2. **Specific Devise or Bequest:** [§723]   A specific gift is a gift of a **particular item** of real or personal property that is capable of being **identified and distinguished** from all other property in the testator's estate. A specific devise or bequest can be satisfied only by the distribution of the specific asset.

   a. **Examples:** A gift of "Blackacre," "all of my household furnishings," "all of my land in Tarrant County"—all of these are specific gifts, because particular property is described thereby. A gift of "the balance in my bank account at First Federal Bank" is specific because, although the amount is unspecified, the gift is nevertheless identifiable and definite, apart from all other funds or property in the testator's estate. [Willis v. Barrow, 119 So. 768 (Ala. 1929)]

3. **Demonstrative Legacy:** [§724]   A demonstrative legacy is a gift of a general amount to be paid from a **specific source or a particular fund**—*e.g.*, "I bequeath $10,000 to my niece Nellie, to be paid out of proceeds from the sale of my Acme stock."

   a. **Comment:** A demonstrative legacy is, in a sense, a hybrid. It is treated the same as a specific bequest to the extent that the fund or property from which it is to be satisfied is on hand at the testator's death. And yet it is treated the same as a general legacy (below) to the extent that it must be satisfied from general assets of the estate. A demonstrative legacy has the advantage of a specific bequest for purposes of determining its priority in the order of abatement, and yet receives the benefits of being treated as a general bequest for purposes of ademption by extinction (*see* below).

4. **General Legacy:** [§725]   A general legacy is a gift that is payable out of the ***general assets*** of the estate and which does not require delivery of any specific asset or satisfaction from any designated portion of the testator's property—*e.g.*, "I bequeath the sum of $10,000 to my nephew Ned."

5. **Residuary Estate:** [§726]   The residuary estate consists of the ***balance*** of the testator's real or personal property on hand after payment of administration expenses, taxes, and claims against the estate, ***and after*** satisfaction of all specific, general, and demonstrative bequests.

D. ADEMPTION

1. **General Rule:** [§727]   If specifically devised property is not in the testator's estate at the time of death, the gift is ***adeemed;*** *i.e.*, it fails. [61 A.L.R.2d 449] This is sometimes referred to as the doctrine of ***ademption by extinction***, to distinguish it from ademption by satisfaction (*see supra*, §§115 *et seq.*).

    a. **Gifts affected:** [§728]   The doctrine of ademption applies ***only*** to ***specific*** devises and bequests. Ademption does not apply to demonstrative or general legacies.

        (1) **Example:** T's will bequeaths "my Cobichon diamond ring to Alan," and bequeaths "$5,000, to be paid out of the proceeds of sale of my Acme stock, to Betty." Thereafter, T's Cobichon diamond ring is stolen; and T sells all of her Acme stock to finance a vacation trip. Neither of these assets is in T's estate at her death. The gift of the Cobichon diamond ring is a specific bequest. Ademption applies; Alan takes nothing. However, the gift of "$5,000, to be paid out of the proceeds of the sale of my Acme stock" is a demonstrative legacy. Ademption does not apply to demonstrative legacies. Betty is entitled to $5,000. Other assets will have to be sold, if necessary, to raise the $5,000 to be distributed to Betty.

    b. **Partial ademption:** [§729]   Ademption need not be of the entire gift; it applies pro tanto where only a portion of the gift has been disposed of. [N.Y. Est. Powers & Trusts Law §3-4.3] If, for example, T executes a will that devises a large tract of land and then sells a portion of the tract, ademption applies to the portion of property not in the estate at T's death. The remaining portion in the estate at death passes to the specific beneficiary.

    c. **Doctrine does not apply to post-death changes:** [§730]   The doctrine of ademption applies only to changes in specifically devised property occurring ***prior*** to the testator's death. Hence, acts done by an executor that affect specific bequeathed property after the testator's death are not subject to the doctrine, and the devisee is entitled to compensation for loss or sale of the property. [Shymer's Estate, 136 Misc. 334 (1930)]

2. **Role of Testator's Intent:** [§731]   At common law and in most states today, application of the ademption doctrine involves an ***objective*** test; the doctrine applies without regard to the testator's probable intent. This is sometimes referred to as the "identity" or

"in specie" theory: The only issue is whether the specifically bequeathed property can be identified as being in testator's estate at his death. [Ashburner v. McGuire, 29 Eng. Rep. 62 (1786)] Thus, it does not matter whether the property is not in the estate due to an act of the testator (*e.g.,* sale of the property), an act of God (*e.g.,* tornado), or an act of a third person (*e.g.,* withdrawal of funds in a bank account pursuant to a power of attorney). [McGee v. McGee, 413 A.2d 72 (R.I. 1980)] If the specifically bequeathed asset is not in the estate **for any reason,** the gift is adeemed. [119 A.L.R. 1383]

a. **Examples**

(1) **Condemnation proceedings:** [§732]   T's will devises Blackacre to B. Between the will's execution and T's death, Blackacre is taken by the state in eminent domain proceedings, and the condemnation award is paid to T's executor after T's death. The gift is **adeemed,** even though it is arguable that since T's loss of ownership was from an act beyond his control, T would have wanted B to have at least the condemnation award. [Ametrano v. Downs, 170 N.Y. 388 (1902)]

(2) **Similar asset:** [§733]   T's will bequeaths "my gold watch to my friend, Alice." After the will's execution, T sells the gold watch and uses the exact amount of the sale proceeds to purchase a gold pendant. Ademption operates, because the testamentary gift was of a gold watch, not some other object. If the subject matter of a specific bequest or devise is sold by the testator, the gift is adeemed, and neither the proceeds nor similar items purchased with the proceeds go to the beneficiary.

(3) **Executory contract:** [§734]   T's will devises Blackacre to S. Thereafter, T enters into a specifically enforceable contract to sell Blackacre to Y. The contract is still executory at T's death. Under the doctrine of equitable conversion (*see* Property Summary), the vendee (Y) is deemed to own Blackacre from the moment the contract becomes specifically enforceable, and the vendor (T) is deemed to own a chose in action—a right to compel payment of the remaining sale proceeds. Thus, T no longer owned Blackacre at his death, and the gift to S is adeemed. S is not entitled to Blackacre nor the remaining proceeds of sale under the contract. [Estate of Hills, 564 P.2d 462 (Kan. 1977)]

(a) **Compare:** In the foregoing example, if T's will did not devise "Blackacre," but instead devised "all of my interest in Blackacre," some courts have held that ademption does **not** apply. Notwithstanding the doctrine of equitable conversion, T did have at death an **interest** in Blackacre—*i.e.,* the right to the remaining contract payments secured by a vendor's lien. Under this rationale, S would be entitled to the remaining contract payments and the security interest.

(b) **Comment:** Moreover, if at T's death, specific performance would not be available because some material condition to the contract's performance had not been satisfied (*see* Property Summary), equitable conversion would not apply. T's interest in Blackacre (the right to the remaining contract payments and the security interest) would pass to S.

(4) **Casualty insurance proceeds:** [§735]   T's will bequeaths "my two-carat diamond ring" to X. The ring is stolen shortly before T's death, and shortly thereafter $10,000 is paid to T's executor under an insurance policy that covered the theft. X is not entitled to the ring because it was not owned by T at her death. X is not entitled to the insurance proceeds because the will did not give X insurance proceeds. The gift to X is adeemed. [*In re* Wright's Will, 7 N.Y.2d 365 (1960)]

b. **Policy:** [§736]   The identity theory (majority rule) has been criticized for failing to take into account the actual intent of the testator, especially in cases in which the property is not in the estate because of something other than a volitional act of the testator. However, the objective approach has the advantage of simplicity of application and predictability of result, and it eliminates speculation as to what testator's actual intent may have been. To permit extrinsic evidence as to testator's probable intent would result in property passing on the basis of oral testimony rather than pursuant to the writing contained in the testator's duly executed will. [McGee v. McGee, *supra*, §731]

c. **Avoiding ademption:** [§737]   Although the courts in many states declare that the testator's intention is immaterial, various techniques have been developed by the courts to avoid the doctrine's application.

(1) **Construction as general legacy:** [§738]   Some courts will classify a bequest as general rather than specific wherever possible, in order to avoid ademption. This constructional approach is encountered most frequently with respect to bequests of ***shares of stock.***

(a) **Example:** T's will bequeaths "my 200 shares of Baker stock" to B and "100 shares of Centex stock" to C. Thereafter, T sells all of her Baker and Centex stock. Since the gift of Baker stock was a specific bequest ("***my*** 200 shares"), ademption applies and B takes nothing. However, most courts reach a different result with respect to the Centex stock. Here the courts seize on the absence of the possessive pronoun "my" and hold that this was not a specific gift of stock for ademption purposes. Rather, it was a general legacy of the ***value*** of 100 shares of Centex stock. This result is reached even if T owned exactly 100 shares of Centex stock at the time she wrote the will. C is entitled to the date-of-death value of 100 shares of Centex stock. [Will of Blomdahl, 258 N.W. 168 (Wis. 1938); Estate of Mahoney, 88 Misc. 2d 499 (1976)]

(b) **Compare:** Suppose, however, that T did not sell the Centex stock and, thereafter, the Centex stock ***split*** two-for-one. The gift of "100 shares of Centex stock" would be treated as a specific bequest for purposes of determining whether the beneficiary is entitled to the stock split (*see infra*, §§752 *et seq.*).

(2) **Construction as referring to property owned at death:** [§739] Even where the language of the gift is such that it cannot be classified as general, it may be construed as referring to an asset in the estate at death rather than an asset owned at the time the will was executed.

    (a) **Example:** T's will devises "the residence which I now own" to B. Normally, such a gift would be construed to refer to the residence owned by T at the time of the will's execution. Under this construction, if T later replaced that residence with another, B would take nothing. However, to prevent ademption, the court may construe the gift as applicable to the residence owned by T *at death.* [Lusk's Estate, 9 A.2d 363 (Pa. 1939)]

    (b) **Example:** Some courts have gone so far as to hold that a gift of "that certain Hudson automobile *now* owned by me" is not adeemed when T thereafter trades that car for a new Hudson which he owned at death. [Estate of Cooper, 107 Cal. App. 2d 592 (1951)]

(3) **Construction as change in form:** [§740]   Ademption does *not* apply where there is only a *slight* change in the form or name of the asset. Of course, there may be a problem in determining what constitutes a change in "form," as distinguished from a change in "identity." Changes in the name of a corporation or partnership are ordinarily considered formal changes, which do *not* result in ademption. Similarly, most courts have held that a gift of "my bank account at Travis Bank" is not adeemed by transfer of the account to another bank: the gift is of the *funds,* wherever located. [Willis v. Barrow, *supra,* §723; *In re* Hall, 160 A.2d 49 (N.J. 1960)]

    (a) **Incorporation of business:** [§741]   Where a will gives the testator's interest in a partnership and thereafter the business is incorporated, *no ademption* occurs since the change is one of form and not of substance. Thus, the beneficiary takes all of testator's interest (now shares of stock) in the business. [Estate of Block, 91 Misc. 2d 92 (1977)]

    (b) **Merger:** [§742]   A merger may result in only a slight change in form. For example, where T's will bequeaths "my eighteen shares of Farmers' Bank stock" to G, and thereafter, Farmers' Bank mergers with Deposit Bank to form Farmers' Deposit Bank, leaving T at death owning eighteen shares of Farmers' Deposit Bank stock, most courts hold that G takes the eighteen shares of stock since the change is purely formal. "The likeness of the new shares to the old is more important than their differences." [Goode v. Reynolds, 271 S.W. 600 (Ky. 1925); U.P.C. §2-607(a)(3)]

(4) **Gifts of proceeds of sale:** [§743]   If the will directs that an item of property be sold and the *proceeds* given to a specific beneficiary, the beneficiary may be entitled to proceeds even if the testator sells the property before his death. Thus, if T's will directs the executor to sell Blackacre and distribute the sale proceeds to B, and thereafter T enters into an installment contract for the sale of Blackacre, receiving some of the installment payments before his death, the

gift is adeemed as to the installments received by T during his lifetime. However, B is entitled to the balance remaining payable after T's death. The theory here is that since the testamentary gift was not of Blackacre but of the sale proceeds, B should receive the sale proceeds whether the sale was made by the testator or by the executor. [45 A.L.R.3d 10]

3. **Statutory Modifications:** [§744]   The Uniform Probate Code and statutes in a number of states have ameliorated operation of the common law rule of ademption in certain well-defined situations.

   a. **Casualty insurance proceeds:** [§745]   By statute in several states, where casualty insurance proceeds for the loss, theft, or destruction of specifically bequeathed property are paid after the testator's death, the beneficiary is entitled to the insurance proceeds. [U.P.C. §2-608(b); Fla. Prob. Code §732.606; N.Y. Est. Powers & Trusts Law §3-4.5]

   b. **Condemnation award:** [§746]   In several states, a statute provides that if specifically devised property is taken by eminent domain before testator's death and the condemnation award is paid *after* death, the specific beneficiary is entitled to the condemnation award. [U.P.C. §2-608]

   c. **Executory contract:** [§747]   Several states have statutes that overturn the common law ademption rule where specifically devised property is subject to an executory contract or installment contract at testator's death. (*See supra*, §734.) Under these statutes, the beneficiary is entitled to all of testator's rights under the contract: the remaining contract payments and any security interest retained by the testator-vendor. [N.Y. Est. Powers & Trusts Law §3-4.6]

   d. **Compare—pre-death payments:** [§748]   The foregoing statutory rules relating to the payment of sale proceeds, condemnation awards, and insurance proceeds on specifically devised property operate *only* to the extent that the proceeds, etc., are paid *after* the testator's death. If the contract is fully performed during testator's lifetime, or if the insurance proceeds or condemnation award are paid to the testator during his lifetime, the statutes have no application. Ademption applies, and the specific beneficiary takes nothing. [N.Y. Est. Powers & Trusts Law §3-4.3] The theory here is that the testator presumably had the opportunity to amend or revise his will to reflect the loss, sale, or taking of the property, but did not do so.

   e. **Changes in securities:** [§749]   Under the U.P.C., where a will makes a specific bequest of securities (*i.e.*, stocks and bonds), the beneficiary is entitled to securities in another entity owned by the testator as a result of merger, consolidation, reorganization, or other similar action initiated by the entity. [U.P.C. §2-607]

   f. **Property under guardianship:** [§750]   Under the U.P.C. and in several non-U.P.C. states, if a person executes a will and later becomes incompetent, and if specifically devised property is sold by the guardian, or a condemnation award or insurance proceeds are paid to the guardian for such property, the devisee is entitled to a general pecuniary legacy equal to the net sale price, condemnation award, or insurance proceeds. [U.P.C. §2-608(a); Fla. Prob. Code §732.606]

(1) **Note:** Other statutes give a narrower remedy in this situation. The specific beneficiary is entitled to the sale proceeds, condemnation award, or insurance proceeds, but only to the extent that the sale proceeds can be traced. [N.Y. Est. Powers & Trusts Law §3-4.6] Under the latter type of statute, if the sale proceeds are expended by the guardian for the ward's care, the gift is adeemed and the specific beneficiary takes nothing.

4. **Satisfaction of Legacies:** [§751] Where, after executing a will, the testator makes a gift to a person who is a general or residuary legatee under the will, the gift may be held to have been in partial or total satisfaction of the legacy—***provided*** the testator intended that result. The "satisfaction of legacies" doctrine is discussed *supra*, §§115 *et seq.*

   a. **Compare:** In general, the doctrine of satisfaction of legacies applies only to general legacies and residuary gifts. It does not apply to specific devises and bequests. Suppose, for example, that T's will bequeaths "my ten-speed Schwinn bike" to B, and thereafter T gives the bike to B. This case does ***not*** involve the doctrine of satisfaction of legacies but, instead, results in ***ademption by extinction*** since the bike will not be in T's estate at his or her death.

E. STOCK SPLITS AND STOCK DIVIDENDS

1. **Introduction:** [§752] Suppose that a will makes a specific bequest to a beneficiary of "my 100 shares of Telecom stock." After the will's execution but before the testator's death, the stock splits two-for-one; or, alternatively, the corporation declares and pays a ten percent stock dividend. Is the beneficiary entitled to the additional shares produced by the stock split or stock dividend?

2. **Common Law**

   a. **Stock splits:** [§753] By majority rule, the specific beneficiary is entitled to the additional shares of stock produced by a stock split. [Fisher v. Paine, 311 P.2d 438 (Or. 1957)] Thus, if the Telecom stock splits two-for-one, the beneficiary is entitled to all 200 shares of Telecom stock.

      (1) **Rationale:** The 200 shares of stock on hand after the stock split represent the same proportionate share of corporate ownership as the 100 shares before the split.

      (2) **What constitutes a specific bequest of stock:** [§754] Suppose that the will did not make a gift of "***my*** 100 shares of Telecom stock" but instead made a gift of "100 shares of Telecom stock" (*i.e.*, without the possessive pronoun "my"). As has been pointed out, if the issue is ademption, many courts have held that this is a general legacy of the ***value*** of 100 shares of Telecom stock. Thus the beneficiary is entitled to the date-of-death value of 100 shares even though testator owns no Telecom stock at his death. (*See supra,* §738.) If, however, testator does not sell the Telecom stock, and it thereafter splits two-for-one, many courts hold that the bequest of "100 shares of Telecom stock" ***is a specific bequest***, meaning that the beneficiary is entitled to the additional

100 shares produced by the split. [O'Neill v. Alford, 485 S.W.2d 935 (Tex. 1972)] Thus a bequest of stock can be classified as a specific bequest for one purpose and as a general legacy for another purpose.

b. **Stock dividends:** [§755]   If the will makes a bequest of "my 100 shares of Telecom stock," and thereafter Telecom declares and pays a ten percent stock dividend, by majority rule the beneficiary is *not* entitled to the additional ten shares of stock produced by the dividend.

   (1) **Rationale:** Stock dividends are paid out of the earned surplus of the corporation just the same as cash dividends. They should be treated as income on the original capital and not as part of the original capital. Thus, stock dividends paid during the testator's lifetime should be treated the same as cash dividends. [Hicks v. Kerr, 104 A. 426 (Md. 1918)]

   (2) **Minority view:** [§756]   Some courts take the position that the value of the original shares is diminished as much by the issuance of a stock dividend as a stock split, and hence, in either case the new shares should go to the legatee of the specific gift.

c. **Compare—post-death splits, dividends:** [§757]   The foregoing rules apply to stock splits and stock dividends occuring during the testator's lifetime. If a stock split or stock dividend takes place *after* the testator's death, the beneficiary is entitled to the stock produced by the split or dividend.

   (1) **Rationale:** The beneficiary owned the stock from the moment of testator's death, subject to the executor's right of possession for purposes of administration. Thus, it was the beneficiary's own stock that produced the split or the stock dividend.

3. **Statutory Solutions:** [§758]   Under the U.P.C. and by statute in several non-U.P.C. states, the specific beneficiary of corporate securities is entitled to additional or other securities of the same entity owned by the testator by reason of action initiated by the entity (*i.e.,* stock splits *and* stock dividends). However, this rule does *not* apply to any additional shares acquired by testator's exercise of a purchase option. [U.P.C. §2-607(a)(2)]

F.   EXONERATION OF LIENS

1. **Majority Rule:** [§759]   At common law and in many states today, if specifically devised property is, at testator's death, subject to a lien that secures a note on which the testator was personally liable, the beneficiary is entitled to have the lien exonerated (unless the will provides to the contrary). In other words, the beneficiary is entitled to demand payment of the debt out of the **residuary estate**, so that the property passes free of any encumbrance or lien. [120 A.L.R. 577] The rationale is that the testator's personal estate was benefited because of the debt, and would have been smaller had the debt been discharged. Thus, the debt should be paid out of the general assets of the residuary estate. [*In re* Budd's Estate, 105 N.W.2d 358 (Wis. 1960)]

a. **Example:** T's will devises Blackacre to A. At T's death, Blackacre is encumbered by a mortgage that secures an indebtedness of $5,000. Under the exoneration of liens doctrine, the mortgage must be exonerated (*i.e.*, the debt must be paid out of the residuary estate) if the secured debt was a ***personal obligation*** of the decedent. [Currie v. Scott, 187 S.W.2d 551 (Tex. 1945)]

b. **Critique:** The doctrine has been criticized on the ground that it is far more likely that the testator intended to give the beneficiary only what the testator owned at death—title subject to the lien. This position has particular force if the property was subject to the lien at the time the will was executed.

c. **Compare—testator not personally liable:** [§760]   The exoneration of liens doctrine applies ***only*** if the decedent was personally liable on the debt involved. If the specifically devised property was subject to a lien but the testator signed a nonrecourse note (or if the testator took title under a "subject to" rather than an "assumption" transaction), such that the testator was not personally liable in the event of a deficiency on foreclosure, there is no exoneration. The beneficiary takes the property subject to the mortgage lien. [Cal. Prob. Code §6176]

2. **Minority Rule:** [§761]   By statute in a growing number of states, liens on specifically devised property are ***not*** exonerated unless the will directs exoneration. A specific devise passes ***subject to*** any security interest existing at the time of death without right of exoneration, and regardless of a ***general direction*** in the will to pay all debts. [U.P.C. §2-609; N.Y. Est. Powers & Trusts Law §3-3.6] Under such statutes, a "just debts" clause directing, *e.g.*, that "all of my just debts be paid as soon as practicable after my death" is a mere general direction to pay debts and is not considered a direction that liens on specifically devised property be exonerated.

X. WILL CONTESTS AND RELATED MATTERS

chapter approach

Questions pertaining to will contests are fairly straightforward. Generally, you will see a disgruntled heir or beneficiary under a former will who believes that he has been "shortchanged" by the present will and so he contests the validity of the will in the probate proceeding. Your approach to this type of question is as follows:

1. Determine whether the will contestant has **grounds** for challenging the will:

    a.   Was the will **improperly executed**—_i.e._, does not meet the statutory formalities?

    b.   Was the will **revoked**?

    c.   Did the testator **lack capacity** at the time of signing? (Watch for insane delusion issues here.) In any case, remember that the standard for testamentary capacity is an easy one to meet.

    d.   Did the testator **lack the intent** to make a will?

    e.   Did someone **unduly influence** the testator—_i.e._, mentally coerce testator into writing a will the way the coercer wanted?

    f.   Was the testator a victim of **fraud** as to the will or a gift in the will?

    g.   Was the will or a gift therein the **result of a mistake**? (For most mistakes, however, the courts do not grant relief.)

2. After you've considered the grounds, decide what relief is available—should the court **set aside** the whole will or merely a part of the will? Remember that a court prefers to distribute property according to the testator's written wishes rather than by intestate succession.

3. The will in your question may have a **no-contest** (in terrorem) clause. If so, note that the majority of jurisdictions hold that such a clause does not trigger a forfeiture **if** the contest was brought in good faith and with probable cause. In any case, challenges to the jurisdiction of the court or a suit to construe the will are **not** will contests.

4. In dealing with issues of **mistake**, keep in mind that the courts are reluctant to change clear language of a will. However, if language is not clear, the court may allow **extrinsic evidence** to correct the ambiguity. If evidence is not helpful, the court falls back on basic rules of construction (_e.g._, interpret the document as a whole, construe to avoid intestacy, favor kin, etc.).

5. Finally, if a will cannot be set aside on the basis of fraud, duress, or undue influence, consider an action **in tort** for wrongful interference with an expected inheritance (a separate suit from the probate proceedings).

A. GROUNDS FOR CONTESTING WILL [§762]

A will "contest" simply poses the issue of whether the document offered for probate is a valid will. The contestant may raise any matter tending to show that the will should be denied probate. While most will contests involve the issues of testamentary capacity or undue influence, a will contest may be based on any of the following grounds:

1. **Defective Execution:** [§763]   The will may be contested on the ground that it was not validly executed (*e.g.*, not signed by the testator). (On the requisites of due execution, *see supra*, §§380- 395; on the proof of due execution that must be established at probate, *see infra*, §§930-935.)

2. **Will Revoked:** [§764]   The will contestants may attempt to show that the will, although validly executed, was revoked by the testator. (*See supra*, §§487 *et seq.*)

3. **Lack of Testamentary Capacity:** [§765]   The contestants may attempt to establish that the testator lacked testamentary capacity at the time the will was executed. (*See infra*, §§780-784.)

4. **Lack of Testamentary Intent:** [§766]   The will may be contested on the ground that the testator did not intend that the proffered document was to serve as his or her will. (*See infra*, §§796-798.)

5. **Undue Influence:** [§767]   The contestants may challenge the will, or a particular gift in the will, on the ground that it was the product of undue influence. (*See infra*, §§799 *et seq.*)

6. **Fraud:** [§768]   The will may be contested on the ground that the will or a gift therein was procured as the result of a fraud perpetrated upon the testator. (*See infra*, §§820 *et seq.*)

7. **Mistake:** [§769]   The contestants may attempt to show that the document was executed, or a gift in the will was made, as the result of a mistake. (*See infra*, §§838 *et seq.*)

B. PROCEDURAL ASPECTS

1. **Time for Contest:** [§770]   The will may be contested either at the time it is offered for probate, or thereafter within the statutory period. In most states, the will contestants may file a contest within six months after the will is admitted to probate. [Cal. Prob. Code §380; *but see* Tex. Prob. Code §93—two years] (On the reason for allowing a will to be contested after it has been admitted to probate, *see infra*, §927.)

   a. **Uniform Probate Code:** [§771]   Under the U.P.C., a will contest is made in a formal testacy proceeding. If the will has been probated in an informal probate proceeding (*see* below), a contestant may initiate a formal testacy proceeding within three years after the decedent's death or within twelve months after the informal probate, whichever is later. [U.P.C. §3-108]

2. **Who May Contest:** [§772]   In most jurisdictions, a party who contests a will is called a "contestant." However, in a few jurisdictions the person is called a "caveator." A person has standing to contest a will only if she is an ***interested party.*** To be an interested party, the person must have a direct interest in the estate, which would be adversely affected by the will's admission to probate. [N.Y. Surr. Ct. Proc. Act §1410]

    a. **Heir or legatee under earlier will:** [§773]   By majority rule, the only persons who are "interested" for purposes of challenging a will are heirs (the people who would take if the will were not admitted to probate) and legatees under an earlier will whose gifts are reduced or eliminated by the will. [Earles v. Earles, 428 S.W.2d 108 (Tex. 1968)] *Note:* An heir who takes more under the will than by intestacy cannot contest the will, nor can a prior legatee who takes the same or a greater interest under the will being offered for probate.

    b. **Creditors cannot contest:** [§774]   Creditors of the decedent are ***not*** "interested" for purposes of having standing to contest a will, because they can assert their claim against the estate whether or not the will is admitted to probate. [Montgomery v. Foster, 8 So. 349 (Ala. 1890)] Also, most courts hold that judgment creditors of an heir have no interest in the ***decedent's*** estate, and thus cannot contest the will so as to procure property for the heir. [Lee v. Keech, 133 A. 835 (Md. 1926)]

    c. **Executor named in earlier will—no standing:** [§775]   By majority rule, an executor or testamentary trustee named in an earlier will has no standing to contest a later will since the fiduciary's only financial interest would be in the commissions to which he would have been entitled if the appointment as fiduciary were not revoked by the later will. [N.Y. Surr. Ct. Proc. Act §1410; 112 A.L.R. 659; 94 A.L.R.2d 1409]

    d. **Estoppel:** [§776]   A legatee who ***accepts benefits*** (*e.g.,* partial distributions) under a will is estopped from later joining in a contest of the will. [Trevino v. Turcotte, 564 S.W.2d 682 (Tex. 1978)]

3. **Necessary Parties:** [§777]   In most states, ***all heirs and all legatees*** named in the will are necessary parties to a will contest and must be given ***notice*** of the proceedings. Merely naming the executor in his representative capacity as defendant is insufficient; the legatees named in the will also must be given notice. [Jennings v. Srp, 521 S.W.2d 326 (Tex. 1975)]

4. **Burden of Proof:** [§778]   In most jurisdictions, the burden is on the ***contestant*** to establish the grounds (*e.g.,* lack of testamentary intent or capacity, undue influence, etc.). [U.P.C. §3-407]

5. **Executor's Defense of Will:** [§779]   The executor has a duty to defend the will. Litigation expenses incurred by the executor are allowed as a charge against the estate even if the will is denied probate.

C. TESTAMENTARY CAPACITY

1. **Legal Test:** [§780] The mental capacity required for making a will involves a different, and lower, legal standard than the capacity to contract. Statutes in most states merely specify that a testator must be of sound mind, leaving elaboration of the statutory test to judicial development. [U.P.C. §2-501] The test for determining whether the testator had the requisite capacity for executing a will consists of four issues:

   a. **Did testator understand the nature of the act he was doing?** [§781] Testator must have **actual knowledge** (mere capacity to understand is not sufficient) of the nature of the act he is undertaking; *i.e.,* he must actually know that he is executing his will.

   b. **Did testator know the natural objects of his bounty?** [§782] Testator must have the capacity to **understand** (not necessarily have actual knowledge of) the relationship between himself and those persons who ought to be in his mind at the time of making his will.

   c. **Did testator know the nature and value of his property?** [§783] Testator must have the capacity to understand the **nature and extent** of his property.

   d. **Did testator understand the disposition he was making?** [§784] Testator must have the capacity to interrelate the foregoing factors and form an **orderly scheme of disposition.**

2. **Insane Delusion:** [§785] A person may have sufficient mental capacity to make a will generally, and yet suffer from an insane delusion which interferes with his ability to formulate a rational plan of disposition. A finding of insane delusion may cause a particular will (or a gift therein) to fail on the ground of testamentary incapacity.

   a. **Definition:** [§786] An insane delusion occurs "where one persistently believes in supposed facts which have no real existence except in his perverted imagination, and against all evidence and probability, and conducts himself, however logically, upon the assumption of their existence." [*In re* Hargrove's Will, 262 App. Div. 202 (1941)] It is a belief in facts that do not exist and which no rational person would believe existed. [Ingersoll v. Gourley, 139 P. 207 (Wash. 1914)]

      (1) **Examples:** Groundless beliefs about family members (*e.g.*, that a child is illegitimate, or that a relative has been stealing from the testator) have been held to be insane delusions. [*In re* Kahn's Will, 5 N.Y.S. 556 (1889)] And a will was held to be the product of an insane delusion where proof supported a finding that the testator, at the time he made his will, was suffering under the warrantless delusion that his seventy-five-year-old wife of many years was cheating on him. [Matter of Honigman, 168 N.E.2d 676 (Ill. 1960)]

   b. **Test:** [§787] A belief can be very illogical, yet not amount to an insane delusion. "Persons do not always reason logically or correctly from facts, and that may be because of their prejudices, or of the perversity or peculiar construction of their minds. Wills, however, do not depend for their validity upon the testator's ability to reason logically, or upon his freedom from prejudice." [*In re* Hargrove's Will, *supra*] The controlling question, therefore, is whether there are **any** facts from which the testator **could** have reasoned, regardless how improperly and regardless of whether the average person would have reached the same conclusion.

c. **Effect of insane delusion:** [§788]   To set aside a will on the ground of insane delusion, it must appear that the delusion had some **effect on the testator's disposition of his property**—*i.e.*, that his will, or some portion thereof, was formulated in reliance on the irrational belief. An insane delusion may invalidate the entire will, or it may affect only a particular gift therein, if it can be shown that the delusion runs only to that particular gift or to the beneficiary thereof. [Estate of Perkins, 195 Cal. 699 (1925)]

(1) **Note—delusion must relate to property:** [§789]   The mere fact that a testator held delusions does not, in itself, constitute testamentary incapacity. The delusions must relate to the property being disposed of, or to the persons concerned, and therefore control the exercise of the testamentary act. [*In re* Heaton's Will, *supra*, §376]

3. **Burden of Proof as to Testamentary Capacity:** [§790]   Some states require a showing that the testator was of sound mind as a prerequisite to admission of the will to probate. The burden of proving mental competency is thus placed on the **will proponents.** [Tex. Prob. Code §88b]

a. **Rebuttable presumption of competency:** [§791]   However, many modern statutes recognize a rebuttable presumption of **competency,** the effect of which is to place the burden on those contesting the will to show that the testator lacked the requisite mental capacity. [U.P.C. §3-407]

b. **Adjudication of incompetency:** [§792]   A proceeding to appoint a guardian or committee to handle an incompetent's property involves a determination of whether the person has the capacity to enter into contracts. Such a determination involves a higher standard than the four-point test for testamentary capacity above. Therefore, an adjudication of incompetency is **evidence** of incapacity but will not support a directed verdict of testamentary incapacity. "One may be capable of making a will yet incapable of disposing of his property by contract or of managing his estate." [Gilmer v. Brown, *supra*, §366]

(1) **Example:** Seven months before T executed his will at ninety-three years of age, a guardian was appointed in legal proceedings on ground that because of age, health, and deteriorating mental condition, T was no longer capable of handling his own affairs. On this ground, the trial judge gave an instructed verdict that T lacked testamentary capacity. The appellate court reversed, holding that a determination of whether to appoint a guardian to handle T's affairs is based on a different test than the four-point test for testamentary capacity; and even if T had mental problems, a jury could find that T had executed his will during a "lucid interval" (a period of time during which T met

the four-point test for testamentary capacity). [Duke v. Falk, 463 S.W.2d 245 (Tex. 1971); *In re* Coe's Will, 47 App. Div. 418 (1900)]

4. **Witness Cannot Testify as to Testator's Legal Capacity:** [§793]   A lay or expert witness may not be asked whether the testator had legal capacity to make a will. The reason for this rule is that "this involves a legal definition and a legal test, and the witness's definition or understanding of capacity to perform the act in a legal manner may differ from the legal standard." [Carr v. Radkey, 393 S.W.2d 806 (Tex. 1965)] For the same reason, a witness cannot be asked whether the testator was suffering from an insane delusion. "A doctor's concept of what constitutes an insane delusion may be quite different from the legal concept." [Lindley v. Lindley, 384 S.W.2d 676 (Tex. 1964)]

   a. **Compare—may testify as to testator's mental condition:** [§794]   A witness can testify as to the testator's mental condition. Competent evidence about the testator's mental condition and ability, or lack of it, which does not involve legal tests, legal definitions, or pure questions of law is admissible. A witness may be asked, assuming she knows or is a properly qualified expert, whether the testator knew or had the capacity to know the objects of his bounty, the nature of the transactions in which he was engaged, the nature and extent of his estate, and similar questions. [Carr v. Radkey, *supra*]

5. **Lucid and Sensible Holographic Will Is Evidence of Testamentary Capacity:** [§795]   In jurisdictions that recognize holographic wills (*see supra*, §455), it is generally held that "a rational and sensible holographic will" prepared by a testator is evidence of the fact that the will was written during a lucid interval. [Carr v. Radkey, *supra*]

D.   TESTAMENTARY INTENT

1. **In General:** [§796]   To be admitted to probate, it must be shown that the proffered document was written and executed with testamentary intent. (*See supra*, §§347 *et seq.*)

2. **Proof That Testator Knew Contents of Will:** [§797]   In the ordinary case, no issue is raised as to whether the testator knew the contents of the will. The will was prepared at testator's direction, and it is presumed that he knew and understood its contents. This *presumption* arises even if testator was blind or illiterate, or if the testator could not read or understand the English language, as long as it is shown that the attorney explained the will to the testator and was satisfied that he understood its contents. [Jedlicka v. Williams, 459 S.W.2d 956 (Tex. 1970)]

3. **Suspicious Circumstances:** [§798]   If, however, the will was prepared and executed under suspicious circumstances, the court may require an affirmative showing that the testator knew and understood its contents.

   a. **Example:** T, unable to read or write, and gravely ill at house of one of the legatees, signed (with an X) a will that disinherited his only child, who was in same house at same time and did not know that her father was executing a will. Neither beneficiary was related to T, and there was no showing that he ever gave anyone instructions to write a will or requested that one be prepared. Since there was no evidence that T knew the contents of the document he had signed, the will was denied probate. [Kelly v. Settegast, 2 S.W. 870 (Tex. 1887)]

E. UNDUE INFLUENCE

1. **In General:** [§799]   A will or a gift in a will may be set aside if it was the result of undue influence—mental coercion that destroyed the testator's free agency and forced him to embody someone else's intentions in his will in place of his own. [*In re* Dunson's Estate, 141 So. 2d 601 (Fla. 1962)] However, mere solicitation of a will does *not* constitute undue influence. [48 A.L.R.3d 961] Importuning, persuasion, and even harassment may influence the testator, but do not constitute undue influence. It is not improper to advise, persuade, etc. as long as testator "remains a free agent," and "the will is his and not that of another." [Ginter v. Ginter, 101 P. 634 (Kan. 1909)]

2. **Legal Test:** [§800]   The test whether a testator has been subjected to undue influence is a subjective one, measured at the time of execution of the will. The burden of proof is always on the person contesting the will, who must establish:

   a. **Existence:** [§801]   The contestants must establish that undue influence *was exerted* on the testator.

   b. **Effect:** [§802]   The effect of the influence must have been to *overpower* the mind and will of the testator.

   c. **Product:** [§803]   The influence must have produced a will (or a gift in the will) that expresses the intent, not of the testator, but of the one exerting the influence, and that *would not have been made but for the influence.* [Rothermel v. Duncan, 369 S.W.2d 917 (Tex. 1963)]

3. **Circumstantial Evidence:** [§804]   Undue influence is usually difficult to prove. Since it is rarely witnessed, it normally can be proved only by circumstantial evidence. However, the evidence must be *substantial* and of probative force; it cannot be based simply on surmise or conjecture. The following four factors are said to be indicia of undue influence; *i.e.*, while no one of them individually is sufficient, the combination of all four may support a finding of undue influence. [Burgess v. Bohle, 63 Cal. App. 2d 165 (1944)]

   a. **Susceptibility:** [§805]   The testator's weakened physical or mental condition may have left him susceptible to undue influence or domination by others. *But note:* This, by itself, does not support a conclusion that the situation was in fact taken advantage of.

   b. **Opportunity:** [§806]   The person alleged to have committed the undue influence had the opportunity to exercise it. *But note:* Again, the mere fact that the opportunity existed does not, by itself, show that the person acted upon it.

   c. **Activity:** [§807]   There was some activity, such as procuring the will or arranging for its preparation, or isolating the testator from his family or from independent legal advice, on the part of the party exerting the influence. [13 A.L.R.3d 381]

d. **Unnatural disposition:** [§808]   The disposition made in the will was "unnatural" in that one child was heavily favored over the others, property was bequeathed to an unrelated party to the exclusion of testator's immediate family, etc.

4. **Undue Influence as to Part of Will:** [§809]   If only one gift in the will was the product of undue influence, the remaining parts of the will are valid, as long as giving effect to the remaining portions does not defeat the overall testamentary plan. [64 A.L.R.3d 277] Where, however, the effect of upholding the unchallenged provisions, while rejecting the tainted gifts, would defeat the testator's presumed wishes for the disposal of his property, the entire will is set aside. [*In re* Estate of Klages, 209 N.W.2d 110 (Iowa 1973)]

5. **Confidential Relationship**

a. **In general**

(1) **Majority rule:** [§810]   By majority rule, the mere existence of a confidential relationship between the testator and a will beneficiary (*e.g.*, attorney-client; doctor-patient; priest-penitent) does ***not***, by itself, give rise to a presumption of undue influence unless the beneficiary played an ***active part*** in procuring the will. [Arnold's Estate, 16 Cal. 2d 573 (1940); 66 A.L.R. 228; 154 A.L.R. 583] However, some courts have indicated that the quantum of evidence necessary to prove undue influence is less where there is a confidential relationship. [McQueen v. Wilson, 31 So. 94 (Ala. 1901)]

(2) **Presumption:** [§811]   A number of courts recognize a rebuttable presumption of undue influence where all three of the following factors appear. Once these elements are present, the burden shifts to the proponent of the will to prove that it was not induced by her undue influence.

(a) **Existence of relationship:** [§812]   A confidential relationship existed between the testator and the beneficiary at the time the will was executed.

(b) **Participation:** [§813]   The beneficiary played some active part in drawing the will, such as by counselling the testator in regard thereto, arranging for an attorney to prepare the will, or engaging in other significant activity in connection with the will's preparation and execution. [13 A.L.R.3d 381] A beneficiary who participates in preparation of a will and occupies a confidential relationship to the testator has a duty to see that the testator receives independent, disinterested advice. [Estate of Swenson, 617 P.2d 305 (Or. 1980)]

(c) **Unnatural disposition:** [§814]   The disposition under the will is "unnatural," in that the beneficiary in question receives far more than the testator might normally be expected to leave to that person.

(3) **Compare—inference:** [§815]   In some jurisdictions, the foregoing factors give rise to an inference only, such as to support a submission of the issue to the jury; the burden of proof does not shift.

(a) **Example:** The only evidence of undue influence was that T was ninety-two years old and suffering from arteriosclerosis when he executed a will that gave $4,000 to each of three daughters and devised his residuary estate to his housekeeper of twenty-five years. A directed verdict admitting the will to probate was affirmed on appeal. Showing that T was in weak physical condition and became more and more dependent on the housekeeper in his later years merely showed the motive and opportunity for exercising undue influence, but did not show that influence had actually been exerted. There was no proof from which an inference of undue influence could reasonably be drawn, and the issue was properly removed from the jury. [Colbeck's Will, 45 App. Div. 2d 796 (1974)]

b. **Gift to testator's attorney**

(1) **In general:** [§816]   It is generally held that the mere existence of the attorney-client relationship, without more, does not give rise to a presumption that a testamentary gift to the attorney was the product of undue influence. In particular, if there has been an ongoing and long-time attorney relationship, and there is no evidence disclosing any pressure or urging by the attorney to make a will in the attorney's favor, the gift should not be set aside. [Swearingen v. Swanstrom, 175 P.2d 692 (Idaho 1946)]

(2) **Presumption of undue influence where attorney prepared the will:** [§817] Where, however, the attorney prepared the will in his favor and supervised its execution, a number of courts have held that a presumption or inference of undue influence arises, especially if other suspicious circumstances exist (*e.g.,* large bequest in relation to size of estate; testator, although he had capacity, was in a weakened mental or physical condition; attorney's arrangement for particular persons to serve as attesting witnesses). [*In re* Heim's Will, 40 A.2d 651 (N.J. 1945); 19 A.L.R. 3d 575] The presumption of undue influence, once it arises, can be overcome only by the clearest and most satisfactory evidence. [*In re* Witt's Estate, 198 Cal. 407 (1926)]

(3) **Independent legal advice:** [§818]   If the will was prepared by another attorney on the basis of independent legal advice, no presumption of undue influence arises. [Frye v. Norton, 135 S.E.2d 603 (W.Va. 1964)] However, preparation of the will by the attorney's office associate based on the attorney's instructions is not the independent and impartial advice necessary to sustain a transaction between the fiduciary and his principal. [*In re* Lobb's Will, 145 P.2d 808 (Or. 1944)]

c. **Illicit relationship:** [§819]   The mere existence of an illicit relationship does not give rise to a presumption or inference of undue influence, but existence of the relationship is a *factor* to be considered along with other factors in determining whether undue influence was exerted. [Reed v. Shipp, 308 So. 2d 705 (Ala. 1975); 76 A.L.R.3d 735] The modern view is that an illicit relationship is **not "confidential"** within the meaning of the rule that gives rise to a presumption of undue influence when a confidential relationship plus other factors exist. [Estate of Spaulding, 83 Cal. App. 2d 15 (1947)]

(1) **Comment:** While the above statement of the rule is found in modern cases as well as older decisions, the actual decisions in cases involving a will in favor of a mistress or paramour tend to reflect the prevailing attitudes of society toward such relationships. Thus, more recent cases tend to reflect a less judgmental attitude toward sexual activities outside the marriage relationship, whereas older decisions appear quicker to find that the illicit activities tainted the will.

6. **Separate Tort Action:** *See infra, §§883 et seq.*

F. FRAUD

1. **In General:** [§820]   A will or testamentary gift that is made as the result of fraud is invalid. To establish fraud, it must be shown that the testator was ***willfully deceived*** as to the character or content of an instrument, or as to extrinsic facts which induced the will or a gift therein.

   a. **Definition:** [§821]   Fraud consists of:

      (i) ***False statements*** of ***material*** facts

      (ii) ***Known to be false*** by the party making the statements

      (iii) Made with the ***intention of deceiving*** the testator

      (iv) Who is ***actually deceived,*** and

      (v) Which ***cause testator to act*** in reliance on such statements.

      [*In re* Roblin's Estate, 311 P.2d 459 (Or. 1957)]

      (1) **Deceit incidentally related to will:** [§822]   Although generally the fraud must be intended to influence the execution or content of a will, deceit directed at some other objective may have incidentally influenced the will as well. For example, a fraudulently induced marriage may not have been intended to procure a will, but a court may find that a will resulting from that marriage is a fruit of the original fraud and must fail. [Estate of Carson, 184 Cal. 437 (1920)]

   b. **Causation:** [§823]   Fraud invalidates a testamentary act only if the testator was in fact ***deceived*** and ***acted in reliance*** on the misrepresentations. There is no basis for challenging a will on grounds of fraud if the same will would have been made regardless of the alleged misrepresentations. [*In re* Roblin's Estate, *supra*]

   c. **Compare—other grounds**

      (1) **Mistake:** [§824]   Innocent misrepresentation does not constitute fraud, although relief may be available on the ground of mistake. (*See* below.)

(2) **Undue influence:** [§825]   Fraud is distinguishable from undue influence in that in undue influence, the testator knows what she is doing but her act is not her own; an element of coercion is present. Fraud involves deception.

(3) **Duress:** [§826]   Fraud is also distinguishable from duress in that duress involves the element of a threat to physically harm the testator. Again, fraud merely involves deception.

2. **Fraud in the Execution:** [§827]   This type of fraud (sometimes referred to as "fraud in the factum") includes cases where the testator was tricked into signing a document not knowing it was a will, or where, by sleight of hand, one "will" was **substituted** for another. Proof of this type of fraud establishes that there was **no testamentary intent.**

   a. **Example:** T signs an instrument upon A's representation that it merely gives A a power of attorney to pay T's bills while T is in the hospital. In fact, the instrument contains provisions devising all of T's property to A.

3. **Fraud in the Inducement:** [§828]   In this type of fraud, the testator has the requisite testamentary intent, but is **fraudulently induced** into making the will (or a particular gift therein). For example, C marries T after representing that he is single, when in fact C is already married. Shortly after the marriage, T executes a will making a substantial gift to C; T dies a year later. If the testamentary gift "was in fact the fruit of the fraud," the gift can be set aside.

   a. **Misrepresentation must be sole inducement:** [§829]   It must be shown that the misrepresentation was the **sole inducement** for testator's making the gift. If there were other inducing reasons for testator to make the gift (e.g., love and affection for the intended beneficiary), the gift will not be set aside. Thus, if in the above example the parties had lived together happily for twenty years, it would be difficult to say that the bequest to C was founded on T's supposed legal relationship with him, and not primarily on their long and intimate relation. [Estate of Carson, *supra*—dictum]

   b. **Knowledge of true facts:** [§830]   There is no fraudulent inducement if the testator knew the true facts. [*In re* Donnelly's Will, 26 N.W. 23 (Iowa 1895)—T knew that her "husband" had another wife]

   c. **Fraud perpetrated by someone other than beneficiary:** [§831]   If fraud has been perpetrated on the testator, it is generally held to be immaterial that the beneficiary was innocent. Thus if someone falsely tells the testator that C is testator's long-lost son, and C has nothing to do with the deception, a testamentary gift to C still would be set aside. The fraud vitiates any testamentary intent to bestow benefits on C. [28 A.L.R. 475]

      (1) **Compare—gifts not a product of deceit:** [§832]   Even where the testator has been fraudulently induced to make a will, the gifts that are **not a product of the fraud** are valid. [Estate of Carson, *supra*] Thus, in the example above,

if the will gave property to B, testator's daughter, the fraud pertaining to "long-lost son" C would ***not*** affect the gift to B.

4. **Fraudulent Prevention of Will:** [§833]   There are occasional cases in which a testator is fraudulently dissuaded from making a will or a testamentary gift. For example, T tells her family that she is going to draw a will and leave all her property to a friend, C. To prevent this, T's daughter tells T that C has just died (which the daughter knows is not true). Believing C to be dead, T decides not to draw any will at all and lets her property pass by intestate succession. C learns about the misrepresentation after T's death. What relief is available?

   a. **No legal remedy available:** [§834]   It is universally held that parol evidence is not admissible, in probate proceedings, to establish that T intended to make a gift to C. The court will not write a will on behalf of the decedent, or identify supposed will beneficiaries on the basis of oral testimony. All testamentary gifts must be contained in a will executed by the decedent; and in the absence of such a writing, the laws of intestate succession must apply.

      (1) **Example:** D alleged that T asked Attorney to prepare a will that included a gift to D; but acting in collusion with T's husband, Attorney purposely omitted the gift but pretended that the gift was made when reading the will aloud to T. The court did not allow reformation of the will. If evidence of D's allegations were admitted, the result would obviously be that the property of a testator would often be disposed of, not according to the directions given in her will, but according to such directions as the parties in interest would be able to show by oral testimony. Although steadfast adherence to the rule requiring that the testator's wishes be reduced to writing in order to be given effect may work a hardship in a particular instance, the policy is "one which the legislature and the courts have deemed to produce the best results in the long run."[Dye v. Parker, 194 P. 640, 195 P. 599 (Kan. 1921)]

   b. **Constructive trust may be imposed:** [§835]   Despite the fact that there is no legal remedy, many courts have imposed constructive trusts for the benefit of the persons who would have been beneficiaries, if proof of the fraud is established by the higher evidentiary standard of "clear and convincing evidence." (*See* Trusts Summary.)

   c. **Tort liability may be imposed:** [§836]   Moreover, modern authorities recognize that the intended beneficiary (D in the above example) may have a cause of action against the perpetrator of the fraud (Attorney above) for tort liability for wrongful interference with an expectancy. (*See infra,* §883.)

5. **Revocation Prevented by Fraud:** [§837]   Suppose that a will beneficiary (B) pretends to revoke T's will by destruction at T's request and in T's presence. In fact, B destroys another document, thereby tricking T into believing that the will has been revoked. Even though it is clear that T would have revoked the will but for the fraud, the will is nonetheless ***admitted to probate*** since it was not validly revoked. However, upon proof of B's deception by clear and convincing evidence, a court no doubt would impose a

constructive trust in favor of T's heirs or the persons she wished to benefit by revoking the will. [Brazil v. Silva, 181 Cal. 490 (1919)]

6.   **Separate Tort Action:** *See infra,* §§883 *et seq.*

G.   MISTAKE

1.   **In General:** [§838]   Where it is claimed that there was a mistake concerning a will, the admissibility of parol evidence to show the mistake and the type of relief available, if any, depends upon the type of mistake claimed. When the alleged mistake relates to **execution** of the document offered for probate, the courts are more likely to accept parol testimony, and grant relief if the mistake is established, than is the case if the alleged mistake relates to the **contents** of the will. This is because an alleged mistake in execution relates to testamentary intent, an issue on which the courts generally admit parol testimony in appropriate cases. (*See supra,* §352.) But where the alleged mistake relates to the contents of an instrument that clearly was executed with testamentary intent, the courts are understandably reluctant to disturb the words contained in the will signed by the testator.

    a.   **Compare—mistake as to revocation:** [§839]   Mistake as a justification for refusing to give effect to a will or some part thereof must be distinguished from mistake as a ground for ignoring a revocation. Relief is much more freely given in the latter situation than for a mistake that results in the making of a will or a testamentary gift. Revocation of a will requires both an act of revocation and the intent to revoke. Since **extrinsic evidence is admissible** on the issue of intent to revoke, evidence is also admissible to show that the intent to revoke was based on a mistake. (*See supra,* §§564 *et seq.,* on dependent relative revocation.)

2.   **Mistake in Execution of Will**

    a.   **Mistake as to nature of instrument:** [§840]   Extrinsic evidence is **always** admissible to show that the testator was unaware of the nature of the instrument he signed (*e.g.,* he believed it to be a power of attorney). Such a mistake relates to the issue of whether the testator had the requisite testamentary intent, without which the will would be invalid. Therefore, if the testator was mistaken as to the nature or effect of the instrument when he signed it, **testamentary intent is lacking,** and probate is denied. [Hildreth v. Marshall, 27 A. 465 (N.J. 1893)]

    b.   **Wrong will signed:** [§841]   Situations where the wrong will is signed occur most often with "mirror" wills, wills containing reciprocal provisions (usually prepared for a married couple). Suppose, for example, that by mistake W signs the will prepared for H, and H signs the will prepared for W. Thus the will signed by W reads: "I, H, leave all my property to my wife, W." And further suppose that the mistake is not discovered until after W dies. In this situation, some courts have denied relief, on the ground that W lacked testamentary intent because she never intended to execute the document she actually signed. [Pavlinko's Estate, 148 A.2d 528 (Pa. 1959)] However, the better and modern view is that the court should grant relief since the existence and nature of the mistake are so obvious. "It would indeed be ironic—if not perverse—to state that because what has occurred is so obvious, and what was intended so clear, we must act to nullify rather than sustain this testamentary scheme. There is absolutely no danger of fraud, and to refuse to read these wills together would serve merely to unnecessarily expand formalism, without any corresponding benefit." [Matter of Snide, 52 N.Y.2d 193 (1981)]

3. **Mistake in the Inducement:** [§842] If the alleged mistake involves the reasons that led the testator to make the will (or the reasons for making or not making a particular gift therein), and the mistake was not fraudulently induced, **no relief** is granted. *Rationale:* Oral evidence as to the testator's purposes, or his reasons for making or not making a disposition, "would open the door wide to fraud" since "the testator is dead, and therefore cannot give his version of the matter." Moreover, if the evidence could be at all effective, two points would have to be established: (i) that the testator was laboring under mistake as to the fact; and (ii) that if the truth had been known he would have made a different disposition. [Bowerman v. Burris, 197 S.W. 490 (Tenn. 1917)]

   a. **Mistake as to relationship or status of beneficiary:** [§843] These mistakes have no effect on the will; it is given effect as written.

      (1) **Example:** T leaves Blackacre to B, under the mistaken belief that B is his nephew. The mistake was entirely T's; neither B nor anyone else misled T. In such a case, the courts will enforce the will as written, including the mistakenly induced gift. [17 A.L.R. 249]

      (2) **Example:** T devises all of her property to her brother and two nephews on the allegedly mistaken belief (not appearing on the face of the will) that her only son is dead. Evidence of the mistake is inadmissible. [Bowerman v. Burris, *supra*]

      (3) **Example:** T's will makes small bequests to two of her children, A and B, and devises her residuary estate to her other two children, C and D. Testimony is offered tending to show that T mistakenly believed that her husband's will left his entire estate to A and B, and that her will was motivated by a desire to equalize distribution of their property among the four children. The evidence is not admissible. There being no evidence of fraud, "courts have no right to vary or modify the terms of a will or to reform it on grounds of mistake." [Carpenter v. Tinney, 420 S.W.2d 241 (Tex. 1967)]

   b. **Limited exception—mistake appears on face of will:** [§844] Some courts have recognized an exception (more often in dictum than in result) if the mistake appears on the face of the will, **and** the disposition the testator would have made but for the mistake can at least be inferred from the instrument. *Rationale:* Since the will discloses that a mistake has been made, it is apparent that giving effect to the will would frustrate the testator's true intent. Also, oral testimony and all of its attendant problems need **not** be relied upon either to establish the mistake or to show how the testator intended to dispose of his property had the mistake not been made. [*In re* Tousey's Will, 34 Misc. 363 (1901)—dictum]

(1) **Example:** T's will reads: "Since my only son, William, was killed in action, I leave everything to the American Red Cross." If William is alive, the will may be set aside.

(2) **Comment:** Cases in which such relief is granted are few and far between, because it is rare for the mistake and the alternate disposition to appear on the face of the instrument. Moreover, even though the will appears to state an erroneous reason for not making a gift to a particular beneficiary, it may be that the testator was not mistaken at all but, instead, chose this more genteel means of explaining a disinheritance rather than disclosing the true reasons.

4. **Mistake as to Contents of Will:** [§845]   Suppose it is contended that a provision was mistakenly omitted from the will, or that a provision contained in the will is not what the testator intended. Is parol testimony admissible to show the existence of the mistake and what the testator intended to provide had the mistake not been made? In general, the answer is a firm *no*, for two reasons. First, this *was* the will that the testator signed, and there is a strong presumption that the testator read the will and knew and understood all of its contents, including each provision thereof. [Downey v. Lawley, 36 N.E.2d 344 (Ill. 1941)] This is true even if the testator did not understand English, as long as the will was explained to the testator and he indicated approval of its terms. [Knutson's Estate, 174 N.W. 617 (Minn. 1919)—will explained to testator in Norwegian] Secondly, the courts are understandably reluctant to allow property to pass, not pursuant to the terms of the duly executed will, but on the basis of oral testimony.

a. **Mistaken omission:** [§846]   Mistakes of omission generally cannot be corrected. Thus if the testator actually intended to make a gift to a particular beneficiary, but the instrument as drafted does not contain the gift, there is generally **no relief** available. [90 A.L.R.2d 934]

(1) **Example:** Although there may be overwhelming, uncontradicted evidence that T intended to make a gift of $1,000 to his friend Sam, if through mistake the will does not include such a gift, evidence is not admissible to show the mistake. Therefore, even if Sam could get the attorney's secretary to show her steno pad and testify that she omitted the clause by mistake, Sam has no claim against T's estate.

(2) **Rationale:** Correction would require the addition of a new provision, and the court cannot reform a decedent's will. A testamentary gift can only be made by a writing contained in a duly executed will.

(3) **Attorney liability:** [§847]   If, in preparing a will pursuant to testator's instructions, the attorney omits a clause that makes a gift to a beneficiary, the attorney is liable to the intended beneficiary for the amount the beneficiary would have received under the will had the clause not been negligently omitted. [Needham v. Hamilton, 459 A.2d 1060 (D.C. 1983)]

b. **Mistake as to meaning of terms of will—in general:** [§848]   It is sometimes contended that the testator "didn't mean" what he wrote in his will; *i.e.,* that he made a mistake in describing a beneficiary or the property that was to be the subject of the gift, or that he was mistaken as to the meaning or legal effect of the terms of the instrument. To what extent, if any, is parol evidence admissible when such a mistake is alleged?

(1) **"Plain meaning" rule:** [§849]   Unless the language of the will is ambiguous (*see infra,* §§854 *et seq.*), the traditional and majority rule is that the will's terms must be construed according to their "plain meaning." Hence, parol evidence (even the testator's own statements as to what was intended) is ***not admissible*** to contradict or alter the ordinary meaning of the will's provisions. If no ambiguity exists, it is the testator's apparent intent that controls—not his supposed actual intent.

(a) **Rationale:** "It is against public policy to permit a pure mistake to defeat the duly solemnized and completely competent testamentary act. It is more important that the probate of the wills of dead people be effectively shielded from the attacks of a multitude of fictitious mistakes than that it be purged of wills containing a few real ones. The latter a testator may, by due care, avoid in his lifetime. Against the former, he would be helpless." [*In re* Gluckman's Will, 101 A. 295 (N.J. 1917)]

c. **Mistake in description of beneficiary or property:** [§850]   A mistake in describing a beneficiary or item of property has no effect on the will. Thus, if the will makes a bequest "to my cousin, William Smith," and if such a cousin exists, evidence, no matter how compelling, is ***not*** admissible to show that "he meant me, his cousin ***Thomas*** Smith." Similarly, if the will makes a bequest of "200 shares of Acme stock," evidence that a mistake was made (*e.g.,* that the testator had given written instructions to make a gift of 300 shares, but the attorney's secretary hit the wrong typewriter key) is not admissible.

(1) **Example:** T's will makes a bequest "to my nephew, William Root." T has a blood nephew, William Root, and a nephew by marriage, William Root. Since in law only a nephew by blood is a "nephew," evidence is not admissible to show which William Root was intended; the blood nephew takes the bequest. [*In re* Root's Will, 40 A. 818 (Pa. 1898)]

(2) **Example:** A Scotsman who had spent all his life in Scotland bequeathed 500 pounds to "The National Society for the Prevention of Cruelty to Children." These words correspond to the official name of a London society which did no work in Scotland and of which the testator had never heard. Near his home was a branch office of "The Scottish National Society for the Prevention of Cruelty to Children," whose activities he knew. The court held the London society should get the money, for the words used have a single plain meaning. [National Society v. Scottish National Society, (1915) A.C. 207]

(3) **Compare:** If, however, there is no organization whose exact name is "The National Society for the Prevention of Cruelty to Children," there would be a

latent ambiguity, and parol evidence would be admissible to cure the ambiguity. (*See infra*, §855.)

d. **Mistake as to meaning or legal effect:** [§851]   According to the prevailing view, if the testator knew and approved the contents of the will, it is immaterial that he mistook the legal effect of the language used. It is what the testator has done, not what he allegedly meant but failed to do, that controls. [Leonard v. Stanton, 36 A.2d 271 (N.H. 1944)] (The attorney-drafter's mistake as to the legal effect of the language used is regarded as the testator's mistake and is binding on him. [Hoover v. Roberts, 58 P.2d 83 (Kan. 1933)])

   (1) **Example:** If the will gives a beneficiary a life estate, evidence is not admissible to show that the testator intended to give the beneficiary, and thought he had given her, some other estate. [*In re* Gluckman's Will, *supra*]

   (2) **Example:** Where the gift of a remainder interest was contingent on the life tenant's dying "intestate," the gift was not effective since the life tenant left a will, even though there was clear evidence that the drafter of the will thought that "intestate" meant "without issue." [Hoover v. Roberts, *supra*]

e. **Liberal (minority) view:** [§852]   Some modern decisions have departed from the "plain meaning" rule, and have ***admitted extrinsic evidence*** to show that the testator meant something other than would be indicated by the words' ordinary meaning. Under this approach, the court admits evidence to determine whether there is an ambiguity that does not appear from the language of the will. If in light of such evidence the will's provisions are susceptible to two or more meanings, the court resolves the ambiguity on the basis of extrinsic evidence under the procedures described in §855, *infra*. If, on the other hand, the court concludes that in the light of all such evidence there is no ambiguity—that the provisions are susceptible of only one meaning—the will is enforced in accordance with that meaning.

   (1) **Rationale:** To determine initially whether the terms of a will are clear, definite, and free from ambiguity, the court must examine the instrument "in the light of the circumstances surrounding its execution so as to ascertain what the parties meant by the language used. Only then can it be determined whether the seemingly clear language of the instrument is in fact ambiguous. Failure to enter upon such an inquiry is failure to recognize that the 'plain meaning' is simply the meaning of people who did not write the document." [Estate of Russell, 69 Cal. 2d 200 (1968)]

   (2) **Example:** T's will devises property to "Robert J. Krause, now of 4708 North 46th Street, Milwaukee, Wisconsin." Under the minority view, extrinsic evidence is admissible to show that a Robert J. Krause lives at that address, but that T did not know him; that Robert *W.* Krause, who lived in the same general area in Milwaukee, was T's longtime friend and employee; that T had mentioned to others that he had made a gift in his will to "Bob Krause"; that T's will left most of his estate to relatives and other employees; and that an earlier will had made a similar gift to "Robert Krause" (sans middle initial and street

address). Noting that there would have been an ambiguity and extrinsic evidence would have been admissible if the will had made a gift to "Robert Krause," the court concluded that "details of identification, particularly such matters as middle initials, street addresses, and the like, which are highly susceptible to mistake, particularly in metropolitan areas, should not be accorded such sanctity as to frustrate an otherwise clearly demonstrable intent . . . when the proof establishes to the highest degree of certainty that a mistake was, in fact, made." [*In re* Gibbs' Estate, 111 N.W.2d 413 (Wis. 1961)]

f. **Mistake in recital of facts of execution:** [§853]   The courts have consistently allowed correction of mistakes of a ***minor or purely formal nature*** that do not relate to the identity of a beneficiary or the description of property. Examples are the misspelling of testator's name [Succession of Crouzeilles, 31 So. 64 (La. 1901)] or insertion of the attorney's name instead of the testator's name in the attestation clause [Gage v. Hooper, 169 A. 925 (Md. 1933)].

H.   AMBIGUITY

1. **Introduction:** [§854]   Parol evidence may be admissible to resolve uncertainties or ambiguities in the will. In such a case, there is no "plain meaning" that can be given to the words used by the testator. The court, in the process of interpreting the will, may admit and rely on extrinsic evidence to resolve the ambiguity. Here there is no concern as to changing the meaning of language or adding words that the testator did not use. Rather, the concern is to ***find*** testator's meaning as to the words she did use. The older decisions, however, draw distinctions according to the kind of ambiguity involved.

2. **Latent Ambiguity:** [§855]   A "latent ambiguity" exists when the language of the will, though ***clear on its face*** in describing a beneficiary or property, is susceptible to ***more than one meaning when applied to the extrinsic facts*** to which it refers. [Will of Frost, 89 N.W.2d 216 (Wis. 1958)] There are two classes of latent ambiguity. One type is where two or more persons or things meet the description in the will (*e.g.,* the will makes a bequest "to my cousin, Mary Smith," and testator has two cousins named Mary Smith; or the will devises "the farm that I own in Marion County," and testator owns two farms in Marion County). The other type is where ***no person or thing*** exactly answers the description in the will, but two or more persons or things meet the description ***imperfectly*** (*e.g.,* the will makes a bequest "to my nephew, John Paul Jones," and testator has a nephew named John Phillips Jones and another nephew named James Paul Jones, but no nephew named John Paul Jones). In these cases, the description of the beneficiary or the gift is imperfect, and uncertainty arises in attempting to determine exactly what the testator intended to give or to whom she intended to give it. It is universally held that ***parol evidence is admissible*** to resolve a latent ambiguity of either type. [94 A.L.R. 26, 47-51] If, however, the extrinsic evidence does not resolve the ambiguity, the gift fails, and the property passes under the will's residuary clause or by intestacy.

a. **Rationale:** Reliance on parol evidence to cure the ambiguity does not have the effect of "rewriting" the will or adding to or contradicting its terms. The extrinsic evidence is merely being received to aid the court in giving meaning to the terms that the testator actually used. [Farrell v. Sullivan, 144 A. 155 (R.I. 1929)] In a sense, it is always necessary to admit extrinsic evidence to identify the beneficiary (does the testator have a cousin Mary Smith; and if so, who is she?) or the subject of the gift (what farmland did the testator own in Marion County?). If this inquiry shows that there is an ambiguity, the ambiguity can be removed by further extrinsic evidence.

b. **Example:** T's will bequeaths a portion of the residuary estate to "Edward Bergner." It turns out that there are two Edward Bergners who might be the intended beneficiaries: a brother Edward G. Bergner and a nephew Edward C. Bergner. The imperfect description may be cured by extrinsic evidence as to which Edward Bergner T intended to benefit. [Nicholl v. Bergner, 63 N.E.2d 828 (Ohio 1945)]

c. **Example:** T's will makes a bequest "to my grandson, William N. Bond." T had two grandsons: Boyd C. Bond (the son of William N. Bond) and William H. Bond (the son of John C. Bond). Extrinsic evidence, including the drafting attorney's testimony as to the testator's declarations, is admissible to cure the ambiguity. [Bond v. Riley, 296 S.W. 401 (Mo. 1927)]

d. **Example:** A devise of "my Lot #6, Square #403," which T did not own, could be shown by extrinsic evidence to have been intended to pass Lot #3 in Square 406, which T did own. [Patch v. White, 117 U.S. 210 (1886)]

3. **Partially Inaccurate Description: *"Falsa Demonstratio Non Nocet"*:** [§856] Where the description is partially accurate and partially inaccurate, it is generally held that the gift may be saved by ***striking out the inaccurate part***—if the remaining language is unambiguous; or, if ambiguous, the ambiguity can be cured by extrinsic evidence. This doctrine is sometimes referred to as *"falsa demonstratio non nocet"* (a mere erroneous description does not vitiate).

a. **Example:** T bequeathed property to "my sister Annie Neary." T had one sister named Annie Flynn and another named Bridget Neary. The court struck out the surname "Neary," leaving the bequest to "my sister Annie," on the basis of extrinsic evidence showing that this was T's probable intent. [Estate of Cawley, 1 R.I. 78 (1920)]

b. **Example:** T left property to "my niece Mary, living in New York." T had a niece named Mary living in Ireland, and a niece named Annie living in New York. Extrinsic evidence showed that T had a much closer relationship with Annie than with Mary. The court therefore struck the given name "Mary," which left the description unambiguous ("to my niece living in New York"). [Estate of Donnellan, 164 Cal. 14 (1912)]

c. **Example:** T's gift of "our former home at Ravenna, Mason County, Illinois, being lot 12, block 2, Max Meyer's addition" was upheld by striking "Ravenna" and "Max" upon a showing that (i) the will was prepared by an attorney in another state, (ii) there was no town named Ravenna in Illinois, (iii) the only Meyer's addition in Mason County, Illinois, was Marguerita Meyer's addition in the town of Havana, and (iv) T owned lot 12, block 2 in Marguerita Meyer's addition. [Armstrong v. Armstrong, 158 N.E. 356 (Ill. 1927)]

    d.   **Compare:** Suppose, however, that testator devises property to "my cousin Henry," and she has a cousin Henry and a cousin Cecil. Here there is no ambiguity and no inaccurate description. Cecil cannot introduce evidence to show that testator intended him to take; the plain meaning rule applies.

4.   **Patent Ambiguity:** [§857]   A patent ambiguity exists where the uncertainty **appears on the face of the will.** (For example, T's will mentions two cousins, "John Smith" and "John Brown," then makes a gift "to my cousin John.") The courts are split as to the admissibility of parol evidence to resolve this type of ambiguity.

    a.   **Traditional view:** [§858]   The traditional view is that parol evidence is **not** admissible to clarify or explain away a patent ambiguity. [Jacobsen v. Farnham, 54 N.W.2d 917 (Neb. 1952); 94 A.L.R. 55] Unlike the situation involving a latent ambiguity, where extrinsic evidence establishes the ambiguity, in this situation resort to extrinsic evidence is not necessary to show the ambiguity. And since extrinsic evidence is not admissible to **show** the ambiguity, it is not admissible to **cure** the ambiguity. In other words, once you get your foot in the door (extrinsic evidence establishes that there is a latent ambiguity), you can open the door; but if you cannot get your foot in the door, the door is closed. Thus, in the above example, the gift fails since the will does not identify which cousin T intended to benefit. [Pickering v. Pickering, 50 N.H. 349 (1870)]

    b.   **Modern trend:** [§859]   A growing number of courts reject the distinction between patent and latent ambiguities, and **admit parol evidence** on testator's intent in **any** case of ambiguity. The rationale is that it is the court's duty to give meaning to the testator's will if it is possible to do so. Parol evidence is not being received for the purpose of "rewriting" the will, but to interpret that which has been written. [Payne v. Todd, 43 P.2d 1004 (Ariz. 1935)]

       (1)   **Note:** In several states, it is provided by statute that mistakes or misdescriptions in the will can be resolved by extrinsic evidence. These statutes apply whether the ambiguity is latent or patent. [Ga. Code Ann. §113-807]

5.   **Type of Extrinsic Evidence Admissible:** [§860]   When extrinsic evidence is admissible, courts generally receive any competent evidence that may bear on the **testator's actual or probable intent.** Thus, evidence of all circumstances surrounding execution of the will; the testator's relationship with the various beneficiaries; the testator's age, health, and understanding at the time of execution; and the testator's knowledge and comprehension of the language used is admissible. [94 A.L.R. 26]

    a.   **Time at which intent ascertained:** [§861]   The extrinsic evidence must reflect on the testator's intent at the time the will was **executed.** [Lydick v. Tate, 44 N.E.2d 583 (Ill. 1942)]

       (1)   **Comment:** Although a will is said to "speak as of the date of the decedent's death," this relates to the effect and operation of the instrument—**not** to its

construction. Where the will is unclear or ambiguous, and thus requires interpretation, it must be construed according to the circumstances existing at the time of its execution.

(2) **Example:** A bequest to "my housekeeper" is interpreted as referring to the testator's housekeeper at the time she made the will, not at the time of her death.

b. **Admissibility of testator's declarations:** [§862]   The courts are in disagreement as to the admissibility of *testator's* declarations as to what she intended at the time she executed the will.

(1) **Majority rule—not admissible:** [§863]   By majority rule, a testator's own declarations are *not* admissible. [Breckheimer v. Kraft, 273 N.E.2d 468 (Ill. 1971)]

(2) **Better view—admissible:** [§864]   The modern and better view is that such evidence *is admissible.* [Bond v. Riley, *supra,* §855—testator's statements to attorney who drafted the will admissible]

(3) **Limited admissions:** [§865]   Some courts admit declarations made by the testator prior to or at the time of executing the will, but reject so-called "fugitive declarations" (those made afterwards). [94 A.L.R. 284] Others admit only indirect assertions of testator's state of mind as opposed to direct statements as to what she intended (*e.g.,* T's statement to B that "you are my favorite niece" would be admissible to show that T had intended to benefit the niece in the will; but the statement that "my will provides for you" would not). [Scheridan v. Scheridan, 207 S.E.2d 691 (Ga. 1974)]

6. **Rules of Construction Where No Evidence of Testator's Intent:** [§866]   Where the meaning of the will is uncertain, and reference to the surrounding circumstances fails to disclose sufficient evidence of testator's probable intent, the courts generally indulge in certain legal presumptions or rules of construction.

a. **Construe as a whole:** [§867]   A will is to be construed as a whole, and conflicting provisions are to be harmonized if possible. Also, every provision of the will should be given effect if it is possible to do so. [Wigglesworth v. Smith, 224 S.W.2d 177 (Ky. 1949)] To overcome inconsistencies, the courts use the following rules:

(1) *Specific provisions control over general provisions.* [Reid v. Voorhees, 74 N.E. 804 (Ill. 1905)]

(2) *Later provisions control over former provisions* (and later codicils over earlier codicils or wills). [*In re* Smith's Estate, 75 So. 2d 686 (Fla. 1954); Osburn v. Rochester Trust & Safe Deposit Co., *supra,* §539]

(3) *Provisions in testator's own handwriting control over typed or printed provisions.*

b. **Construe to avoid intestacy:** [§868]   Where two constructions are equally possible, courts choose the one that avoids intestacy in whole or in part. The courts presume from the very fact that the testator made a will that she intended to avoid intestacy and to have **all** of her property pass under the will. [Holmes v. Welch, 49 N.E.2d 461 (Mass. 1943); Wiechert v. Wiechert, 294 S.W. 721 (Mo. 1927)]

c. **Construe in favor of kin:** [§869]   Where two interpretations are possible, and the testator's blood relatives would take under one interpretation but not under the other, courts generally construe the will in favor of the relatives and against "strangers." [40 Cal. L.R. 63]

d. **Meaning of words:** [§870]   Words in the will are to be given their ordinary meaning.

   (1) **Example:** A gift of "cash" ordinarily does not include stocks and bonds; likewise, a gift of "land" would not convey a leasehold. [*In re* Chamberlain's Estate, 46 Cal. App. 2d 16 (1941)]

   (2) **Compare—will drafted by nonlawyer:** [§871]   But keep in mind that the fundamental rule of construction is to discern the testator's intent. Hence, contrary results have been reached, particularly where dealing with holographic wills drawn by laypersons. Where the will was drawn by an illiterate or poorly educated testator, courts occasionally have been willing to give words other than their usual meaning.

      (a) **Example:** Where an illiterate testator drafted his own will leaving the "balance of my money" to his mother, it was held that "money" passed the balance of the testator's property, both real and personal. [*In re* Estate of Miller, 48 Cal. 165 (1874)]

      (b) **Example:** An illiterate testator drafted his own will, leaving his estate to his "children." The court admitted evidence showing that testator's children were dead when he executed his will, and that he had meant to name his grandchildren. [*In re* Schedel, 73 Cal. 594 (1887)]

   (3) **Technical terms:** [§872]   Technical terms used in the will (*e.g.*, "per stirpes") are to be construed in their technical sense—at least where the will has been drafted by an attorney. [Lombardi v. Blois, 230 Cal. App. 2d 191 (1964)]

   (4) **Personal effects:** [§873]   Frequently, problems are encountered with gifts of "personal property," "personal effects," or "belongings" in a will. Generally, these phrases are construed narrowly and are held to encompass only items of tangible personal property intimately associated with the person (clothing, jewelry, furs, perhaps automobiles, etc.). [94 A.L.R.2d 1106] Again, however, if there is any evidence of testator's probable intent, the latter controls.

I. NO-CONTEST CLAUSE

1. **Effect of No-Contest Clause:** [§874]   A no-contest clause (sometimes called an *in terrorem* clause) is a will clause that provides that any person who contests the will shall *forfeit all interests* he otherwise would have received under that will. Of course, if a beneficiary under the will contests the will and the contest is successful, the no-contest clause falls with the will, and the contestant's rights upon intestacy or under a prior will are not affected by the in terrorem provision. Suppose, however, the beneficiary loses the contest? There is a split of authority as to the validity and effect of no-contest clauses.

    a. **Majority rule:** [§875]   In most states and under the Uniform Probate Code, a beneficiary who unsuccessfully contests the will does *not* forfeit the legacy if the court finds that the beneficiary challenged the will in *good faith* and on the basis of *probable cause.* [Estate of Seymour, 600 P.2d 274 (N.M. 1979); 125 A.L.R. 1135; U.P.C. §3-905] However, the forfeiture provision is given effect if the beneficiary had no reasonable basis for contesting the will.

        (1) **Rationale:** Giving effect to the forfeiture provision in all cases in which the contest was unsuccessful might discourage a person who had a legitimate basis for challenging the will from doing so. Such clauses should not be given effect so as to discourage meritorious litigation. "If fraud, coercion and undue influence . . . can be covered up and made secure by the insertion of a forfeiture condition in a will, . . . we may be putting another weapon into the hands of the racketeer." [Barry v. American Security & Trust Co., 135 F.2d 470 (D.C. Cir. 1943)—dissenting opinion]

    b. **Minority rule:** [§876]   A minority view gives full effect to no-contest clauses even if the losing contestant had probable cause for challenging the will. [Miller's Estate, 156 Cal. 119 (1909); Barry v. American Security & Trust Co., *supra*]

        (1) **Rationale:** In will contests based on lack of testamentary capacity, and to some extent in contests on undue influence grounds, the testator's character, habits, and personal traits are put in issue. A testator should be allowed to protect her reputation as well as her dispositive plan from post-death attack.

        (2) **New York view:** [§877]   By statute in New York, a no-contest clause is given effect despite the presence of probable cause for bringing the contest. However, the following *exceptions* are recognized by the statute: (i) a contest on ground that will was *forged or revoked,* if the contest was based on *probable cause;* (ii) objection to the *jurisdiction* of the court (*e.g.*, a challenge to probate of a will on the ground that testator was a domiciliary of another state); (iii) a contest brought on *behalf of an infant or incompetent;* or (iv) an action to *construe* the will's terms. [N.Y. Est. Powers & Trusts Law §3-3.5]

    c. **Florida view—clause unenforceable:** [§878]   Reflecting a policy that no heir should be discouraged from bringing a will contest, Florida statute provides that no-contest clauses are unenforceable in all cases. [Fla. Prob. Code §732.517]

2. **Actions That Do Not Constitute a Contest:** [§879]   A challenge to the will based on lack of testamentary capacity or undue influence clearly triggers a no-contest clause. But what about other actions brought by a beneficiary? While the answer to this question turns in part on the language of the no-contest clause, it is generally held that the following actions do **not** result in a forfeiture.

   a. **Construction suit:** [§880]   An action brought to construe the will does not challenge the will's basic validity, but is simply asking: What did testator mean? What interests were created? [49 A.L.R.2d 198] This includes an action to establish that a provision in the will violates the Rule Against Perpetuities. [*In re* Harrison's Estate, 22 Cal. App. 2d 28 (1937)]

   b. **Objection to jurisdiction of court:** [§881]   A challenge to the will's probate on jurisdictional grounds (*i.e.*, that the decedent was domiciled in another state) does not challenge the will's validity, but merely seeks to have the will probated in the proper state. [Maguire v. Bliss, 22 N.E.2d 615 (Mass. 1939)]

   c. **Challenge to appointment of or accounting by executor:** [§882]   A challenge to the appointment of an executor or to the accounting made by that person is not a challenge to the will. Enforcement of a forfeiture on such grounds would be against public policy, as it would tend to prevent challenge of the executor's actions on behalf of the estate. [Estate of Wojtalewicz, 418 N.E.2d 418 (Ill. 1981)]

J. **TORT LIABILITY FOR WRONGFUL INTERFERENCE WITH EXPECTED INHERITANCE**

1. **In General:** [§883]   Even if an heir or intended beneficiary is not able to set aside a will or testamentary gift on the ground of fraud, duress, or undue influence, he may be able to obtain a tort recovery for wrongful interference with his expected inheritance. [Restatement (Second) of Torts §774B] Although an heir apparent or a beneficiary named in a living person's will has only an "expectancy," in recent years courts have recognized a cause of action for wrongful interference with that expectancy, drawing an analogy to tort cases dealing with wrongful interference with a contractual or business relation. [22 A.L.R.4th 1223]

   a. **Example:** H and his second wife W raised H's daughter P from childhood. When H died, he left his entire estate to W, who then established a revocable trust that would make gifts to P and others on W's death. P alleged that W (eighty years old, in poor health, and under the defendants' care and constant supervision) decided to amend the trust so as to name P as sole beneficiary; that W instructed her attorney to prepare the amendment; and that the defendants, upon learning of this, falsely persuaded W that P did not love her, was not concerned about her, and was not worthy of receiving her estate. They told W that they were the only ones who cared for her, that they should be rewarded by being left her estate, and that they would withdraw the care and comfort upon which she had become dependent if she did not amend the trust to leave the estate to them. The court held that P's complaint stated a cause of action for tortious interference with an expected bequest. [Davison v. Feuerherd, 391 So. 2d 799 (Fla. 1980)]

2. **Proof Required:** [§884]   To recover, the plaintiff has the burden of proof to establish:

   (i)   The *existence* of her expectancy;

   (ii) That the defendants *intentionally interfered* with her expectancy;

   (iii) The interference involved *conduct tortious in itself,* such as fraud, duress, or undue influence;

   (iv) That there is a reasonable certainty that the devise to plaintiff *would have been received but for* defendants' interference; and

   (v)   Damages.

   [Nemeth v. Banhalmi, 425 N.E.2d 1187 (Ill. 1981)—facts similar to Davison v. Feuerherd, *supra;* plaintiff was primary beneficiary under two earlier wills]

   a.   **No relief available in probate proceedings:** [§885]   Some courts impose an additional requirement that the plaintiff must have attempted to pursue a remedy in probate proceedings, or else must show that no remedy is available in probate proceedings. [McGregor v. McGregor, 101 F. Supp. 848, *aff'd,* 201 F.2d 528 (10th Cir. 1951)—no attempt to probate alleged lost will]

3. **Compare—Tort Recovery for Suppression of Will:** [§886]   To be distinguished from the "expectancy" cases are cases in which the plaintiff alleges that the defendant wrongfully suppressed a will in plaintiff's favor. Courts have always recognized a cause of action on this ground, since the gravamen of the complaint is that the plaintiff *had* a property interest given to him by the decedent's will, and that the defendant wrongfully interfered with that property interest.

   a.   **Example:** W destroyed her husband's will (allegedly containing a legacy to P) because she was dissatisfied with its provisions. Two years later, W sought probate of the will as a lost will. Although the will was admitted to probate, under the rules governing probate of lost wills (*see supra,* §§548 *et seq.*), there was insufficient evidence to establish P's legacy in the probate proceedings. P then sued for a tort recovery and won, the court holding that the decision of the probate court regarding P's legacy was *not* res judicata. The probate court merely decided that the preliminary proof required by statute to enable the court to pass upon the legacy had not been furnished. "The issue here, whether as a matter of fact the will contained a legacy to plaintiff, never reached the stage of decision in probate court." Thus, in this tort case, P could prove his legacy and that W intentionally interfered therewith. [Creek v. Laski, 227 N.W. 817 (Mich. 1929)]

XI.   PROBATE AND ESTATE ADMINISTRATION

chapter approach

This chapter gives you a general understanding of the estate administration process. Most of this information is not likely to be tested in great detail on a law school exam (although you may see a question on abatement, the nonclaim statute applicable to creditors' claims, or the powers and duties of an executor). Nevertheless, a careful reading of this chapter will be important to a general understanding of exam questions. For example, you won't be thrown by unfamiliar terminology such as "ancillary administration," "formal probate," or "guardian ad litem."

A.   OVERVIEW OF ESTATE ADMINISTRATION PROCESS

1.   **Terminology:** [§887]   Strictly speaking, "probate" refers to the proceeding in which an instrument is judicially established as the duly executed last will of the decedent (or, if there is no will, the proceeding in which the decedent's heirs are judicially determined). After the will is admitted to probate (or the heirs are determined) and a personal representative is appointed, the administration of the decedent's estate begins. Estate administration is the process whereby the decedent's assets are marshalled, the debts and liabilities are discharged, and the remaining assets are distributed according to the will or the intestacy statutes. Technically, you **probate** a decedent's will, and you **administer** the decedent's estate; however, the term "probate" is commonly used to refer to all steps in the process of estate administration ("probate administration," or "the probate process").

2.   **Steps in the Process:** [§888]   While the procedures vary in detail from state to state, the following steps are involved in administering a decedent's estate in all jurisdictions.

   a.   **Opening the estate—probate:** [§889]   The first step in the estate administration process is to "open" the probate proceeding. The decedent's last will is offered for probate, and its due execution is proven. (*See infra*, §§930-935.) Or, if the decedent left no will, the decedent's intestate heirs are judicially determined. At the same proceeding, the decedent's personal representative (executor or administrator) is appointed by the court and is issued letters testamentary or letters of administration evidencing the authority to act on behalf of the estate. Only a duly appointed personal representative has the authority to act on behalf of the estate, *e.g.*, by giving a binding receipt and release upon collection of a bank account in the decedent's name. [Brobst v. Brobst, 155 N.W. 734 (Mich. 1916)]

   b.   **Collecting the decedent's assets:** [§890]   The personal representative is under a duty to collect and conserve the decedent's assets. Title to a decedent's real and personal property **vests immediately** in the decedent's legatees, devisees, or heirs, subject to the personal representative's right to possess the assets for purposes of paying creditors' claims and winding up the decedent's affairs. [Tex. Prob. Code §37]

(1) **No hiatus in title:** [§891]   There is no hiatus or gap in the ownership of or title to any of the assets. The assets are owned by the decedent up to the moment of death, and immediately after death the assets are owned by the legatees, heirs, or devisees. It may take some time before the identity of the owners is determined (*e.g.*, if the decedent's will is contested), but once that ownership is determined, title ***relates back*** to the moment of death.

(2) **Personal representative's right of possession:** [§892]   The personal representative is entitled to take possession of the decedent's assets, selling them if necessary to satisfy claims against the estate. Thus, in estates that are likely to be in administration for a fairly long period, it is customary to have all securities that were in the decedent's name re-registered in the personal representative's name, so that income from the assets will be collected by the representative. However, in many instances (and particularly for assets such as tangible personal property) the personal representative does not assert this right of possession and, instead, leaves the assets in the physical possession of the surviving family members.

c. **Family allowance, homestead, and exempt property set-aside:** [§893]   Upon petition by the appropriate surviving family members, and upon approval by the court, the personal representative pays a family allowance, fixes any homestead right granted by the state (or pays the allowance in lieu of homestead), and makes a set-aside of any exempt personal property. (*See supra*, §§303-316.)

d. **Creditors' claims:** [§894]   The personal representative gives ***notice*** by publication to creditors of the estate (and gives personal notice to secured creditors), and pays or disallows creditors' claims. (*See infra*, §§992 *et seq.*).

e. **Taxes:** [§895]   The personal representative is responsible for filing all tax returns on behalf of the decedent or the decedent's estate, and is personally liable to see that all taxes are paid. Actual payment of the tax, however, is from estate assets.

(1) **Decedent's final income tax return:** [§896]   Invariably, the personal representative has to file at least one tax return even if the estate is too small to require the filing of a state inheritance tax return or federal estate tax return. The personal representative must file an income tax return that reports income for the decedent's final taxable year.

(a) **Example:** X, who (as with most individuals) was a calendar year taxpayer, dies on May 19, and in due course E is appointed executor of X's estate. On April 15 of the following year, E must file the decedent's final income tax return, which will report X's income from January 1 to May 19. (*See* Income Tax I Summary.)

(2) **Income from estate assets:** [§897]   If the estate includes income-producing assets, all of the income from such assets will be received by the personal representative during the period the estate is in administration. The personal representative must select a taxable year (either a fiscal year or a calendar year)

for the estate. If the estate has more than $600 of income in any taxable year, the personal representative must file a fiduciary income tax return (Form 1041) reporting such income.

(3) **Death taxes:** [§898]   Depending on the size of the estate, the personal representative may be required to file a state inheritance tax return and a federal estate tax return. (*See* Estate and Gift Tax Summary.)

f.   **Distribution:** [§899]   After payment of funeral expenses, expenses of administration, and claims against the estate, and after payment of any tax that may be due, the personal representative distributes the assets remaining on hand to the will beneficiaries or heirs. In most jurisdictions, this final distribution is made after a hearing at which the probate court enters a decree of distribution and discharges the personal representative from any further duties and all liabilities.

3.   **Court-Supervised vs. Unsupervised Administration**

a.   **Majority rule—supervised administration:** [§900]   In most jurisdictions, all steps in the probate administration process are subject to the court's supervision and control. Before the personal representative can take any of the required actions on behalf of the estate (payment or disallowance of creditors' claims, sale of an asset to pay claims or expenses, distribution to a beneficiary or heir, etc.), court approval must be obtained at a hearing after notice is given to all interested parties. Although a number of jurisdictions permit a testator to provide in the will that some acts can be taken without court approval (*e.g.*, private or public sale of real or personal property), except for purely ministerial acts, virtually every action taken on behalf of the estate involves strict court supervision. The personal representative is seen as a representative of the court in winding up the decedent's affairs.

b.   **Independent administration:** [§901]   Until the 1970's, only two jurisdictions utilized procedures allowing estates to be administered independent of court supervision. In Texas, a testator may designate an "independent executor," and may provide in the will that no action shall be taken in the probate court in regard to the estate other than the probate of the will and the filing of an inventory, appraisement, and list of claims of the estate. After the will has been probated and the independent executor has been appointed, the executor proceeds to administer the estate entirely on her own, without the many routine court appearances required in a supervised administration. [Tex. Prob. Code §145] The state of Washington has a similar procedure if the testator executed a "nonintervention will," which provides that the estate is to be administered without the intervention of any court. [Wash. Rev. Code Ann. §11.68.010] Both of these procedures recognize that most probate administrations are harmonious, nonlitigious affairs in which the surviving family members desire to wind up the decedent's estate with a minimum of formality and expense.

c.   **Uniform Probate Code:** [§902]   Drawing upon the Texas and Washington experience, the U.P.C. provides for both "unsupervised administration" and "supervised administration."

(1) **Unsupervised administration:** [§903]   Under an unsupervised administration, the personal representative administers and distributes the estate without court supervision, meaning that the notices and hearings attendant to a court-supervised administration can be dispensed with. (*See infra*, §§964 *et seq.* for a detailed discussion of the personal representative's duties.)

(2) **Supervised administration:** [§904]   Under the U.P.C.'s supervised administration provisions, court approval must be obtained before a distribution of the estate may be made. [U.P.C. §3-503] However, a personal representative may still exercise most other administration powers (*e.g.*, pay claims or the family allowance, sell property, etc.) *without* court approval. [U.P.C. §3-504] Under the U.P.C., all administrations are unsupervised unless a supervised administration is requested by the personal representative himself or by any interested party (beneficiary, heir, creditor). [U.P.C. §3-502] The court considers the request for supervision and, if granted, supervises the distribution. Moreover, the court may direct a supervised administration proceeding even though the will directs that the administration is to be unsupervised. [U.P.C. §3-502]

d. **Other jurisdictions:** [§905]   Informal probate under the Uniform Probate Code has the advantage of simplifying the administration of estates. Nevertheless, a number of states have declined to adopt a similar procedure on the ground that such advantages do not outweigh the opportunities for abuse by dishonest or incompetent representatives created by insufficient judicial policing. Even in these latter jurisdictions, however, the desirability of providing an alternative to formal proceedings has been recognized in a few situations.

(1) **California:** [§906]   In California, for example, statutes now permit *limited* administration of *community property* in the decedent's estate. [Cal. Prob. Code §§202-204] Basically, these provide that only the *decedent's one-half share* of the community property is subject to probate—and then *only if* it passes to someone other than the surviving spouse. In addition, the surviving spouse may continue to manage and control *all* community assets (including those properly bequeathed by the decedent to others). (*See* Community Property Summary.)

e. **Informal administration procedures:** [§907]   In the case of a very modest estate, no formal administration or court involvement may be needed to wind up the decedent's affairs. Many jurisdictions encourage informal family settlements (*see infra*, §1023), and a number of states have simplified administration procedures for handling small estates (*see infra*, §§1030-1032).

4. **Jurisdiction and Venue:** [§908]   Primary probate jurisdiction is in the state of the decedent's *domicile at the time of death*.

a. **In rem jurisdiction:** [§909]   A probate proceeding is in rem; that is, it conclusively determines as against all persons the title and ownership of the decedent's property that is subject to the court's jurisdiction.

b. **Venue**

    (1) **Resident:** [§910]   Under statutes found in nearly all states, venue for probate and estate administration lies in the *county of the decedent's domicile* at the time of death. [U.P.C. §3-202]

    (2) **Nonresident:** [§911]   In most states, where a nonresident left property located in the state, venue is proper in any county where the decedent *owned property*, or where *any debtor* of the decedent resides. [Fla. Prob. Code §733.101]

c. **Ancillary administration:** [§912]   Where the decedent owned property located in another state, *ancillary* probate and administration proceedings are required in the other state in order to clear title to property. [U.P.C. §3-202] The ancillary administrator takes possession of the property within his jurisdiction, satisfies the claims of creditors within that state, and then distributes the surplus, if any, to the principal executor or administrator.

d. **Choice of law rules:** [§913]   As a general rule, all questions as to the validity or construction of a will are settled in the place of *primary administration* (domicile), and once determined are accepted as binding in the ancillary proceedings. [U.P.C. §3-202] However, because of the situs rule, determinations made by the court handling the primary administration may not always be recognized as conclusive on questions regarding title to land in another state. (*See* Conflict of Laws Summary.)

B. PROOF OF WILLS IN PROBATE

1. **Duty to Produce Will:** [§914]   By statute in many states, a person who has possession of a decedent's will must present the will to the probate court within a specified period. Failure to produce the will ("will suppression") results in *civil liability* to the beneficiaries harmed thereby, and in some states results in criminal liability. [*See, e.g.,* D.C. Code §18.111]

2. **Who May Offer Will for Probate:** [§915]   A will may be offered for probate by *any person interested in the estate*: the named executor, a beneficiary named in the will, an intestate heir of the decedent, or even a creditor having a claim against the estate.

3. **Time Within Which Will Must Be Probated:** [§916]   In all states, a will must be offered for probate within a specified number of years after the decedent's death, or the decedent is deemed to have died intestate.

    a. **Uniform Probate Code:** [§917]   Under the U.P.C., a will must be offered for probate within *three years* after the decedent's death. If no will is probated within the three-year period, the presumption that the decedent died intestate becomes conclusive. [U.P.C. §3-108]

4. **Informal vs. Formal Probate**

    a.   **Common law:** [§918]   At common law, the probate procedure could take one of two forms.

        (1)   **Probate in common form:** [§919]   Probate in common form was *an ex parte proceeding* in which no notice to interested parties was required. The will proponent offered the will for probate, the attesting witnesses testified as to due execution, and the will was admitted to probate. Unless the will was contested within a prescribed period of time, the order admitting the will to probate became final. Common form probate was frequently used, since most probates are harmonious and uncontested.

        (2)   **Probate in solemn form:** [§920]   Under a probate in solemn form, *notice* was required to be given to all interested parties, who could appear to challenge the probate proceeding.

    b.   **Uniform Probate Code:** [§921]   The U.P.C. authorizes the two forms of probate recognized at common law, but gives them different names:

        (1)   **Informal probate:** [§922]   An informal probate is an ex parte proceeding, held before a *registrar* rather than the court, under which *no notice* is given to interested parties. [U.P.C. §§3-301–3-306] This procedure is used when there is no likelihood that the will is going to be contested; although after a will has been admitted in the informal proceeding, a contestant can initiate formal probate proceedings within three years after the decedent's death.

            (a)   **Limitations:** [§923]   The informal probate procedure may *not* be used where the decedent left a "series of testamentary instruments (other than a will and its codicil), the latest of which does not expressly revoke the earlier." [U.P.C. §3-304] Also, an informal proceeding may not be used where there is a contest of the will. [U.P.C. §3-401]

        (2)   **Formal testacy proceeding:** [§924]   A formal testacy proceeding is, as the name suggests, a formal adjudication in which it is determined whether the decedent left a valid will. Such a proceeding may be brought by any interested party (i) to obtain a *formal adjudication* that a will should be admitted to probate, (ii) to *set aside or prevent informal probate* of a will, or (iii) to obtain an order that the decedent died *intestate*. The proceeding is held before the *court* after *notice* to interested parties. Notice is by person or mail to known interested parties (heirs, devisees named in the will), and by publication to unknown heirs. [U.P.C. §§3-401–3-413]

    c.   **Majority rule:** [§925]   Several states on the east coast continue the common form/solemn form probate of the common law, and several non-U.P.C. states have adopted the U.P.C.'s informal probate/formal probate procedures. However, in most states, probate is a formal, adjudicative proceeding in which *notice* must be given to all interested parties.

5.   **Burden of Proof**

   a.   **In probate:** [§926]   At the time the will is offered for probate, the ***will proponents*** have the burden of proving that the will was duly executed. [*In re* Schillenger's Will, 258 N.Y. 186 (1932)]

   b.   **After will admitted to probate:** [§927]   If the challenge to the will's execution is made after the will is initially admitted to probate, the burden of proof ***shifts to the contestants***. [Curtis v. Curtis, 481 F.2d 549 (D.C. Cir. 1972)]

   (1)   **Comment:** At first blush, the foregoing statement looks like a contradiction in terms. How can the issue of proper execution be raised ***after*** the will has been admitted to probate? Due execution should have been in issue at the initial probate proceeding. It must be remembered, however, that in most cases the will is offered for probate just a few days or weeks after the testator's death. At that point in time, the parties who might contest the will may not have had time to determine the facts surrounding the will's execution and may not have determined whether they want to contest on this ground. Most states' procedures recognize this, by allowing probate of the will upon formal (and uncontested) testimony, and then giving the contestants a period of time (usually six months) in which to challenge on various grounds, including improper execution. (*See supra*, §§762 *et seq.*) If the contestants do appear at the probate proceeding and raise the issue of proper execution, the will proponents have the burden of proof on the issue of due execution; if the contestants raise the issue thereafter, ***they*** have the burden of establishing that the will was not duly executed.

   c.   **Proof of execution cannot be waived:** [§928]   The requirement of formal proof of due execution cannot be waived by the admission of opposing parties or by consent of all concerned parties. Even if all interested parties want the instrument to be admitted to probate, if the probate court finds that it was not properly executed, or if there is no evidence of due execution, probate must be denied. An instrument that has not been properly executed is ***not*** a will. [Hopkins v. Hopkins, 708 S.W.2d 31 (Tex. 1986)]

6.   **Whether Will Was Validly Executed Is a Question of Fact:** [§929]   If the fact finder determines, on the basis of testimony by a handwriting expert, that the testator's signature was forged, the will is not entitled to probate even though disinterested, credible attesting witnesses testify that they saw testator sign the will. [Estate of Sylvestri, 44 N.Y.2d 260 (1978)] If there was evidence to support the jury finding, that finding will not be disturbed on appeal. While the probate judge ordinarily rules on the validity of a will, many states provide for trial by jury upon the motion of any party. [N.Y. Surr. Ct. Proc. Act §502(1)]

7.   **Proof**

   a.   **Testimony of attesting witnesses:** [§930]   In most states, both attesting witnesses must testify in open court as to the facts surrounding execution of the will. That testimony must show that the requirements of due execution were complied with. [D.C. Code §18-504] (In several states, it is provided that the testimony can be taken by the court clerk rather than in open court if probate is unopposed.) Some states are much more liberal and require the testimony of only one attesting witness. [Tex. Prob. Code §84]

b. **Absent or unavailable witness:** [§931]   If one witness is dead or incompetent, or cannot be located, it is usually provided that her testimony can be dispensed with and the will can be admitted to probate on the testimony of the other attesting witness. If a witness resides outside the county (some jurisdictions) or outside the state (other jurisdictions), it is usually provided that the absent witness's testimony can be taken by deposition or interrogatory. If all the attesting witnesses are dead, incompetent, or otherwise unable to testify, proof of the handwriting of the testator and of at least one of the attesting witnesses is required in most states.

c. **Attestation clause:** [§932]   A well-drafted will invariably contains an attestation clause which, appearing beneath the testator's signature line and above the signature lines for the attesting witnesses, recites the facts of due execution.

   (1) **Example:** "On the above date, _____, the testator, declared to us, the undersigned, that the foregoing instrument was her last will and testament, and she asked us to attest the will and her signature thereto. She then signed the will in our presence, we being present at the same time. We then signed the will at the testator's request, in her presence, and in the presence of each other, each of us being of the opinion that the testator was of sound and disposing mind and memory on the date hereof."

   (2) **Prima facie evidence:** [§933]   An attestation clause is prima facie evidence of the facts recited therein. Accordingly, when a will contains an attestation clause, it can be admitted to probate even though the attesting witnesses' memories fail them and they have no recollection of the circumstances surrounding the will's execution. [Katz's Will, 277 N.Y. 470 (1938)] The will can be admitted even if the witnesses' testimony is hostile to the will's probate. [Jones v. Whiteley, 533 S.W.2d 881 (Tex. 1976)]

      (a) **Example:** One attesting witness testifies that he had not signed in T's presence, and that in fact the signature on the will was forged. Notwithstanding this hostile testimony, the court can find that the will is admissible to probate. "A full attestation clause reciting compliance with all formalities of execution and signed by the witness is prima facie evidence of the validity of the will, although the witness' memory is faulty, or he contradicts the facts stated in the clause, or where he is dead." [Jones v. Whiteley, *supra*]

   (3) **Not a substitute for attesting witnesses' testimony:** [§934]   Unlike a self-proving affidavit, however, a will cannot be admitted to probate on the strength of an attestation clause alone. The attestation clause can be used to corroborate evidence of due execution (testimony of the attesting witnesses, or

proof of testator's and witnesses' signatures), but it is not a substitute for such evidence. (*See* self-proved wills, below.)

    d.   **Self-proved will:** [§935]   Where a self-proving affidavit was executed at the time the will was executed (or thereafter), the will is **admissible** to probate on the strength of the affidavit. (*See supra*, §448.) The procedures described above apply only if the will was not self-proved.

8.   **Will Written in Foreign Language:** [§936]   A will written in a foreign language may be admitted to probate under the same procedures that apply to an ordinary will, except that the will must be accompanied by an English translation. [Fla. Prob. Code §733.204]

9.   **Lost Wills:** [§937]   All states have procedures whereby a will that has been lost or accidentally destroyed can be admitted to probate. Since questions concerning alleged lost wills arise most frequently in the context of the issue of revocation, this topic is discussed *supra*, at §§548-556.

C. APPOINTMENT AND QUALIFICATION OF PERSONAL REPRESENTATIVE

1.   **Nomenclature**

    a.   **Executor:** [§938]   An executor is a person **named in the will** to serve as personal representative. The executor's appointment is evidenced by the court's issuance of **letters testamentary**, which show the executor's authority to act on behalf of the estate.

    b.   **Administrator:** [§939]   An administrator is a personal representative **appointed by the court** to administer an intestate estate. The administrator's appointment is evidenced by **letters of administration**.

    c.   **Administrator c.t.a.:** [§940]   Where the decedent's will does not name an executor or the named executor fails to act for some reason, the person appointed to administer the estate is titled an **administrator with will annexed**, or administrator c.t.a. (standing for *cum testamento annexo*).

    d.   **Special or temporary administrator:** [§941]   Where it is necessary to obtain the **immediate** appointment of a personal representative prior to the formal appointment of a permanent executor or administrator, a special administrator may be appointed. [U.P.C. §§3-614–3-618] This might occur where there is a will contest, meaning that appointment of the named executor is in doubt during the pendency of the contest; or where there is a dispute over priority of appointment between various heirs. In some jurisdictions, the person holding this position is called a temporary administrator.

    e.   **Successor personal representative:** [§942]   Where an executor or administrator properly begins to serve but ceases to act for some reason, a successor executor or administrator is appointed by the court.

f.   **Uniform Probate Code:** [§943]   The U.P.C. uses one term, *personal representative*, in lieu of the more specialized terms such as executor and administrator. [U.P.C. §1-201(30)]

g.   **Guardian**

(1) **Guardian of the person:** [§944]   A guardian of the *person* of a minor child is charged with the custody and care of the child and is responsible for the child's upbringing. A child's parents are, of course, the child's **natural guardians**. A parent may designate a guardian of the person for his children in the will. The nomination is *not* binding on the court, but is given considerable weight. If minor children are orphaned and no guardian is designated in either parent's will, or if the parents left no will, the guardian is selected from a list that, in most states, gives **preference to grandparents**, uncles and aunts, and other kin, in that order. (Of course, the statutes do not indicate which grandparents, maternal or paternal, or which uncle or aunt, is to be selected.) One of the primary reasons a couple with minor children should have wills is to take advantage of the opportunity to designate who will be responsible for raising their children if the children are orphaned.

(2) **Guardian of the estate:** [§945]   If a minor inherits property and no provision has been made for the property's management (*e.g.*, by a settlement in trust), it may be necessary to appoint a guardian of the minor's *estate*. This situation would be encountered if the child were orphaned, but it also could arise if either or both parents are living, if, for example, the child is given a legacy by an uncle's will. In most states, a personal representative **cannot make a distribution to a minor;** only a duly appointed guardian can give the personal representative a binding receipt and release for the distribution. Although a parent is guardian of the child's person, he or she has *no* authority to handle the child's estate. In many states, guardianship laws are unusually cumbersome and restrictive: The guardian must give **bond** (with annual premiums), must make **annual accountings**, can invest only in savings accounts and government bonds, and cannot expend anything other than income for the child's benefit **without court approval**. If a will does not designate a guardian of the person, a guardian is selected from a statutory list that, typically, gives preference to parents, grandparents, uncle and aunts, and other kin, in that order.

(a) **Distributions of small amounts of property:** [§946]   Many jurisdictions have statutes that permit distribution of small amounts of tangible or intangible personal property from an estate or trust to the parents of a minor beneficiary or heir. [Fla. Guard. Laws §744.301—up to $5,000]

(b) **Distributions to custodian under Uniform Gifts to Minors Act:** [§947]   To provide an alternative to distributions into a guardianship with its attendant problems and expenses, several states have amended their version of the Uniform Gifts to Minors Act to authorize distributions from an estate or trust to a custodian for the minor heir or beneficiary under the state's Uniform Gifts to Minors Act ("U.G.M.A."). [N.Y. Est.

Powers & Trusts Law §7-4.9; Tex. Rev. Civ. Stat. Ann. art. 5923-101] A U.G.M.A. custodianship provides **flexible management and administration powers** without the court involvement and expenses attendant to a guardianship administration.

(3) **Guardian ad litem:** [§948]   A guardian ad litem is a person appointed by the court to represent the interest of a minor or incompetent heir or beneficiary when no guardian has been appointed and the party's interests are not otherwise represented. The court may appoint a guardian ad litem even though a guardian has been appointed, if the court feels that the representation may be inadequate. An example of this latter situation would be where the guardian has an interest that is adverse to that of the ward. A guardian ad litem also may be appointed to represent the interests of unborn, unascertained, or unlocatable persons. A guardian ad litem may be appointed at any time by the court on its own motion. [Fla. Prob. Code §731.303(5)]

2. **Qualification of Personal Representative:** [§949]   To be eligible for appointment as a personal representative, a person must have the **capacity to contract**. Thus, minors and incompetents are ineligible to serve. Several states go beyond this and provide for disqualification from appointment for drunkenness, conviction of a felony, etc. [Fla. Prob. Code §733.302; 175 A.L.R. 784]

a. **Conflict of interest:** [§950]   The mere fact that the person seeking appointment has a claim against the estate or some interest adverse to that of the estate does not by itself disqualify him from appointment. [Boyles v. Gresham, 263 S.W.2d 965 (Tex. 1954); 18 A.L.R.2d 633] *Rationale:* It "has ever been the policy of the law . . . that every citizen making a will has the right to select according to his own judgment the person or persons whom he would have execute it." [Estate of Svacina, 1 N.W.2d 780 (Wis. 1942)]

b. **Nonresidents:** [§951]   In a few states, nonresident individuals are disqualified from acting as personal representatives. [*See, e.g.,* Penn. Stat. Ann. tit. 20, §3157] Even more frequently, foreign corporations are disqualified. In other states, nonresident individuals may act as executors, but not as administrators. [Cal. Prob. Code §§405.1-405.6]

3. **Priority for Appointment:** [§952]   In all states, statutes fix the order of priority for appointment as a personal representative of an estate. The Uniform Probate Code provisions are representative: (i) person named in will as executor; (ii) surviving spouse (if will beneficiary); (iii) any other will beneficiary; (iv) surviving spouse; (v) any other heir; and (vi) if forty-five days after decedent's death, any creditor. [U.P.C. §3-203]

4. **Bond:** [§953]   In most states, the personal representative must give a fiduciary bond (typically, for double the value of personal property in the estate) **unless** bond is waived by the will.

a. **Uniform Probate Code:** [§954]   Under the U.P.C., bond is not required in informal probate proceedings unless the will expressly requires that the executor give bond. In formal testacy proceedings, the court can dispense with the necessity of a bond even if there is no will provision waiving bond. [U.P.C. §3-603] In either type of proceeding, however, any person with an interest in the estate (including a creditor) may demand that the personal representative give bond. [U.P.C. §3-605]

5. **Compensation:** [§955]   The personal representative is, of course, entitled to compensation for performance of his services. In most states, a ***statutory rate*** of compensation (based on the size of the estate) applies, absent a contrary will provision. [Cal. Prob. Code §§900-903]

   a. **Will provision:** [§956]   If the will specifies the amount or rate of compensation for the personal representative, and the personal representative accepts the appointment, the will provisions are binding; thus, the personal representative cannot thereafter attempt to claim the higher fees authorized by statute. Acceptance of the appointment constitutes an acceptance of the decedent's offer of compensation, and the personal representative is bound by the contract. [19 A.L.R.3d 520] If, however, the personal representative performs ***extraordinary services*** beyond those ordinarily involved in an estate administration, the court may award additional compensation for such extraordinary services. [19 A.L.R.3d 543]

   b. **Uniform Probate Code:** [§957]   Under the U.P.C., a personal representative is entitled to "a reasonable compensation" for his services. If a will provides for compensation of the personal representative and there is no contract with the decedent regarding compensation, the personal representative may renounce the provision before qualifying and be entitled to "reasonable compensation" rather than the amount stated in the will. [U.P.C. §3-719]

   c. **Reasonable compensation:** [§958]   As noted above, the U.P.C. provides for "reasonable compensation" of personal representatives. Also, a common practice in will drafting is to provide that the personal representative shall be entitled to "reasonable compensation" in lieu of the mode of compensation provided for by statute. In implementing such a provision, the standard practice is to look to rates of compensation that prevail in the community, including fiduciary fees charged by banks and trust companies for serving as personal representative. In some jurisdictions, the local court promulgates a fee schedule to be used as a guide in determining reasonable compensation.

   d. **Waiver:** [§959]   If the will names the surviving spouse or some other family member as executor, it is quite common for the executor to waive the right to compensation and serve as personal representative at no cost to the estate. There may be tax advantages in doing so, as compensation received by the personal representative is taxable as ordinary income under the federal income tax. If no compensation is paid to the executor, the estate will not be entitled to a deduction for this item under the federal estate tax or state succession tax. However, under current tax laws, very few estates pay estate or succession taxes. (*See* Estate and Gift Tax Summary.) In such a case, loss of an estate tax deduction for this item would be of only theoretical concern.

(1) **Example:** T dies leaving a will that bequeaths her entire estate to her daughter D and names D executor. Under state law, D would be entitled to receive $8,000 in compensation for her services. D should waive the right to compensation. Since she will receive T's entire estate in any event, the only effect of accepting the compensation will be to increase D's taxable income by $8,000.

(2) **Compare:** If, however, T's estate will have to pay a federal estate tax or state succession tax, whether D should accept the compensation (thereby entitling the estate to an $8,000 deduction at the cost of D's having taxable income) or waive compensation should be determined by comparing the estate's marginal estate tax bracket to D's marginal income tax bracket.

6. **Termination of Appointment:** [§960]   Certain events result in termination of a representative's appointment and authority. These include: death or disability, resignation, judicial determination of misconduct, judicial ruling that a prior determination of testacy was incorrect, entry of an order closing the estate, or passage of one year after a closing statement is filed. [U.P.C. §§3-609–3-612]

   a. **Resignation:** [§961]   Once appointed, the personal representative *cannot* merely resign. She is charged with the fiduciary duties and responsibilities set forth below until the court that appointed her has accepted her resignation. This usually requires an accounting that shows all receipts and disbursements, and a transfer of the assets of the estate to the successor personal representative.

   b. **Removal:** [§962]   The personal representative may be removed (and letters of appointment revoked) wherever she is shown to have been guilty of misconduct in administration, or to be lacking in any of the qualities required for a personal representative. [U.P.C. §3-611] Failure to perform any of the duties required of the personal representative, or acting in adverse interest or hostility to the estate or the beneficiaries, constitutes grounds for removal. [Estate of Palm, 68 Cal. App. 2d 204 (1945)] However, "the removal of a personal representative chosen by the testator is a drastic action which should be taken only when the estate . . . is endangered," and mere animosity between the executor and other beneficiaries does not constitute grounds for removal. [Estate of Beichner, 247 A.2d 779 (Pa. 1968)]

D. DUTIES AND LIABILITIES OF PERSONAL REPRESENTATIVE

1. **Qualification:** [§963]   Before letters testamentary or letters of administration are issued, the personal representative must file with the court a statement accepting the appointment. [U.P.C. §3-601] In most states, the personal representative must give a fiduciary **bond** (*see supra*, §§953-954).

2. **Powers and Duties:** [§964]   Unlike a trust, which may continue for the lifetime of one or more beneficiaries, an estate administration is usually of short duration. Accordingly, the personal representative's powers and duties are limited to those required to manage and preserve the decedent's assets during the period of administration.

a. **Marshalling assets:** [§965]   The personal representative's initial duty is to *take possession or control* of the assets belonging to the decedent. The representative must do everything required to obtain possession of and care for all such assets. In carrying out this responsibility, the representative is granted the same powers that an *absolute owner* would have [U.P.C. §3-715], and is empowered to maintain an action to recover possession of property or to determine title to it [Fla. Prob. Code §733.607].

   (1) **Exception:** [§966]   Any real or tangible personal property may be left with, or surrendered to, the person presumptively entitled to it unless possession of such property by the personal representative is necessary for purposes of administering the estate.

   (2) **Only probate assets:** [§967]   The estate assets that are subject to the personal representative's management and control do *not* include nonprobate assets, such as property that passes by right of survivorship (*e.g.*, joint tenancy) or by the terms of a contract (*e.g.*, insurance proceeds), or property held in a trust, even where the decedent held a power of revocation or power of appointment.

   (3) **Duty not to commingle assets:** [§968]   The personal representative may not commingle estate assets with his own, either in making investments or otherwise. Accordingly, the representative should open a separate bank account in the name of the estate.

b. **Inventory:** [§969]   The personal representative must file an inventory of property of the estate, listing it with *reasonable detail* and including for each listed item its *estimated fair market value* as of the date of the decedent's death. [Fla. Prob. Code §733.604] Several states require that one or more appraisers must be appointed to value estate assets, while in other states the appointment of an appraiser is optional. [Fla. Prob. Code §733.605]

c. **Accounting:** [§970]   In most states, the executor or administrator must render periodic accountings to the probate court, typically within twelve months after appointment and successive annual accountings thereafter. The personal representative cannot be discharged until his *final accounting* has been approved by the probate court.

d. **Care and preservation of assets:** [§971]   The personal representative must exercise *reasonable care* in preserving the assets of the estate. Basically, he must manage the estate with the degree of care that a prudent person would exercise in managing his own affairs, with an eye towards preservation of the property. This includes a duty to insure property for which casualty insurance is usually obtained, the duty to prevent property from being taken or damaged by the acts of others, and the duty to pay taxes thereon.

e. **Investments:** [§972]   The representative's *primary duty* is to *preserve* the estate—not to invest it and make it productive. Consequently, in most states, the representative has no inherent power to invest funds belonging to the estate. However, monies belonging to the estate should be deposited in a bank account in the estate's name. [Cal. Prob. Code §585] Also, a duty to invest may be implied from the circumstances, particularly if the administration will remain open for an extended period of time. And, of course, if the will permits or directs the executor to invest, he may do so.

(1) **Exception:** [§973]   The duty to preserve the estate imposes on the representative the duty to sell assets or change investments where necessary to avoid loss or unreasonable risk of loss to the estate.

f.   **Carrying on decedent's business:** [§974]   In most states, the personal representative ordinarily has **no duty or authority** to carry on a business owned by the decedent. If he does so without authorization in the will or prior court approval, he is **personally liable** for any losses and, of course, is personally accountable for the profits. [58 A.L.R.2d 365]

(1) **Authority may be conferred:** [§975]   Authority to continue the operation of the decedent's business may be conferred by the will, or by express consent of all beneficiaries, heirs, and other persons interested in the estate. Upon petition, the court may authorize the representative to continue the decedent's business.

(2) **Minority rule:** [§976]   Under the Uniform Probate Code and in several non-U.P.C. states, the personal representative may continue any unincorporated business or venture in which the decedent was engaged at the time of death for a period of **four months**. Also, the representative may continue the business throughout the period of administration, if the business is incorporated by the representative and no interested party objects. [U.P.C. §3-715 (24)] In addition, the representative may consent to the reorganization, merger, or consolidation of any corporation or other business enterprise. [U.P.C. §3-715(19)]

g.   **Sale or mortgaging of estate assets:** [§977]   In most jurisdictions, the representative has the power to sell property of the estate **only** when authorized by the **will or court order**. A sale of estate assets generally will be authorized by the court when necessary to pay debts of the estate, to provide funds for the payment of bequests, or to prevent loss to the estate (if, for example, the assets are declining in value). Also, if the decedent was bound by a specifically enforceable contract to convey or transfer real or personal property, the court may authorize the representative to make the conveyance or transfer pursuant to the contract.

(1) **Borrowing:** [§978]   The representative may be authorized to borrow on the credit of the estate and to give a mortgage on estate assets where necessary to pay estate debts or expenses of administration.

(2) **Will provision:** [§979]   If the decedent's will confers a specific power to sell or mortgage real property or a general power to sell any asset of the estate, the personal representative may sell, mortgage, or lease real property without court order for cash or credit, with or without security; and such actions need not be justified by a showing of necessity. [Fla. Prob. Code §733.613]

(3) **Uniform Probate Code:** [§980]   Under the U.P.C., a personal representative need not obtain specific authorization to sell or mortgage assets, since this power is granted by the Code. [U.P.C. §3-715(23)] The representative is prohibited from selling, etc., only when express restraints have been imposed upon him under the will or by court order.

h. **Leases:** [§981]   If authorized by the will or court order, the personal representative may execute a lease of any asset belonging to the estate. Usually, there is some statutory limit on the term of such leases. [*See, e.g.,* Cal. Prob. Code §842—10 years] Leases are generally authorized by the court only where consistent with the *normal use* of the property (*e.g.,* an apartment house), or where necessary to *obtain funds* for the estate.

(1) **Uniform Probate Code:** [§982]   Again, the U.P.C. permits leasing of assets without court authorization, unless the representative has been specifically restrained therefrom. [U.P.C. §3-715(23)]

3. **Fiduciary Duties Generally:** [§983]   A personal representative is subject to the fiduciary duties and standards of conduct that apply to fiduciaries generally.

a. **Standard of care, skill, and prudence:** [§984]   A personal representative is held to the general standard of care that applies to trustees. [Fla. Prob. Code §733.602] Therefore, he must observe those standards in dealing with estate assets that would be observed by a prudent trustee dealing with the property of another. If the representative has special skills or is named personal representative on the basis of representations of special skills or expertise, he is under a duty to use those skills. [Liberty Title & Trust Co. v. Plews, 60 A.2d 630 (N.J. 1948); Fla. Prob. Code §737.302; *and see* Trusts Summary]

b. **Duty of loyalty—no self-dealing:** [§985]   The personal representative owes a duty of undivided loyalty to the estate that he represents. In general, a personal representative cannot "wear two hats" (his fiduciary "hat," representing the estate, and his personal "hat," representing his individual interest) in any transaction with respect to the estate. Thus, a personal representative cannot sell assets to the estate nor buy assets from the estate. Also, the personal representative cannot borrow estate funds for his personal use, no matter how well-secured the loan may be, and no matter how fair the rate of interest may be. (*See* Trusts Summary.)

(1) **Rationale:** The theory underlying the self-dealing rules is *not* (or at least not necessarily) that the personal representative would act dishonestly or would use the fiduciary office to personal advantage. Rather, it is that the personal representative is not in a position to make a completely objective, impartial judgment if his personal interest is affected by the transaction. Should this particular asset be sold (or purchased); and if so, on what terms? The personal representative's judgment as to the wisdom of a particular course of action may be affected, no matter how slightly, if his own personal interest is involved.

(2) **Exceptions:** [§986]   It is generally held that a personal representative may be allowed to buy or sell an estate asset from or to himself *if authorized by the probate court* (after notice to interested parties) upon a finding that the action is in the estate's best interests. Also, the *testator may waive* the self-dealing rules by an express provision to that effect in the will (*e.g.*, if the will gives the executor an option to purchase a particular asset in the estate).

4.   **Liabilities:** [§987]   As is true of any fiduciary, a personal representative is liable for any losses resulting from bad faith actions, mismanagement, or breach of a fiduciary duty (including the duty not to self-deal). [U.P.C. §3-712]

   a.   **Torts:** [§988]   At common law and in most states today, an executor or administrator is *personally liable* for any torts committed by him (or by his servants or agents) in the course of administration of the estate. He is, however, entitled to *reimbursement* from the estate for any such liability, *provided* that (i) he was not personally at fault, and (ii) there was no breach of duty of care by him in incurring the liability (*e.g.*, the tort was committed by agent or employee selected with reasonable care).

   b.   **Contracts:** [§989]   By majority rule, the personal representative is *personally liable* on any contracts entered into on behalf of the estate unless the contract relieves him from liability. However, he is entitled to be *reimbursed* from the estate for any such obligation, *provided* the contract was within his powers and was executed in the course of proper administration of the estate. Of course, if the estate is insolvent, the loss will fall upon the representative personally.

   (1)   **Rationale:** The personal representative is in a better position than the contracting party to know whether the estate's assets are sufficient to cover the obligation.

   (2)   **Provisions that relieve personal representative of liability:** [§990]   Signing a contract as "Sam Jones, Executor" does not eliminate personal liability but merely reflects the representative capacity. However, signing a contract "Mary Jones Estate, by Sam Jones, Executor" reflects that the *contract is with the estate* (not the executor) and eliminates personal liability.

   (3)   **Minority rule:** [§991]   In several states, a personal representative is *not* personally liable on the estate's contracts unless (i) he fails to reveal his representative capacity, or (ii) the contract provides for personal liability. [N.Y. Est. Powers & Trusts Law §11-4.7; Fla. Prob. Code §733.619 – exception for contracts for attorney's fees]

E.   CREDITORS' CLAIMS

1.   **Notice to Creditors:** [§992]   One of the personal representative's first acts is to give notice by publication to creditors of the estate, advising of the pendency of the administration and when and where claims must be filed. After such publication, the "nonclaim"

period commences to run. Secured creditors must be given notice by registered or certified mail.

2. **Nonclaim Statutes:** [§993]   In most states, creditors' claims must be filed within a specified period of time; otherwise, the claim is barred notwithstanding that the statute of limitations otherwise applicable to the claim has not run. [Fla. Prob. Code §733.702—3 months; U.P.C. §3-801—4 months] The statute applies to all claims: matured and contingent, liquidated and unliquidated, contract and tort. The purpose of the short nonclaim period is to facilitate the winding up of the decedent's estate, so that the estate can be distributed to the heirs or beneficiaries free of any concern about creditors' claims.

   a. **Secured claims:** [§994]   A secured creditor who fails to file a claim within the nonclaim period loses the opportunity to collect from estate assets on the basis of the decedent's personal liability on the debt. However, the creditor's ability to enforce the lien is ***not*** affected by the failure to file. [U.P.C. §3-803(c)] (As a practical matter, this means that the secured creditor will be paid in full; otherwise he will foreclose on the lien.)

   b. **No publication of notice:** [§995]   It is usually provided that if notice to creditors is not published in accordance with the statute, claims against the estate are barred within a specified number of ***years*** after the decedent's death. [U.P.C. §3-803(a)(2)—3 years]

   c. **Minority rule:** [§996]   In several states, a creditor who does not file claims within the time prescribed by statute is not barred. The only consequence is that the creditor loses priority and is not paid until after all creditors who made timely filings have been paid. [N.Y. Surr. Ct. Proc. Act §1802; Tex. Prob. Code §322] In these states, failure to file a claim within the time prescribed by the statute has significance ***only if*** the estate is partially insolvent.

3. **Priority of Claims:** [§997]   In all states, statutes fix the order in which claims against the estate are to be paid. Typically, it is provided that claims are to be paid in the following order: (i) administration expenses; (ii) funeral expenses and expenses of last illness (up to a stated dollar amount); (iii) family allowance; (iv) debts given preference under federal law (tax claims, etc.); (v) secured claims (up to value of security interest); (vi) judgments entered against the decedent during his lifetime; and (vii) all other claims. [Cal. Prob. Code §950; Fla. Prob. Code §733.707]

F. ABATEMENT

1. **Introduction:** [§998]   Abatement is the process of reducing testamentary gifts in cases where the estate assets are not sufficient to pay all claims against the estate and satisfy all bequests and devises. The testator can specify the source of funds from which claims against the estate are to be paid, and the order in which testamentary gifts are to be abated; the rules set out below apply ***if there are no contrary directions*** in the will.

2. **Classification of Testamentary Gifts:** [§999]   The classes of gifts that can be made by a will are discussed *supra*, §§722-726.

3. **Common Law:** [§1000]   At common law and in a handful of states today, all gifts of personal property, of whatever class, abate before dispositions of real property. [Edmunds, Administrator v. Scott, 78 Va. 720 (1884)] The historical reason for this rule was that title to land passed directly to the heirs or devisees, and the personal representative had the power to sell such real property only if the personal estate was insufficient to satisfy all estate claims.

   a. **Order of abatement:** [§1001]   In states following the common law, the order of abatement is:

      (i) *Personal property* passing by *intestacy* (if there is a partial intestacy for some reason) is first used to satisfy administration expenses and claims against the estate.

      (ii) After this class of assets is exhausted (or if, as in the ordinary case, there is no partial intestacy), personal property in the *residuary estate* is used.

      (iii) Next to be abated are *general* legacies, which abate pro rata.

      (iv) Then *demonstrative* legacies.

      (v) Finally *specific bequests* of personal property abate pro rata.

      (vi) Only after *all* personal property has been exhausted is *real property* used to satisfy estate claims and expenses. Real property dispositions abate in the same order: any real property passing by intestacy, then real property in the residuary estate, and last to be abated are specific devises of real property.

   b. **Qualification:** [§1002]   A few jurisdictions nominally apply the common law rule (*i.e.*, that all gifts of personal property abate before any gifts of land), but temper the rule if the court finds that the testator intended to charge the general and specific bequests on the residuary realty. Such an intent is found whenever the will contains a residuary clause that "blends" (*i.e.*, makes no distinction between) land and personal property: "I give all of my residuary estate, both real and personal property. . . ." In such cases, gifts abate in the order set out below.

4. **Modern Law (Majority View):** [§1003]   In most states today, the distinction between real property and personal property has been abolished, at least insofar as abatement *between* categories of gifts are concerned. Thus, the order of abatement is:

   (i) *Real or personal property* passing by partial *intestacy* is first exhausted.

   (ii) Next, the *residuary estate* (both real and personal property) is abated.

   (iii) Next are *general* legacies, which abate pro rata.

   (iv) Finally, *specific* devises and bequests can be reached.

   [U.P.C. §3-906]

a. **Abatement within categories:** [§1004]   In a number of states, while no distinction is made as to real and personal property *between* categories, the distinction continues to be drawn *within* categories. Thus, personal property passing by partial intestacy abates before intestate real property; and personal property within the residuary estate abates before real property in the residuary estate. [Thompson v. Thompson, 236 S.W.2d 779 (Tex. 1951)]

b. **Demonstrative legacies:** [§1005]   Demonstrative legacies are treated in the same category as specific gifts—at least to the extent that the property from which the gift was to be satisfied is in the estate at death. However, demonstrative legacies are classified the same as general legacies, and abate pro rata with general legacies, to the extent that the fund or property from which payment was directed is *insufficient* to satisfy the demonstrative legacy.

c. **Variations:** [§1006]   There are numerous local variations in the operation of the above rules. In some jurisdictions, if gifts of the same class are made both to blood relatives and to others who are not related to the testator, the gifts to the nonrelatives abate first. [Cal. Prob. Code §752] In some states, gifts to the testator's surviving spouse do not abate until other gifts of the same category are exhausted. [Fla. Prob. Code §733.805]

G. SOURCE OF PAYMENT OF DEATH TAXES

1. **State Inheritance Taxes:** [§1007]   An inheritance tax is considered a tax on the right to inherit. In states that have inheritance taxes, the tax rates and exemptions turn on the amount given to the beneficiary and the beneficiary's relationship to the decedent. Unless the testator specifies otherwise in the will, the burden of the tax is on the *recipient* of the gift. Thus, if testator's will makes a bequest of $25,000 to F, and if an inheritance tax is payable by reason of this bequest, the burden of the tax is on F and must be paid out of F's legacy.

   a. **Estate taxes:** [§1008]   Until the 1970's, a majority of states had inheritance taxes as their primary succession tax. The remaining states had estate taxes which (as with the federal estate tax) are tied to the value of assets passing at death rather than the amount passing to each beneficiary as heir. Today, however, a majority of states have estate taxes, most of which do nothing more than absorb the "credit for state death taxes" allowed against the estate tax under Internal Revenue Code section 2011. (*See* Estate and Gift Taxes Summary.) In such states, the source of payment of the state tax is the same as for the federal estate tax, discussed below.

2. **Federal Estate Tax**

   a. **Majority rule:** [§1009]   A majority of states follow common law principles in holding that federal (and state) estate taxes, as with other debts of the estate, are payable out of the *residuary* estate (absent a contrary will provision). This applies to all assets that generate estate tax, *including nonprobate assets* such as joint tenancy properties passing by right of survivorship and revocable transfers.

b. **Exception:** [§1010]   The burden-on-the-residue rule is subject to an exception created by federal statute. To the extent that the federal estate tax is attributable to life insurance proceeds or property over which the decedent held a general power of appointment, such proceeds or properties bear their pro rata share of the federal estate tax, subject to the following qualifications. [I.R.C. §§2206, 2207]

   (1) **Contrary provision:** [§1011]   Testator can always make whatever will provision she deems appropriate as to the source of payment of the estate tax.

   (2) **Marital deduction:** [§1012]   If the life insurance proceeds or general power of appointment disposition qualify for the federal estate tax marital deduction, the federal statutes provide that such dispositions are relieved of any burden of the estate tax. (For the rationale for this exception, *see infra*.)

c. **Apportionment statutes:** [§1013]   A substantial number of states have enacted apportionment statutes under which the estate tax is ratably apportioned ***among all beneficiaries*** of the estate: testamentary beneficiaries and beneficiaries of nonprobate dispositions, subject to the following qualifications. [U.P.C. §3-916; Cal. Prob. Code §970]

   (1) **Contrary provision:** [§1014]   A testator can provide in the will that the apportionment rule shall not apply to her estate by expressly providing that the estate tax shall be paid from a specified source (*e.g.*, the residuary estate).

   (2) **Marital, charitable deduction:** [§1015]   A common feature of these statutes is that dispositions qualifying for the federal estate tax (or state succession tax) marital deduction or charitable deduction are not subject to pro rata apportionment. The rationale for this exception is that an estate tax deduction is available only for the net amount passing to the spouse or charity (*i.e.*, after all charges, including taxes). If these gifts were reduced by the taxes attributed to them, the deductions would be reduced and higher taxes would have to be paid.

H. ENTITLEMENT TO INCOME DURING PERIOD OF ADMINISTRATION

1. **Introduction:** [§1016]   The administration of an estate often takes a substantial period of time, and the classification of testamentary gifts determines the rights of the respective beneficiaries to earnings, interest, and profits on the estate assets.

2. **Specific Gifts:** [§1017]   A specific devise or bequest carries with it the right to ***all earnings***, profits, or other accessions produced by the particular property ***after*** the testator's death. [Fla. Prob. Code §738.05] Thus, a devisee of real property is entitled to rent that becomes due on the property after the testator's death. On the other hand, the devisee is ***not*** entitled to rents that became due during the ***testator's lifetime***, even though such rents are not paid until after testator's death. Such rental income is a general asset of the estate.

a. **Bond interest, cash dividends:** [§1018]   The specific legatee of a bond is entitled to interest accruing on the bond *after* the testator's death. Likewise, dividends declared *after* the testator's death pass to the specific legatee. Dividends declared to stockholders of record during the testator's lifetime, though paid to the executor after the testator's death, do *not* pass to the legatee of specifically bequeathed stock.

b. **Stock dividends, stock splits:** [§1019]   If the will makes a specific gift of stock, the beneficiary is entitled to stock dividends and stock splits declared *after* the testator's death. *Rationale:* The specific beneficiary owned the stock from the date of testator's death, subject to the executor's possession for purposes of administration. [Estate of Marks, 255 A.2d 512 (Pa. 1969)]

3. **General Legacies:** [§1020]   In most states, a general legatee ("I bequeath $10,000 to my nephew Ned") is *not* entitled to interest on the legacy if it is paid within *one year* after testator's death. If not so paid, the general legatee is entitled to interest at the legal rate, beginning one year after the testator's death (unless the will provides otherwise). [Cal. Prob. Code §162] The legal rate of interest varies, but in most states it is six percent. Under the Uniform Probate Code, interest on a general legacy begins to run one year after appointment of a personal representative (unless the will indicates a contrary intent). [U.P.C. §3-904]

4. **Residuary Gifts:** [§1021]   The residuary beneficiaries own all testamentary assets not specifically devised or bequeathed, after payment of all claims and satisfaction of all legacies. Thus, all earnings and profits not used to pay interest on general legacies and not belonging to the recipients of specific gifts are added to and become a part of the residuary estate.

I. INFORMAL ADMINISTRATION PROCEDURES

1. **Introduction:** [§1022]   A major purpose of the estate administration process is to *clear title* to assets in the decedent's name, and to cause the records to reflect the *new ownership* of the persons who have succeeded to the decedent's property. In many instances, however, the decedent's estate is a modest one, consisting primarily of tangible personal property. In this situation, the decedent's successors may not need a court order or formal administration proceeding to deal with the decedent's assets or wind up his affairs. Insofar as the title-clearing function of probate is concerned, it is only where the decedent owned assets that evidence legal title by a document (a deed, as to realty; a stock certificate, as to securities; a certificate of title, as to an automobile) that a court proceeding may be required to establish the ownership rights of the decedent's successors. Recognizing that a formal administration proceeding is not necessary for modest-sized estates, all jurisdictions authorize one or more of the following simplified administration procedures.

2. **Informal Family Settlements:** [§1023]   If the decedent's estate is a small one (meaning that the authority of "letters of administration" is not needed to collect his assets), creditors' claims can be satisfied informally, and decedent's family can reach an amicable agreement as to the proper distribution of his assets, there is no need to subject the surviving family members to the expenses and delays of a formal estate administration.

They can wind up his affairs informally. [Heinz v. Vawter, 266 N.W. 486 (Iowa 1936)] Statutes in several states recognize this principle by providing that there must be an affirmative showing that an estate administration is needed before letters of administration will be issued by the probate court. [Tex. Prob. Code §§88(d), 178(b)] Moreover, empirical studies have shown that many small estates are handled informally even in the absence of statutory authority. [Stein, Probate Administration Study: Some Emerging Conclusions, 9 Real Prop., Prob. & Trust J. 596 (1974)]

a. **Example:** D dies survived by his wife and several adult children. D and his wife lived in an apartment (meaning that title to real property is not involved). Aside from the couple's checking account, a joint savings account (which passed to the wife by right of survivorship), and a life insurance policy that names the wife as beneficiary, D's "estate" consists of the furniture and furnishings in the apartment and his personal effects. In this situation, it may occur to the wife and children that there is no need to have a formal administration of D's estate—and they are right. The wife can pay the funeral bill and the expenses of D's last illness out of the savings account; and she can pay the gas bill and the monthly rent out of the checking account just as she did last month. If the wife decides to sell the Sony color TV set, she is not going to have to furnish evidence of her title for such items; *possession* is ten-tenths, not just nine-tenths, of the law. Here, D's successors, whether claiming under a will that is not probated or claiming as heirs, do not need any probate court involvement to wind up his affairs. (If D died intestate, meaning that a portion of the estate passed to his adult children, the children are not likely to assert any claim to his property as against their mother. The children's greatest concern is likely to be, not their rights as heirs, but that they may be called upon to support their widowed mother who has been left such a modest estate.)

b. **Comment:** The rights of the surviving family members are further supported by the rule that title to a decedent's assets passes immediately and automatically to his legatees or heirs, subject to the personal representative's right of possession for purposes of administration. The effect of this provision is to legitimate the legatees' or heirs' simply taking possession of the decedent's property.

3. **Affidavit Procedures:** [§1024]   Suppose, in the foregoing example, that the wife and children are able to handle D's estate informally except for two items: the certificate of title to the family car, which is in D's name (the wife now wants to sell the car); and a $2,000 bank account, which stands in D's name with no survivorship provisions. Even here it may not be necessary to take out formal estate administration proceedings.

a. **Bank accounts:** [§1025]   As a general rule, a bank cannot safely pay over an account in a decedent's name to anyone other than the decedent's duly authorized personal representative; only the representative can give the bank a binding "receipt and release" that will protect the bank against claims of others (*e.g.*, the decedent's creditors). [Brobst v. Brobst, *supra*, §889] However, statutes in a number of states permit collection of small bank accounts by a notarized affidavit signed by the decedent's heirs. The bank is protected if it pays over the account pursuant to the affidavit. [Miss. Code Ann. §81-5-63—$1,000 per bank; N.Y. Surr. Ct. Proc. Act §1310—not to exceed $10,000 in the aggregate]

b. **Automobile certificates of title:** [§1026] Similarly, a number of states permit the transfer of an automobile certificate of title to the decedent's heirs upon an affidavit signed by the heirs. [D.C. Code Ann. §20-357; Iowa Code Ann. §321.47; Tex. Penal Code art. 1436-1, §35]

4. **Probate of Will as Muniment of Title:** [§1027] Suppose, in the example above, that the family lived in a house, not an apartment, and that title to the family home is in D's name. Except for the residence, the estate can be handled informally under the procedures described above. In most states, it would be necessary to have a formal estate administration, so that the land title records would include a probate decree showing that all creditors' claims were satisfied and that D's successors are now the owners of the property. Absent such a decree, the surviving family members could not sell or otherwise deal with the real property. The last deed in the chain of title would show D as record owner, and getting his signature on the next deed out is going to be rather difficult.

a. **Muniment of title:** [§1028] In a few states, even in this situation it would *not* be necessary to have a formal estate *administration*. Upon a finding that there are no unpaid debts of the decedent, the will is simply admitted to probate (*i.e.*, its due execution is proven as in the ordinary case). The will (which names the devisees, and thus the new owners) and the order admitting it to probate become part of the county records and constitute a "muniment of title"; *i.e.*, a link in the chain of title that has the same effect as a deed. No other steps usually involved in an estate administration (appointment of a personal representative, etc.) are required. [Tex. Prob. Code §89] If land is located in more than one county, a certified copy of the will and the order admitting it to probate are filed of record in the second county, and constitute a muniment of title in that county as well. Since title insurance companies and title examiners will accept deeds signed by the parties named in the will, this procedure is effective to clear title to the decedent's lands (as well as to other assets title to which is in the decedent's name).

b. **Statutory proceeding to determine heirship:** [§1029] Several states have a similar procedure that can be used if the decedent left *no will*. Upon a hearing, the court enters a decree declaring that the decedent died intestate, that he was survived by the indicated family members, and that their respective intestate shares are as set forth in the order. The court decree becomes a part of the county records, and serves as a link in the chain of title. [Tex. Prob. Code §48]

5. **Administration of Small Estates:** [§1030] Nearly all states authorize simplified administration procedures for small estates. The appropriate family member files a verified petition stating that the value of the decedent's estate is less than a certain amount prescribed by the statute. The probate judge (in some states) or court clerk (in other states) then issues an affidavit that serves the same function as letters testamentary or letters of administration (*see supra*, §889). Acting under the authority of the affidavit, the family member proceeds to collect accounts receivable or bank accounts standing in the decedent's name, reregister securities now in the decedent's name, or take whatever other actions are necessary to wind up the decedent's affairs.

a. **What constitutes small estate:** [§1031]   The size of estate that qualifies for this streamlined procedure varies from jurisdiction to jurisdiction. [D.C. Code §20-357—$10,000; Fla. Prob. Code §735.201—$25,000; N.Y. Surr. Ct. Proc. Act §1301—$10,000; Tex. Prob. Code §137—$50,000]

b. **Very large estates can qualify for "small estate" administration:** [§1032]   At first blush, it would appear that in states such as New York with its $10,000 limit, only truly modest estates (*e.g.,* the estate of someone who qualified for the food stamp program) can qualify for a small estate administration. However, this is not the case. First, it must be remembered that "estate" means only the ***probate*** or testamentary estate; it does not include nonprobate assets. (*See supra,* §§7-11.) Secondly, in several states the amount of the qualifying estate is determined after deducting the family allowance, exempt personal property set-aside, and the homestead. [Tex. Prob. Code §§137-144] Thus, if title to the decedent's $200,000 family home was held in a joint tenancy or tenancy by the entireties (or if it qualifies as a homestead), if the decedent's bank accounts and certificates of deposit had right of survivorship provisions, and if the decedent's principal wealth consisted of life insurance policies and employee death benefits under qualified retirement plans, it might even be possible for a millionaire's estate to qualify for a "small estate" administration.

APPENDIX

REPRESENTATIVE INTESTACY STATUTES

A. UNIFORM PROBATE CODE

As of 1986, fourteen states had enacted the Uniform Probate Code: Alaska, Arizona, Colorado, Idaho, Maine, Michigan, Minnesota, Montana, Nebraska, New Jersey, New Mexico, North Dakota, Pennsylvania, and Utah. (Several other states have adopted a number of U.P.C. provisions in revising their probate laws.) However, not all of the Uniform Probate Code states have enacted the U.P.C. intestate succession rules without modification. The intestate distribution rules are set forth in U.P.C. sections 2-101 through 2-114.

1. **Intestate Share of Surviving Spouse**

    a. **Survived by issue, all of whom are issue of surviving spouse:** Where all of the decedent's issue are also issue of the surviving spouse (*e.g.*, a one-marriage situation), the surviving spouse takes the *first $50,000 plus one-half* the balance of the estate. The remaining one-half passes to the issue by representation.

        (1) **Rationale:** "This section gives the surviving spouse a larger share than most existing statutes on descent and distribution. In doing so, it reflects the desires of most married persons, who almost always leave all of a moderate estate or at least one-half of a larger estate to the surviving spouse when a will is executed. . . . Moreover, in the small estate (less than $50,000 after homestead allowance, exempt property, and allowance), the surviving spouse is given the entire estate if there are only children who are issue of both the decedent and the surviving spouse; the result is to avoid protective proceedings as to property otherwise passing to their minor children." [U.P.C. §2-102, Official Comment]

    b. **Survived by issue, some of whom are not issue of surviving spouse:** Where the decedent is survived by issue of an earlier marriage, the surviving spouse takes *one-half* of the estate, and the remaining one-half passes to the decedent's issue.

        (1) **Example:** W dies intestate. She is survived by her husband H, by her daughter A (child by a former marriage), and by sons B and C (children of her marriage to H). Because W was survived by issue of another marriage, the first-$50,000 rule does not apply. H inherits one-half of W's estate. The remaining one-half passes to A, B, and C (one-sixth each).

    c. **Survived by parents but not survived by issue:** If the decedent is not survived by issue but is survived by one or both of his or her parents, the surviving spouse takes the first $50,000 *plus* one-half the balance of the estate. The remaining one-half passes to the parents or the surviving parent.

    d. **Not survived by issue or parents:** If the decedent is not survived by issue or parents, the *entire* estate passes to the surviving spouse.

2. **Not Survived by Spouse:** Where the decedent is not survived by a spouse but is survived by issue, the estate passes to the issue.

   a. **Issue take by representation:** If the issue are all of the *same degree* of kinship to the decedent, they take *equally.* If they are of unequal degree, those of more remote degree take by representation. [U.P.C. §2-103(1)]

   b. **Representation defined:** "If representation is called for by this Code, the estate is divided into as many shares as there are surviving heirs in the nearest degree of kinship and deceased persons in the same degree who left issue who survive the decedent, each surviving heir in the nearest degree receiving one share and the share of each deceased person in the same degree being divided among his issue in the same manner." [U.P.C. §2-106]

3. **Not Survived by Spouse or Issue:** If the decedent is not survived by a spouse or by issue, the estate passes to the parents (one-half each) or to the surviving parent (all).

4. **Not Survived by Spouse, Issue, or Parents**

   a. **Brothers and sisters and their issue take by representation:** If there are no surviving issue or parents, the decedent's brothers and sisters and the issue of deceased brothers and sisters take by representation.

   b. **Grandparents or the issue of grandparents:** If the decedent is not survived by spouse, issue, parents, or the issue of parents, one-half of the estate passes to maternal grandparents or the issue of maternal grandparents, and one-half passes to paternal grandparents or the issue of paternal grandparents. As to each half, the grandparents or the surviving grandparent take. If there is no surviving grandparent, the issue of the grandparents (uncles, aunts, and their issue) take by representation. If there is no surviving grandparent or issue of grandparent on the paternal or the maternal side, the entire estate passes to the relatives on the other side.

   c. **No inheritance beyond issue of a grandparent:** If the decedent is not survived by spouse, issue, parents or their issue, or by grandparents or their issue, the estate *escheats* to the state.

5. **120-Hour Survival Rule:** "Any person who fails to survive the decedent by 120 hours is deemed to have predeceased the decedent for purposes of homestead allowance, exempt property, and intestate succession." [U.P.C. §2-104]

   a. **Where no proof of survival by 120 hours:** If the time of death of the decedent or of the person who otherwise would be an heir cannot be determined, and it cannot be established that the person survived by 120 hours, "it is deemed that the person *failed to survive* for the required period."

   b. **Where result would be escheat:** The 120-hour survival rule does *not* apply if the result would be an escheat. Thus, if the decedent's only living relation is an uncle who died forty-eight hours after the decedent, the estate passes by inheritance to the uncle (and thence to the uncle's devisees or heirs). If, however, the uncle left two children (the decedent's first cousins) who survived the decedent by more than 120 hours, the uncle is deemed not to have survived the decedent. The estate would pass by inheritance to the two cousins.

6. **Community Property States**

   a. **Separate property:** Under the U.P.C.'s rules for community property states, the surviving spouse's share of the decedent's separate property is determined under the rules (including the "first-$50,000" rule) described above.

   b. **Community property:** The one-half of community property that belongs to the decedent passes to the surviving spouse. [U.P.C. §2-102A] The other one-half does not pass by inheritance; the surviving spouse already owns it. The bottom line, though, is that the surviving spouse ends up with the entire community estate.

B. FLORIDA PROBATE CODE

The Florida Probate Code, which was enacted in 1975, adopted several of the Uniform Probate Code rules governing inheritance, wills, and probate law. However, Florida is *not* regarded as a "U.P.C. state." The selective adoption of only a handful of the U.P.C. provisions reflects that the U.P.C. was consulted to provide guidelines, but not a blueprint, for probate revision. The intestate succession rules are set forth at Florida Probate Code sections 732.101 *et seq.*

1. **Intestate Share of Surviving Spouse**

   a. **Survived by descendants, all of whom are descendants of surviving spouse:** Where all of the decedent's descendants are also descendants of the surviving spouse, the surviving spouse takes the first $20,000 *plus* one-half the balance of the estate. The remaining one-half passes to the descendants. "Property allocated hereunder to the surviving spouse to satisfy the $20,000 shall be valued at the fair market value on the date of the decedent's death." [Fla. Prob. Code §732.102]

   b. **Survived by descendants, some of whom are not descendants of surviving spouse:** If the decedent is survived by descendants by an earlier marriage, the surviving spouse takes *one-half* of the estate. The other one-half passes to the descendants.

      (1) **Example:** H dies intestate. He is survived by his wife W, by his son A (child by his former marriage), and by daughter B (child by his marriage to W). Since H was survived by a descendant from another marriage, the first-$20,000 rule does not apply. W inherits one-half of H's estate. The remaining one-half passes to lineal descendants—here, to A and B (one-fourth each).

   c. **Not survived by descendants:** If there is no surviving lineal descendant of the decedent, the surviving spouse takes the entire intestate estate.

2. **Not Survived by Spouse:** If there is no surviving spouse, the entire intestate estate passes to the decedent's *lineal descendants* per stirpes. [Fla. Prob. Code §§732.103, 732.104]

3. **Not Survived by Spouse or Descendants:** If the decedent is not survived by a spouse or by lineal descendants, the estate passes to the decedent's father and mother equally, or to the survivor of them.

4. **Not Survived by Spouse, Descendants, or Parents:** Where the decedent is not survived by a spouse, descendants, or parents, the estate passes to the descendants of parents (brothers, sisters, and the descendants of deceased brothers and sisters) *per stirpes.*

5. **Not Survived by Spouse, Descendants, Parents, or Descendants of Parents:** If the decedent was not survived by a spouse, descendants, parents, or the descendants of parents, one-half of the estate goes to the decedent's paternal kindred, and the other half goes to the maternal kindred.

   a. **Grandparents or surviving grandparent:** As to each one-half, that one-half goes to the maternal (or paternal) grandparents or to the survivor of them.

   b. **Descendants of deceased grandparents:** If there is no surviving maternal (or paternal) grandparent, that one-half passes to maternal (or paternal) uncles, aunts, and descendants of deceased uncles and aunts, per stirpes.

   c. **No surviving kindred on one side:** If there is no kindred on one side surviving, the entire estate passes to the kindred on the other side.

6. **No Inheritance Beyond Grandparents or Descendants of Grandparents:** Florida has adopted the U.P.C.'s *"laughing heir" rule,* which cuts off inheritance by persons related beyond the grandparent or descendant of grandparent level.

   a. **Exception for kindred of decedent's last deceased spouse:** While generally there is no inheritance beyond grandparents or the descendants of grandparents, the Florida Probate Code carves out this exception: Instead of an escheat, the estate "shall go to the kindred of the last deceased spouse of the decedent as if the deceased spouse had survived the decedent and then died intestate entitled to the estate." [Fla. Prob. Code §732.103(5)] While this provision will avoid an escheat in many cases, there nonetheless would be an escheat if (i) the decedent had never married, or (ii) there are no living grandparents or descendants of grandparents of the last deceased spouse.

7. **Uniform Simultaneous Death Act:** The Florida legislature did *not* adopt the U.P.C.'s rule that a person must survive the decedent by 120 hours in order to take as an heir. Instead, the legislature retained the Uniform Simultaneous Death Act rule. [Fla. Prob. Code §732.601] *(See supra, §86.)*

C. ILLINOIS PROBATE ACT

The statutes governing descent and distribution are in article II of the Illinois Probate Act.

1. **Intestate Share of Surviving Spouse:** If the decedent is survived by a spouse and by one or more descendants, the spouse takes *one-half* of the estate. The remaining half passes to the descendants per stirpes. If the decedent is not survived by descendants, the entire estate passes to the spouse.

2. **Not Survived by Spouse:** If the decedent is survived by descendants but not by a spouse, the estate passes to the descendants *per stirpes.*

3. **Not Survived by Spouse or Descendants:** If the decedent is not survived by a spouse or by descendants, the estate passes to the decedent's parents, brothers, and sisters in *equal* shares.

    a. **Comment:** The Illinois distributive plan is unusual in treating parents on the same basis as brothers and sisters. In most states, if the decedent is not survived by spouse or issue, the entire estate passes to the parents or to the surviving parent. In other states, the estate passes to parents if both survive and one-half passes to the surviving parent if only one survives.

    b. **Only one parent survives:** If only one parent survives, the surviving parent takes a *double* portion.

    c. **Descendants of deceased brothers and sisters:** Descendants of deceased brothers and sisters take *per stirpes.*

    d. **Example:** X dies intestate, unmarried and without descendants. X is survived by his mother M, by sisters A and B, and by nephews X, Y, and Z (children of his deceased brother C). Since X's father did not survive, M takes a double portion or two-fifths. A and B each take one-fifth. C's three children take one-fifteenth shares.

4. **Not Survived by Spouse, Descendants, Parents, or Descendants of Parents:** If the decedent is not survived by a spouse, descendants, parents, or the descendants of parents, one-half of the estate goes to the decedent's maternal kindred, and the other one-half goes to the paternal kindred.

    a. **Grandparents or surviving grandparents:** As to each one-half, that half goes to the maternal (or paternal) grandparents, or to the survivor of them.

        (1) **Comment:** Unlike the rule with respect to parents, *grandparents* are the *preferred takers* as against their descendants. Descendants of grandparents take only if both grandparents on that side predeceased the intestate.

    b. **Descendants of deceased grandparents:** If there is no surviving maternal (or paternal) grandparent, that one-half passes to maternal (or paternal) uncles, aunts, and descendants of deceased uncles and aunts, per stirpes.

c. **No surviving kindred on one side:** If there is no surviving kindred on one side, the entire estate passes to the kindred on the other side.

   (1) **Example:** Y dies intestate, unmarried and without descendants. Her nearest relations are two uncles on her father's side (descendants of her paternal grandparents). Y's maternal grandparents and their descendants predeceased her, although Y has living relations who are the issue of her maternal great-grandparents. The entire estate passes to her two uncles, to the exclusion of her more remote maternal kindred. [Ill. Prob. Act §2-1(e)]

d. **No surviving grandparents or their descendants:** If the decedent was not survived by spouse, grandparents, or the descendants of grandparents, one-half of the estate passes to the maternal great-grandparents or the survivor of them, or if no surviving great-grandparent, to their descendants per stirpes. The other one-half passes to the paternal great-grandparents or their descendants in the same manner. If there are not surviving great-grandparents or their descendants on one side, the entire estate passes to the great-grandparents or their descendants on the other side. [Ill. Prob. Act §2-1(f)]

e. **No surviving great-grandparents or their descendants:** If the decedent has no kindred nearer in relationship than great-grandparents or the descendants of great-grandparents, the estate passes *per capita* to the decedent's *nearest kin*; *i.e.*, the estate passes "in equal parts to the nearest kindred of the decedent in equal degree (computed by the rules of the civil law) and without representation." [Ill. Prob. Act §2-1(g)]

f. **Escheat:** If the decedent has no known kindred, the estate escheats. Real property escheats to the county in which it is located. Personal property escheats to the county of which decedent was a resident.

D. NEW YORK ESTATES, POWERS AND TRUSTS LAW

In New York, the term "distributee" is used in lieu of "heir." "Distributee" is defined as "a person entitled to take or share in the property of a decedent under the statutes governing intestate distribution." [N.Y. Est. Powers & Trusts Law §1-2.5]

1. **Intestate Share of Surviving Spouse**

   a. **Survived by two or more children or their issue:** If the decedent is survived by two or more children (or by the issue of two or more deceased children), the surviving spouse takes money or personalty not exceeding $4,000 *plus* one-third of the balance of the estate. The other two-thirds passes to the children and the issue of deceased children, per stirpes.

   b. **Survived by one child (or issue of one deceased child):** If the decedent is survived by one child (or by the issue of one deceased child), the surviving spouse takes money or personalty not exceeding $4,000 *plus one-half* of the balance of the estate. The remaining one-half passes to the child (or to the issue of the deceased child, per stirpes).

c. **Survived by parents but not by issue:** Where the decedent is survived by parents but not by issue, the surviving spouse takes *$25,000 plus one-half* of the balance of the estate. The other one-half passes to the parents (one-fourth each) or the surviving parent (one-half, if only one parent survived).

d. **Not survived by issue or parents:** If the intestate is not survived by issue or parents, the entire estate is inherited by the surviving spouse.

e. **When spouse is disqualified to be a distributee:** A spouse is disqualified from taking as a distributee if:

   (i)   There is a final decree of divorce or annulment.

   (ii) A final decree of separation had been rendered against the surviving spouse.

   (iii) The surviving spouse obtained a divorce in another jurisdiction, which is not recognized as a valid divorce in New York.

   (iv) The marriage is bigamous or incestuous.

   (v)   The spouse abandoned decedent, and the abandonment continued until decedent's death.

   (vi) The surviving spouse failed or refused to support the decedent.

   [N.Y. Est. Powers & Trusts Law §5-1.2]

2. **Not Survived by Spouse:** If the decedent is survived by issue but not by a spouse, the estate passes to the issue *per stirpes,* except that if they are in *equal degrees* of kinship to the decedent, they take *equal shares.*

   a. **Per stirpes distribution:** Suppose that the decedent, a widow, was survived by son A; by three grandsons P, Q, and R (children of her deceased son B); and by X and Y (children of her deceased daughter C). The distribution is per stirpes: One share for each family line. A takes one-third; P, Q, and R each take one-ninth; and X and Y each take one-sixth.

   b. **Per capita distribution:** Suppose the same facts as above, except that A also predeceased the intestate, leaving no issue. Since all the distributees are in the same degree of kinship to the decedent (grandchildren), they take per capita. Therefore P, Q, R, X, and Y each take one-fifth shares.

3. **Not Survived by Spouse or Issue:** If the decedent is survived by one or both parents but is not survived by a spouse or issue, the estate passes to the *parents equally* if both survive, or all to the surviving parent if only one survives.

a. **Exception:** A parent *cannot inherit* from his child *if* he failed or refused to support the child or abandoned the child when the child was under the age of twenty-one. (This provision was exempted from the general lowering of the legal age from twenty-one to eighteen in 1974, since parental support of children under age twenty-one is still required.) The estate is distributed as though the disqualified parent predeceased the intestate. [N.Y. Est. Powers & Trusts Law §4-1.4]

4. **Not Survived by Spouse, Issue, or Parents**

a. **Descendants of parents:** If the decedent is not survived by a spouse, issue, or parents, the estate passes to the decedent's brothers and sisters and the issue of deceased brothers and sisters, per stirpes. However, if the distributees are all in the same degree of kinship to the intestate they take per capita.

b. **Grandparents:** If the intestate was not survived by parents or the issue of parents, the estate passes *in equal shares* to the surviving grandparents or grandparent. Thus, the shares could be one-fourth, one-third, one-half, or all, depending on the number of grandparents who survive. If only one grandparent survives, she takes the entire estate *even though other predeceased grandparents left issue* who survived the intestate.

c. **Issue of grandparents:** If the decedent was not survived by grandparents, the estate passes to the issue of the grandparents in the nearest degree of kinship to the decedent per capita.

   (1) **No split between maternal and paternal lines:** In most states, at this point the statute distributes one-half the estate among the kindred of the maternal grandparents and the other one-half among the kindred of the paternal grandparents. Not so in New York. The entire estate goes to those in the nearest degree of kinship to the intestate, in equal shares.

      (a) **Example:** Decedent's nearest relations are two uncles (brothers of her father) and an aunt (sister of her mother). The two uncles and the aunt each take a one-third share.

   (2) **Per capita distribution:** Per stirpes distributions are limited to the decedent's issue, brothers, sisters, and the issue of brothers and sisters. [N.Y. Est. Powers & Trusts Law §4-1.1] When inheritance is by more remote kin, the relations in the nearest degree of kinship take all.

      (a) **Example:** Suppose, in the example immediately above, the decedent's aunt also predeceased her, leaving three children who survived. The decedent's nearest relations, then, are her two uncles on her father's side, and her three first cousins on her mother's side. The two uncles take the entire estate (one-half each). The first cousins take nothing.

d. No inheritance beyond issue of a grandparent

(1) **Escheat:** If the intestate is not survived by a spouse, issue, parents or their issue, or by grandparents or their issue, the decedent's estate escheats to the state.

(2) **Exception:** If the decedent was at the time of his death under age eighteen or had been adjudicated an incompetent, and if he was survived by one or more great-grandparents, the estate passes to the surviving great-grandparents per capita. If the minor or incompetent was not survived by great-grandparents but was survived by the issue of great-grandparents, the estate passes to those issue in the *nearest degree* of kinship to the intestate. An escheat occurs only if the minor or incompetent was not survived by great-grandparents or the issue of great-grandparents.

(3) **Rationale:** The purpose of this provision is to cover the situation where the person would not be able to avoid an escheat by writing a will. (A person must be age eighteen to have the capacity to make a will.)

E. CALIFORNIA PROBATE CODE

1. **Community Property:** The decedent's one-half of the community property passes by intestacy to the surviving spouse (who already owns the other one-half). Thus the surviving spouse succeeds to ownership of the entire community estate, regardless of whether the decedent was survived by issue. [Cal. Prob. Code §§100, 6101, 6401]

2. **Quasi-Community Property:** Quasi-community property is treated the same as community property for succession purposes. If the decedent (the "acquiring spouse") left a will, it can dispose of only one-half of the quasi-community property. The other one-half passes to the surviving spouse. If the acquiring spouse left no will, the surviving spouse takes all of the quasi-community property: one-half passes by inheritance to the surviving spouse; one-half is already owned by the surviving spouse. [Cal. Prob. Code §§66, 6101]

   a. **What constitutes quasi-community property:** Quasi-community property is property acquired by a spouse while *domiciled in another jurisdiction* which would have been classified as community property had it been acquired under the same circumstances while the spouse was domiciled in California. It also includes property acquired in exchange for real and personal property which would have been classified as quasi-community property. This provision applies to personal property wherever located and to real property situated in California. Because of the situs rule, the quasi-community property statute does *not* apply to real property located in another jurisdiction.

3. **Election Doctrine:** As discussed in §260, where one spouse purports to make a testamentary disposition of the entire interest in community assets (and not just his one-half community share), the surviving spouse is put to an election. She may take "under" the will, accepting whatever benefits are given by the will. If she does so, she relinquishes her one-half community interest in the assets disposed of by the will. Alternatively, the

surviving spouse may elect to take "against" the will, and claim the one-half community to which she is entitled by law. If she does so, she relinquishes all interests devised to her by the decedent's will. This same election doctrine applies if the acquiring spouse's will purports to devise the entire interest in quasi-community property.

4. **Separate Property: Intestate Share of Surviving Spouse**

   a. **Survived by two or more children or their issue:** If the decedent is survived by two or more children (or the issue of two or more deceased children), the *surviving spouse inherits one-third* of the decedent's separate property. The other two-thirds passes to the children and to the issue of deceased children, per stirpes. [Cal. Prob. Code §§240, 6401, 6402]

   b. **Survived by one child or issue of one child:** If the decedent is survived by one child (or by the issue of one deceased child), the surviving spouse takes *one-half* of the decedent's separate property. The other one-half passes to the child, or to the issue of the one deceased child. [Cal. Prob. Code §§240, 6401, 6402]

   c. **Not survived by issue:** If the decedent is not survived by issue but is survived by parents or the issue of parents, the surviving spouse inherits *one-half* of the decedent's separate property. The other one-half passes to the parents or to the surviving parent. If neither parent survives, that one-half is inherited by the decedent's brothers and sisters or their issue, per stirpes. [Cal. Prob. Code §§240, 6401, 6402]

   d. **Not survived by issue, parents, or issue of parents:** If the decedent is not survived by issue, parents, or the issue of parents, the *entire* estate passes to the surviving spouse. [Cal. Prob. Code §6401]

5. **Not Survived by Spouse:** If the decedent is not survived by a spouse but is survived by issue, the *issue take per stirpes.*

   a. **Example:** H dies intestate. His wife predeceased him. H is survived by children A and B and by grandchildren X, Y, and Z (children of H's deceased child C). The distribution is per stirpes, or by right of representation. A and B each take one-third shares. The one-third that would have passed to C had she survived to be an heir passes by representation to X, Y, and Z (one-ninth each).

   b. **Strict per stirpes:** A strict per stirpes distribution is made when the decedent is not survived by children, and the takers of the estate are grandchildren and great-grandchildren. (If all of the takers are grandchildren, they take equal shares since they are all in the same degree of kinship to the intestate. [Cal. Prob. Code §§240, 6402]) Under a strict per stirpes distribution, the stirpes (shares) are determined at the *first generational level* (*i.e.*, the child level) regardless of whether there are any living takers at that level.

      (1) **Example:** H dies intestate. His wife and his three children (A, B, and C) predeceased him. H is survived by grandson B, Jr. (B's child), and by grand-

daughters X, Y, and Z (C's children). Since the heirs are all in the same degree of kinship to H, the four grandchildren each take one-fourth shares.

(2) **Example:** Same facts as above, except that grandchild Z also predeceased H, leaving a child (Z, Jr.) who survived H. Thus H is survived by grandson B, Jr., by granddaughters X and Y, and by great-grandchild Z, Jr. Since the takers are not in same degree of kinship to H, the distribution is on a strict per stirpes basis. A one-half share is taken by B's issue, and a one-half share is taken by C's issue. Thus, B, Jr. takes one-half of the estate; X, Y, and Z, Jr. each take one-sixth shares. [Maud v. Catherwood, *supra,* §75; Lombardi v. Blois, *supra,* §872]

(3) **Comment:** This is a minority position. Most jurisdictions take a "per capita with representation" approach, under which the stirpes or shares are determined at the first generational level at which there are living takers. Under the majority approach, B, Jr., X, Y, and Z, Jr. would each take one-fourth shares.

6. **Former Community Property and Former Separate Property:** California applies some unusual rules to property that is traceable to the decedent's marriage to a deceased spouse. [Cal. Prob. Code §6402.5] These rules *do not apply* if the decedent is survived by spouse or by issue; in that case the rules summarized above apply to the entire estate, regardless of its source. These rules *do apply* if the decedent is not survived by a spouse or issue, but is survived by the issue, parents, or issue of parents of the *previously deceased spouse.* (These rules *do not apply* if the decedent is *not* survived by the issue, parents, or issue of parents of the previously deceased spouse. In that case the source of the property is irrelevant; the entire estate passes to the decedent's kin.)

   a. **Former community (and quasi-community) property:** The general purpose of the statute is to divide any property that was formerly the community property (or quasi-community property) of the decedent and the predeceased spouse between the decedent's kin and the predeceased spouse's kin. Former community property (which is the share that is to go to the predeceased spouse's kin) consists of:

   (1) *One-half of the community property* in existence at the death of *the predeceased spouse.*

   (2) *One-half of any community property,* in existence at the death of the predeceased spouse, which the decedent *received from the predeceased spouse* by gift, will, or inheritance.

   (3) *Community property* in which the predeceased spouse had an incident of ownership and which vested in the decedent *by right of survivorship* on the predeceased spouse's death.

   (4) *Property* that was set aside for the decedent as a *probate homestead* on the predeceased spouse's death.

b. **Former separate property:** The general purpose of the statute is to give the former separate property of the predeceased spouse to that spouse's kin. Former separate property is separate property of the predeceased spouse that passed to the decedent by gift, will, inheritance, or right of survivorship.

c. **Devolution:** Former community property and former separate property passes to the predeceased spouse's issue, per stirpes. If there are no surviving issue of the predeceased spouse, it passes to that spouse's parents or surviving parent; or, if neither parent is living, to the predeceased spouse's brothers and sisters and their issue, per stirpes.

7. **Not Survived by Spouse or Issue:** If the decedent is not survived by a spouse or by issue, the estate passes to the ***decedent's parents*** (one-half each) or surviving parent (all).

   a. **Not survived by parents:** If the decedent is not survived by either parent, the decedent's estate is inherited by his ***brothers and sisters*** and their issue, per stirpes.

   b. **Caveat:** The rules described in this section do not apply to former community property and former separate property under the rules described above.

8. **Not Survived by Spouse, Issue, Parents, or the Issue of Parents:** If the decedent is not survived by any immediate family, the estate passes to his ***nearest kin*** as determined by the statutory rules of consanguinity. The degree of kinship is determined by counting the number of steps from the claimant to the common ancestor, and then adding the number of steps from the common ancestor to the decedent. The sum of these two counts is the degree of relationship of the claimant to the decedent. The claimant related in the closest degree takes as next of kin. [Cal. Prob. Code §6402]

   a. **Co-claimants:** Where co-claimants are related in the same degree, the person who traces through the closest common ancestor takes ***to the exclusion*** of the other. If two or more claimants in the same degree trace through the same ancestor, they share equally.

   b. **Escheat:** If there are no next of kin, the estate escheats to the state. [Cal. Prob. Code §6801]

9. **Ancestral Property:** If the decedent is not survived by a spouse or by issue, any property in the decedent's estate that came by gift, will, or inheritance from the separate property of a parent or grandparent shall go to that parent or grandparent or, if dead, to the parent or grandparent's heirs. [Cal. Prob. Code §6402.5]

10. **Minor Decedent:** If a decedent dies under age eighteen and unmarried, any property that came to the decedent by succession from a parent shall go to the other issue of the parent, per stirpes. [Cal. Prob. Code §6402]

F. TEXAS PROBATE CODE

1. **Community Property:** Inheritance of community property is governed by Texas Probate Code section 45.

    a. **Survived by descendants:** On the death of a spouse, her one-half community interest passes to her descendants.

        (1) **Example:** W dies intestate. She is survived by her husband H and by two children: A and B. W's one-half community share passes by intestacy to A and B. H takes his one-half community—not by inheritance, but because death has dissolved the community and has forced a division of the community estate. Thus, H owns one-half of the property (his one-half); A and B own one-fourth each (W's one-half, passing by intestacy).

    b. **Strict per stirpes:** Descendants of a deceased child "shall inherit only such portion of [the] property as the parent through whom they inherit would be entitled to if alive." [Tex. Prob. Code §45] This is referred to as a strict per stirpes distribution, because the stirpital shares are determined at the first generational level regardless of whether there are any living takers at that generational level.

        (1) **Example:** W dies intestate. Her two children predeceased her. W was survived by her husband H; by her grandson G (child of her deceased son S); and by three granddaughters W, X, and Y (children of her deceased daughter D). H takes his one-half community share. W's one-half community passes by inheritance to G (one-fourth) and to W, X, and Y (one-twelfth each).

    c. **Not survived by descendants:** If the decedent is not survived by children or more remote descendants, the surviving spouse succeeds to the entire community estate. Parents and collateral relations never inherit community property. The deceased spouse's one-half community passes to the surviving spouse by intestacy. The other one-half does not pass by intestacy; the surviving spouse already owns it.

2. **Separate Property; Survived by Spouse:** Inheritance of separate property owned by a married person is governed by Texas Probate Code section 38(b).

    a. **Survived by descendants**

        (1) **Separate personal property:** *One-third* of the decedent's separate property passes to the surviving spouse if the decedent is survived by descendants. The other two-thirds passes to the descendants.

        (2) **Separate real property:** The surviving spouse takes a *life estate in an undivided one-third* of the descendant's separate real property. The remaining estate passes to the descendants.

(a) **Example:** W dies intestate owning separate personal property and separate real property. W is survived by her husband H and by three children, A, B, and C. The separate personal property passes as follows: H inherits one-third, and the remaining two-thirds passes to A, B, and C (two-ninths each). The separate real property passes: a life estate in one-third to H; the remainder passing to A, B, and C. (The statute uses the term "remainder" in two different senses. The children take the "remainder" following the life estate in the future interests sense; they also take outright ownership of the remaining two-thirds in the "all the rest" sense.)

b. **Not survived by descendants**

(1) **Separate personal property:** If the decedent is survived by a spouse but not by descendants, *all* separate personal property passes to the *surviving spouse.*

(2) **Separate real property:** If the decedent is survived by a spouse but not by descendants, decedent's separate real property passes *one-half to the spouse* and one-half to the decedent's parents and collateral kin under the rules set out below.

3. **Not Survived by Spouse:** Inheritance of the estate of a single person is governed by Texas Probate Code section 38(a).

a. **Survived by descendants:** If the decedent is survived by *all* of his children, they take equal shares. If the decedent is survived by children and by the descendants of deceased children, the distribuiton is per stirpes.

b. **Per stirpes or per capita?** If the decedent is not survived by children but is survived by grandchildren, it is not clear whether the grandchildren take under a "strict per stirpes" basis (as they would if community property were involved; *see supra*), or under a per capita with representation basis, under which the shares are determined at the first generational level at which there are living takers. A literal reading of section 43, dealing with per stirpes versus per capita distributions, would suggest that the grandchildren take on a per capita with representation basis. This is how property is distributed among collateral kindred. However, it has been argued persuasively that, for reasons of legislative history, the statute should not be construed literally when grandchildren are involved. [*See* Bailey, "Intestacy in Texas: Some Doubts and Queries," 32 Tex. L. Rev. 497, 513 (1954)] This same problem is encountered, as to separate property, if the decedent was survived by his spouse and by grandchildren.

c. **Not survived by descendants**

(1) **Survived by both parents:** If both parents survive the decedent, each parent takes *one-half* of the estate.

(2) **Survived by one parent:** If only one parent survives the decedent, that parent takes *one-half* of the estate. The other one-half passes to the decedent's brothers and sisters and their descendants, per stirpes.

(3) **Not survived by parents:** If neither parent survives the decedent, the entire estate passes to the *decedent's brothers and sisters* and their descendants, per stirpes.

d. **Not survived by parents or descendants of parents:** If the decedent was not survived by parents or the issue of parents, the estate is divided into two "moieties," one for maternal kin and the other for paternal kin. As to each half, if both grandparents survive, each takes one-half of that one-half, or one-fourth of the total estate. If only one grandparent survives, he takes one-fourth and the other one-fourth passes to descendants of grandparents, per stirpes. If neither grandparent survives, that one-half share passes to the issue of the grandparents.

e. **No "laughing heir" statute:** If there are no grandparents on the maternal (or paternal) side, that one-half passes to the maternal (or paternal) great-grandparents and their descendants on that side, or to great-great-grandparents and their descendants, "and so on without end, passing in like manner to the nearest lineal ancestors and their descendants." Unlike the U.P.C., Texas has *no limit* on the degree of relationship that qualifies one to take as an heir.

4. **120-Hour Survival Required:** Texas Probate Code section 47 adopts the 120-hour rule of the Uniform Probate Code, including the presumption of nonsurvival by 120 hours if there is no evidence of survival, and also including the exception if the result would be an escheat. (*See* discussion of U.P.C., *supra* this appendix.)

REVIEW QUESTIONS

FILL IN
ANSWER

1. Barney, a New York resident, dies intestate. Barney owned real and personal property in New York, and also owned a farm, a herd of cows, and two tractors in Iowa. In distributing Barney's estate, does the New York intestacy statute apply to all of Barney's assets? _____

    a. Suppose that Barney and his sister also owned land in Ohio as joint tenants with right of survivorship. Is intestate distribution of the Ohio land governed by New York law or Ohio law? _____

2. H dies without a will. He is survived by his wife W, his children A and B, and his mother M. Does M take an intestate share of H's estate? _____

    a. H left an estate of personal property worth $100,000 and real property worth $200,000. If H was a resident of a state that has enacted the Uniform Probate Code, what intestate distribution should be made? _____

    b. Suppose, instead, that H was a resident of a community property state, and that the $300,000 in assets were community property. What intestate distribution should be made? _____

3. Sarah, a widow, dies intestate. She is survived by her father Frank, her son Al, two grandchildren (Billy and Bob) by her deceased daughter Betty, and one grandchild (Curtis) by her deceased son Charley.

    a. Does Frank take an intestate share of Sarah's estate? _____

    b. Do the three grandchildren (Billy, Bob, and Curtis) take equal shares of Sarah's estate? _____

    c. Suppose, instead, that Al also predeceased Sarah, leaving no issue, meaning that grandchildren Billy, Bob, and Curtis were Sarah's nearest kin. Do the three grandchildren take equal shares of Sarah's estate? _____

4. After living in Tennessee for many years, Jack and Jill move to a community property state, bringing with them 2,000 shares of Old Grandad Inc. common stock which Jack acquired from his earnings at a distillery. Jack dies intestate survived by Jill and the couple's two children Peter and Piper. Does Jill take the 2,000 shares of Old Grandad stock by inheritance? _____

    a. Suppose, instead, that Jill dies intestate survived by Jack, Peter, and Piper. Do the 2,000 shares of Old Grandad stock pass by inheritance through Jill's estate? _____

5. Martha has a child (Cliff) out of wedlock. Cliff is placed for adoption and is adopted by Henry and Winnie Holt. Some years later, Martha dies; then Martha's mother Gertrude dies intestate. Does Cliff have inheritance rights in his natural grandmother's estate? _____

    a. Suppose, instead, that Henry dies; then Henry's father George dies intestate. Does Cliff have inheritance rights in his adoptive grandfather's estate? _____

6. Phil has a child (Art) by his first marriage. Thereafter, Phil marries Beulah and they have two children (Bonita and Carla). Beulah does not adopt Art. If Beulah dies intestate, does Art have inheritance rights as a half-blood? _____

    a. Phil and Beulah die; then Carla dies intestate, survived by her siblings Art and Bonita. Does Art take one-half of Carla's estate? _____

7. Donald and Rachel, who are married but have no children, are killed instantly when their car strikes a concrete abutment. Rachel's nearest kin are her mother and father. Donald (who had a modest estate) left a will bequeathing "all my property" to his brother Ronnie; Rachel (who owned assets worth $500,000) died intestate. Ronnie contends that all or a substantial portion of Rachel's estate passed by intestacy to Donald, and thence under Donald's will to him. Is he right? _____

    a. Suppose, instead, that although Rachel was pronounced dead at the scene of the accident, Donald died at a local hospital two hours later. Does Ronnie end up with ownership of a share of Rachel's estate? _____

8. Pauline gives land worth $25,000 to her son Roderick on his twenty-fifth birthday. Two years later, Pauline dies intestate survived by Roderick and two other children. She leaves an estate valued at $300,000. Is Roderick entitled to one-third of Pauline's estate notwithstanding the lifetime gift to him? _____

9. Tony's will makes several bequests, including a bequest of $50,000 to his daughter Eileen. Two years before his death, Tony gives $20,000 to Eileen. Is Eileen nevertheless entitled to the $50,000 bequest? _____

10. Glenda dies intestate survived by four children and several grandchildren. Five months after Glenda's death, one of her children (Denise, who has two children) disclaims one-half of her interest in Glenda's estate. Is Denise's disclaimer effective? _____

    a. At the time Denise disclaimed, Acme Finance had a $125,000 judgment against her. Can Acme reach the share of Glenda's estate that Denise purported to disclaim? _____

11. Rambo is charged with murdering his father. In plea-bargaining, Rambo pleads guilty to the lesser charge of voluntary manslaughter. Is Rambo entitled to inherit from his father's estate? _____

    a. Suppose, instead, that the case goes to trial, and Rambo is acquitted of both of murder and the lesser charge of manslaughter. Is Rambo entitled to inherit from his father's estate? _____

12. Lucian, a resident of a common law state, dies leaving a will that bequeaths $22 to his wife Tammy ("$1 for each miserable year I spent with her"), and the remainder of his estate "to my faithful and efficient secretary, Lola LaTour, in consideration for her thoughtful and many services." Lucian left an estate valued at $200,000. Tammy has retained you to represent her. She wants to know: Is she entitled to more than $22 from Lucian's estate? _____

    a. In addition to leaving a $200,000 estate, three years before his death Lucian gave his brother Morris securities worth $100,000. Do Tammy's rights extend to the securities given to Morris? _____

    b. Suppose, instead, that Lucian had transferred the securities to a revocable trust that named Morris as trustee to pay the income to Lucian for life, and on Lucian's death to distribute the principal to Morris free of the trust. Do Tammy's rights extend to the securities settled in the revocable trust? _____

13. H and W own Blackacre as community property. H, thinking that Blackacre (worth $100,000) was his because he had purchased it out of his salary, dies leaving a will that states: "I own Blackacre as my separate property. I devise the fee simple title therein to my brother Bernie. I give all the remainder of my [$200,000] estate to my wife if she survives me; otherwise to my brother Bernie." W contends that since Blackacre was community property, she owns one-half of it, and that she also takes H's residuary estate under his will. Is she right? _____

14. Mona and Frank live in a community property state. Without Frank's knowledge, Mona gives securities worth $20,000 to Marcie, her daughter by a former marriage. Can Frank set the gift aside? _____

15. Ferd and Ann, who were married and lived in California for many years, move to a common law state, bringing with them securities worth $200,000. The securities were community property even though the stock certificates were registered in Ferd's name as owner. Three years later, Ferd dies leaving a will that bequeaths "all my property" to his sister. Does Ann have any rights in the securities, given that Ferd is listed as their owner? _____

16. Tom is married to Wanda, and they have one child (Chauncey) at the time he executes his will bequeathing "all my property to my wife Wanda if she survives me, otherwise to my mother Mabel." Thereafter, Tom and Wanda adopt a child (Andrew); then Wanda dies. Tom dies without having revoked or modified his will. He is survived by Mabel, Chauncey, and Andrew.

   a. Does Chauncey have any rights in Tom's estate? _____

   b. Does Andrew have any rights in Tom's estate? _____

   c. Suppose the same facts, except that Tom's wife Wanda also survived him. Does Andrew have any rights in Tom's estate? _____

   d. Suppose now that (i) shortly after Andrew's birth, Tom took out a $10,000 life insurance policy that named Andrew as beneficiary, and (ii) Wanda predeceased Tom. Does Andrew have any rights in Tom's estate? _____

17. Ruth, an elderly widow, is an ardent fan of television evangelist Brother Billie Bob Boon and his PTP ("Pass the Plate") Club. She executes a will that bequeaths two-thirds of her $500,000 estate to the PTP club, and the remaining one-third to her daughter Desire. Ruth dies twenty days after executing the will. The will was not the product of undue influence and, despite Ruth's conviction that Brother Billie Bob was "a messenger of the Lord" with healing powers, the PTP gift was not the product of an insane delusion. Desire contends that the testamentary gift to the PTP Club is invalid. Is there any basis for her claim? _____

18. Are each of the following accurate statements of the law?

   a. An instrument that makes no disposition of property cannot be admitted to probate as a will. _____

   b. The right to make a will is both a natural and a constitutional right; and while the legislature may fix reasonable limits on the power of testation, it can neither withhold the right altogether nor place excessive restrictions thereon. _____

   c. In many jurisdictions, a will is valid if it complies with the law in effect at the time of execution *or* death. _____

d. In determining whether the instrument-maker had testamentary intent, an objective test is applied. The requirement of testamentary intent is judged by a "reasonable person" standard—*i.e.,* whether such a person would consider the instrument and words used to be testamentary in nature. _____

e. If an instrument signed by a person in the presence of attesting witnesses begins by declaring, "I, [name] , declare this instrument to be my Last Will," there is a conclusive presumption that the instrument was written and signed with testamentary intent. _____

19. Tommy, who is seventeen years old, executes a will bequeathing all of his property to his mother. Tommy dies ten years later; he never married and he is survived by his mother. Is Tommy's will admissible to probate? _____

20. Larry executes a will that bequeaths his rare book collection to State College. Thereafter, Larry sends a typewritten, signed letter to his friend Moe, stating that "I have decided to give my rare books to you rather than to State College. You can have them when I die." When Larry dies, is Moe entitled to the rare books? _____

21. Ted Smith, whose nickname is T.S., types out his will on a portable typewriter. In the presence of two neighbors (who sign as attesting witnesses), Ted signs the will with his initials, "T.S." On Ted's death, is the will admissible to probate? _____

22. Wendy executes what purports to be her last will and testament. The document contains three bequests, followed by Wendy's signature, two more bequests, a date, and the attestation and signatures of subscribing witnesses. On Wendy's death, is the will admissible to probate? _____

a. Suppose instead that the material following Wendy's signature consisted of a statement that "this is the sum and substance of my dispositions," followed by the attestation clause and witness signatures. On Wendy's death, is the will admissible to probate? _____

b. If it is shown that the two bequests following Wendy's signature were added *after* the will was signed and witnessed, can they be given effect? _____

c. Is the will invalid if Wendy failed to declare to the witnesses (by words or conduct) that the instrument was her will? _____

23. T asks X and Y to "witness my will." However, X and Y sign the will before T signs. Is the will admissible to probate? _____

24. Smith asks Bill and Marion to witness his will, which he signs in their presence in his dining room. Smith then goes into his kitchen for a glass of water, whereupon Bill and Marion sign the document. Is the will admissible to probate? _____

a. Would the will be admissible to probate if Smith had passed out in the kitchen when the witnesses were signing the will? _____

25. Tim's will devises his residuary estate to his friend Harry as trustee of a trust for the benefit of Tim's wife Lucille. Harry signs the will as one of the two attesting witnesses. Is Harry disqualified from receiving compensation or from serving as trustee by reason of his witnessing the will? _____

a. Suppose the same facts, except that the will provides: "The trustee shall pay the trust income to my wife Lucille for life, and on Lucille's death the trustee shall distribute the trust principal to Harry free of the trust." Again, Harry signs the will as one of the two attesting witnesses. Is the will admissible to probate? _____

b. Suppose again that Harry is given the trust remainder by the will, but Harry was ***not*** one of the two witnesses to the will. Two years after the will is executed, Tim executes a codicil that (i) bequeaths $10,000 to his nephew Norman and (ii) reaffirms and republishes his will. Harry is one of the two attesting witnesses to the codicil. Does the interested witness statute apply to the gift to Harry?   _____

26. Agnes dies leaving a typewritten will that was dated and signed by her and also signed by Seth and Trevor immediately below the will's attestation clause, which recites that "each of the undersigned witnesses signed in the testator's presence and in the presence of each other." Seth testifies that Agnes' brother brought the will to him for signing and that he did not sign the will in Agnes' presence. Is the will admissible to probate?   _____

a. Suppose the same facts, except that (i) the will was handwritten by Agnes, and (ii) the court finds that Seth did not sign in Agnes' presence. Is the will admissible to probate?   _____

27. After Tom's death there is found in his safe deposit box a signed and dated instrument that bequeaths all of his real and personal property. The document is entirely in Tom's handwriting exept for the third paragraph, which is partially handwritten and partially typed: "I bequeath ***Blueacre,*** my ranch in Fayette County, to my brother Bob." "Blueacre" is typewritten. If the state permits holographic wills, is the document admissible to probate?   _____

a. Suppose the document was not dated. Is it admissible to probate?   _____

28. Tess, who moved away from home at an early age, writes her sister Trudy a three-page letter that describes Tess's activities and the weather, asks about Trudy's family, and states how lonely she is. At the top of page three of the letter, Tess writes: "The only thing that comforts me is that after I am gone you and your children will get everything I own, and our good-for-nothing brother Bob won't get a dime." The letter is signed by Tess and dated. After Tess's death, Trudy offers the letter for probate. Should it be admitted to probate as a holographic will?   _____

29. After Zoe's death, three sheets of paper in her handwriting are discovered inside a family Bible. The pages are unnumbered and consist of separate, unnumbered paragraphs devising Zoe's property to various persons. The first sheet was written with a ball point pen, the second with a pencil, and the third with a blue felt tip pen. The third page concludes with Zoe's signature and the date. Can the three pages be considered a valid holographic will?   _____

30. P is involved in a serious auto crash and finds himself bleeding profusely. He tells the three ambulance attendants that he wants his $500 camera to go to his niece Q, and asks them to witness the request as his will. The attendants note the request in their written report of the accident filed the next day. P recovers from his injuries and dies of a heart attack five months later. May Q offer the written accident report for probate?   _____

a. Suppose, instead, that P's oral bequest was of his five-acre ranch, not a camera. May Q offer the written accident report for probate?   _____

31. Ruth executes a will that provides, "I am about to swim the English Channel. If anything happens to me, I want all my property to go to my sister Sarah." Ruth swims the channel in record time, but dies in an automobile accident five years later. Does Sarah take Ruth's estate under the will?   _____

32. T executes a will leaving all his property to R and S in equal shares. Thereafter, T marries M. Then T dies without having revoked or modified his will; he is survived by M, R, and S. Is T's will revoked by operation of law?   _____

a. Suppose the same facts, except that T and M also adopted a child A. Is T's will revoked by operation of law? _____

33. Stanley executes a will leaving his estate to his wife Vera if she survives him, otherwise to Tim. The will names Vera as executor and Tim as alternate executor. Several years later, Vera divorces Stanley, who thereafter dies without remarrying or changing his will. Stanley is survived by Vera and Tim. Does Vera take Stanley's estate under the will, and is Vera entitled to appointment as executor of Stanley's estate? _____

   a. Suppose the same facts, except that one year after the divorce Stanley and Vera reconcile and remarry. Does Vera take Stanley's estate under the will, and is Vera entitled to appointment as executor of Stanley's estate? _____

34. Ted executes a will that bequeaths $10,000 to Ann, $5,000 to Betty, and his residuary estate to Carolyn. A year later, Ted executes a will that bequeaths $5,000 to David and his residuary estate to Elsie. The second will makes no mention of the earlier will. Should both wills be admitted to probate? _____

35. Bill decides to revoke his will by burning it. He places the will in a stove with numerous other papers and sets them afire. Unbeknownst to Bill, only the upper corner of the will is burned; all the provisions of the will still can be read. Has the will been revoked? _____

   a. Suppose, instead, that Bill burned a pile of papers in the stove, but did not know that his will (which was completely consumed by the flames) was in the pile of papers. Has the will been revoked? _____

36. Paula writes to her attorney, "I hereby instruct you to destroy and negate my present will." The letter is entirely in Paula's handwriting and is signed and dated by her. The jurisdiction recognizes holographic wills.

   a. If the attorney does not destroy the will, has Paula's will been revoked? _____

   b. If the attorney does destroy the will pursuant to Paula's instructions, has the will been revoked? _____

37. Andy Albertson's will bequeaths $15,000 to Ben, $5,000 to Celia, and his residuary estate to Della. Thereafter, Andy crosses out the $15,000 bequest to Ben and writes in the margin, "Cancelled. A.A." Is this an effective revocation of the gift to Ben? _____

38. Beulah's will is executed in duplicate: *i.e.*, **two copies** are signed and witnessed. The bond paper copy is left with the attorney for safekeeping; Beulah takes the signed carbon copy home with her and places it in her desk. After Beulah's death, the executed carbon copy cannot be found, but the bond paper copy is found in the attorney's possession. Should it be admitted to probate? _____

   a. Suppose the same facts, except that after Beulah's death, the copy left with the attorney cannot be found, but the carbon paper copy is found in Beulah's desk. Should the carbon copy be admitted to probate? _____

39. Phil executes a will leaving his estate to Robert and Steve in equal shares. Some years later, Phil executes a new will in which he "hereby revoke[s] all earlier wills and codicils." The second will leaves Phil's estate to Robert. Shortly before his death, Phil destroys the second will with the intent to revive and restore his first will. Is the first will entitled to probate? _____

40. Randy executes a will that contains this provision: "I give my ranch in Collin County and several items of personal property that are important to me to the persons named in a list that

I plan to prepare in the future and attach to my will." Thereafter, Randy types, dates, and signs a list that says, "Pursuant to the provisions of my will, I give my ranch in Collin County to my brother Danny, my golf clubs to my cousin Lanny, my Mercedes 500SL to my friend Manny, and $5,000 to my niece Nanny." After Randy's death, the list is found stapled to her will.

a. Is the gift of the ranch valid? _____

b. Is the gift of the golf clubs valid? _____

c. Is the gift of the Mercedes valid? _____

d. Is the $5,000 bequest valid? _____

41. Hershel transfers stocks and bonds worth $200,000 to his friend Tom as trustee: To pay the trust income to Hershel for life, then to Sarah for life, and on the death of the survivor of Hershel and Sarah to pay the trust principal to Nellie. Hershel reserves the power to revoke or modify the trust. Thereafter, Hershel executes a will that states, "I bequeath my residuary estate to my friend Tom, as trustee, such residuary estate to be added to the trust which I established during my lifetime." Shortly before his death, Hershel amends the trust by a written instrument that is signed by him but not witnessed. Under the amendment, on the death of Hershel and Sarah, the trust principal is to be paid to Nellie and Noah in equal shares. Is the testamentary gift valid? _____

42. Gertie executes a will that devises her estate to her husband Hobart and her son Seth in equal shares, and that names Hobart as executor. Thereafter, Gertie and Hobart adopt a child: Carol. Two years later, Gertie executes a codicil to the will that names her brother Bill as executor in place of Hobart. Gertie dies; she is survived by Hobart, Seth, Carol, and Bill. Is Carol entitled to a share of Gertie's estate as a pretermitted child? _____

43. Xavier's will bequeaths his farm Blueacre to William. Thereafter, Xavier tells William that he is thinking about bequeathing the farm to Terry, whereupon William offers to manage and improve the property and split the income with Xavier if he will agree not to revoke the bequest. Xavier orally assents. Despite William's extensive improvements to Blueacre, Xavier executes a codicil revoking the bequest and leaving Blueacre to Terry. Can William enforce the agreement? _____

44. A and B execute a joint will wherein each leaves all his or her property to the other for life, and on the death of the survivor of A and B, all of their property is to go to S and D in equal shares. Some time later, B executes a codicil that leaves all his property to D. Do either A or S have any right to enforce the original bequest? _____

a. Would the result be different if the bequests were made "in consideration of the agreement by the other not to revoke? _____

45. Homer's will bequeaths 1,000 shares of AT&T stock to Betty and devises his residuary estate to Martha. Betty predeceases Homer, leaving a child (Cuthbert) who survives Homer. Betty leaves a will that devises all of her property to her husband Bob. Does Cuthbert take the AT&T stock? _____

a. Suppose the same facts, except that Betty survived Homer but died two days later. Does Cuthbert take the AT&T stock? _____

b. Suppose that the bequest of the AT&T stock was "to Betty if she survives me." Does Cuthbert take the AT&T stock? _____

46. Donald's will bequeaths his residuary estate "in equal shares to my son Dewey, my friend Huie, and my cousin Louie."

    a. Huie predeceases Donald, leaving a child (Herkie) who survives Donald, as do Dewey and Louie. Does Herkie take a one-third share of Donald's residuary estate? _____

    b. Suppose instead that Dewey predeceases Donald, leaving a child (Duckie) who survives Donald, as do Huie and Louie. Does Duckie take a one-third share of Donald's residuary estate? _____

47. Bert's will devises Greenacre "in equal shares to the children of my brother Vern." At the time the will is executed, Vern has three children: Alan, Bruce (both of whom were born to Vern's wife Martha), and Charlie (who was born out of wedlock; Vern's secretary was the mother). Thereafter, Vern adopts a child (Donna), and Alan dies survived by his daughter Alice. Then Bert dies, and his will is admitted to probate. Two years after his death Vern and Martha have another child, Elsie.

    a. Does Alice take a share of Greenacre? _____

    b. Does Charlie take a share of Greenacre? _____

    c. Does Donna take a share of Greenacre? _____

    d. Does Elsie take a share of Geenacre? _____

48. Mona's will contains the following bequests: "(A) I bequeath my Rembrandt painting to Patricia. (B) I bequeath my 200 shares of Ibix common stock to Ralph. (C) I bequeath 100 shares of Kytek common stock to Stanley. (D) I give, devise, and bequeath the rest, residue, and remainder of my estate to Tammy."

    a. Mona is killed in a house fire in which the Rembrandt is also destroyed. After Mona's death, her executor collects $100,000 in insurance proceeds to compensate for the loss of the Rembrandt. Is Patricia entitled to the $100,000? _____

    b. Suppose instead that the Rembrandt was destroyed two months before Mona's death and the insurance proceeds were collected by Mona shortly before her death. Is Patricia entitled to the $100,000? _____

    c. Before her death, Mona sold all of her Ibix stock and invested the sale proceeds in Series E Bonds. Is Ralph entitled to the Series E bonds? _____

    d. Suppose instead that Ibix Corporation was acquired by Goliath Corporation in a merger. As a result of the merger, Mona received 100 shares of Goliath stock in exchange for her 200 shares of Ibix stock. Is Ralph entitled to the Goliath stock? _____

    e. Also before her death, Mona sold all of her Kytek stock and invested the sale proceeds in Butane common stock. Does ademption apply to the gift to Stanley? _____

49. Zack owns 100 shares of NuGrowth common stock. He executes a will that provides: "I bequeath 100 shares of NuGrowth common stock to Tess." Thereafter, NuGrowth declares a two-for-one stock split, and two years later NuGrowth declares a ten percent stock dividend. As a result, Zack owns 220 shares of NuGrowth stock at his death.

    a. Is Tess entitled to the additional 100 shares of NuGrowth stock produced by the stock split? _____

      b.   Is Tess entitled to the additional 20 shares of NuGrowth stock produced by the stock dividend?   ————

      c.   Suppose instead that NuGrowth declared the stock dividend two months *after* Zack's death. Is Tess entitled to the additional 20 shares of NuGrowth stock produced by the stock dividend?   ————

50.   Trudy executes a will that devises her summer cabin to Bess. Thereafter, Trudy borrows $10,000 and gives the lender a mortgage on the cabin as security for the loan. When Trudy dies, the loan has not been repaid. Bess has taken the position that the executor must pay off the loan out of the residuary estate so that title to the summer cabin will pass to her free of the mortgage lien. Is Bess correct?   ————

51.   Rupert's will bequeaths $20,000 to his son Alex, $20,000 to his son Ben, and his residuary estate [$500,000] "to my beloved daughter Daphne." The will further provides: "Anyone who contests this will, or any part thereof, shall forfeit his legacy and shall take nothing hereunder." Alex's wife Agnes is outraged by the will, and feels strongly that the will was the product of Daphne's undue influence. Can Agnes contest the will?   ————

      a.   Suppose that Alex contests the will on the ground of undue influence, but the court finds no such influence. Are Alex's rights under the will thereby forfeited?   ————

52.   Wilbur's will makes modest bequests to each of his children and bequeaths his residuary estate to ESP Incorporated "because they have enabled me to talk to my dear, departed wife Ethel." Wilbur's children contest the will on the grounds of testamentary incapacity and insane delusion. Should they prevail?   ————

      a.   Would the result be different if Wilbur had been adjudicated insane several months prior to his executing the will?   ————

53.   Hortense's will makes a bequest of $50,000 to Tom Trickey, the attorney who prepared the will, and devises her residuary estate to her sister Sue. Sue contends that the gift to Trickey was the product of undue influence. Should she prevail?   ————

54.   Michael executes a will that bequeaths $500,000 to Elise. After his death, several of Michael's heirs move to set aside the gift on the ground that Elise tricked Michael into making the bequest by falsely representing that she would use the funds to start a religious order. If the heirs can prove that Elise made such a false representation, is this enough to invalidate the gift?   ————

      a.   Suppose instead that Michael made the bequest believing that Elise would start a religious order, even though Elise made no representation to that effect. Should the gift be invalidated?   ————

55.   Jack executes a will that bequeaths "$5,000 to my nephew Curtis" and devises the remainder of his estate to Edward. After Jack's death, Edward challenges the gift to Curtis. He offers evidence that Jack made the gift to Curtis because of a mistaken belief that Curtis was Jack's nephew when in fact they were unrelated. Is the evidence admissible?   ————

      a.   Curtis offers evidence that the amount of the bequest was intended to be $50,000, not $5,000, and that the attorney's stenographer made a mistake in incorrectly typing $5,000. Is the evidence admissible?   ————

56.   Brewster, a professor of history, bequeaths $50,000 "to my college." Brewster received a B.A. degree from Adams College, a PhD from Baker College, and taught for twelve years

at Clarendon College. Is extrinsic evidence admissible to show that Brewster intended the bequest for Adams College?

57. Professor Mens Rea summarizes his lecture on administration of estates by noting, "The informal probate procedure of the Uniform Probate Code has the advantage of safeguarding against possible abuse by the personal representative of the estate, but it does not really simplify the standard procedure." Is he correct?

58. Hans dies leaving a handwritten will that is signed by one witness. The state does not recognize holographic wills. Despite the lack of two witnesses, all of Hans' family members who would be heirs if there were no will petition the court to have the will probated and waive all rights they may have as heirs. Should the will be admitted to probate?

59. Barbara's will, which contains an attestation clause, is signed by Ralph and Gina as attesting witnesses but is not self-proved. When the will is offered for probate, Ralph testifies that he has no recollection of signing the will at all, let alone in Barbara's presence; Gina testifies that Barbara's brother brought the will to Gina's house for her signature and Barbara was not present. In light of this testimony, should the court deny probate of the will?

60. Antonio's will names his son Lino as the executor of his estate. When Antonio dies, Lino is sixteen years of age but highly intelligent (he is a sophomore in college) and quite familiar with the nature and responsibilities of an executor. Is Lino qualified for appointment as executor?

61. Greta is appointed executor of the estate of Heinrich. Greta decides that the sale of certain real property (not specifically bequeathed by the will) is necessary to pay creditors' claims. The will does not give the executor an express power of sale. Must Greta obtain a court order to sell the real property?

  a. Greta retains a broker to sell the real property. Subsequently, the purchaser (Petra) sues Greta for false representations by the broker concerning the condition of the property. Can Greta be held liable to Petra?

  b. If Petra obtains a judgment against Greta, is Greta entitled to reimbursement from Heinrich's estate?

62. Sven dies leaving a will that names his friend Lars as executor. Shortly after the will is probated, Lars properly publishes notice to creditors. Seven months later—after the state's nonclaim period has run—Nils presents a claim for $5,000 based on a promissory note signed by Sven. Nils points out that he, Lars, and Sven were all good friends, that Nils had loaned Sven the $5,000 to meet a pressing personal obligation (and that Lars knew of the loan), and that Lars knows that Sven would have wanted the loan paid off before any assets of the estate were distributed. Should Lars pay the $5,000 to Nils?

63. Ramona's will bequeaths $10,000 to her daughter Maria, $20,000 to her son Miguel, and her Corona stock (worth $6,000) to her neighbor Zapata. After administration, Ramona's estate has assets (including the Corona stock) worth $27,000.

  a. Will Zapata's gift be paid in full?

  b. Should Maria and Miguel receive the same amount under the will?

64. Nigel's will bequeaths $100,000 to his nephew Reginald. Nigel dies on February 15. After considerable dispute among the heirs and beneficiaries, a representative for the estate is

appointed by the court on December 10. Is Reginald entitled to interest on the $100,000 bequest from February 15 of the following year?

    _____

65.   Isadore dies leaving a will that bequeaths his estate to his daughter Rebecca and his son Malachi in equal shares. Isadore's modest estate consisted of a nine-year-old sedan, the furniture and furnishings in his apartment, $1,500 in cash, a $5,000 savings account, and a $50,000 life insurance policy that names Rebecca and Malachi as co-beneficiaries. Will it be necessary to probate Isadore's will and take out a formal administration of his estate?

    _____

ANSWERS TO REVIEW QUESTIONS

1.	**NO**	The New York intestacy laws apply to the New York assets and to all of Barney's personal property wherever located, including the cows and tractors in Iowa. However, under the situs rule, disposition of the Iowa farmland is governed by the Iowa intestate succession statute. [§4]
a.	**NEITHER**	The joint tenancy estate was a nonprobate asset and thus not subject to intestate succession laws. Title to the land passes to Barney's sister by right of survivorship. [§9]
2.	**NO**	In all states, a parent never inherits if the intestate was survived by a spouse and descendants. [§20]
a.	**DEPENDS**	If H's children A and B are also W's children, W would take $50,000 plus one-half the balance of H's estate, $125,000 (total to W being $175,000). A and B would share the remaining estate (one-fourth of the balance, or $62,500, each). But if either A or B were H's child by a former marriage, the U.P.C.'s first-$50,000 rule would not apply. Rather, W would take one-half of the estate ($150,000), and A and B would take one-fourth each ($75,000). [§17; *and see* Appendix]
b.	**SPLIT OF AUTHORITY**	In California and states that have enacted the U.P.C., W would succeed to the entire community estate. In Texas, W would continue to own her one-half community share, but H's one-half community would pass by intestacy to A and B (one-fourth each). [§§39-41; *and see* Appendix]
3.a.	**NO**	In all states, a parent never inherits if the intestate was survived by descendants. [§20]
b.	**NO**	When there is one living taker at the child level, the distribution is per stirpes—that is, by right of representation. Al takes one-third, Betty's children Billy and Bob take one-sixth each, and Curtis takes one-third. [§§21-22]
c.	**SPLIT OF AUTHORITY**	In most states, the distribution would be by "per capita with representation," and the grandchildren would take equal shares by inheritance since there were no living takers at the child level. However, some states make a "strict per stirpes" distribution, under which Curtis would take one-half, and Billy and Bob would take one-fourth each. [§§73-75]
4.	**SPLIT OF AUTHORITY**	If Jack and Jill moved to California or Idaho, the stock would be classified as quasi-community property, and Jill would inherit the stock. If, however, the move was to one of the community property states that does not have a quasi-community property statute, the stock would be Jack's separate property and would pass under the intestate succession rules applicable to separate property. [§§42-44]
a.	**NO**	Even in states with quasi-community property statutes, if the nonacquiring spouse predeceases, she has no interest in the quasi-community property to pass by will or inheritance. [§43]
5.	**SPLIT OF AUTHORITY**	In most states, a child who is adopted by a new family has no inheritance rights from his natural parents or the natural parents' kin. However, a few states permit inheritance from and through the natural parents notwithstanding the adoption by a new family [§§54-58]

a. **YES**   All states have discarded the common law "stranger to the adoption" rule. With respect to the adopting family, an adopted child has the same inheritance rights as a natural child. [§52]

6. **NO**   The half-blood doctrine applies only to inheritance among collateral kin (*i.e.*, brothers and sisters). Art, a stepchild, has no inheritance rights in Beulah's estate unless he can invoke the equitable doctrine of "adoption by estoppel" based on an unperformed agreement to adopt. [§§68-70]

a. **SPLIT OF AUTHORITY**   Under the U.P.C. and in most states, Art would take one-half of Carla's estate. However, in some states, half-bloods take half as much as whole bloods, meaning that Art would inherit one-third and Bonita would inherit two-thirds of Carla's estate. In still other states, Art would take nothing, and Bonita would inherit Carla's entire estate. [§§79-84]

7. **PROBABLY NOT**   If the Uniform Simultaneous Death Act applies, and there is no sufficient evidence that the parties died otherwise than simultaneously, Rachel's estate will pass as though she survived Donald, and Rachel's parents will inherit her estate. But if the evidence shows that Donald survived Rachel by a measurable period of time, he would take an intestate share of her estate and that share (determined under the rules of intestate succession) would pass under Donald's will to Ronnie. If the state has enacted the U.P.C.'s 120-hour rule, Donald could not take as an heir because he failed to survive Rachel by 120 hours. [§§85-88, 91, 96-97]

a. **SPLIT OF AUTHORITY**   Here there is sufficient evidence that Donald survived Rachel, and the Simultaneous Death Act does not apply. In states that have enacted the Act, Donald would have inherited all or a substantial share of Rachel's estate [*see* §§18-19], and that share would pass under Donald's will to Ronnie. But if the state has enacted the U.P.C.'s 120-hour rule, Donald could not take as an heir because he failed to survive Rachel by 120 hours, and Rachel's parents would inherit her estate. [§§91-92, 96-97]

8. **PROBABLY YES**   At common law (and in a few states today), the lifetime gift to Roderick would be treated as presumptively being an advancement, and thus would be taken into account in making the intestate distribution. However, most states either have reversed the presumption (*i.e.*, a lifetime gift to an heir is presumptively **not** an advancement) or require that the intent to make an advancement must be evidenced by a writing signed by the donor **or** the donee. Absent evidence of intent that the gift was to be an advancement, or absent a writing, the lifetime gift to Roderick would be disregarded in distributing Pauline's estate. [§§103-106]

9. **SPLIT OF AUTHORITY**   In most states, a lifetime gift to a general legatee in a previously executed will is presumptively intended to have been in partial satisfaction of the legacy. In such states, Eileen would have to overcome this presumption by proof of Tony's intent; otherwise she would receive only $30,000 under the will. However, statutes in a number of states require that such a lifetime gift is to be treated as in partial satisfaction of the legacy **only if** shown by a writing signed by the donor **or** the donee. [§§115-117, 122-126]

10. **YES**   While at common law an heir could not disclaim an intestate share, nearly all states now have statutes permitting heirs (as well as will beneficiaries) to disclaim their interest in a decedent's estate. Partial disclaimers are expressly permitted. Thus Denise takes one-half of her one-fourth share (total of one-eighth) of Glenda's estate, and the other one-eighth (the disclaimed portion) passes to Denise's children as though Denise had predeceased Glenda. [§§136-137, 144]

a.	**SPLIT OF AUTHORITY**	In most states, a disclaimer is effective as against the creditors of the disclaiming party. However, in several states, a disclaimer cannot be used to defeat creditor's claims. [§§149-150]
11.	**DEPENDS**	Under the U.P.C., a person who feloniously and intentionally kills the decedent forfeits his interest in the decedent's estate. While a felony conviction is conclusive, in the civil action relating to distribution of the father's estate, the court could find that Rambo feloniously and intentionally killed his father. [§§165-167] In non-U.P.C. states, the rules governing forfeiture by a killer of the decedent vary widely. [§§151-164]
a.	**DEPENDS**	In states where the killer forfeits his interest in the decedent's estate, a conviction is conclusive evidence. However, even if the party is found ***not guilty***, the court could find in the civil action (where the evidentiary test is "a preponderance of the evidence," not "beyond a reasonable doubt") that the party wrongfully brought about the death of the decedent. [§§158-159]
12.	**YES**	All but a handful of the common law states give a surviving spouse a right of election to take a statutory share (usually one-third or one-half) of the deceased spouse's estate. Tammy is entitled to receive the elective share amount upon filing a notice of election within a prescribed period of time. [§§189, 194, 219] In addition, and depending on the particular state's laws, Tammy may be entitled to homestead rights, an exempt personal property set-aside, and a family allowance over and above the amount of her elective share. [§§303, 310, 313]
a.	**PROBABLY NOT**	In states that apply the "illusory transfer" doctrine, the elective share statute does not apply to irrevocable transfers with no retained controls. In other states, Tammy could not reach these assets via her elective share unless she was able to show that Lucian's motive or intent was to defeat her elective share rights. The U.P.C.'s "augmented estate" concept does not apply to irrevocable transfers made more than two years before death. [§§229-230, 235-236, 238]
b.	**SPLIT OF AUTHORITY**	Absent a statute dealing with the question, the courts are divided on whether property in a revocable trust is subject to the surviving spouse's elective share right. However, the U.P.C. and statutes in several other states expressly provide that assets settled in a revocable trust are subject to the elective share. [§§237-238, 247-256]
13.	**NO**	H's will put W to an election. She can claim her one-half interest in Blackacre to which she is entitled under the community property laws. But if she does so, she must relinquish the testamentary gift of the residuary estate. If W wants to take H's residuary estate under the will, she must allow the will to pass title to her one-half interest in Blackacre to Bernie. [§§260-263]
14.	**DEPENDS**	First, it is unclear whether the securities were separate or community property. If they were Mona's separate property, Mona was completely free to give them to Marcie. (Remember, though, that all assets are presumptively community property unless they are affirmatively shown to be separate property.) But what if the securities were community property? In several states, neither spouse can make gifts of community property without the other spouse's written consent. In these states, Frank could set the gift aside in its entirety during Mona's lifetime, or as to his one-half share after Mona's death. However, in most states, Frank can set aside the gift only if he can prove that the transfer was in fraud of his community rights. [§§274-281]
15.	**YES**	All courts that have considered the question have ruled that Ann's ownership rights will be recognized under the theory of resulting trust or constructive trust. If the state

has enacted the Uniform Disposition of Community Property Rights at Death Act, Ann's one-half ownership interest is recognized by statute, and she does not have to rely on a resulting trust or constructive trust theory to establish her rights. [§§282-284]

16.a.	**SPLIT OF AUTHORITY**	Aside from Louisiana (with its forced heirship rules), in most states the answer is no. The pretermitted child statute applies only to children born or adopted **after the will's execution**. However, in a minority of states children alive when the will is executed are pretermitted unless the will mentions them or there is other evidence of an intent that they were not to share in the estate. In these states, Chauncey would be entitled to his intestate share of Tom's estate. [§§285-287, 289-297]
b.	**YES**	In all states with pretermitted child statutes, the statute applies to after-adopted as well as afterborn children. Thus, Andrew is entitled to an intestate share of Tom's estate. [§§286, 298]
c.	**PROBABLY NOT**	In most states, the child is not pretermitted if the will bequeathed substantially all of the estate to testator's spouse **and** the spouse was also a parent of the child. [§§296-297]
d.	**PROBABLY NOT**	In most states, the child is not protected by the pretermitted child statute if he was provided for by lifetime settlement. The life insurance proceeds would qualify as a lifetime settlement. [§295]
17.	**PROBABLY NOT**	Desire's only basis would be some restriction on testamentary gifts to charity; however most states place no restrictions on such gifts. And while a few states have "mortmain" statutes that void such gifts in a will executed shortly before death, there is a serious question as to such statutes' constitutionality. [§§317-319]
18.a.	**NO**	An instrument that does not dispose of property may still be a will even if it does nothing more than name an executor, revoke an earlier will, or exercise a power of appointment. [§§325-330]
b.	**NO**	Except in Wisconsin, the right to make a will is **not** regarded as a natural right. The power of testation is entirely subject to legislative control and (according to dictum in several cases) could be withheld altogether. [§§339-340]
c.	**YES**	The U.P.C. expressly so provides, and this is the rule by statute or case decision in nearly all states. [§§341-342]
d.	**NO**	It is testator's **subjective** intent that governs: She must have actually intended the words to operate as her will. [§347]
e.	**NO**	The overwhelming majority view is that such facts give rise to a presumption that the instrument was written with testamentary intent, but the presumption is **rebuttable**. [§§349-351]
19.	**NO**	In all but a handful of states, a testator must be eighteen years of age or older to have capacity to make a will. (An exception is sometimes made for persons who are married or in the armed forces.) Capacity is determined at the time the will is executed. [§§370-371]
20.	**NO**	The letter is not admissible to probate as a will since it was not executed with the required formalities; *i.e.,* it was not witnessed by attesting witnesses. [§380]
21.	**YES**	Signing with a nickname or initials is a valid signature. [§397]

22.	**SPLIT OF AUTHORITY**	In most states and under the U.P.C., there is no requirement that testator's signature be at the end of the will or in any particular place. As long as the two bequests were present at the time the will was executed, they would be given effect along with the rest of the will. Some states with a "signature at the end" requirement would give effect to all provisions **above** Wendy's signature, but would not give effect to the two bequests following her signature. *And note:* Some states with a "signature at the end" requirement would declare the entire will void. [§§400-409]
a.	**YES**	Even in states with the "signature at the end" requirement, it is generally held that if the words that follow testator's signature are of an informal or nondispositive nature, they can be disregarded as surplusage. Furthermore, Wendy signed at the logical or literary end of the will. [§§404, 409]
b.	**NO**	Only words that were present when the will was executed can be given effect. Moreover, these facts do not invoke the "signature at the end" rule, because the two bequests were not part of the duly executed will. [§410]
c.	**SPLIT OF AUTHORITY**	Most states and the U.P.C. do **not** require "publication" of a will; in these states, Wendy's will would be admissible to probate. In states that impose a publication requirement, the will would not be admitted to probate. [§§414-416]
23.	**YES**	In nearly all states, the order of signing is immaterial as long as all the parties sign as part of a contemporaneous transaction. Nor does it matter whether the testator's signature is below those of the attesting witnesses. [§§417-418]
24.	**DEPENDS**	Most state statutes require that the witnesses sign in the testator's presence. In states that apply the "conscious presence" test, it would be a close case (depending on whether the kitchen is next to the dining room, whether there is a wide doorway, etc.) as to whether the witnesses signed in Smith's presence, but the court probably would hold that they did. In states that apply the "line of sight" test, it would be necessary to show that the witnesses were in Smith's line of sight when they signed. [§§419-421]
a.	**NO**	If Smith was unconscious when the witnesses signed, the attestation would not meet either the scope of vision or conscious presence test. [§§419-421]
25.	**NO**	A person designated as trustee or executor in the will is not **beneficially** interested within the meaning of the interested witness statute. While Harry will be paid for serving as trustee, this is compensation and not a gift. [§433]
a.	**YES**	Even though Harry is an "interested witness" within the meaning of the statute, this does not affect the validity of the will (assuming that it was otherwise validly executed). However, under most statutes, the gift to Harry of the remainder interest would be purged (void) since Harry (a friend) would not be an heir if Tim had died intestate. [§§427-431]
b.	**NO**	The gift to Harry is not invalidated when he witnessed a codicil that did not make (or increase) a gift to him. The codicil actually operates against Harry's interest, since the $10,000 bequest will reduce the size of the trust in which Harry is given an interest. [§440]
26.	**DEPENDS**	In view of the recitals in the attestation clause, the court (or jury) could find that the will was validly executed (*i.e.*, that Seth signed in Agnes' presence) even in the face of Seth's hostile testimony. [§§443-446]
a.	**DEPENDS**	In states that recognize holographic wills, the will would be admissible to probate upon proof that it was entirely in Agnes' handwriting. Seth's signature would not be

needed. However, in states that (i) do not give effect to holographic wills and (ii) require the witnesses to sign in the testator's presence, the will would be denied probate. [§§419, 455]

27. **YES**

Even though a holographic will (or at least its material provisions) must be entirely in testator's handwriting, "Blueacre" can be disregarded as surplusage since it is not necessary to complete the will or its meaning. The instrument does make a gift, in Tom's handwriting, of "my ranch in Fayette County." [§§456-459]

a. **SPLIT OF AUTHORITY**

In most states, a holographic will does not have to be dated to be valid. However, a few states require that a holographic will must be dated. [§§463-464]

28. **PROBABLY NOT**

Although the letter makes "testamentary noises," the likely finding of a court is that the letter was not written with testamentary intent; *i.e.*, the letter itself was not intended to serve as a will. It is more likely that Tess's statement in the letter referred to a will that she had already made or was thinking about making. [§§465-467]

29. **YES**

The fact that the three pages may have been written at separate times (in view of the different writing instruments used) would not defeat the presumption of integration where there is continuity in the provisions and Zoe's signature indicates her intent that the pages constitute her will. [§§468-469, 576-580]

30. **PROBABLY NOT**

Most states do not recognize oral wills. And while some states permit oral wills for dispositions of personal property, the will must be uttered during the person's last sickness. When P recovered from the accident and died of independent causes several months later, it can be shown that the will was not uttered in P's last sickness. [§§471-475]

a. **NO**

In nearly all states that allow oral wills, such wills can dispose of personal property only. [§473]

31. **DEPENDS**

The court must determine whether Ruth's statement was intended to operate as a condition to the will's taking effect or merely the motivation for making a will. If Ruth would otherwise die intestate, the court probably would uphold the will (particularly since several years have elapsed since occurrence of the "inoperative" event). [§§478-484]

32. **SPLIT OF AUTHORITY**

Under the U.P.C. and in most states with statutes dealing with this problem, the will would be partially revoked only. M would take an intestate share of T's estate; the remaining estate would pass to R and S. Under some statutes, however, the will would be revoked in its entirety because of the subsequent marriage. In states without statutes on the question, T's marriage would have no effect on the will. In all cases, M would have rights under the elective share statute as well as the right to a homestead, exempt personal property set-aside, and family allowance. [§§493-500]

a. **SPLIT OF AUTHORITY**

In a few states, marriage followed by birth of issue revokes a previously executed will. In most states, however, the will would not be revoked, but M would have rights as a pretermitted spouse (as set out in the preceding answer), and A would have rights as a pretermitted child. [§§496, 298-301]

33. **NO (as to both questions)**

In nearly all states today, divorce revokes all testamentary gifts and administrative appointments in favor of the ex-spouse, and the will is read as though the former spouse predeceased the testator. Thus, Stanley's estate would pass to Tim, and Tim would be appointed executor. In a small minority of states, however, the divorce would have no effect on the will, and Vera would take Stanley's estate. [§§503-510]

a.	**YES**	In states with revocation-by-divorce rules, it is usually provided by statute or case decision that if the couple remarry, the revoked provisions are revived. [§511]
34.	**YES**	There is only a partial inconsistency between the two wills, and there is an implied revocation of the first will only to the extent of inconsistent provisions. The second will should be read as a codicil to the first will. Thus Ann takes $10,000, Betty takes $5,000, and the residuary gift to Carolyn in the first will is revoked by implication. David takes $5,000 and Elsie takes the residuary estate under the "codicil." [§§523-526]
35.	**NO**	Revocation by physical act requires that a material part of the will must have been physically acted upon. [§§528-529]
a.	**NO**	The physical act of destruction must be accompanied by a present intent to revoke the will, and here there was no such intent. Since the will was destroyed, it will be necessary to satisfy the "proof of lost wills" statute in order to gain its admission to probate. [§§533, 548-555]
36.a.	**NO**	The letter cannot effect a revocation by subsequent instrument because the letter did not itself reflect a present intent to revoke the will. The testator's own words must constitute the revocation. [§§520, 534]
b.	**NO**	Revocation by physical act by another person must be at testator's direction *and in testator's presence.* Since the will was physically destroyed, it would be necessary to satisfy the "proof of lost wills" statute in order to gain it admission to probate. [§§534, 548-555]
37.	**SPLIT OF AUTHORITY**	Most states allow partial revocations by physical act; in these jurisdictions the revocation would be effective. However, a minority of states do not recognize partial revocations by physical act; in these jurisdictions, Ben would take the bequest notwithstanding Andy's attempted revocation. [§535-538]
38.	**PROBABLY NOT**	If wills are executed in duplicate, both copies must be accounted for before either can be probated. If the copy last seen in testator's possession cannot be found after diligent search, there is a presumption that testator destroyed it by physical act with the intent to revoke it. Unless the presumption of revocation can be overcome by proof (*e.g.*, that it was accidentally destroyed), the will cannot be probated. [§§541, 545-546]
a.	**YES**	No presumption of revocation arises because the copy in Beulah's possession and control was found after her death. The fact that the instrument offered for probate is not the bond paper copy does not matter. [§§541, 545-546]
39.	**SPLIT OF AUTHORITY**	Under the U.P.C. and in several "minority rule" states, the first will is revived upon proof that this was testator's intent. However, the majority rule is that revocation of a second will does *not*, by itself, revive or restore an earlier will. In these states, since the second will was revoked based on a mistake of law as to the validity of the first will, it is possible that the *second* will could be probated under the doctrine of dependent relative revocation. [§§557-570, 574-575]
40.a.	**NO**	The typewritten list cannot be incorporated by reference because it was not in existence at the time the will was executed. Also, the typewritten list had no independent significance; its only purpose was testamentary (*i.e.*, to dispose of property at death). [§§581-583, 593-596]

b.	**SPLIT OF AUTHORITY**	The gift would be valid in states that have enacted the U.P.C. provision giving effect to a list that disposes of *tangible personal property*. In states without such a rule, the gift would be invalid for the reasons given above. [§591]
c.	**DEPENDS**	The answer set out in b., above, applies *if* the Mercedes was Randy's personal automobile and was not used in her trade or business. The U.P.C. rule regarding lists of tangible personal property does not apply to trade or business assets. [§591]
d.	**NO**	Same answer as in a., above. The U.P.C. rule applies to *tangible* personal property and does not apply to intangible property such as cash or securities. [§591]

41.	**YES**	This is a pour-over gift, valid in all states that have enacted the Uniform Testamentary Additions to Trusts Act or its equivalent. The gift is valid even though (as here) the trust is later amended by an unwitnessed instrument. However, in a few states execution of the trust would have to have been acknowledged before a notary public in order to receive a valid pour-over gift. [§§597-603]

42.	**SPLIT OF AUTHORITY**	Under the doctrine of republication by codicil, the will is deemed to have been executed on the date of the last codicil thereto, meaning that Carol is treated as having been adopted *before* the will's execution. In states whose pretermitted child statutes protect only afterborn and after-adopted children, Carol has no rights. However, in states that give protection to children alive when the will was executed, Carol would take a share as a pretermitted child. [§§607-609]

43.	**NO**	The U.P.C. and many states require that any contract to make a gift by will and any promise not to revoke a will must be in writing and signed. Several states have the further requirement that existence of the contract be referred to in the will. But even in states without such a statute, the oral agreement is actually a contract for the sale of land, meaning that the Statute of Frauds applies. [§§613-616, 639]

44.	**PROBABLY NOT**	While a few courts would imply an agreement not to revoke in the case of a joint will containing reciprocal provisions, most would hold that B can revoke the will absent an *express* agreement not to revoke. [§§616-619, 628-631, 641]
a.	**DEPENDS**	If the revocation occurred *after* A's death, the express agreement would give S the right to impose a constructive trust on the property. However, a revocation prior to A's death affords no relief in most states *if* B gives A notice of the revocation. [§§643-645]

45.	**DEPENDS**	Whether Cuthbert takes by substitution under the lapse statute depends on Betty's relationship to Homer and the scope of the state's lapse statute. If Betty was Homer's child or grandchild, in all states the lapse statute would apply and Cuthbert would take. If Betty was Homer's grandparent or the descendant of a grandparent, Cuthbert would take in states that have enacted the U.P.C. or a similarly broad lapse statute. If, however, Betty was not related to Homer, the lapse statutes found in most states would not apply. The bequest would lapse, and the AT&T stock would become part of the residuary estate that passes to Martha. [§§660-665, 669]
a.	**DEPENDS**	If the jurisdiction has enacted the U.P.C.'s 120-hour rule, Betty would be treated as having predeceased Homer since she failed to survive him by 120 hours. Whether Cuthbert takes the bequest under the lapse statute would depend on Betty's relationship to Homer, as explained above. In states that have not adopted the 120-hour rule, Betty would have taken the AT&T stock under the will since she survived Homer; the stock would then pass to Bob under Betty's will. [§659]

b.	**PROBABLY NOT**	In nearly all states, the lapse statute (and the U.P.C.'s 120-hour rule) does not apply if the testamentary gift was contingent on the beneficiary's surviving the testator. Since Betty failed to meet the condition of the gift, the gift fails according to its terms and the stock would pass to Martha under the residuary clause. However, a small minority of states would apply the lapse statute (assuming it is otherwise applicable) because there was no gift over in the event of Betty's nonsurvival. [§§659, 667-668]
46.a.	**NO**	The lapse statutes found in most states would not apply because Huie was not related to the testator. Most states apply a "no residue of a residue" rule, under which the one-third share that lapsed would "fall out of the will" and pass by intestacy—to Dewey. Dewey would end up with two-thirds and Louie one-third of the residuary estate. Under the U.P.C. and in other states that have a "surviving residuary beneficiaries" rule, Dewey and Louie would each take one-half of the residuary estate. [§§673-675]
b.	**YES**	Since this case is covered by the lapse statute in all jurisdictions, neither the "no residue of a residue" rule nor the "surviving residuary beneficiaries" rule applies. [§676]
47.a.	**DEPENDS**	Alice does not take a share if the state has a narrow lapse statute that applies only if the predeceasing beneficiary was a descendant of the testator. Instead, the "class gift rule" applies, and Greenacre passes in equal shares to Vern's children who survived the testator. But under the U.P.C. and the broader lapse statutes found in many states, the lapse statute would apply and, since most courts hold that the lapse statute overrides the class gift rule, Alice would take a share of Greenacre under the lapse statute. [§§661-664, 706-709]
b.	**PROBABLY NOT**	In most states, a gift to someone's "children" does **not** include children born out of wedlock absent a showing of contrary intent. And while the U.P.C. provides that such a gift presumptively includes children born out of wedlock to the **mother**, a child born out of wedlock is not included in a gift to the **father's** "children" unless the father openly acknowledged the child as his own. Under a few modern decisions, however, a gift to "children" presumptively includes children born out of wedlock. [§§693-696]
c.	**PROBABLY YES**	Nearly all jurisdictions have discarded the common law "stranger to the adoption" rule. Donna would take a share **if** she was legally a child when she was adopted. If Donna was an adult when she was adopted, the courts are divided on whether she would be included in the gift. [§§688-692]
d.	**NO**	Under the "rule of convenience," the class closed on the testator's death. Only Vern's children who were alive (or in gestation) when the testator died share in the gift. [§§713-715]
48.a.	**SPLIT OF AUTHORITY**	Unless the state has enacted a statute affecting the question, Patricia does not take. Since the Rembrandt was specifically bequeathed and was not in Mona's estate at her death, ademption applies. Patricia is not entitled to the $100,000 because the will bequeathed a painting, not insurance proceeds. In these states, the $100,000 becomes a part of the residuary estate which passes to Tammy. However, under the U.P.C. and by statute in several states, Patricia would be entitled to the casualty insurance proceeds. [§§727-728, 735, 745]
b.	**NO**	Even the U.P.C.-type statute applies only to the extent that the casualty insurance proceeds are paid **after** the testator's death [§748]

c.	**NO**	This was a specific bequest ("*my* 200 shares"). Ademption applies since Mona did not own any Ibix stock at her death. Ralph is not entitled to the Series E bonds because the will gave him Ibix stock, not bonds. [§§727-728, 738]
d.	**PROBABLY YES**	Most courts hold that where new stock is acquired as the result of a merger, the change is one of form and not of substance, and thus ademption does not apply. The U.P.C. and statutes in several states expressly so provide. [§742]
e.	**NO**	Since the bequest was of "100 shares" and not "*my* 100 shares" of Kytek stock, most courts would classify this gift as a general legacy for ademption purposes. Ademption does not apply to general legacies. Stanley is entitled to the date-of-death value of 100 shares of Kytck stock. [§738]
49.a.	**YES**	By majority rule and by statute in several states, a specific bequest of stock carries with it any additional stock produced by a stock split during the testator's lifetime. For purposes of the stock split rule, this gift would be classified as a specific bequest even though the gift was not of "*my* 100 shares" of stock. [§§752-754, 758]
b.	**SPLIT OF AUTHORITY**	Most courts have ruled that, unlike stock produced by a stock split, a specific bequest of stock does **not** include stock dividends declared during the testator's lifetime. Under the U.P.C. and by statute in several states, however, stock dividends are treated the same as stock splits. [§§755-758]
c.	**YES**	Tess owned the stock from the moment of Zack's death, and thus the stock dividend was declared on **her** shares of stock. [§§757, 1019]
50.	**SPLIT OF AUTHORITY**	A majority of states hold that Bess is entitled to have the lien exonerated since the testator was personally liable on the note secured by the mortgage. However, the U.P.C. and a growing number of states have discarded the "exoneration of liens" doctrine. In these states, the lien is not exonerated unless the will directs exoneration. [§§759-761]
51.	**NO**	Alex has a direct interest in the estate (and would be benefitted if the will were set aside), but his wife does not. Agnes is not an interested party because she is neither an heir nor a legatee named in an earlier will. [§772]
a.	**DEPENDS**	Under the U.P.C. and in most states, Alex would not forfeit the legacy even though he lost the will contest *if* the court finds that the contest was brought in good faith and with probable cause. However, a minority of jurisdictions would hold that Alex had forfeited his legacy even if he had probable cause for challenging the will. [§§874-876]
52.	**DEPENDS**	Wilbur seems to have had the capacity to know the natural objects of his bounty. Further facts would have to be developed to determine whether he had sufficient capacity to understand the nature of the act he was doing, know the nature and value of his property, and understand the disposition he was making. And while most persons might conclude that Wilbur's belief that he had communicated with a dead person is, at best, illogical, a jury might find that such a belief is not so irrational as to constitute an insane delusion. [§§780-789]
a.	**POSSIBLY**	Although the adjudication would be admissible as evidence of incapacity, it is **not** conclusive. Determination of whether a person should be adjudicated incompetent involves a different (and more stringent) legal test than determination of capacity to make a will. [§792]

53.	**DEPENDS**	In many states, where an attorney prepares a will in his favor and supervises its execution, a presumption or inference of undue influence arises, especially if other suspicious circumstances exist. More facts would have to be developed, *e.g.*, whether there was a long and ongoing attorney-client relationship, circumstances surrounding the will's preparation and execution, etc. [§§816-818]
54.	**PROBABLY NOT**	It must also be shown that the misrepresentation was the *sole* reason for the bequest. If Michael had other inducing reasons (affection, esteem, etc.), the gift would not be set aside. [§§828-830]
a.	**NO**	The gift could not be set aside for mistake, because none appears on the face of the will. Nor do the facts, without more, indicate undue influence upon the testator. [§843]
55.	**PROBABLY NOT**	Absent a showing of fraud, parol evidence of mistake as to the inducement for a bequest is generally not admissible. [§§842-844]
a.	**NO**	Unless there is an ambiguity, extrinsic evidence is never admissible to overturn the plain meaning of a will. [§§845, 849]
56.	**YES**	There is a latent ambiguity in the description of the beneficiary, and extrinsic evidence is admissible to cure the ambiguity. [§855]
57.	**NO**	The opposite is more nearly correct. While the U.P.C. informal probate procedures have distinct advantages in simplicity, it is arguable that they may provide a greater opportunity for abuse because of lenient notice requirements and lack of court supervision of the personal representative. [§§900-906]
58.	**NO**	Since the instrument was not properly executed, it cannot be probated because it is *not* a valid will. [§928]
59.	**NOT NECESSARILY**	The attestation clause is prima facie evidence of the facts recited therein (*i.e.*, that Ralph and Gina signed in the testator's presence). The trier of fact could find that the will was validly executed notwithstanding Ralph's poor memory and Gina's hostile testimony. [§§929, 933]
60.	**NO**	In addition to good moral character, etc., a personal representative must have *contractual* capacity—which thereby excludes minors. [§949]
61.	**SPLIT OF AUTHORITY**	Under the U.P.C. and in several states, a personal representative is given the power to sell or mortgage estate assets by statute, and she need not obtain court authorization unless she desires to do so. However, many states require court authorization unless the will grants a power of sale. [§§977-980]
a.	**YES**	A representative is personally liable to third persons for acts committed by her *or her agents* in administering the estate. [§988]
b.	**DEPENDS**	Since Greta was not personally at fault, she is entitled to reimbursement *provided* she exercised reasonable care in hiring and instructing the broker regarding the sale. [§988]
62.	**NO**	The claim has been barred by the nonclaim statute and is no longer a valid obligation of the estate. If Lars pays the $5,000, he will be personally liable to the estate. [§§992-993]

63.a.	**YES**	In nearly all states, general legacies abate before specific bequests are abated. [§§1001-1003]
b.	**NO**	General legacies abate pro rata. After distributing the stock to Zapata, there will be $21,000 on hand. Miguel should receive $14,000 and Maria $7,000. [§1001-1003]
64.	**SPLIT OF AUTHORITY**	In most states, a general legatee is entitled to interest at the legal rate commencing one year after testator's death. Under the U.P.C., however, interest would not commence until one year after appointment of the personal representative (*i.e.*, the following December 10). [§1020]
65.	**PROBABLY NOT**	It is likely that Isadore's children can wind up Isadore's estate informally. In many states, transfer of title to the car and collection of the bank account can be handled by a statutory affidavit procedure. Even if this is not the case, the estate may qualify for a small estate administration under special statutory procedures. In determining whether the estate qualifies for small estate administration, the life insurance would not be counted because it is a nonprobate asset. [§§1022-1032]

SAMPLE EXAM QUESTION I

Trudy, a widow, died three months ago. Trudy's duly executed will, dated June 1, 1984, contained the following provisions:

FIRST, I bequeath my 1982 Lincoln Continental and my 500 shares of Rand Corp. stock to my daughter Ann.

SECOND, I bequeath 300 shares of Safeco Corp. stock to my son Bill.

THIRD, I bequeath $50,000 to my son Charlie.

FOURTH, I give, devise, and bequeath all the remainder of my estate to my children, Ann, Bill, and Charlie, in equal shares.

All three of Trudy's children survived her. However, Charlie died thirty days after Trudy (and before Trudy's will had been admitted to probate), leaving his wife Claudine as sole beneficiary under his will. Charlie also left two children who were not mentioned in his will. An investigation shows that in 1985 Trudy gave 300 shares of Safeco stock to her son Bill, and later that year Trudy traded in her Lincoln Continental on a new Cadillac. In 1984, the Rand Corp. stock split two-for-one, and early this year Rand Corporation merged into Amtex Corporation. The day after Trudy's death a new stock certificate arrived for 1,000 shares of Amtex stock registered in Trudy's name.

After all debts, taxes, and administrative costs have been paid, there remains the following property for distribution: a 1985 Cadillac, 600 shares of Safeco stock, 1,000 shares of Amtex stock, and a $125,000 savings certificate registered in Trudy's name.

What are the rights of Trudy's three children or their heirs in the assets of Trudy's estate? Explain fully.

SAMPLE EXAM QUESTION II

Tony Testator, fully competent mentally, suffered from multiple sclerosis and had great difficulty in writing. In 1984, under no mental or physical coercion, and using an old stationer's will form as a rough guide, Tony dictated to Sandy Oaks, the practical nurse who was caring for him, the following instrument, which was typewritten by Sandy on one side of a single sheet of paper. When Sandy completed her typing, the instrument was as set out below. (The handwritten portions were added as hereinafter stated.)

I, Tony Testator, do make this, my Last Will and Testament.

After my just debts are paid, I devise all the rest and residue of my estate to my nephew, Arnold Smith, and I name Arnold as my executor, to serve without bond.

Subscribed and sealed by the above-named Testator, *Tony Testator* , as and for his Last Will and Testament in the presence of us, who were all present at the same time, and who in Testator's presence, and in the presence of each other, have subscribed our names as witnesses.

By *Sandy Oaks*
July 1, 1984

Witnesses:

Arnold Smith
Arnold Smith

Tony then called in Arnold Smith and Roger Jones and said to them: "Gentlemen, I would like you to witness my will." Tony managed, with some difficulty, to pick up a pen and to place it at the left side of the space where his handwritten name appears in the attestation clause. He started to write, but it was apparent that he had little control over his movements. Sandy, without more, firmly superimposed her hand over Tony's and guided it, the effect being a legible signature. Sandy then wrote "By Sandy Oaks" and "July 1, 1984." Arnold wrote his name and then Roger signed, inadvertently writing Arnold's name below Arnold's signature instead of his own. Tony then said "thanks" to Arnold and Roger, and they departed.

Tony died last month, survived by his nephews Arnold and Benny, his nearest kin. Disappointed that he did not share under the instrument, Benny has retained counsel to contest the will or otherwise assert any rights he might have in Tony's estate. Arnold has retained you to protect his right to Tony's entire residuary estate. Discuss with him the legal issues which the case presents and your conclusion as to the ultimate distribution of the estate assets.

SAMPLE EXAM QUESTION III

Frank Foley married Ann White in 1960, and in 1962, a child, Lonnie, was born of the marriage. Frank and Ann were divorced in 1975, and in 1978, Frank married Betty Black.

In 1979, Frank duly executed a will in which, after making cash bequests of $5,000 to each of three brothers and two sisters (totaling approximately five percent of his net estate), he left the residue of his estate as follows: "One-half thereof to my wife Betty and the remaining one-half to my child Lonnie." In 1981, Frank adopted Ronnie Black, Betty's child by a previous marriage. In 1985, Lonnie died survived by two minor children, Peter and Paul.

On January 20, 1986, Frank consulted his attorney and told her to prepare a new will, revoking all prior wills, and disposing of his estate as follows: $10,000 to each of the brothers and sisters named in the 1979 will, one-half of the residue to his wife Betty, and the remaining one-half in equal shares to his adopted son Ronnie and his two grandsons, Peter and Paul. While Frank was in the office, the attorney had her secretary type a memorandum correctly setting forth Frank's requests. After reading over the memorandum, Frank signed it and the attorney gave him a xerographic copy of the signed memo.

Frank died of a heart attack on January 24, 1986. The 1979 will was found in his desk with the word "CANCELLED" written diagonally across the face of the will. Testator's initials ("F.F.") and "1/21/86" appeared just under the word "Cancelled," all writing being in Frank's hand. The memo concerning the new will was found with the 1979 will.

Frank was survived by Betty, Ronnie, Peter, and Paul, and the brothers and sisters named in the 1979 will. Who is entitled to share in Frank's estate and in what shares? Discuss all issues raised by these facts.

SAMPLE EXAM QUESTION IV

Thelma, a 78-year-old widow, suffered from the infirmities of advanced age. On July 1, 1986, she entered a nursing home. Martin, a practical nurse and former neighbor of Thelma's, was a frequent visitor in the nursing home, coming to see Thelma. He would often feed her and provide other minor assistance. On December 15, 1986, Martin suggested to Thelma that she should have a new will because the tax laws were recently changed (which was true). On December 20, 1986, Counsel, an attorney, came to the nursing home at Martin's request. Counsel prepared and supervised the execution of a new will which devised the bulk of Thelma's estate to Martin. Counsel then asked Thelma to give him the old will "because it is now obsolete." Thelma acceded to this request and handed the document to Counsel. After returning to his office, Counsel wrote "VOID" across each page of the old will and placed it in the file with the new will. Under the old will, all of Thelma's estate was devised to her grandson Harry.

Thelma died on April 15, 1987, while still in the nursing home. An investigation shows that Thelma's grandson Harry, her sole heir, never visited Thelma or called the nursing home to inquire about his grandmother's condition, even though Harry lived in the same city. Harry consults you as to the legal status of each of the two wills and the possibility of his inheriting Thelma's estate. What advice would you give to Harry? Discuss the controlling legal issues.

SAMPLE EXAM QUESTION V

Lucy, who was single, duly executed a will in 1983 which provided as follows:

1. I bequeath fifty shares of General Bank stock to my sister Alice.

2. I devise my home to my sister Barbara.

3. I give, devise and bequeath the rest of my estate to my brothers, Charles, David, and Edward.

4. I intentionally make no provision for my sister Frances.

In 1984, Lucy sold her home to Byers for $50,000. The sale was pursuant to an installment contract under which Byers paid $5,000 down and agreed to pay Lucy $500 per month until the balance (with interest) was paid in full. A deed to the home was placed in escrow, to be delivered to Byers upon full payment of the contract price. The note was secured by a vendor's lien on the property. At the time of sale, Lucy told Byers that if she died before the price was paid in full, Byers was to pay the balance to Lucy's brothers.

In 1985, General Bank paid a 100 percent stock dividend, as a result of which Lucy received an additional 50 shares of stock. Also in 1985, Lucy's brothers Charles and David died. Charles was survived by a widow and two adopted children. David, who never married, had no children.

Lucy died in 1986. Her estate contained 100 shares of General Bank stock; the note and vendor's lien from Byers (with an unpaid balance of $35,000 when Lucy died); and other assets worth $100,000. Lucy was survived by her sisters Alice, Barbara, and Frances, her brother Edward, and the widow and two adopted children of her brother Charles. How should Lucy's estate be distributed? Explain fully.

SAMPLE EXAM QUESTION VI

John Johnson died leaving a purported last will and testament dated August 1, 1984. The will was in John's handwriting and his signature was affixed at the bottom. To the left of John's signature were the signatures of Louise (John's housekeeper), Fred (John's uncle and only living blood relative), and Byron (John's neighbor).

John's will left his $10,000 savings account (which was registered jointly in Louise's and his name) to Louise, his stamp collection and automobile to Byron, and his residuary estate to Uncle Fred.

In 1986, John became seriously ill. Just before the ambulance arrived to take him to the hospital, he called Louise and Byron to his bedside and gave his savings passbook to Louise and his stamp collection to Byron, saying "I won't be coming back so you can have these now."

John died two days later. Not counting the savings account and the stamp collection, John's estate included the following assets: $75,000 in stocks and bonds; a checking account with a $12,000 balance; and a Mercedes automobile purchased in 1986. (John had traded in his 1980 Volkswagen as a downpayment for the Mercedes.)

Should the purported will be admitted to probate and who should receive each of the assets mentioned? Discuss your reasoning and conclusions.

SAMPLE EXAM QUESTION VII

Martha died two months ago, leaving as her sole heirs four children: Andy, Bob, Carol, and David. Martha had executed a will with all appropriate formalities in 1979; the will was witnessed by two neighbors. Although Martha asked the neighbors to "witness my will," neither neighbor knew the contents of the will, which had been prepared by Martha's lawyer. The will contained the following provisions:

1. I devise Blackacre to my son Andy.

2. I bequeath $8,000 and all of the paintings in the master bedroom of my home to my daughter Carol.

3. I bequeath $10,000 to my college.

4. I bequeath $25,000 to my son David with the hope and expectation that he use a portion of this money to provide educational assistance to and/or custodial care for his son Dwayne.

5. I give my residuary estate to my good friend, Mary Wilson.

6. I have not forgotten my son Bob. However, it is my intention that he shall not, under any circumstances, share in my estate.

Other pertinent facts are as follows: Martha, a retired college professor, earned an undergraduate degree from Central State College, a master's degree in education from Mega University, and taught for fifteen years at Elysian College. Her grandson Dwayne was injured in a car accident in 1978, in which he suffered brain damage. In November 1980, Martha mortgaged Blackacre, and the unpaid balance on the mortgage note was $15,000 at her death. Mary Wilson died in March of 1982, leaving her mother as her sole heir at law. When Martha was confined to her bed shortly before her death, she had a number of valuable paintings moved from other parts of her house to her master bedroom so that she might enjoy them; this more than doubled the value of paintings in the room.

What distribution should be made of Martha's estate? Explain fully.

SAMPLE EXAM QUESTION VIII

In 1978, Chester Testator, then a widower, entered into a written agreement wherein he agreed to devise Blackacre, an undeveloped tract of land then worth $150,000, to his son Abel if Abel would assist him in his business for a period of ten years or until Chester's earlier death. Chester also had a daughter Betty. In 1980, Chester duly executed a will that contained the following provisions:

1. I bequeath legacies of $25,000 to each of my children, Abel and Betty.

2. I recognize my obligation to my son Abel in assisting me in my business, and I therefore bequeath to him the further sum of $150,000.

3. I devise Blackacre to my son Abel for life, with remainder over to my daughter Betty.

Betty was named residuary beneficiary and executor. At the date of execution of the will, Blackacre had not appreciated in value.

In 1986, Chester married Wilma, a wealthy widow. They died in an automobile accident on their wedding trip. Chester was killed instantly; Wilma died a week later without ever regaining consciousness. She died intestate leaving an only child, Doris. Wilma knew nothing of the agreement with Abel. Abel, Betty, and Doris, all of whom are adults, survive.

Betty has offered Chester's 1980 will for probate. Because of the development of a "theme park" in the vicinity, Blackacre had recently skyrocketed in value, and of Chester's total assets (before estate taxes but after payment of all other claims, charges, and expenses) of $1,000,000, it represents $750,000 thereof. Abel has fully performed the agreed services.

Abel has retained you to advise him as to his rights under the agreement and the will, and as to his best course of action. Discuss the distribution of the assets, considering the rights of Abel, Betty, and Doris, and setting forth your reasoning for conclusions reached. (Assume that all documents were validly executed according to law. Also, disregard the impact of possible estate taxes on your conclusions.)

SAMPLE EXAM QUESTION IX

Margaret Mills, age 73, lived with her daughter Amelia ever since her husband died ten years ago. Amelia has taken care of Margaret's financial affairs, and in the last few years Margaret's declining health has required Amelia to be a nurse as well as financial advisor. Margaret has been very thankful for Amelia's help and has often told her friends that she planned to take care of Amelia in her will.

One day while taking a walk, Margaret fell and broke her hip. She was rushed to the hospital and was told she would have to have surgery. Amelia told her mother that it was time to make her will and that she had arranged for a lawyer to come to the hospital. Margaret said that if that was what Amelia thought was best, she would tell the lawyer what to write and she would sign it.

Clyde Attorney visited with Amelia and Margaret the next day, and Margaret told him to draft her will so that she could execute it before her surgery. Clyde went back to his office and drafted a will in accordance with Margaret's instructions, as follows:

ITEM I. I bequeath $25,000 to my good friend, Ann Wilkes.

ITEM II. I give my son John Mills one-fifth of my property, both real and personal, wheresoever situated.

ITEM III. I give all the rest, residue, and remainder of my property, both real and personal, to my beloved daughter Amelia Mills.

Clyde Attorney returned to the hospital and found Margaret about to go into surgery. She said she was too tired to read her will but asked Clyde if he had done what she told him. He said he had, and she executed her will in the presence of Amelia and two nurses. The nurses signed as witnesses to the will.

Margaret recovered from surgery and returned home. John Mills wrote his mother and said he was joining the gay alliance. Margaret was so upset that she had Clyde Attorney draft a codicil to her will revoking Item II. Margaret duly executed the codicil.

Two years later, John returned home to see Margaret and attend Ann Wilkes' funeral. He and Margaret had a long talk, and Margaret decided it was time to make peace with her son. She took the codicil out of her desk, tore it up, and threw it in a wastebasket.

Margaret died two days later, leaving an estate valued at $200,000 after all debts and expenses. She was survived by John and Amelia, her only children.

John Mills comes to see you and wants his mother's will set aside because of the actions of his sister Amelia at the time the will was prepared. Should John prevail, and if so, how will the estate be distributed? If the will stands, how will the estate be distributed? State the reasons for the conclusions that you reach.

SAMPLE EXAM QUESTION X

Tim Brown went to a program at his church, sponsored by the local bar assocation, on estate planning and the need for the average citizen to have a will. After the meeting, Tim decided he needed a will. Concluding that he did not own enough property to warrant paying a lawyer to draft his will, Tim wrote the following handwritten statements on a yellow legal pad:

I, Tim Brown, being of sound mind, leave my estate as follows:

ITEM I: I give my good friend Herb Hanson all of my fishing equipment and my twenty-five-foot boat.

ITEM II: I give my church, First Baptist Church of Smithville, the sum of $10,000.

ITEM III: All the rest of my property I give to my sister Jane Brown.

After writing the will, Tim took it over to his preacher's house and asked the preacher and his wife if they would witness the will. They said that they would be happy to, and the preacher thanked Tim for the generous gift to the church. The preacher and his wife signed at the bottom of the page, and then Tim signed the will just above their signatures. Tim took the will home and placed it in his desk drawer.

About a year later, after a dispute with members of his church, Tim left the First Baptist Church and joined the Glory Baptist Church of Smithville. After he joined the Glory Church, Tim crossed out the words "First Baptist Church" and wrote in "Glory Baptist Church" in Item II of his will. He then initialed the change in the margin and put the will back into his desk.

Tim died four weeks ago and his will has been offered for probate by his sister Jane. Jane has notified First Baptist Church and Glory Church about the will. Discuss the issues as to the validity of the will, and who will take the $10,000 under Item II.

ANSWER TO SAMPLE EXAM QUESTION I

Ann: Daughter Ann takes the 1,000 shares of Amtex stock and one-third of the residuary estate. Trudy's will made a specific bequest of "my 500 shares" of Rand stock. Since a specific devisee of stock is entitled to additional shares produced by a stock split declared after the will is executed, Ann would have been entitled to all 1,000 shares of Rand stock. But then Rand Corporation was merged into Amtex Corporation. At common law and in a few states, this would result in ademption of the bequest of Rand stock. However, the U.P.C. and most states hold that since this was a change of form and not of substance, the specific legatee of stock gets the equivalent shares in the new corporation which are produced by a merger, consolidation, reorganization or similar action.

Ann has no claim, however, to Trudy's Cadillac. A specific bequest of an item that is not in the testator's estate at her death is adeemed. Since the 1982 Lincoln Continental was not in Trudy's estate at her death the bequest to Ann is adeemed. Ann has no claim to the Cadillac; it was not bequeathed to her.

Bill: Son Bill takes one-third of the residuary estate. The authorities are divided on whether Bill is also entitled to an additional 300 shares of Safeco stock (*i.e.*, over and above the 300 shares that Trudy gave him in 1985) or whether the 1985 gift was in total satisfaction of the legacy. At common law and in states not having statutes on the question, there is a rebuttable presumption that the 1985 gift was intended as in total satisfaction of the legacy. Under the U.P.C. and in states with statutes on the question, the gift would not be treated as in satisfaction of the legacy unless there was a writing signed by the donor or donee evidencing such an intention. Here, because there was no writing signed by either Trudy or Bill evidencing such an intention, the gift would not be treated as in satisfaction of the legacy. Moreover since there are sufficient shares of Safeco stock in Trudy's estate to satisfy the bequest, ademption would not apply.

Charlie's heirs: Charlie's wife Claudine takes $50,000 plus one-third of Trudy's residuary estate. Charlie was alive when Trudy died, and thus the gifts to Charlie did not lapse. Since Charlie owned this portion of Trudy's estate as of her death, upon his own death thirty days later, the property passed under Charlie's will to Claudine. The fact that Trudy's will was not probated and the property had not been distributed before Charlie's death does not matter. His rights under the will relate back to Trudy's death.

Charlie's two children have no claim to the $50,000 or Charlie's share of the residuary estate under the lapse statute. But do they have any claim to this or any other part of Charlie's estate under the pretermitted child statute? In states whose pretermitted child statutes apply only to afterborn children, the children have no claim if they were alive when Charlie executed his will. But even if they were afterborns (as to Charlie's will), or if the state's pretermitted child statute applies to children alive when the will was executed, if Claudine is their mother they would not have any claim under the pretermission statutes found in most states. In most jurisdictions, the statute does not apply if the testator devised substantially all of his estate to his spouse, the parent of all his children.

Thus, the residuary estate, consisting of the 1985 Cadillac, either 300 or 600 shares of Safeco stock (depending on whether the doctrine of satisfaction of legacies applies), and $75,000 ($125,000 - $50,000) in the savings certificate should be divided in equal shares between Ann, Bill, and Claudine.

ANSWER TO SAMPLE EXAM QUESTION II

The first issue is whether the will was validly executed. Under the most stringent will execution statutes, to be valid the will must have been: (1) signed by the testator (or by another person at testator's direction and in his presence), (2) at the end of the will, (3) in the presence of two witnesses, present at the same time. There must also have been: (4) two attesting witnesses, (5) both of whom signed in testator's presence and (6) in the presence of each other. Finally, (7) the testator must have declared to the witnesses that the instrument is his will.

In this case, this seven-point test was met. (1) Tony did sign the will. Any mark made by the testator, intended to be his signature, satisfies the signature requirement. While Tony needed to have his hand guided, the mark that was made (with Sandy's guidance) was his mark, not Sandy's; it was his volitional act. (Policy supports this result: Persons suffering from multiple sclerosis should be able to execute wills too!) Besides, even if a court were reluctant to find that Tony actually signed the will, the signature requirement would be satisfied by resort to the alternate test: If it is deemed that Sandy signed Tony's name, this would have been done at Tony's (tacit) request and in his presence.

(2) Tony signed at the end of the will. The fact that he did not sign on the designated signature line is a bit sloppy, but it does not alter the fact that Tony did impress his signature, and that his signature was at the end of the will.

There is no problem as to elements (3), (4), (5), (6), or (7). There were two witnesses, both present when Tony signed, who then signed the will as attesting witnesses in Tony's presence and the presence of each other. Tony also declared to them that the instrument involved was his will.

What of the fact that Roger Jones inadvertently signed Arnold Smith's name rather than his own? This is the toughest part of the case. Benny has a very good argument that a witness's signature must be just that—the witness's signature. Benny will argue that policy supports this view; otherwise, anyone could come in and say, "I know that that second signature does not give my name, but I am the person who inadvertently signed it that way." This claim is a bit too implausible and is fraught with potential for fraudulent claims.

While a court may rule for Benny on this issue, I would argue (and I believe persuade the court) that the evidence does show that Roger Jones did make the second mark. In general, the signature requirement (whether that of the testator *or of the witnesses*) is liberally construed. Any mark, intended as such, suffices. Thus, such signatures as "Dad," "Skip," "SMJ," and even "X" have been upheld. Arnold will argue persuasively that Roger Jones did sign at the indicated place and did intend for that mark to be his signature. Furthermore, the statute has been complied with literally: The will was signed by two witnesses. We can prove that and that is all we have to prove. Under oath, Arnold and Roger will each testify, "Yes, I signed that."

Another issue here concerns the fact that Arnold, one of the two attesting witnesses, is the sole beneficiary under the will. This does not affect admissibility of the will to probate in any state (except Louisiana), but may affect Arnold's share in the estate. Under the U.P.C. and in states that have abolished the "interested witness" rule, there would be no problem: Arnold would take the entire estate. However, in states that have a "purging" interested witness rule, that voids the gift to a witness who is also a beneficiary, Arnold would take the lesser of (i) the bequest in the will or (ii) the amount that he would have taken if the will were not executed (*i.e.*, his intestate share). Since Arnold and Benny are Tony's sole heirs, in these states, Arnold would take one-half and Benny the other one-half of Tony's estate. (Note that some states with purging statutes have a further qualification: The interested witness statutes do not apply if the will can be proved without the witness-beneficiary's testimony. In these states, it might be possible to avoid the purging rule upon proof of due execution based on Roger Jones' testimony.)

ANSWER TO SAMPLE EXAM QUESTION III

The 1979 will was revoked by physical act in 1986. The new will was never validly executed. As a result, Frank died intestate. The following is a chronological analysis of the events giving rise to this result.

The 1981 adoption of Ronnie Black made Ronnie a pretermitted child as to the 1979 will. The pretermitted child statute treats after-adopted children the same as afterborn children. If the 1979 will were probated, Ronnie would be entitled to an intestate share of Frank's estate. The statute would apply because there was no intent expressed in the will to omit Ronnie. Also, there was no evidence of a lifetime settlement to Ronnie; and even though Betty is Ronnie's natural parent, she was not left substantially all of Frank's estate under the will (she gets less than one-half).

Lonnie's death in 1985 caused a lapse of her gift under the 1979 will. Since Lonnie was a descendant of the testator, Lonnie's gift would pass to her children under the lapse statute. Peter and Paul would share Lonnie's one-half of the residue *if* the 1979 will could be probated.

However, the 1979 will cannot be probated beause it was effectively revoked by the testator's physical act on January 21, 1986. The cancellation was written across the face of the will, and it physically touched the words of the will. There is no evidence refuting Frank's clear intent to revoke the will by this act, and there is no evidence refuting the fact that Frank himself revoked the will. Such a written cancellation is an effective revocation in all states.

The 1979 will cannot be saved by the doctrine of dependent relative revocation ("DRR"). Although Frank apparently wished to create a new dispositive plan under a new will, and was no longer going to need the 1979 will, the revocation of the 1979 will was premature. Frank did not attempt to execute the new will before he died. Therefore, he could not have been relying on the validity of the new will when he revoked the old one. Since his revocation of the 1979 will was not based or dependent upon any mistake of law as to the validity of another disposition, DRR does not apply.

The 1986 memorandum cannot be probated as Frank's will because it was never properly executed. Although the memorandum was signed by Frank, it was not witnessed by attesting witnesses.

Thus, since Frank died without a valid will, his estate will pass to his heirs under the state's intestacy statute. Under the U.P.C., Frank's wife Betty is entitled to one-half of the estate (not $50,000 plus one-half, because Peter and Paul are not her lineal descendants). Ronnie (Frank's adopted son) takes one-fourth of the estate, and Peter and Paul take one-eighth each by representation.

ANSWER TO SAMPLE EXAM QUESTION IV

If Harry can prove either that Thelma lacked testamentary capacity at the time the new will was executed or that she was subjected to undue influence, he will inherit his grandmother's entire estate. The attempted revocation of Thelma's old will, under which Harry is the sole beneficiary, was ineffective.

Harry may have a difficult time proving lack of testamentary capacity. Harry will have the burden of proof and must show that Thelma did not have sufficient capacity to understand: (1) the nature and extent of her property, (2) who the natural objects of her bounty were, (3) the nature of the disposition she was making under the will, and (4) the interrelation of these factors into a scheme or plan of distribution. The fact that Thelma was in a nursing home and suffered from the infirmities of old age is not, by itself, sufficient evidence to satisfy this burden. Harry must come up with hard evidence that Thelma lacked one of these four requirements. Nothing in the facts given suggests that any such evidence exists.

Harry has a much better chance of proving that the will was executed as the result of undue influence. Although Harry still has the initial burden of proof to show undue influence, he has ample evidence to get his case started. In most states, a presumption of undue influence arises where there is a confidential relationship between testator and the will beneficiary, the beneficiary actively participates in the drawing of the will, and the will makes an unnatural disposition (*e.g.*, favors an unrelated party over relatives). Here Harry should be able to establish that a confidential relationship existed between Martin and Thelma because of the nurse-patient relationship that had developed and because of the heavy reliance Thelma placed on Martin for care and companionship. Since Martin procured the will's preparation and the will makes an unnatural disposition (by favoring Martin over grandson Harry), a presumption of undue influence will arise. The burden would then shift to Martin to rebut the presumption. (In some states, these facts would raise an inference of undue influence, but the burden of proof would not shift.)

Once the burden of proof shifts to Martin, he will have a very difficult time disproving that undue influence existed. Thelma was susceptible to undue influence because of her condition and because she was somewhat isolated in a nursing home. Martin had the opportunity to exert undue influence since he was caring for her. Since Martin procured the will and it makes an unnatural disposition of Thelma's property, the various facts support a finding of undue influence, thus rendering the execution of the new will invalid.

The revocation of the old will was invalid for two reasons: (i) the same undue influence that rendered the execution of the new will invalid would render the revocation of the old will invalid; and (ii) the physical revocation was not performed by Thelma herself. If a will is physically revoked by another, the revocation must be at testator's direction and in testator's *presence*. The failure to satisfy the presence requirement nullifies the revocation, regardless of any undue influence issue. The words of revocation in the new will do not operate to revoke the old will because the new will was a product of undue influence, and is void in all respects.

Thus, Thelma's old will should be admitted to probate, and Harry will take the whole estate.

ANSWER TO SAMPLE EXAM QUESTION V

The Stock: Alice of course takes at least fifty shares of General Bank stock. But does she take the additional fifty shares produced by the stock dividend? First, it should be noted that the bequest of stock is a specific one. (The absence of the words "*my* fifty shares" does not make the bequest a general one. Only in ademption cases will the courts seize on the absence of the possessory pronoun "my" in order to classify a bequest of stock as a general bequest.) At common law and in some states today, a specific bequest of stock includes additional shares produced by a stock split after the will is executed, but does not include additional shares produced by a stock dividend. In these states, Alice would take only the fifty shares. However, under the U.P.C. and by statute in several other states, Alice is entitled to the additional shares, whether they were the result of a stock split or a stock dividend; in these states Alice would take all 100 shares.

The Home: Since Lucy entered into a contract for the sale of her home after the will was executed, at common law and by majority rule, the devise of the home to Barbara would be adeemed because a gift of specific property that is not in the estate at the testator's death fails. Even though, because of the escrow arrangement, legal title was still in Lucy at the time of her death, under the doctrine of equitable conversion Lucy did not own real property, but only a contract right, at her death. Since the will did not bequeath the note or contract to Barbara, ademption applies, and in some states Barbara takes nothing.

Under the U.P.C. and by statute in several states, however, Barbara is entitled to the remaining purchase price on the property sold, to the extent unpaid at Lucy's death. In these states, Barbara would be entitled to the $35,000 unpaid balance. The money already paid to Lucy under the contract is not covered by the statute and would be included in Lucy's residuary estate.

Regardless of which of the above rules applies, Lucy's instructions to pay the balance of the purchase price to her brothers were ineffective. These oral instructions were an attempted testamentary act, not executed with the requisite formalities of due execution, and therefore they will not be enforced. Furthermore, the instructions could not be considered part of the contract since, being oral, they were subject to the Statute of Frauds.

The Residue: Since David predeceased Lucy, the gift to David of a share of the residuary estate lapsed at his death, and since David left no descendants, the lapse statute does not apply. Then what happens to David's share? The bequest was not a class gift because Lucy named the brothers by name, thus indicating that Lucy was not "group-minded" in making this gift. By majority rule, there can be no "residue of a residue"; thus, David's share of the residue would "fall out of the will" and pass by intestacy: One-fifth shares would go to Alice, Barbara, Edward, and Frances; and one-tenth shares would go to each of Charles' two children. By majority rule, Frances would take a share even though she was specifically disinherited by the will, since the will's language has no application to property passing under the intestacy statutes.

Under the U.P.C. and by statute in several states, there would be no lapse of David's residuary gift. Under these states' "surviving residuary beneficiaries" rule, David's share would pass to the surviving residuary beneficiaries: one-half to Edward and one-half as described in the next paragraph.

Charles also predeceased the testator. Under the narrow lapse statutes found in several states, the lapse statute would not apply since Charles was not a descendant of the testator. Thus, either two-thirds of the residuary estate would pass by intestacy (if the "no residue of a residue" rule applies), or Edward would take the entire residuary estate (if the "surviving residuary beneficiaries" rule applies). However, the more liberal lapse statutes found in many states (and that of the U.P.C.) would apply in favor of Charles' two children since Charles was a brother of the testator. (The lapse statute provides that the gift is shared by Charles' issue; the gift does not pass under Charles' will or by intestacy.) Lapse statutes operate in favor of adopted children as well as natural born children. Thus, Charles' two children would take either one-third or one-half of the residuary estate, depending upon whether the "no residue of a residue" rule or the "surviving residuary beneficiaries" rule applies.

ANSWER TO SAMPLE EXAM QUESTION VI

Admission of Will to Probate: John's will is valid even if the jurisdiction does not recognize holographic wills. A valid will does not have to be typewritten. The only thing that is important is whether it has been properly executed. Here, it appears that the requirements of execution have been satisfied: (1) John signed the will at the end thereof. (2) The will was witnessed by two (actually, three) witnesses. (3) The fact that a witness may have been interested does not affect the validity of the will. (4) No state requires that an attestation clause be included in a will. If the will had contained an attestation clause, its recitals would have been prima facie evidence that the testator "published" the will, and that the witnesses signed in testator's presence, etc. Since there is no attestation clause, the required facts will have to be established by the witnesses' court testimony. It appears, however, that such proof will not be difficult in this case. Therefore, the will should be admitted to probate.

Distribution of the Assets

Stamp Collection and Savings Account: The stamp collection passed to Byron by inter vivos gift. The bequest of the stamp collection was adeemed by John's last minute gift to Byron ("ademption by satisfaction"). This is probably also the result with respect to the joint savings account given to Louise. Under the law of gifts, it is possible that mere delivery of the passbook may not be considered a completed gift of the amount on deposit. If that is the case, there is still no problem because then the money would still be in the estate, and thus Louise's bequest would not have been adeemed. She would take under the will rather than by gift. Moreover, the facts state that the savings account was a joint one. If the joint account had survivorship provisions, the entire account would pass to Louise by right of survivorship. If the account was in tenancy in common form, John's one-half interest in the account would pass to Louise either under the will or by the last minute gift.

Automobile and residuary estate: The other assets present more of a problem because the witnesses to this will were all "interested" (*i.e.*, also beneficiaries under the will). The U.P.C. and several states have abolished the "interested witness" rule. In these states, the assets will be distributed according to the will. The stock, bonds, and checking account pass to Fred under the residuary clause; the Mercedes passes to Byron. Under the facts of independent significance doctrine, the bequest of "my automobile" will be interpreted to mean the one owned by John at his death; so it is irrelevant that at the time John wrote the will he had a Volkswagen.

Things would be different, however, if the jurisdiction had a "purging" statute. Although the interested witness situation does not affect the will's admissibility to probate in any state (except Louisiana), the bequests to interested witnesses would be purged. Thus, the bequest of the Mercedes to Byron would be purged, as would any portion of the savings account that was subject to John's will (*see* discussion above). But Fred would be able to take his bequest. Under the "whichever is least" rule, an interested witness who is also an intestate heir may take the lesser of the intestate share or the bequest amount. Here, since Fred would inherit John's entire estate if there were no will, the gift to Fred would not be purged. Note that the supernumerary rule, another exception to purging statutes, would not help since all three witnesses were interested; there were not two disinterested witnesses among them.

ANSWER TO SAMPLE EXAM QUESTION VII

The fact that the attesting witnesses did not know the contents of the will has no relevance. No state requires that an attesting witness know the will's contents. Some states have a "publication" requirement, under which the witnesses must know that they are serving as witnesses to a will, but it is clear from the facts that both witnesses here knew they were attesting a will.

In most states, Andy would be entitled to have the $15,000 mortgage on Blackacre paid out of the residuary estate. Under the doctrine of exoneration of liens, liens on specifically devised property are exonerated. Under the U.P.C. and by statute in a number of states, however, this doctrine has been abolished. In these states, absent a contrary will provision, the specific beneficiary takes the property *subject to* any lien against it, and in these states, Blackacre would pass to Andy subject to the mortgage.

Carol of course takes $8,000 under paragraph 2. Under the facts of independent significance doctrine, the bequest to Carol includes all of the paintings in the master bedroom. While Martha's subsequent actions of moving a number of paintings into the bedroom had the practical effect of increasing the bequest to Carol, this is perfectly valid. Although the doctrine requires that the fact have a legal significance apart from its effect on the will, it is clear from the facts of this question that Martha's act had a lifetime motive or purpose: She wanted to enjoy the paintings.

Paragraph 3 presents a problem: Which institution is to take the gift to Martha's "college"? There are three institutions that may have been intended. This is a case of latent ambiguity, because the ambiguity does not arise until the terms of the will are applied to the facts and it is determined that Martha had an association with three different colleges (or only two, if Mega University is determined not to be within the meaning of "college"). Extrinsic evidence (including, for example, the testimony of the attorney who prepared the will) is admissible to show which school was intended. If the extrinsic evidence does not cure the ambiguity, the gift will fail for want of identifying a beneficiary, and the $10,000 will become part of the residuary estate.

David takes $25,000 under paragraph 4. Despite Martha's comments regarding her "hope and expectation," David takes the money free of any trust or other enforceable obligation to use the funds for the indicated purpose. The words used are precatory words; they have no binding effect. David may do whatever he wishes with the money.

The bequest of the residuary estate to Mary Wilson lapsed since Mary predeceased the testator. The lapse statute found in most states would not be applicable on two counts: Mary was not related to the testator, and Mary left no issue who survived the testator. Since the lapse statute does not apply, Mary Wilson's mother takes nothing. Rather, Martha's four children inherit one-fourth shares of the residuary estate. Although Martha expressly disinherited Bob in her will, this provision has no effect on property passing by intestate succession (majority rule). When property passes by intestacy for any reason—here, by a lapse in the residuary estate—title passes to the heirs by force of the intestacy statutes. Thus, Bob takes one-fourth of the residuary estate by inheritance.

(*Note:* Under New York's "negative bequest" rule, the provision disinheriting Bob would be given effect, and the residuary estate would pass by intestacy to Andy, Carol, and David in equal shares.)

ANSWER TO SAMPLE EXAM QUESTION VIII

The Contract: Whether Abel can enforce his right to Blackacre under the contract with Chester depends on state law. Under the U.P.C. and in many states, the contract would be enforceable even though not referred to in the will, because it was evidenced by a writing signed by the parties. Since Abel's agreement with his father amounted to a contract for the sale of land, the Statute of Frauds applies; however, it appears that the written contract satisfied the Statute of Frauds.

In a minority of states, a contract relating to making a gift by will can be established only by provisions in the will stating that a contract does exist and setting forth the contract's material terms. In these states, Abel could not enforce the contract and would be limited in his recovery to quantum meruit for the reasonable value of his services (unless the will gift in paragraph 2 satisfies Abel's claim; *see* discussion below).

Assuming, however, that an enforceable contract did exist, Chester breached the contract. The agreement was for Abel to get fee simple title to Blackacre, not for him to get a cash sum equal to Blackacre's 1978 value plus a life estate in the property. Betty may argue that the breach occurred in 1980 when Chester executed the will, and thus the statute of limitations has run on Abel's remedy for breach of the contract, but she would lose this argument. The breach did not occur until Chester died without having made the agreed-upon gift in his will.

The proper remedy in this situation is to admit the will to probate and then impose a constructive trust in favor of the contract beneficiary. Abel should take Blackacre under a constructive trust.

Abel's and Betty's Legacies: The next question is whether Abel is also entitled to the $150,000 legacy. Abel will argue that the cash bequest was entirely separate from the agreement regarding Blackacre, and that he should get both. Betty will argue that the language of the devise ("recognizing my obligation to my son") shows that Chester intended the $150,000 gift to be in lieu of an outright devise of Blackacre, thus putting Abel to an election: He can take the $150,000 plus a life estate in Blackacre under the will, or he can take a fee in Blackacre under the contract; he cannot take both. Betty's argument should prevail. The language describing the $150,000 gift stated that it was related to Chester's obligation for Abel's helping in his business; this is the same consideration that supported the agreement for Chester to devise Blackacre to Abel. Furthermore, to give Abel both $150,000 and Blackacre (now worth $750,000) would give him over ninety percent of the estate. Chester clearly intended for Betty to have something of value (remainder interest in Blackacre plus residuary estate). Therefore, the better solution is for Abel to take Blackacre under a constructive trust and let the $150,000 fall into the residuary estate—subject to Wilma's (and now her daughter Doris') claims.

Of course, Abel and Betty would each take the $25,000 bequeathed to them in paragraph 1 of the will.

Doris' Interest: Although Chester and Wilma were both fatally injured in the automobile accident, Wilma survived Chester by a week. Therefore, neither the Uniform Simultaneous Death Act nor the U.P.C.'s 120-hour rule applies.

Many states have "pretermitted spouse" statutes that provide that marriage subsequent to the execution of a will partially revokes the will to allow the "pretermitted spouse" a share of the estate. Here, Wilma would have rights as a pretermitted spouse since she was not mentioned in the will and there is no mention of a prenuptial agreement waiving her rights in Chester's estate. Under the statute found in many of these states, Wilma would take an intestate share of Chester's estate. (In a few states, the pretermitted spouse statute would revoke the will in its entirety.) Since Wilma died intestate, her share of Chester's estate would pass to Wilma's only child Doris. In calculating Wilma's intestate share, Blackacre would not be included assuming that Abel is successful in establishing a constructive trust. Property subject to a valid contract to devise is not part of the estate because the testator had no dispositive rights over it at the time of his death.

However, Doris (as Wilma's heir) will succeed to a share of Chester's estate only if the jurisdiction has a pretermitted spouse statute. Without such a statute, Doris has no interest. Although most states have elective share statutes, allowing a spouse to take a statutory share of the estate regardless of what is in the will, the right of election dies with the surviving spouse. Thus Wilma's right of election was extinguished by her death before making the election. Neither Doris nor a personal representative can exercise the right for her. Doris then receives nothing.

ANSWER TO SAMPLE EXAM QUESTION IX

John has two possible grounds for challenging Margaret's will: (1) Amelia exercised undue influence upon Margaret, and (2) Margaret lacked testamentary capacity at the time the will was executed. However, John is not likely to prevail on either ground.

Although Margaret was very dependent upon Amelia, there is no indication that Amelia exercised undue influence over her mother. She recommended that Margaret make a will and she arranged for the lawyer, but it does not appear that Amelia influenced the terms of the will. Although Amelia was present during Margaret's interview with the attorney, the directions concerning the will's terms came from Margaret, not Amelia. The terms of the will were consistent with Margaret's past comments to friends that "she planned to take care of Amelia in her will." It was a natural distribution for Margaret to leave more to the child who lived with her and who took care of her. John has the burden of proving that Amelia's influence overpowered Margaret's mind and will. The mere existence of the opportunity to exert influence, susceptibility to influence due to illness and age, and the fact of an "unnatural disposition" are not, by themselves, sufficient to establish that undue influence was exerted. John must show that Margaret's free agency was destroyed, and the facts as presented do not warrant such a finding. In fact, they probably do not even warrant submission to a jury.

The fact that Margaret was in a hospital and had a broken hip does not indicate a lack of testamentary capacity. There is no indication that her mind was unclear from pain or drugs. She knew the nature and extent of her property, the natural objects of her bounty, and understood the disposition she was making. It is also clear that she understood the nature of the act that she was doing, i.e., making a will. Also, Margaret lived several years past the execution of the will. Her mind was clear; she remembered the terms of the will; she had further contact with Clyde Attorney concerning the codicil. Obviously, if the will had not reflected her testamentary intent, she would have changed it.

Furthermore, it was not necessary for Margaret to have read the will before executing it. She had dictated the terms herself, and Clyde Attorney had correctly assured her that these terms were all included in the will. She knew what she was signing, and the execution was valid.

Thus John's grounds for contesting the will are very weak. It is highly unlikely that he could meet his burden of proof for establishing undue influence or lack of testamentary capacity. But if John were to prevail and the will were set aside, the estate would be distributed as though Margaret died intestate. John and Amelia would each inherit one-half of the estate.

If the will stands, Ann Wilkes' estate or heirs take nothing. Since Ann predeceased Margaret and no alternative taker was named in Item 1, the gift to Ann lapsed and fell into the residuary estate. Even if Ann Wilkes left issue, the gift would not be saved by the lapse statute found in most states, because the predeceased beneficiary must not be related to the testator for the statute to apply; that is not the case here. The $25,000 bequest was a general legacy which, upon lapse, falls into the residuary estate.

John will take one-fifth of the $200,000 estate, or $40,000. The codicil that disinherited him was validly revoked by physical act. By majority rule, the revocation of a codicil by physical act restores the will to its original terms (i.e., those before the modifying codicil was executed).

Amelia takes the residuary estate, or $160,000. Even though the lapsed gift to Alice falls into the residuary, Amelia gets only four-fifths of it. Item II gave John one-fifth of Margaret's property, real and personal.

ANSWER TO SAMPLE EXAM QUESTION X

Tim's will was validly executed and is entitled to probate. The will was entirely in Tim's handwriting and was signed by him. If Tim was a resident of a state that recognizes holographic (*i.e.*, handwritten, unattested) wills, the will would be entitled to probate. The signatures of the two witnesses would be unnecessary to the will's validity.

Even in states that do not recognize holographic wills, however, the will would be admissible to probate because it was validly executed. To be valid, the testator must have signed the will at the end thereof in the presence of two witnesses, both of whom signed in the testator's presence and in the presence of each other. The facts show that these requirements were met. It is true that both witnesses signed before Tim signed. However, it is generally held that the exact order of signing the will is not critical as long as it is all part of one continuous transaction, as was the case here. Since Tim and the witnesses did not execute a self-proving affidavit, proof of due execution will have to be by the testimony of the attesting witnesses in open court, but that should not be a problem.

The fact that the preacher and his wife served as attesting witnesses does not create a problem either. Even in states, that have an "interested witness" rule (prohibiting a witness who is also a will beneficiary from taking under the will), the statute only strikes down *direct* bequests to a witness. Although the preacher might be seen as indirectly benefiting from the bequest to the church, this would not make him an "interested witness" within the meaning of the statute. Moreover, the U.P.C. and several states have abolished the interested witness rule.

More of a problem than the issue of execution of the will is the change in its terms. In states that do not recognize holographic wills, Tim's attempted change of the beneficiary from First Baptist Church to Glory Baptist Church is ineffective. Words added to a will after it has been executed are not given effect because they are unattested words. Only the words that are part of the will at the time it is executed have testamentary effect. Thus, Glory Baptist Church does not take the $10,000 bequest.

But does First Baptist Church take? A minority of states do not recognize partial revocations by physical act. In these states, First Baptist Church would take the bequest notwithstanding the attempted revocation because Tim's striking of the words "First Baptist Church" would be without legal effect. However, most states do give effect to partial revocations by physical act. In these states, First Baptist Church would take nothing; the $10,000 bequest would lapse and fall into the residuary estate, which passes to Jane Brown. Nor could First Baptist Church successfully argue that the doctrine of dependent relative revocation should be applied. It is true that Tim acted under a mistake of law as to the validity of another disposition; *i.e.*, he mistakenly thought that he could make a new gift to Glory Baptist Church by his interlineation. However, it is clear from the facts that Tim's intent to revoke the gift to First Baptist Church was independent of his intent to make a gift to Glory Baptist Church. To disregard the revocation would be contrary to Tim's intent, for Tim made it clear that he did not want First Baptist to take.

In states that give effect to holographic wills, Tim's change of the beneficiary from one church to the other would be valid, and Glory Baptist Church would take the $10,000. There is no requirement that a holographic will be written at one time or at one sitting. Interlineations and crossouts on a holographic will are given full effect as long as the evidentiary test is met: It must be shown that the will, and its interlineations and crossouts, are entirely in the testator's handwriting. On the facts given, this test could easily be met.

TABLE OF CASES

Dodge, Estate of - §664
Donigian's Will, *In re* - §545
Donnellan, Estate of - §856
Donnelly's Will, *In re* - §830
Donnor, Estate of - §199
Downey v. Lawley - §845
Drafts v. Drafts - §711
Duke v. Falk - §792
Duncan's Estate, *In re* - §152
Dunson's Estate, *In re* - §799
Dutill v. Dana - §155
Dye v. Parker - §834

Earles v. Earles - §773
Eaton v. Brown - §480
Edmunds, Administrator v. Scott - §1000
Edwards v. Edwards - §283
Emerson, Estate of - §339
Estate of - *see* name of party
Estes, Estate of - §352

Fairweather v. Nord - §458
Fanning, Estate of - §293
Farmers' Bank & Trust Co. v. Harding - §562
Farrell v. Sullivan - §855
Ferguson v. Ferguson - §481
Fisher v. Paine - §753
Fleming v. Morrison - §§351, 353
Fogo v. Griffin - §215
Fortney, Estate of - §691
Fowles, Matter of - §595
Frolich Estate, *In re* - §675
Frost, Will of - §855
Frye v. Norton - §818

Gaff v. Knight - §444
Gage v. Hooper - §853
Gardner, Estate of - §293
Garey, Estate of - §57
Gibbs' Estate, *In re* - §852
Gilkey's Will, *In re* - §456
Gilmer v. Brown - §§366, 792
Ginter v. Ginter - §799
Givens v. Girard Life Insurance Co. - §278
Glomset, Estate of - §291
Gluckman's Will, *In re* - §§849, 851
Goode v. Reynolds - §742
Gordon v. Parker - §417
Gould v. Chaimberlain - §525
Gould v. Stafford - §475
Gradwohl v. Campagna - §81
Gratton's Estate, *In re* - §477
Green v. Davis - §420
Griffin v. Driver - §653
Gristy v. Hudgens - §275
Grotts v. Casburn - §518

Hall, *In re* - §740
Halpern's Estate, *In re* - §231
Hanson, Estate of - §33
Hardenburgh v. Commissioner - §136
Hargrove v. Taylor - §164
Hargrove's Will, *In re* - §§786, 787
Harrell v. Hickman - §636
Harrison's Estate, *In re* - §880
Hatheway v. Smith - §581
Hatzistefanou, Estate of - §379
Heaton's Will, *In re* - §§376, 789
Heien v. Crabtree - §72
Heim's Will, *In re* - §817
Heinz v. Vawter - §1023
Hertrais v. Moore - §507
Heyer v. Flaig - §501
Heyer's Estate, *In re* - §653
Hickman's Estate, *In re* - §327
Hicks v. Kerr - §755
Hildreth v. Marshall - §840
Hills, Estate of - §734
Hinson v. Hinson - §457
Hockaday v. Lynn - §50
Hoenig, Estate of v. Commissioner - §145
Hoffman, Will of - §696
Holmes v. Welch - §868
Honigman, Matter of - §786
Hoover v. Roberts - §851
Hopkins v. Hopkins - §928
Hopper, Estate of - §586
Hopson v. Ewing - §352
Howard v. Howard - §275
Hunt's Estate, *In re* - §441

In re - *see* name of party
Inda v. Inda - §231
Ingersoll v. Gourley - §786
Irving Trust Co. v. Day - §339

Jacobsen v. Farnham - §858
Jedlicka v. Williams - §797

Jennings v. Srp - §777
Jeruzal v. Jeruzal - §233
Jewett v. Commissioner - §143
Jezo v. Jezo - §182
Johnson v. McDowell - §116
Johnson's Estate, *In re* - §270
Jones v. Brown - §506
Jones v. Whiteley - §§445, 933
Jordan, Estate of - §436

Kahn's Will, *In re* - §786
Katz's Will - §933
Kauffman's Estate, *In re* - §354

Wilkes v. Wilkes - §699
Will of - *see* name of party
Willis v. Barrow - §§723, 740
Windsor v. Leonard - §236
Winter's Will, *In re* - §409
Witt's Estate, *In re* - §817
Wojtalewicz, Estate of - §882
Wolf v. Rich - §653

Wolf, Estate of - §270
Wolfe's Will, *In re* - §523
World's Gospel Union v. Barnes' Estate - §514
Wright's Will, *In re* - §735

Young's Estate, *In re* - §585

Zschernig v. Miller - §174

INDEX

F

FACTS OF INDEPENDENT SIGNIFICANCE
in general, §§593-596
nontestamentary acts, §§593-595
test for application, §596
FAMILY ALLOWANCE, §§313-316
FRAUD
See Will Contests

G

GENERAL LEGACY, §§117, 725

H

HALF-BLOODS
ancestral property, §82
common law, §80
in general, §§79-84
HOLOGRAPHIC WILLS
date of execution, §§463-464
definition, §333
handwriting, §§456-459
surplusage rule, §458
typed portions, §457
in general, §§455-470
intent, §§465-467
extrinsic evidence, §467
interlineations, §§468-470
signature, §§460-462
HOMESTEAD, §§303-309
HOMESTEAD ALLOWANCE, §309

I

ILLEGITIMATE CHILDREN
See Children Born Out of Wedlock
IN TERROREM CLAUSES
See No-Contest Clause
INCORPORATION BY REFERENCE
application, §581
in general, §§581-592
ineffective deed, §§588-590
oral statements, §592
requirements, §§582-586
tangible personal property, §591
validation effect, §587
INTEGRATION
in general, §§576-580
proof of, §§578-580
INTERESTED WITNESSES
See Witnesses
INTESTACY, §1
See also Intestate Succession
INTESTATE SUCCESSION
adopted children. *See* Adopted Children
ancestral property, §§33-34
children born out of wedlock. *See* Children Born Out of Wedlock
choice of law, §4
community property, §§35-48
distribution
ancestral property, §§33-34
children, §§20-23
descendants, §§20-23
escheat, §§31-32
grandchildren, §§21-23, 73-78
in general, §§11-34

parents, §§24-25
surviving spouse, §§14-19
escheat, §§31-32
estate, §§5-10
grandchildren, §§21-23, 73-78
half-bloods. *See* Half-Bloods
in general, §§1-48
intestacy, §1
laughing heir statutes, §30
parents, §§24-25
posthumous children. *See* Posthumous Children
stepchildren. *See* Stepchildren
surviving spouse, §§14-19

J

JOINT WILLS
contract issue, §628
in general, §§628-636
survivor's rights, §§634-636
terminology, §§629-633
joint will, §§629-631
mutual wills, §633
reciprocal wills, §632

K

KILLER OF INTESTATE OR TESTATE
common law, §§151-156
constructive trust, §155
nature of homicide, §156
title does not pass, §154
constructive trust, §155
conviction required, §§158-159, 167
corruption of blood, §§168-169
joint tenancy, §163
life insurance, §162
statutory solutions, §§157-160
tenancy by the entireties, §166
Uniform Probate Code, §165
wills, §162

L

LAPSED GIFTS
death of beneficiary, §§656-659
120-hour survival rule, §659
Uniform Simultaneous Death Act, §658
general legacy, §§669-672
in general, §656-684
lapse statutes, §§660-667
application, §660
contrary will provision, §§667-668
scope, §§661-664
substitute takers, §§660, 665
residuary gift, §§669-672
specific gift, §§669-672
void gifts, §§677-684
LAUGHING HEIR STATUTES
See Intestate Succession
LOST WILLS
as proof of revocation, §556
burden of proof, §§548-555
cause of nonproduction, §§550-552
contents, §§553-555
due execution, §549
in general, §§548-556
probate of, §§548, 937

gilbert
LAW SUMMARIES

Titles Available

Administrative Law
Agency & Partnership
Antitrust
Bankruptcy
Basic Accounting for Lawyers
Business Law
California Bar Performance Test Skills
Civil Procedure
Civil Procedure & Practice
Commercial Paper & Payment Law
Community Property
Conflict of Laws
Constitutional Law
Contracts
Corporations
Criminal Law
Criminal Procedure
Dictionary of Legal Terms
Estate and Gift Tax
Evidence

Family Law
Federal Courts
First Year Questions & Answers
Future Interests
Income Tax I (Individual)
Income Tax II (Corporate)
Labor Law
Legal Ethics
Legal Research & Writing
Multistate Bar Exam
Personal Property
Property
Remedies
Sales & Lease of Goods
Securities Regulation
Secured Transactions
Torts
Trusts
Wills

Also Available:

First Year Program
Pocket Size Law Dictionary
Success in Law School Handbook

Gilbert Law Audio Tapes
"The Law School Legends Series"

Bankruptcy
Civil Procedure
Commercial Paper
Constitutional Law
Contracts
Corporations
Criminal Law

Criminal Procedure
Evidence
Family Law
Federal Income Taxation
Future Interests
Law School ABC's
Law School Exam Writing

Professional Responsibility
Real Property
Remedies
Sales & Lease of Goods
Secured Transactions
Torts
Wills & Trusts

*All Titles Available at Your Law School Bookstore,
or Call to Order: 1-800-787-8717*

Harcourt Brace Legal and Professional Publications, Inc.
176 West Adams, Suite 2100
Chicago, IL 60603

Notes

Notes